CHICANO/LATINO HOMOEROTIC IDENTITIES

ARLAND REFERENCE LIBRARY OF THE HUMANITIES
OL. 2117
ATIN AMERICAN STUDIES
OL. 16

Latin American Studies

David William Foster, *Series Editor*

CHICANO/LATINO HOMOEROTIC IDENTITIES

David William Foster

Routledge
Taylor & Francis Group
New York   London

First published by Garland Publishing, Inc.

This edition published 2013 by Routledge

Routledge	Routledge
Taylor & Francis Group	Taylor & Francis Group
711 Third Avenue	2 Park Square, Milton Park
New York, NY 10017	Abingdon, Oxon, OX14 4RN

*Routledge is an imprint of the Taylor & Francis Group,
an informa business*

Library of Congress Cataloging-in-Publication Data

Chicano / Latino homoerotic identities / edited by David
   William Foster.
                         p. cm. — (Garland reference library of the
      humanities ; vol. 2117. Latin American studies ; vol. 16)
         ISBN 9780815332282 (hbk)
         ISBN 9781138970274 (pbk)

      1. Gays' writing, American—History and criticism.
      2.

American literature—Mexican American authors—History and
criticism. 3. American literature—Hispanic American authors—
History and criticism. 4. Gays' writing, Latin American—
History and criticism. 5. Homosexuality and literature—
United States—History. 6. Homosexuality and literature—
Latin American—History. 7. Group identity in literature. 8.
Lesbians in literature. 9. Gay men in literature. I. Foster,
David William. II. Series: Garland reference library of the
humanities. Latin American studies ; vol. 16.
PS153.G38C48   1999
810.8'03538'08664—dc21   99–15048
                                                                                               CIP

Paperback cover design by Caroline Lifshey.

SERIES PREFACE

The monographs in Garland's Latin American Studies series deal with significant aspects of literary writing, defined broadly and including general topics, groups of works, or treatments of specific authors and movements. Titles published have been selected on the basis of the originality of scholarship and the coherency of the theoretical underpinnings of the critical discourse. Cognizant of the fact that literary study is an ongoing dialogue between multiple voices, established topics and approaches complement attempts to revise the canon of Latin American literature and to propose new agendas for their analysis. Studies will also focus on interdisciplinary approaches, the bridging of national and linguistic divisions, subaltern studies, feminism, queer theory, popular culture, and minority topics. The series includes only studies written in English.

David William Foster

Contents

Preface

The papers included in this volume began with a research symposium held at Arizona State University in November 1997 on queer issues in Hispanic culture. Approximately half of the papers in this volume have their origin in that symposium. However, we made the decision not simply to publish what was presented at the symposium, but to utilize it as the core for assembling essays that would focus exclusively on Chicano/Latin queer studies. The reason for this, as will become evident from reading Manuel de Jesús Hernández-Gutiérrez's superb concluding study, is that the interfacing of queer and Chicano/Latino still produces a certain level of discomfort among Chicano/Latino scholars. Certainly, Latina lesbian work has proceeded with considerable enthusiasm and brilliant results, although not always within the bosom of academic programs. However, the record for gay male Chicanos and Latinos remains thin, both in terms of cultural production and in terms of scholarly examination. It is for this reason that, if there is any disproportionate representation here, it is in favor of *los vatos*, precisely because there is so much work to be done.

Clearly, the emphasis of interest here lies with Chicano culture, not only because Chicano represent the largest group of U.S. Latinos, but because Arizona State University, as a large metropolitan state institution, necessarily has an enormous programmatic emphasis on such issues. We are, however, pleased to include essays dealing with Puerto Ricans/Neoricans. One essay, that of José B. Alvarez IV, deals with homoeroticism in Cuban literature, which is continuous with Cuban cultural interests in the U.S. and directly related to the legitimacy of gay identity—or the lack therefore—of Cuban American writers. By the same token, Kanishka Sen's essay on the early twentieth-century theater of the Mexican Xavier Villaurrutia concerns questions of homophobic gay invisibility that are directly pertinent to the extensions of Mexican culture in Chicano culture. Carmen de Urioste focuses on a relatively forgotten phenomenon of U.S. Latino culture, those writers whose Hispanic roots do not belong to one of the three dominant groups—the Chicano, the Puerto Rican/Neorican, and the Cuban American—but rather, in the case of Ana María Fagundo, are in fact Spanish.

A comment about the institutional distribution of these papers. Because Chicano studies are particularly strong at Arizona State and because the Spanish graduate program has a particular emphasis on culture studies, including queer studies, the purpose of the research symposium in which this volume originates was to showcase the work being done at this institution. Most of the individuals represented here have published elsewhere on issues pertinent to the volume, and several have already begun to develop a scholarly agenda that is specifically queer inflected. The research volumes *Latin American Writers on Gay and Lesbian Themes; A Bio-Critical Sourcebook* and *Spanish Writers on Gay and Lesbian Themes; A Bio-Critical Sourcebook* (both published by Greenwood Press) were organized at Arizona State, and the three classroom anthologies, *Literatura hispanoamericana; una antología, Literatura española; una antología,* and *Literatura chicana, 1965-1995: An Anthology in Spanish, English, and Caló* (all three published by Garland Publishing), all of which have as one organizing strand the inclusion of homoerotic writing, were organized at Arizona State. Although this volume is not intended as a sample of the Arizona State program, its relationship to the Research Symposium and to the Spanish graduate program at that university serves indirectly to attest to one point of reference in Hispanic education in the United States where it has been possible to incorporate a queer emphasis.

But I wish to return to Hernández-Gutiérrez's essay. The reader will find here not only a registry of those Chicano/Latino publications that constitute a primary source for the identification of a queer tradition in Chicano/Latino writing (included is Arizona State's own resident playwright, Guillermo Reyes, represented in this volume with a fragment from his *Deporting the Divas*), but also a careful analysis of how queer studies have begun to and can continue to enrich academic reasearch on Chicano/Latino culture.

All essays included here are original contributions and have not appeared elsewhere, with one exception. Catronia Rueda Esquibel's contribution is reproduced from *Signs: Journal of Women in Culture and Society* 23.3 (1998) with permission of the University of Chicago.

CHICANO/LATINO HOMOEROTIC IDENTITIES

Chicanas in Love
Sandra Cisneros Talking Back and
Alicia Gaspar de Alba "Giving Back
The Wor(L)D"

Susana Chávez-Silverman

*The subject is what speaks, writes, reads, and it is no
more than that. Silence is death. Desire lives, then, in its
inscription.*

> —Catherine Belsey, "Postmodern Love" 687

*Black queer female sexualities . . . represent discursive
and material terrains where there exists the possibility
for the active production of speech, desire, and agency.*

> —Evelynn Hammonds, "Black (W)holes" 141 [1]

*The power of the word and the pleasures of the female
body are intimately related.*

> —Elaine Marks in Farwell 78

Is it true, as Catherine Belsey has claimed recently, that "the postmodern condition brings with it an incredulity toward true love"
("Postmodern Love" 683)? I will not attempt to answer this question,
dangerously loaded as it is with terminological—not to say philosophical—landmines: *the* postmodern, true, love. However, naive or
daring as it may seem, love is indeed my topic, love and women
(overdetermined though this coupling may be), women in love, or,
more precisely, women poets as they represent themselves in love. The

3

postmodern Chicana writer, I will claim, does not tend to exhibit this incredulity toward true love. Of course, she is not alone, for, as Belsey reminds us (should we need reminding), "no amount of skepticism does away with desire" ("Postmodern Love" 683).

In this essay, I explore the relationship between love and female agency in representations of subjectivity in the recent poetry of Chicana authors Sandra Cisneros and Alicia Gaspar de Alba. In earlier versions of this essay, I posed the following couple of essentially rhetorical questions: are women in love a fateful, ill-fated link in patriarchy's chain, irrevocably bound to, inevitably contained by the master narrative even when—or, more insidiously still, precisely because— they attempt to position themselves against or outside the master's domain? Or is something else possible, in the oft-cited but still poignantly resonant words of Mexican poet Rosario Castellanos, "otro modo de ser, más humano y libre"?

I confess I set Sandra Cisneros up as the "fall girl," her poetry constituting the unfortunately affirmative answer to the first question; Alicia Gaspar de Alba's writing, on the other hand, embodied the (positively-coded) affirmative answer to the second question. A literary boxing match, with only one possible winner. Very binary. Not very postmodern. Subsequent reformulations of my argument have led, I hope, to a less hierarchizing, more subtle and complementary reading of both Cisneros's and Gaspar de Alba's poetry. I am attempting to take up, here, Chicana feminist scholar Chela Sandoval's challenge to U.S. Third World feminists to "point out the differences that exist among all women not in order to fracture any hope of unity among women but to propose a new order—one that provides a new possibility for unity *without the erasure of differences* (Sandoval in Martin 283; emphasis added). In addition, I have found Evelynn Hammonds' argument about the interdependency of black female sexuality and black *lesbian* sexuality compelling for my articulation of an analogous connectedness between Chicana sexuality and Chicana lesbian sexuality. "Theorizing about black lesbian sexuality," writes Hammonds, "is crucially depen- dent upon the existence of a conception of black women's sexuality in general. . ..we cannot understand [the one] without understanding it in relation to [the other]" (136).

Sandra Cisneros was featured in 1995, along with Denise Chávez, Ana Castillo, and Julia Alvarez—"as girlfriends"—on the cover of *Vanity Fair*. Another indicator of mainstream success, she has also achieved literary "crossover" status, leaving Arte Público and Third

Woman Presses, with whom she published *The House on Mango Street* and *My Wicked Wicked Ways* respectively, for Random House and Knopf, who brought out *Woman Hollering Creek* and *Loose Woman.* Cisneros was perhaps best known (before winning the MacArthur "genius" award in 1995) as the creator of one of the most convincing child narrators in recent fiction, Esperanza from *Mango Street.* In her other works, however, the theme of women in love predominates.

Sandra Cisneros's self-presentation, both in ostensibly autobiographical formats and in her literary works, often manifests, at the same time, an avowedly feminist stance and what I call a "self-tropicalizing" tendency. Both can be seen in the following quotes from a March 1995 interview with Cisneros by Catherine Craddock and Claudia Meléndez in *El Andar.* The interviewer asks Cisneros about possible criticisms of her (unflattering) portrayal of men, to which she responds: "Sometimes people . . . say I have been real one-sided with the male characters, but I feel that there is much worse going on than what I've written about. . . . I think I have been rather lenient on them" (16). Later, the interviewer comments on Cisneros's "evol[ution] into a more erotic poet," and she responds thus: "Well, Latinas are very sexual, that's something that makes us Latinas; we are really sexual and we are not afraid about that sexuality . . . it's in our bodies . . . it's in our colors, in the food. . . . Look at the way the earrings wiggle and jiggle. There's a wiggle in everything we do . . . one of the things I look for as a writer is to discuss those things that are taboo subjects" (16). When the interviewer presses Cisneros on the reception of this "erotic" work by the "conservative Latino community," she disavows her just-invoked ethnic connection—an odd elision—claiming that she "mainly hang[s] around with a gay crowd . . . and artists" (19). I will only point to the disconcerting contradictions in Cisneros's linking of Latinas to a "wiggle" which she characterizes as at once essential to the culture as a whole and "taboo." The disturbingly essentializing claim to authenticity and representativity implicit in her comments is then undermined by her peculiar disavowal of the "traditional" Latino sector.

The allure of the Latina "wiggle" is, undeniably, rather compelling, and not just in the dominant discourse. In the final paragraph of her book-length study, *Women Singing in the Snow: A Cultural Analysis of Chicana Literature*, published last year, preeminent Chicana scholar Tey Diana Rebolledo concludes:

> If Chicanas can gain acceptance of being complex figures, of being
> good girls and more, they might be satisfied . . . at the same time, the
> figure of the wicked woman, the troublemaker . . . is a very appealing
> one. It is an image that Chicana writers are not only willing to accept
> and to integrate, but one that they enthusiastically and passionately
> embrace. (206)

But of course, Chicanas *are* "good girls and more," in the dominant as
well as traditional Chicano discourse, which always already allow the
"hot tamale" or "luscious Latina" alongside the good mother/ virgin.
Cisneros's and Rebolledo's embrace, their self-tropicalizing recirculation of the dominant culture's images of Chicanas must be seen as
stereotypical. Lest we think this embrace an empowering move, let us
recall the function of the stereotype according to the late art historian
Craig Owens: "the stereotype . . . functions to reproduce ideological
subjects that can be smoothly inserted into existing institutions of . . .
sexual [and, I would add, racial and ethnic] identity. Stereotypes treat
the body as an object to be held in position, subservience, submission;
they disavow agency" (194).

A glance at Cisneros's titles confirms her enthusiastic "embrace" of
these hypereroticized, stereotypical images. Also, the *frisson* provoked
by Cisneros's South of the Border-brand "wickedness" registers
abundantly in the blurbs on the brilliantly-colored, almost doggedly
multiculti jacket on the hardcover edition of *Loose Woman*. "These
poems are firecrackers and tequila," finds Native American Joy Harjo.
"Fierce, intoxicating," from Cuban-born Cristina García; "sassy, tangy,
intimate," says Dominican-born Julia Alvarez, who praises Cisneros's
voice as "naughty with all we girls were taught not to say out loud—or
even whisper."

Interesting to me, without tarrying to deconstruct the internalized
racism in these comments, is comparing the self-tropicalizing,
effusively eroticized praise of *Loose Woman* by mainstream heterosexual Latin American-born Latina authors, such as Alvarez and
García, to the more muted comment by Chicana writer Ana Castillo,
who has written and lived, variously, lesbian, bisexual, and straight
subject positions. Castillo's blurb, exquisitely lyrical, is itself a circular,
playful meta-poem, seeming to double back upon itself rather than
referring to the same collection blurbed by Alvarez, García et al: "some
[poems] sheer jade and some for the jaded, a noose for the lover on the
loose, a net for the next novio." Reassuringly normative after all—the

nongender specific "lover" slides into "novio"—Castillo's praise nevertheless is strongest and most convincing (and convinced) when she leaves off the paean to heterosexual seduction scenarios and observes: "sometimes they are simply love poems in wonderment of life and death. At all times, Sandra Cisneros has penned poetry of utterly divine language and imagery."

I do find a certain tension in *Loose Woman* between the speaker's "looseness"/ "wickedness" and a lowering of her guard, rhetorically speaking, in terms of heterosexual politics, a shifting of focus from the would-be transgressive Chicana in love to a female speaker with a profound love of words. However, the former subject position predominates in Sandra Cisneros' poetry, both in *Loose Woman* and in her earlier collection, *My Wicked Wicked Ways*.[2] The following two texts exemplify Cisneros's poetic embodiment, in her most recent work, of the "wicked woman" and "troublemaker," espoused by Rebolledo as the images of "complexity" aspired to and "passionately embrace[d]" by contemporary Chicana writers.

In "You Bring Out the Mexican in Me," the collection's second text, notions of power and danger (nuclei of potential empowerment or containment in discursive constructions of sexuality) are relativized and inverted in relation to their meaning in dominant discourse, yet they are linked by the deployment of an unproblematized, essentialist trope of "Mexicanness."

> You bring out the Mexican in me.
> The hunkered thick dark spiral.
> The core of a heart howl.
> The bitter bile.
> The tequila *lágrimas*[3] on Saturday all
> through next weekend Sunday.
> You are the one I'd let go the other loves for,
> surrender my one-woman house.
> Allow you red wine in bed,
> even with my vintage lace linens.
> Maybe. Maybe. (4)

In this first stanza, the female speaker scripts love as *renuncia* (renunciation), but the traditional femaleness of this gesture is inverted by the performatively male actions carried out: a heavy drinking binge,[4] giving up promiscuity, allowing the house to become a sector domesticated by love. In the next two stanzas, the speaker begins to represent her loose or dangerous side, brought out by the love of the "you" the text addresses. The poem is structured as a series of parallel paradigmatic substitutions, sometimes nearly synonymous, other times antonymic, but all subsumed, in terms of history, geography, and popular culture, under the sign of "Mexicanness."

> You bring out the colonizer in me.
> The holocaust of desire in me.
> The Mexico City '85 earthquake in me.
> The Popocatepetl/Ixtaccíhuatl in me.
> The tidal wave of recession in me.
> The Agustín Lara hopeless
> romantic in me.
> The *barbacoa taquitos*[5] on Sunday in me.
> The cover the mirrors with cloth in me. (5)

I find the third stanza, cited above, particularly troubling, as Alice in Wonderland-like, the speaker's body now has engulfed several cataclysmic historical events, absolutely decontextualized and brought to bear narcissistically as signifiers of the speaker's raging, out-of-control (Mexican) passion. This dehistoricized, trivializing invocation of the Holocaust ("of desire"), for example, is even more disturbing when located in a series which concludes with "barbacoa taquitos"! The last two stanzas move into a more direct form of self-definition, using overdetermined icons of Mexican culture, both positive and negative—"the filth goddess Tlazoltéotl," Virgen Guadalupe, diosa Coatlicue—from which the speaker derives (specifically female) power only to abdicate it in the final stanza, in an apotheosis of "Mexicanness" signified by the intensified presence of Spanish, and a by a "way of loving" which is at once self-abnegating and completely possessive.

> *Quiero ser tuya.* Only yours. Only you.
> *Quiero amarte. Atarte. Amarrarte.*
> Love the way a Mexican woman loves. Let
> me show you. Love the only way I know how. (6)

Significantly, the speaker signals both her Mexicanness and its lack: "the way a Mexican woman loves" reveals the trace of performativity, of difference from itself, while the hyper-Mexicanness suggested in the

Spanish—both phonetically and semantically—enacts the disavowal of this reading.

"Loose Woman," the final poem in this eponymous collection, again scripts the swaggering, "dangerously" powerful persona found in "You Bring Out the Mexican in Me." Although not precisely about a woman in love, the text deploys gendered and sexualized imagery along a crosscultural, transhistorical axis. The speaker recodes her identity as powerful and dangerous by conceding to an unnamed (but obviously patriarchal) third person plural ("They") the truth in their naming of her.

> They say I'm a beast.
> And feast on it. When all along
> I thought that's what a woman was.
>
> They say I'm a bitch.
> Or witch.
> I've claimed
> the same and never winced. (112)

These terms—beast, bitch, witch—are all firmly entrenched along the *puta* (whore) axis of the virgen/puta binary, although the speaker's level of comfort and seamless self-identification varies according to the epithets.

> They say I'm a *macha*, hell-on-wheels,
> *viva-la-vulva*, fire and brimstone,
> man-hating, devastating,
> boogey-woman lesbian.
> Not necessarily,
> but I like the compliment. (112)

The third stanza, above, reveals the speaker's fixation on the lesbian as powerful, masculine, hypersexualized, and frightening, overlapping with the dominant culture's image of the (butch) lesbian. Even as she appears to flirt, in an assertively nonhomophobic move, with the *semantic* possibilities of being a lesbian ("but I like the compliment"), the speaker hastily beats her (admittedly coy and ambiguous) retreat from this reality ("not necessarily").

In the fourth stanza, when the speaker opens her mouth to defend herself from the mob, what issues forth are not words but rather, disconcerting in this assumedly feminist reversal poem, images from fairy tales—diamonds and pearls, consumer goods from the province of fairy queens, or toads and serpents, seemingly related to a case of PMS:

> Diamonds and pearls
> tumble from my tongue.
> Or toads and serpents.
> Depending on the mood I'm in. (112-13)

In the final stanza, the speaker becomes fully present to and embodies the loose/ wicked persona attributed to her by the judgmental voice of patriarchy throughout the poem:

> I'm Bitch. Beast. *Macha.*
> *¡ Wáchale!*
> Ping! Ping! Ping!
> I break things. (115)

Has she, in fact really "broken" anything? In attempting to enact a reversal *from within*, Cisneros's move in *Loose Woman* replicates the "positive images" response (of black artists and cultural workers) critiqued by Cornel West, following Stuart Hall. West reminds us that there is no unmediated access to what "the real Black [or Chicano] community" is; he warns that this notion is "value-laden, socially loaded and ideologically charged" (28). In attempting to positively empower this subject position, the I who speaks in Sandra Cisneros's *Loose Woman* seems naively unaware of the need, already clearly articulated by Gloria Anzaldúa in 1987 (and many other Chicana feminists, before and since), of "*unlearning* the puta/virgen dichotomy" (*Borderlands* 84). A nonparodic recirculation—indeed, embodiment— of available stereotypes (slut, Scarlett O'Hara, Coatlicue, bitch, perra, lesbian, not to mention golden earrings, mangoes, incense galore) suggests the failure to recognize that looseness/wickedness is always already allowed to Chicanas. It simply constitutes the negative side of the Marianista-Misoginista binary of Hispanic culture, and repeats stereotypes of wantonness overdetermined for Chicanas in the dominant Anglo culture as well. To reverse the valency without problematizing the underpinning structure is to risk inevitable containment.

We must remember, however, the tradition(s) from which Sandra Cisneros emerges.[6] Mestiza sexuality, in the Mexican and Chicano traditions, has been an oxymoron. From the disparaging, mysoginistic representation of woman's sexuality as *rajada* (slash) in Octavio Paz's *El laberinto de la soledad (The Labyrinth of Solitude;* 1950; 1959) through more recent, asexualized versions of the sainted mother in Chicano (male) narrative, the Chicana *as* sexual, present to herself and giving voice to her *own* sexuality, is a fairly recent phenomenon. In 1984, when the editors of *Third Woman* wanted to produce a Chicana/ Latina lesbian issue, they found that "very few professional writers— be they creative or critical—have actively pursued a lesbian political identity" (8). Although the situation has changed dramatically in the ensuing years, nevertheless in 1989, when *Third Woman: The Sexuality of Latinas* was published, Norma Alarcón, Ana Castillo and Cherríe Moraga wrote: "our sexuality has been hidden, subverted, distorted within the 'sacred' walls of the 'familia'—be it myth or reality—and within the even more privatized walls of the bedroom . . . in the journey to the love of female self and each other we are ultimately forced to confront father, brother, and god (and mother as his agent)" (9).

And so, in 1994, the speaker of Sandra Cisneros's *Loose Woman* does indeed articulate a sexual voice, in open confrontation with "father, brother, and god"—and even with "mother," with the good girl in her self. Even if the subject position and sexuality of her poetic speaker ultimately is contained by the master narrative of heterosexual romance, we must recognize the importance, particularly within the phallocentric Chicano tradition, of Cisneros's *giving voice* to Chicana sexuality. It is *this* achievement—this *voz*—to which Julia Alvarez calls attention when she praises the poems of *Loose Woman* as "Naughty with all we girls were taught not to say out loud—or even whisper."[7]

It is not the *presence* of signs of "looseness" in Sandra Cisneros's poetry that I find problematic. Before moving to a consideration of Alicia Gaspar de Alba's poetry, let me mention briefly the work of Latina lesbian poet-photographer Marcia Ochoa, who traffics in many of the same signs deployed by Cisneros in *Loose Woman*, to vastly different effect. As Yvonne Yarbro-Bejarano notes in a recent essay, "Marcia Ochoa restructures [through photographic and verbal representation] a colonized reality [the female body] by rearranging its parts to create a different reality" ("The Lesbian Body" 189). In an artist's statement Ochoa claims: "If I can't be Carmen Miranda, I can't

be a Nazi dyke either—I'm too boy to be Latina, but I'm too Latina to
be a boy" (quoted in Yarbro-Bejerano, "The Lesbian Body" 190). In
this carefully-calculated self-portrait, we can observe some of the same
concepts and images which circulate in the Cisneros poem "You Bring
Out the Mexican in Me," but with a difference. Whereas the Cisneros
poem seems to rest content on an uncritical, fragmentary juxtaposition
of images, such as Dolores del Río, Manifest Destiny, tequila, lace, and
so forth, Ochoa's statement layers images in a functional manner,
purposefully disavowing, for example, the Carmen Miranda comparison that Cisneros's texts solicit. For Ochoa, Carmen Miranda is too
Latina-femme; on the other hand, the traditional butch image is rejected
for its excess Anglo-ness: in other words, the butch in Ochoa problematizes the Latina, and vice versa.

Without producing the closure implicit in an ethical adjudication
between heterosexual and lesbian Chicana eroticism, I am interested in
contrasting literary self-representations of Chicanas in love, looking for
what are, to me, the most compelling, counterhegemonic discursive
instances, locating texts, in other words, that enact the enticing promise
of Cheryl Clarke's lesbian poetics: "To imagine Black women's
sexuality as a polymorphous erotic that does not exclude desire for men
but also does not privilege it. To imagine, without apology, voluptuous
Black women's sexualities" (cited in Hammonds 139).

Many recent lesbian theorists caution against the tempting but
facile move to script "the lesbian" as essentially *anything*. "Lesbian
bodies," writes Cathy Griggers, "are not essentially counterhegemonic
sites of culture, as Wittig might like to theorize. The lesbian may not be
a woman, as [Wittig] argues ... yet she is not entirely exterior to
straight culture ... lesbians are inside and outside, minority and
majority, *at the same time* " (129). Australian critic Annamarie Jagose,
in her potently provocative recent study *Lesbian Utopics*, focuses on
various textual attempts to theorize a perfect lesbian space as altogether
elsewhere, hence utopian (2) and concludes, following Foucault, that
positing the lesbian as utopic, outside the dominant conceptual
framework, essentializes this category as transgressive or subversive
while failing to recognize the category's implication within the
networks of power (9).

It is within this theoretical framework—acknowledging the tension
between the temptation of the transgressive and the refusal to allow the
figure of the lesbian to completely inhabit an essentialized exteriority to
the dominant discourse—that I read Alicia Gaspar de Alba's *Beggar*

on the Cordoba Bridge (1989).[8] I read this meticulously structured, steeped in paradox, four-part collection under the sign of a voyage of discovery. Unlike the notion of "exiting" with which Bonnie Zimmerman reactivates for the lesbian bildungsroman the traditional Western trope of the voyage, through the hostile heterosexual patriarchy to eventually arrive at the brave new world of lesbianism (249), Gaspar de Alba's speaker is not going elsewhere, but rather *back* to the *frontera* (frontier), which, through her journey, is reactualized as a hybrid, porous geosexual space, full of longing and pain.

Like musical movements, the four aptly titled sections of *Beggar on the Córdoba Bridge* signal the speaker's odyssey through a brief heterosexual marriage, a tentative initial sexual tryst with an anonymous Blonde, and an affair with a closeted Latina, all recorded in poems in the second section, entitled "Bad Faith." Gaspar de Alba's move toward a "se(m)erotics," to use Elizabeth Meese's term—toward an explicit textualization of lesbian desire—begins with the poem "Dark Morning Husband." This four-stanza poem has a narrative structure: it moves temporally from night toward dawn, spatially from outside to in, out, in to end—literally—on the border between in and out, on the threshhold, *en el umbral*. In terms of the textual I, there is a move from initial visceral desire (expressed by the speaker to herself, as throughout the poem),

> You meet a woman on the street
> outside a gay bar. Blonde hair,
> open red shirt, nipples
> like tiny fists.
> She looks you over down
> the loose curve of shoulders
> arms and hips. Your massive thighs
> twitch in the dark.

through actualization of desire,

> Inside the red
> glare of the dance floor,
> she jams bone and muscle
> against your flesh, asks you
> for a light.

You take the Blonde
to her motel, watch her urinate,
help her strip
the blankets from the bed.
She tastes of menthol
and sour beer. . .

through an anagnorisis,

She smells of secrets.
Her odor clings to your finger-
tips. You cannot lie.

which culminates, finally, in an explosion of rage at the threshhold:

She trembles at the way
you smash your hands
into the wall, bare your teeth.
When you leave you kick
the door.

The rage emanates from but is unable, yet, to productively disavow the
inevitable capitulation to the heterosexual imperative:

Somewhere,
a dark morning husband
waits for you to get home (21).

Why can't the speaker's rage smash *through* the wall, kick *down* the
door? Why is her self articulated as monstrous, "bar[ing] her teeth"?[9]
Why is the Blonde *qua* Blonde foregrounded, repeatedly inscribed with
a capital B? Against whom is the speaker's rage directed, the Blonde,
the "dark morning husband," herself? These and other related questions
are explored in several key poems of the collection.

"Leaving 'The Killing Fields,'" for example, is highly significant.
In this text we learn that the "dark morning husband" of the earlier
poem has been left, just as the speaker leaves the movie theater. The
"leaving" metaphor also functions as a sign for the speaker's coming
out:

I leave the movie and the dog-eared
shadows of trees, the afternoon
light, the smell of popcorn
remind me of you, white man
stalking my dreams like Jack
and his magic seeds. At night
I hear helicopters pumping over
the roof, radio waves, the click-
click of telegrams on your pink
tongue. Wherever you are,
you must hear the same sounds,
you must remember the trench
we slept in, the hole that Alice
found, the rabbit chasing her
to a land far away from you.
Remember the eggshells littered
in the closet and my fingers
cake-sweet with blood. The cock
crowing in your belly warned you,
the gray hairs showing on your head,
the white space growing in our bed.
Five years ago I left you
wolfless: goodbye Peter, hello
Rita Mae Brown.

The images used to characterize the then-husband ("white man")
develop a threatening, sinister, phallic portrait: he "stalk[s her]
dreams"; helicopters "pump" and telegrams "click-click. . .on [his] pink
tongue" which seems, in this context, hardly sensual, instead grotesque,
mechanical, and thrusting. The marital bed is represented as a
battleground; it is a "trench," a "hole" from which the speaker ("Alice,"
with obvious echoes of Lewis Carroll; this is also the English version of
the poet's own name) flees "to a land far away from [him]." We glean
other important details from this oddly dreamlike text. Ultimately the
"white man," older and alone in what was once the marriage bed, seems
not sinister but pathetic as the speaker leaves him "wolfless: goodbye
Peter, hello/Rita Mae Brown," in an intertextual nod to her emergent
lesbianism. In the final stanza, we learn that the husband was the
speaker's only male lover:

Today the memory of your body
looms immense, a tree trunk
sliding into the earth, into the black
mud and the blood on the car seat.
I took you between my thighs
at sixteen, the only man
who ever dropped his seeds there.
No roots, Jack, no golden eggs.
Just a slow chafing of thighs
and the taste of popcorn (27).

The configuration of images here returns us to "Dark Morning
Husband," the man's overdetermined whiteness correlating with the
rage-inducing encounter with the "Blonde," the notion of leaving the
husband "wolfless" resonating with the speaker "baring her teeth,"
wolf-like, in the earlier poem. The sex act in this final stanza is
demystified, a crass, hyperfunctional "dropping of seeds," ultimately
sterile in the reproductive ("no golden eggs") as well as erotic or
emotional ("no roots") sense.[10] As "Leaving 'The Killing Fields'"
remits the reader back to "Dark Morning Husband," so it also urges us
forward, to "Bad Faith."

"Bad Faith" gives the title to the collection's second section; it is
the third in a triptych of pivotal texts which deal specifically with
ethnicity and sexuality. In "Dark Morning Husband" the speaker
explores her lesbianism, but the encounter with the Blonde proves
unsatisfactory. The lover's very "Blonde-ness," the closeted speaker's
lesbian lust and the need to hide the encounter from her husband, her
sense of the inauthenticity of the situation, all produce a physical rage
in the speaker. The husband in "Leaving 'The Killing Fields'" is
portrayed in a negative (although not completely unsympathetic) light,
because of his whiteness and maleness, both overdetermined. In "Bad
Faith," the physical signs of dissimulation—passing—are not what
disturb the speaker about her closeted femme Latina lover:

It's not that wild
cinnamon lips, plumfrost
cheekbones and henna highlights upset me.

Rather, she laments the psychic energy her lover must expend daily to pass,

> But you come home
> bent, eyes and mouth
> smudged
> by the stories you have told all day:

and the untenable—invisible—position it puts her in,

> movies, Kahlúa crepes,
> Sundays at the mercado
> with a man who's really me.[11]

The speaker's coming out to herself is not imbued, as I've mentioned previously, with the sort of teleological value implicit in Bonnie Zimmerman's lesbianism-as-exit model. In fact, the nonlinear "mapping" (a psychic, ethnic, and sexual cartography) is implicitly critical, I would argue, of the tautological "journey home" of many autobiographical lesbian coming out stories privileged by Anglo feminism. In the third section of *Beggar. . .*, titled "Gitanerías" (Gypsy Things), Gaspar de Alba desplays an intimate understanding of flamenco music's *altibajos*, whose musical genre sign she deploys synaesthetically to suggest her speaker's psychosexual *vaivenes*— variations on flamenco's topnote of desire—in the section's subtitles: "Frenesí" (Frenzy), "Soledad" (Solitude), "Libertad" (Liberty), "Confusión" (Confusion), and "Pasión" (Passion).

> Someone tells me I am strangely/aggressive today, and I say *yes, I'm practicing/to be a vampire"*; "we're too old for this furtive touching of hands"; "She knows what they need, what/she too would like to have . . . the other two delve into each other's mouths/as she folds herself into the firm triangle of breasts." "A womanhood as fresh and damp as these two flowers rooted in my heart. Perhaps one morning/ I will awaken to an insistent knocking"; "She is not the lady I want./ I go back to the dark carpet and close my eyes,/thirsting for her voice, letting myself bleed/softly into the earth"; *"It could all be so simple,* she thinks. . . ./She will move only/when a brown hand grazes her thigh, and then she/will move forever." (35-38)

These juxtaposed fragments from "Gitanerías" exemplify the sense of movement, of a journey back and forth through frustration, loneliness, voyeurism, flashes of rage, disavowal, and lust, during which the speaker arrives, finally, at an erotic epiphany which is also, implicitly, profoundly political: the representation of *Chicana* lesbian desire fulfilled, metonymically figured by the image of the brown woman's hand grazing the speaker's thigh. The difference here, in relation to the figurations of lesbian desire we have seen in the previous texts, is profound. Unlike the speaker's painfully closeted subjectivity in "Dark Morning Husband" and "Bad Faith," here she represents herself as an out lesbian, claiming the ex-centric (vampiric) aggressiveness which historically has encoded lesbianism. Her desired lover is also an out Chicana lesbian (she knocks on the door of the speaker's heart "insistent[ly]"; her "brown hand" is a political as well as erotic emblem and ethnic marker), not like the passing Latina femme of "Bad Faith" or the menthol and beer tasting, illicit Blonde of "Dark Morning Husband." Indeed, the impact of "Gitanerías" is only fully revealed intertextually. The overarching bridge metaphor is particularly apt as, like the speaker who moves back and forth, between and among two worlds as she crosses over the Córdoba Bridge connecting El Paso and Ciudad Juárez, the reader constructs meaning for the collection by weaving among and between the texts in a shuttle-like move that defers closure and privileges interconnectedness.

Although I will argue that Alicia Gaspar de Alba's poetics are ultimately too theoretically sophisticated to fall prey to the seductive utopianism inherent in much critical and creative work by lesbians and feminists of color, there is a sense in which the yearning for the "brown hand," as expressed in "Gitanerías," can *only* be utopian. It is not that Gaspar de Alba posits Chicana lesbianism as altogether outside patriarchy, or outside the world. However, we must take note of the future and, especially, the conditional tenses piling up on each other in the juxtaposed lines I cited earlier: "would like," "perhaps," "I will awaken," "it could all be . . . ," "she will move." It is the poignant expression of *desire* for the Chicana lesbian that defers the brown woman as presence for, as Catherine Belsey reminds us, "utopias represent objects of desire . . . they also tend to indicate a place for passion within an alternative social order, and in utopian writing of the modern period it is possible to trace a deepening critique of the increasing domestication of desire . . . and its confinement within the nuclear family" (*Desire* 186).

I contend that Gaspar de Alba is well aware of the danger of containment inherent in *sustainedly* utopian figurations of lesbian desire. What she does with the image of the "brown hand," with the notion of Chicana lesbian love, anticipates, I believe, Annamarie Jagose's critique of Gloria Anzaldúa's deployment of the mestiza as *embodiment* of the border as utopic site of cultural fusion and hybridity. As Jagose points out, "despite [*Borderlands/La Frontera's*] promotion of the *mestiza* as the site of confluence and intermixture . . . there is an undeniable sense in which the very concept of the *mestiza* depends on concepts of diversity, distinction, and difference" (156). Therefore, Jagose continues, "any prioritization of the *mestiza* must not be due to her alleged ability to secure a space beyond the border's adjudication of cultural difference but due to her foregrounding of the ambivalence that characterizes the operation of the border"(157). Alicia Gaspar de Alba defers closure at the individual and iconically essentialist level of the brown woman's loving hand and moves into the textualization of Chicana lesbian collectivity—in, not beyond, the borderlands—in the final section, titled "Giving Back the World." Here, the eponymous poem:

> Women, we crawl out of sleep with the night
> still heavy inside us. We glean the darkness
> of our lives from the people who loved us
> as children: Abuelitas teaching us to pray,
> Papás we remember in pictures, Tías and Tíos
> holding our hands at the matinee.
>
> Now, we are mothers or aunts, widows, teachers,
> or tortilleras, beggars gathered in a deep
> field of dreams. We offer our capacity
> to grow—like hair, like night. We root
> ourselves in the bedrock of our skin
> and suck on the blue milk of morning. (50)

In this text, the speaker articulates her subjectivity within a plurality which is inclusive, yet diverse, "women," whom the poem interpellates in its very first utterance. The first stanza grounds this subjectivity in tradition and *familia*. However, lest this text be read as atavistic nostalgia for or reinscription of "family values" *a lo Chicano*, the speaker emphasizes aspects of the culture that are to be

remembered, incorporated, but put behind us: Abuelita taught us
religion and Papá is present only as the figuration of an absence: in
photos. The second stanza tells us to move on, to move *into* a world of
women gathered together in "a deep field of dreams." And yet, this is
not an end in itself, not *the* end, because the image of the "field of
dreams" sends us irremediably back to the beginning. We return,
through this leitmotiv, to the "body of dreams," the Río Grande, to the
eroticized borderspace of the collection's opening poem, titled "La
frontera."

In the opening section, also titled "La frontera," the speaker maps
out her geocultural and familial history in poems about iconic Mexican
and Chicano figures: *brujas, duendes, curanderas, La Malinche* and *La
Llorona*, her El Paso/Ciudad Juárez border childhood. Resonating now
with the erotic and ideological coming (out) to consciousness chron-
icled in "Bad Faith" and "Gitanerías," which culminates in "Giving
Back the World," the borderspace as resignified by Gaspar de Alba in
Beggar on the Córdoba Bridge is what I call a *fronterótica*:[12]

> La frontera lies
> wide open, sleeping beauty.
> Her waist bends like the river
> bank around a flagpole.
> Her scent tangles in the arms
> of the mesquite. Her legs
> sink in the mud
> of two countries, both
> sides leaking sangre
> y sueños.
>   I come here
> mystified by the sleek Río Grande
> and its ripples and the moonlit curves
> of tumbleweeds, the silent lloronas,
> the children they lose.
> In that body of dreams,
> the Mexicans swim for years,
> their fine skins too tight to breathe.
> Yo también me he acostado con ella,
> crossed that cold bed, wading
> toward a hunched coyote. (5)

Is this woman or river? Erotic reverie or anguished geopolitical lament? In Alicia Gaspar de Alba's postmodern *borderotics*, it is both/and, not either/or, as we can see in the polysemous final image of the "coyote": timeless emblem of Southwestern outlaw freedom, or outlaw mercenary bordercrosser. In *Beggar on the Córdoba Bridge*, the figure of the Chicana lesbian and, in a broader sense, the textualization of a *fronterótica*—by this I mean a theoretically sophisticated refiguration of both "the border" (vis-à-vis traditional Chicano renditions) and of a specifically Chicana lesbian desire (vis-à-vis heterosexual Chicana eroticism and Anglo lesbian feminism)—which I claim as the collection's project, do not serve, in an Anzaldúan and ultimately recuperable, utopian sense, to heal the *brecha*, because Alicia Gaspar de Alba's poetics do not attempt to foreclose but rather to foreground, in Annamarie Jagose's sense, the deep ambivalence, the differentiation and hybridity, of the border.

Let me conclude by returning to the issue with which I began this essay: Chicanas in love and their fate. In Sandra Cisneros's *Loose Woman,* in all but a very few poems, such as "Bay Poem from Berkeley" (40), or the challenging, gorgeous "With Lorenzo at the Center of the Universe, el Zócalo, Mexico City" (60-63), the speaker merely inverts the valencies, attempting to adscribe a positive charge to stereotypical images and actions always already allowed women (especially Chicanas) in dominant heterosexist discourse. To her credit, like her sisters "las girlfriends" (Denise Chávez, Ana Castillo, Julia Alvarez) and others, Sandra Cisneros articulates, in the face of its persistent silencing and pathologizing, both in Chicano heterosexual and the dominant Anglo culture, a self-present, vibrant Chicana sexuality. However, I do not think it coincidental that Cisneros has been embraced by the literary mainstream in this country, for in *Loose Woman* particularly, she is giving back to the dominant culture something comfortable, something familiar: what they (think they) already know about Chicanas. For Alicia Gaspar de Alba, on the other hand, a Chicana in love is an unabashedly (brown) woman-loving woman. So, although her complex and lyrical *borderotics* is nourished by the shifting ground, the ambivalence, and hybridity of the *frontera* and not by a "dangerously utopic" lesbian separatism, it is clear to me that—tropical-femme packaging notwithstanding—Gaspar de Alba's "crossing over" into mainstream success will take more than a wink and a wiggle.[13]

NOTES

1. I owe to Evelynn Hammonds's incisive, elegant "Black (W)holes and the Geometry of Black Female Sexuality" a more productive way of reading Sandra Cisneros with (instead of merely against) Alicia Gaspar de Alba. My argument is indebted to her clear articulation, in "Black (W)holes," of the interconnectedness of representations of black female sexuality and black *lesbian* sexuality.

2. My critique of the sexual politics of Sandra Cisneros's poetry in no way is meant to imply a criticism of her literary accomplishments. I find her a prodigiously talented stylist, especially in prose. See my analysis of her short story "Eyes of Zapata" in "Inside the U.S. Latino Gender B(l)ender."

3. tears

4. Although the representation of tears is usually encoded as feminine in Anglo culture, in my experience, this is less true within a Hispanic (I include Spain, as well as Latin America and the U.S. Chicano/Latino) context; any lingering trace of the feminine resonating principally from the dominant culture is further attenuated by the overdetermined maleness of drinking (especially tequila) and the hangover.

5. barbacued tacos

6. I, as a biracial, non-Catholic who self-identifies as a Chicana, only partially inhabit this subject position; I would venture a guess that Cisneros's "bad girl" persona might seem more appealing, seem a more viable subversion of the hegemonic position assigned to woman, had I been raised exclusively within the Catholic, patriarchal, Hispanic paradigm.

7. Of course, Alvarez's comment presupposes a unitary Latina subject ("we girls"), flattening out racial, ethnic, national, class, religious, and sexual differences. But that is the subject for another essay.

8. Just *how* compellingly antihegemonic a text it is is hard to predict from the Carmen Miranda-femme, hothouse-flower pink cover of the volume it's incongruously housed in, to the volume's near-Commodores-sounding title, *Three Times a Woman.*

9. Note the similarity between this image of the painfully closeted lesbian as monstrous and Sandra Cisneros's use of the "beast" imagery to signify both patriarchy's naming of her *and* her claiming her self as bad girl. For Gaspar de Alba, the violent monster is a sign of inauthenticity, closetedness, whereas for Cisneros, the beast signifies positive, transgressive power.

10. It is interesting that although the speaker, in her remembered version of the sex act, acknowledges the man's phallic power (the memory of his body "looms immense," he is represented as a "tree trunk," he "dropped his seeds

there") the text functions as a subtle refusal of this power and of male privilege and even as a revisionary rewriting of heterosexual intercourse: "I *took* you between my thighs" and "No roots, Jack, no golden eggs," boasts the female speaker, undermining thus heterosexuality's male dominant, compulsorily procreative paradigm.

11. Although there is no specific textual reference to the ethnicity of the lover in "Bad Faith," signs of her—and the speaker's—*latinidad* abound, for example: "Sundays at the mercado," and the exclamations of her coworkers, in Spanish: "*Qué suerte*, they moan. . . ."

12. This term is copyrighted. I coined it during the 1993 American Studies Association convention in Boston in a discussion with Deena J. González and Alicia Gaspar de Alba. Readers may notice how melodious borderotics sounds in English too.

13. This essay is for my sister, Laura Chávez Silverman, in whose East Village apartment I completed an earlier version. I would like to thank Florence Moorhead-Rosenberg, who was particularly helpful with the wording of my conclusion, and my colleague Margaret Waller, for her theoretical and stylistic queries and suggestions. Thanks also to the anonymous readers for *Chasqui*, for their painstaking readings; their insightful comments were invaluable in revisions of this essay.

Chueco Sexualities
Kaleidoscopic I's and Shattered Mirrors
Cecilia Rosales

*We are beings who are looked at in the spectacle
of the world.*

—Jacques Lacan

INTRODUCTION

During this decade, we have witnessed the emergence and rapid
evolution of queer theory. Be it as members of an academic
community, as consumers of the cultural production offered by mass
media, or simply as silent witnesses in a crowded street, we have all at
least once had an encounter with what now has come to be called queer.
For many scholars and theorists, queer emerges as a coalition formed
by gay, lesbian, and feminist discourses, and its most evident
characteristic is that it resists and escapes the dichotomies that dazzle
the Cartesian mind by destabilizing the apparently natural and given
relation between chromosomal sex, sexual desire, and gender.

One of the main problems in using queer theory arises when it is
blinded by its own borders. We cannot simply establish and propose
analytical and theoretical models for cultural production that are alien
to the culture in which queer theory first emerged. However, more than
queer, gender is perhaps the most problematic category, since this
social construct is always given, yet almost automatically dismantled
with the same tools that created it in white discourses. Outside the
United States, gender is inextricably related to such variables as social
class. It is therefore difficult to approach other cultures taking as a point
of departure the political connotation and the "in your face" attitude of

many queer-identified groups, of which Queer Nation is only one example.

It is impossible to look for queer visibility in many so-called Third World countries where freedom of speech is only a chimera and where the individual's sexuality is controlled and governed by the state. Manifestos like "I Hate Straights" or slogans like "We're queer. We're here. Get used to it." belong within U.S. white culture, but can hardly be extrapolated. To ignore the historical moment and the touchstone that the 1960s have proven to be for gay and feminist liberation movements would be naive. "Flower power" and the Stonewall riots of 1969 have as their Latin-American counterparts bloody episodes of militant youths concerned more with their daily survival within the repressive political regimes of the times than with sexuality. From this perspective, any attempt to theorize and define nonwhite homoerotic identities outside the United States' culture from a quite central theoretical standpoint, as is in this case queer theory, will inevitably result in a flawed pastiche, and, needless to say, in an additional imposition of patriarchal domination in the inextricable monologue of power that emerges in trying to form a new discourse for/of the *other* derived from the discourse of domination: Too much "fathering," too much "othering."

Since the early 1990s queer theory has provided a safe "playground" for culturalists, feminist, gay, and lesbian scholars. However, it has also become a popular stage for transvestism, since it frequently allows homophobic perspectives to "pass" as queer.

WHAT YOU SEE IS WHAT YOU GET?

Undoubtedly, the realm of the visual has dominated every aspect of our lives for the last half of this century. It is through images that we differentiate ourselves from others: how different or how alike we are in relation to others determines our position within a group. Gender, as opposed to chromosomal sex or sexual desire, depends largely on—or is constructed through—the visual characteristics of oneself. The masculine or feminine traits of a specific subject will depend on such things as dress codes, color preferences, biomechanics, bodily display. It has everything to do with the way we dress up and make up according to, or in opposition to, what has been established as "masculine" or "feminine." However, as I have already tried to problematize earlier, vision and image making and interpreting is intimately related to the way we understand a specific culture. The gaze, the look, the screen, and ultimately the camera through which images are made legible to us both define and prescribe gender "(id)entities."

Mary Ellen Wolf's photo essay "Out of Frame: Border(line) Images"[1] questions and problematizes gender and "otherness" as it documents transvestites' lives on the Mexico-United States border. Wolf's work, as we will "see," deals with the interstices of a hyphenated subculture in a literal (-) and metaphorical sense. It is interesting to note that these politically silenced counterparts provide an unfathomed dialogue with the center of queer theory. Through their daily lives, they probe, prove, and contradict the central tenants of queer theory produced in the United States. Their self-representations and practices on the United States-Mexico border become the margin on which the ever-evolving script of queer theory is questioned and corrected.

Such terms as Mexican-American, cross-dressing and border-crossing, need the hyphen in order to convey their meaning. In the first instance the rule that justifies the use of the hyphen is that it is required to join "coequal" terms. Here, clearly, the hyphen is used to indicate an antinomy, as the nouns in hyphenated national identities known to us have nothing that is "coequal." Metaphorically, the hyphen in itself constitutes a border separating two concepts that together convey one meaning, but separately embrace a series of dissimilarities. In Wolf's portrayal of transvestites "passing" off as women, her lens is at once what separates and confronts the image portrayed (Mexican male bodies) with the connotation conveyed (gender blending), thus rendering "borders" intelligible.

CHUECO REVENGE?

Chueco (figure 1) is the Spanish word for "crook" or "crooked." It can be used as a noun or as an adjective, and it refers to that which is not straight or aligned; that is, anything bent, curved, angular, twisted, or distorted; or to any act or person who is false, tricky, dishonest, fraudulent, or deceptive. In Mexican slang, *chueco* also refers to the practice of a transvestite passing as a woman, be it on stage, on the streets, or in bed, which represents the ultimate *chueco* achievement. This photograph helps elucidate the whole concept of transvestisim and gender, since as Wolf points out:

For many years Lourdes worked as a barmaid and dancer in several
border cities. This *image* taken from a particular *photo* from her
scrapbook references what I have come to know as *chueco*. . . .
Chueco highlights that moment in image *making* and image *viewing*
when you *want to believe*, when you *act as if* what you see is what
you get. Yet you really can't be sure. (498, my emphasis)

Hence, *chueco* is the convergence of the problematic connotations
of such terms as *image* versus *photo*; *viewing* versus *making*; *wanting
to believe* versus *act as if*. The first term in these dichotomies—image,
viewing, wanting to believe—denote more naturalness and less politics
as opposed to the latter—photo, making, act as if—and it is precisely in
the interstices that separate and unite such concepts that gender is
constructed and fought (fucked?) back. Let us juxtapose Wolf's account
of *chueco* with Butler's notions of gender vis-à-vis performativity in
the following excerpt of her most cited *Gender Trouble*:

That the gendered body is performative suggests that it has no
ontological status apart from the various acts which constitute its
reality [image]. This also suggests that if this reality is fabricated
[photo] as an interior essence, that very interiority is an effect and
function of a decidedly public and social discourse [making], the
public regulation of fantasy trough the surface politics of the body
[viewing], the gender border control [want to believe] that
differentiates inner from outer, and so institutes [as if] the 'integrity'
of the subject. (136)

OH FATHER, FORGIVE US OUR TRESPASS/ING

Let us open another border metaphor. The contested grounds for a
queer identity have been waged over the perpetual need for
unfixedness: the need to defer the limiting characteristics that would
irrevocably define identity, and by so doing, render it meaningless. In a
similar fashion, the border *chueco*, instead of being ousted from the
center, finds him/herself crossing the border without paying tolls. In
Mexico, it is not uncommon to see transvestites living double lives.
During the day many work—are exploited—at the center of the border-
town economy, in menial service tasks at the *mercado* or in beauty

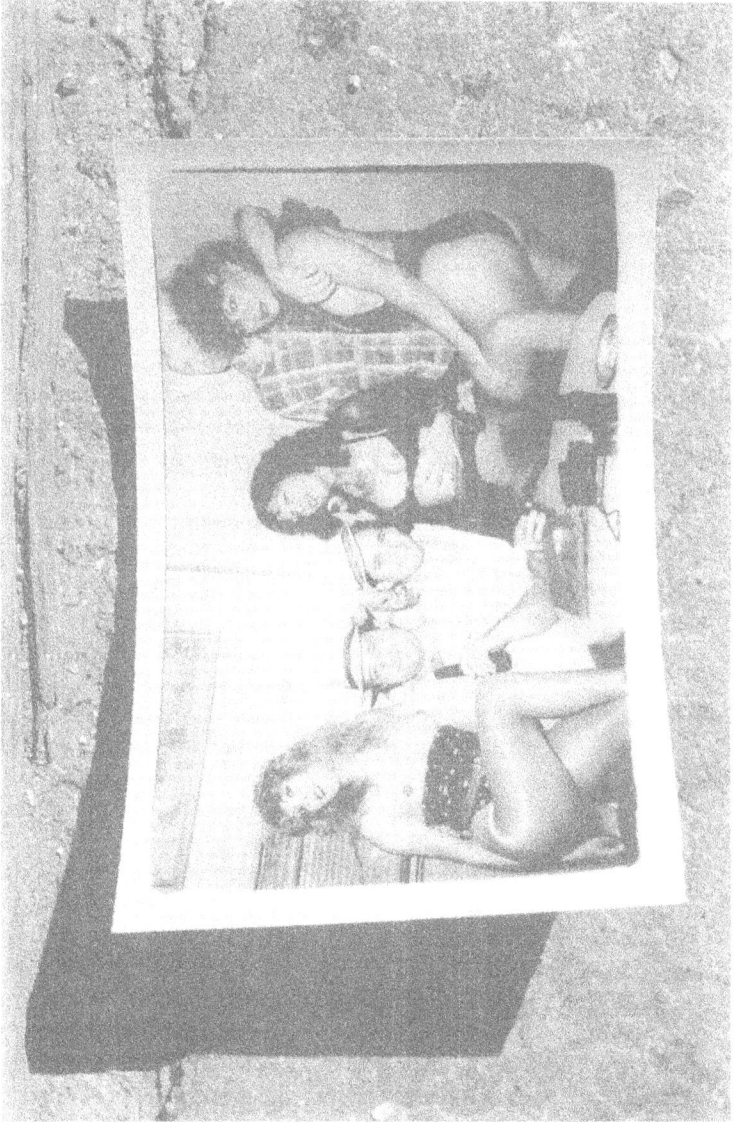

Fig. 1

parlors. But at night they capitalize on the product that they create, possess, and sell. Two different economies, one supported by a system of classes, the other by distinctions of gender, where the American male representing patriarchy is exploited/cheated by the very same object of desire he insists on creating.

While "passing," these transvestites are also trespassing in several ways. Since, as Wolf states, they aren't allowed to cross the physical border to enter U.S. territory, they sell their services on the Mexican side, where it is illegal to cross-dress (497). The project operated by patriarchy undercover agents—*granaderos*/policemen—consists of policing even the rupture of the heterosexual norm. It is important here to consider how threatening transvestites are to a phallogocentric society that mocks itself for being the incarnation of the "macho," as is in this case Mexican society ("phallologocentric" is here a meld of "phallocentric" and "logocentric").

"Graciela and the Virgin" (figure 2), "The Last Time I Saw Sonia" (figure4), and "Cynthia and Jesus" (figure 5) refer us to a different kind of trespass. The iconography and the construction of their altars tell us about their "naturalness," since Mexican society has "proudly" defined itself as mostly Catholic. Graciela's and Cynthia's altars devote an important space to the virgin—their selves seem to represent the other part of the antinomy, the whore—and implicit in this iconography is the Mary Magdalen position that Graciela and Cynthia assume. This virgin/whore dichotomy is well enacted in Graciela's poses. The marked difference in her facial and bodily expression (figure 2) and in "Graciela and Compañero" (figure 3) seems to obey a shift in spaces, thereby reconstructing herself coming out of the door's threshold that mediates the inner—the true Graciela—from the outer world which provides her with social constructions for her transvestite gestures: gender, in this case. In this same shot, Graciela's friend assumes an interesting pose. Why is he wearing sunglasses? Is it as a protection from the "look" of the outer world? Does he wants to conceal his identity? Is he blind? Whatever the reason, his attitude is totally different from the one of the white males in *Chueco* (figure 1) who face the camera with no shame and who find pride in being accompanied by such good looking "chicks."

Returning to the altars, whether they function as elements that nourish these individuals—in that they convey a sense of belonging to a wider group, popular culture, and iconography—or not, they do suggest the transvestite's self-consciousness as a trespasser.

Fig. 2

Fig. 3

Sonia's altar is less conventional but strikingly interesting. Timidly, while at the same time provocatively, Sonia poses facing the camera (figure 4) next to—and reflected in—her altar, composed of a trio of objects arranged diagonally as if they represented a hierarchy: in the upper left corner an image of the Sacred Heart of Jesus, in the middle a magazine clipping of a handsome man dressed in a tuxedo, and lastly, in the lower right corner, a rustic mirror in which we see the reflection of Sonia's profile while she faces directly toward the camera. A schizophrenic representation of the self, perhaps?

The order in which Sonia has arranged her altar tells us about her idealization of these things. Kaja Silverman, in *The Threshold of the Visible World,* theorizes about love, idealization, and the apparatuses involved in the process of understanding and approaching the visual. In describing the complex dynamics involved in the process of idealization, she states:

> When the subject idealizes what is most culturally valorized, the idealized object becomes almost automatically fetishized, in the Marxist rather than the Freudian sense of the word. Affirmed both representationally and psychically, it begins to seem intrinsically more valuable that the other objects, substantially superior. Although the subject has constituted that object as an ideal, he or she often falls prostrate before it, in a thrall of fascinating luster. (40)

Sonia's altar is only complete with her facial image. Wolf's photograph, however provides the spectator with a body dressed in an animal-print body suit. In ascending order, Sonia seems to represent the animal instinct, as suggested by the tiger-like print; the mirror, besides the Lacanian connotation, seems to represent the idealization of the self-constructed image that Sonia, as transvestite, has chosen; the scrap of the handsome white male appears to be an intermediate space within the parameter of perfection between the paradigm of earthy and divine beauty.

NO-MAN'S LAND

It is in this destabilizing complex flux—that is the border—wherein lies the essence of *chueco* identity. It is not only the mobility of the floating population on the border, but also the mobility of the semantic spheres, which purports to stabilize and delimit identity in a fixed parameter and in a decipherable way, that allows these "aliens" free access to the ironically fenced and guarded border. Geographically the United States-Mexican border has become the stage for government's aggression towards "others," but metaphorically it seems a veritable no-man's land in terms of the salient definitions of identity.

Transvestism, drag, cross-dressing, transsexualism, bisexualism until recently had been "bastard" practices within the array of "identified" sexualities. These practices and the individuals identified with them could hardly fit into the established—either/or—binarisms of homosexual/heterosexual, female/male. From what we can tell from Wolf's, photographs these transvestites find pride in making themselves up and in constituting themselves as a different kind. In this respect, Marjorie Garber's *Vested Interests* sheds some light on the notion of the so-called third "sex" or "term" and its political connotations. Garber proposes three examples of how the "third" is a good site of resistance from binarisms and compulsory intelligibility, since it causes a meaning crisis. She employs opposite semantic fields to prove how "third" is always neither, representing the space of resistance inscribed in the hyphen.

I find Garber's proposal attractive since she exploits the connotative border that the third represents. She exemplifies it as follows:

> The Third World is only a "third" in that it does not belong to one or another of two constructed regions, the developed West and what used to be described as the Communist bloc. What the so-called Third World nations have in common is their relative poverty and their largely non Caucasian population and the fact that they were once subjected to Western rule. . . . As for the third actor, it will be recalled that this was Sophocles' remarkable contribution to the development of Greek classical drama. . . .Yet the "third actor" did not play a single part, but rather several different roles within a given play. Only three speakers conversed on stage *at a time*, but the number of characters, the number of parts, was not confined to three. . . . [I]t is not itself *a* third *one* ; it is rather something that challenges the possibility of harmonious and stable binary symmetry. The "third" dimension in the Lacanian psychoanalysis, the *Symbolic*, is likewise not a realm apart, but the transference onto the level of the signifying chain of those binary structures that in the Imaginary dimension, relate everything back to a fictional "one." (11-12)

Fig. 4

Fig. 5

Again, this fictional "one" takes us back to the "true" model, the true self that these transvestites try to perform and that seems to haunt them in the exact same way as heterosexual women are haunted with idealized parameters of physical beauty. Wolf's lens seems interested in exploring the relationship between white pop culture's icons and Mexican transvestites. "Your Eyes on Mine" (figure 6) elaborates on the subject's consciousness of the "male" gaze at the same time that it reinstates the "eye" in five different ways: first, and foremost, the title already interprets what the camera is constructing; secondly, the shadow covering Madonna's face serves at once to veil and to reinscribe the idealized object; the more evident oval mirror; the subject's eyes and the omnipresent lens. In already constructing herself as other in front of the camera that at the same time reads all legible signs, the Madonna wannabe will inevitably be deceived with the picture, since, as Silverman proposes:

> [T]he gaze does not photograph us directly, but through the cultural representations which intervene between it and us—representations which Lacan calls the "screen." Although we often treat these representations as simple mirrors, they do not so much reflect us as cast their reflection upon us. They are carriers of—among other things—sexual, racial, and class difference. For these reasons, the subject not always occupy the field of vision happily. (57)

Earlier, I have suggested the dangers of extrapolating gender norms from one culture to another. Interestingly enough, "Your Eyes on Mine," "Celestina, the Tarot Reader," and "Deyanira on Good Friday" shift the attention from the typical altars in Mexican popular culture, as seen in the previous shots, to emblematic figures in contemporary United States' culture. Madonna, Marilyn Monroe, and the Statue of Liberty, respectively, appear in these shots as idealized figures that both identify and repel the transvestites' own conception of themselves. The "woman" in "Your Eyes on Mine" has clearly and consciously invested in portraying the "look" of the now queer superstar. In the same fashion, Celestina's eyebrow design and hairdo seem to echo the Marilyn Monroe worn and torn poster that appears on the wall next to her bed (figure 8). For those of us familiar with Spanish literature, the "preferred reading" in "Celestina, the Tarot Reader" (figure 7) would focus on the connotation of the proper name: Celestina, Fernando de

Fig. 6

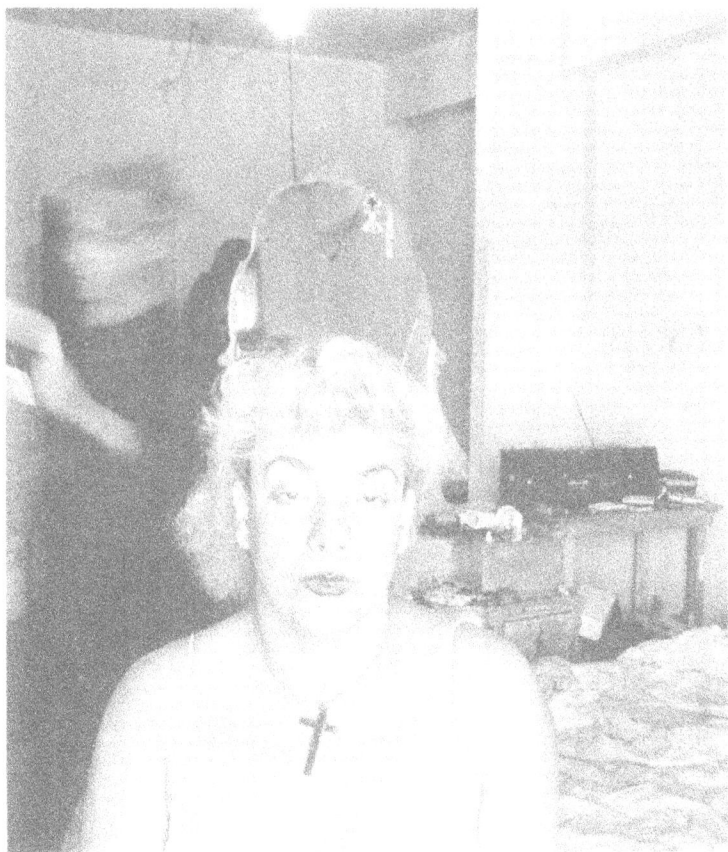

Fig.7

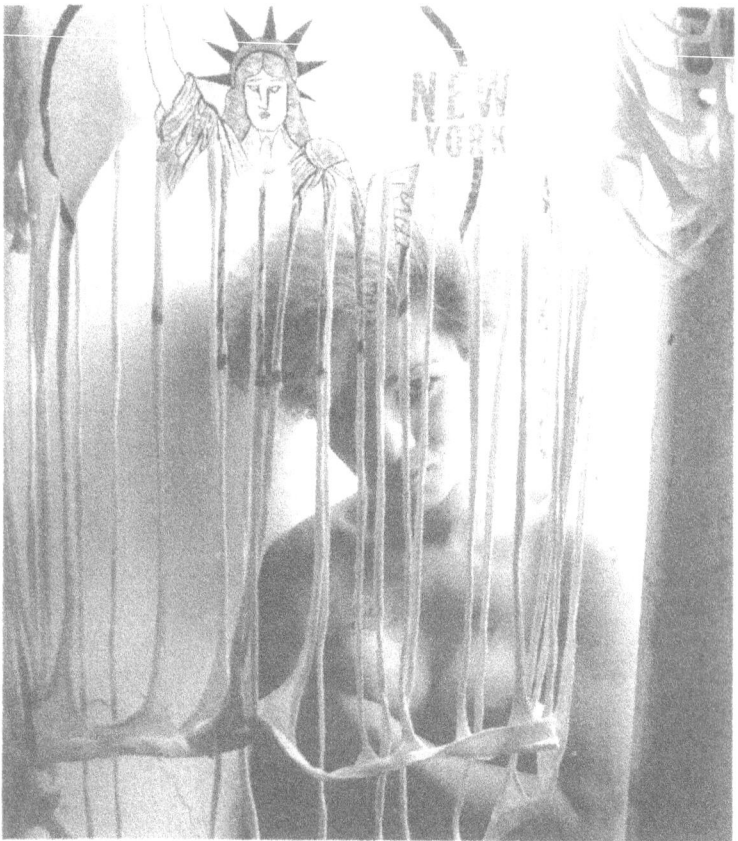

Fig.8

Rojas's immortal late-Medieval character represents the rupture with the old patriarchal-ecclesiastical order and emerges as a capitalist-individualist prostitute in the midst of Spanish conservatism. Within the Judeo-Christian tradition it is very common to hear proper names such as Adam, Joseph, or Mary, but on rare occasions one hears of Cain or Salome, which proves the fear and metonymic move from an abstract concept, which in this case would be lust or evil, to the *locus* of the proper name. The tarot reader's choice could then have been a political act in that if familiar with Celestina's story—be it by means of the now so popular *telenovelas* or simply as an awkward reference—she shows no fear for the "determinism" implicit in such a proper name.

The underlying oxymoron in "Deyanira on Good Friday" (figure 8) is found in that the exact same object that seems to liberate her—the Statue of Liberty—also confines her. According to Wolf :

> I had just met her about twenty minutes before. . . . She was very wild, jumping around. I loved her T-shirt and it was my idea to hang it up. At the time she was crossing the Rio Grande every night to trick—a very fearless and dangerous practice. Perhaps she liked that Statue of Liberty because that is how she viewed herself—mobile and free. But I can't ask her now because she dropped out of sight that same week. I lost track of her. (497)

Though the *mise-en-scène* would direct our reading toward Deyanira's liberty, her expression tells us more about confinement behind the bars that the same Statue of Liberty creates, and it also reminds Deyanira and the viewer of how she is not free.

The same could be said in relation to Sonia (figure 4), whose mirror reflects the distance between her and the white male in the magazine scrap.

It would be fair to remember that while transvestites strive to "pass" as women, they are not the only ones striving to pass as white. One needs only to watch Mexican television from time to time to see how the Mexican-ness portrayed by popular actors has nothing to do with the stereotypical image that the Mexican national identity project sought to reflect. A vast majority of the population, I would say, invests considerable amounts of time and money in "prosthetic" accessories that help them convey a "First World look." Michael Jackson might have been the most famous person with that strange disease that bleaches people, but back home it is called Mother of Pearl Bleaching Cream and is widely used among low-income females.

US/THEM

Transvestites and drag queens on the Mexican-United States border are involved in a dialectic far more complicated than white, middle-class heterosexual male transvestites in the United States. They do not form coalitions among themselves, nor self-help groups for their friends and family. Manifestations of public outwardness, such as parades and political marches are also notably absent. Their border crossing is at once literal and metaphorical, and on both sides of the border they are illegal "aliens" accused of gender b(l)ending. These "aliens" are subjected to the pressures of the structures of alienation and the apparatuses of power that subjectivize them as *other*, as outsiders. In theorizing transvestism at/from the margins of the Río Grande, the ghost of patriarchal domination/coercion is ever present. Questions such as whether *chueco* is a political act emerge and remain unanswered. Though my "reading" of this particular practice and my conversation with Mary Ellen Wolf's photographical work is in fact political and positioned at instances at the center of the dominant discourse within queer theory, the hyphen to which I myself belong in this "-" American nomenclature keeps me from imposing my reading of *chueco* into the practice itself. As T. Minh-ha Trinh cleverly suggests:

> A conversation of "us" with "us" about "them" is a conversation in which "Them" is silenced. "Them" always stands in the other side of the hill, naked and speechless, barely present in its absence. Subject of discussion, "them" is only admitted among "us," the discussing subjects, when accompanied or introduced by an "us" member, hence the dependency of "them" and its need to acquire good manners for the membership standing. The privilege to sit at a table with "us," however, proves both uplifting and demeaning. It impels "them" to partake in the reduction of itself and the appropriation of its otherness by a detached "us" discourse. (127)

Nevertheless, and regardless of any positionality, it is impossible to divest *chueco* of its potentially subversive powers, especially when surviving leaves little time for a political agenda. It is well known that transvestites, transsexuals, cross-dressers and drag queens have had a hard time fitting in and complying with the norm of gay, lesbian, and feminist theory. The most common concern for many feminists is that transvestites reinscribe the norms of patriarchal domination, while at the same time they parody "women." The question to be asked here is why would women feel demeaned? Though cross-dressers rework the specificities of gender as a social construct to "make up," it is also true that in so doing they make manifest the absurdity of such constructions. What is woman? A dress and a good pair of pantyhose?

Janice Raymond, among other feminists who criticize transgender practices, claims they are of no political use. In her essay entitled "The Politics of Transgenderism" she writes:

> That some men find gender relief, sexual pleasure, and/or stardom and financial profit in this mimicry does nothing to challenge the political power of the normative, dominant, powerful class of men that the male gender bender still belongs to. Cross-dressing could be more accurately perceived as another form of male self expression and exhibitionism. . . .
>
> The claim for tolerance, based on the notion that transgenderism in all its forms is a form of gender resistance, is alluring but false. Instead, transgenderism reduces gender to wardrobes, hormones, surgery and posturing—anything but real sexual equality. A real sexual politics says yes to a view and reality of transgender that transforms, instead of conforming to gender. (223)

I cannot help but find Raymond's words puzzling. Transgenders are not necessarily compelled to be a part of the theoretical-political network around queer studies, and they do not pride themselves on defying patriarchy—most of them have been unable to come out of the closet! While I recognize that Raymond refers to white male transgenderists, her resistance to tolerance based on the claim that transgender is anything "but real sexual equality" is hard to accept. Feminists, gays, and lesbians who are gender benders frequently reproduce heterosexual norms. They do not have to cross-dress to do so, and yet nevertheless deserve tolerance. The politicization of sexuality here seems to coerce the individual to assume a specific posture and to display it in daily life. Is a woman a feminist solely because she chooses not to wear a bra?

The transvestites portrayed by Wolf are anything but powerful. Raymond's suggestion that cross-dressers should be reduced to "exhibitionists" ignores the real risk faced by Wolf's transvestites, who imperil their very lives every time they dress up and walk in the streets or when they do *chueco*. We cannot discuss here what compels these individuals to cross-dress or to work as prostitutes—sociologists and psychiatrists have already said enough without ever satisfying anyone. I would like to assume that they enjoy it, that it is a choice, a form of self-expression, and that should suffice to grant them tolerance; they certainly have not had it easy in an extremely repressive Mexican society.

Raymond seems to refer to Judith Butler's claim that gender is not something that you put on, and that not all drag is subversive. However, she fails to consider the performative aspect. In *Bodies That Matter* Butler emphasizes the aspects of her work that have much been misunderstood. She spends considerable time explaining why performativity (in its literal and theatrical sense) is not to be understood as drag. Many have understood drag and performance as performativity and have invested transvestism and cross-dressing with a political subversive power, which, as I stated earlier, is not necessarily the case. In Butler's words:

> [P]erformativity cannot be understood outside of a process of iterability, a regularized and constrained repetition of norms. And this repetition is not performed *by* a subject; this repetition is what enables a subject and constitutes the temporal condition for the subject. This iterability implies that "performance" is not a singular "act" or event, but a ritualized production, a ritual reiterated under and through constraint, under and through the force of prohibition and taboo, with the threat of ostracism and even death controlling and compelling the shape of the production, but not, I will insist, determining it full in advance. (95)

In physical and metaphorical borders, code switching and cross-dressing are necessary skills. *Chueco* practices, thus, are often performed at the border. The American *maquiladoras*, for example can do on the Mexican border what is illegal in the United States; underage American teenagers come to the border to get inebriated, and many Mexicans drive *chueco* cars and speak a *chueco* Spanish. In this sphere of perpetual ebb and flow that is the border, national identities are challenged, assumed, de/constructed. But what is national identity but a freaked fixed notion of what everyone in a specific geographical domain should be like? Mexican national identity seems at times to be intertwined with machismo, in stereotypes like the ones portrayed by Pancho Villa or the ones pictured by Hollywood. The recently deceased Octavio Paz maintained in his *The Labyrinth of Solitude* that these "macho-like" stereotypes were too deep in the Mexican's psyche to be questioned or reelaborated, and that they were part of Mexican-ness.

In what I consider a very delicate issue, from a Chicano political perspective, this is totally awkward. Just a few miles from the border into the United States, Chicano and Mexican-American groups tend to value anew and to reinstitutionalize emblems and symbols of "Mexican-ness" that were once used by the patriarchy/state to give the sense of an interior coherence that many inside the country strive continuously to reject. But when one is contesting from within the Mexican border and not from without, it is difficult to swallow hook, line, and sinker. Gloria Anzaldúa's *Borderland/La frontera*, for example, glorifies Mexican traditions and icons in order to counteract racism, colonialism, and more general attitudes that desecrate Mexican culture. Furthermore, she sets the utopian quest for an ethnic queer nation, and in so doing, follows the Mexican philosopher José Vasconcelos' Cosmic Race project, ignoring the political dangers of such a move and the classist and racist remarks in Vasconcelos' work.

So allow me now to use the term "drag" with a different denotation, although I am not quite sure that one is not implied in the other. I am referring to the verb "to drag" for we all drag things, ideas, habits, and registers that help us constitute our sexual and national identities, vexed and perplexed as they may be. As Wolf's photographs show, Graciela, Sonia, Deyanira, and Celestina drag the old preconceived notions of masculinity and femininity, while at the same time they drag emblems and icons of Mexican-ness that they superimpose on their idealized Anglo idols. The result is a neither/nor, a hyphen. Interestingly, the Spanish word for hyphen is *guión*, which would translate back to English as "script." In the elaboration of their discourse, these transvestites reject the script of marginality and shame that society seems to confer on them; they find liberty in the hyphen, in their border lives.

In conclusion, I would like to question national identity and equate it with gender, since it seems to be in that interstice where *chueco* could be politically invested. Mary Wolf, in sharing her experience with her "subjects," recalls: "I've heard it said that you can abandon both your nationality and your sexual identity on the banks of the Rio Grande. I have spent many afternoons at the apartment house where identities are crafted on a daily basis" (497). With Wolf's idea in mind, what follows is a fragment of one of Judith's Butler most read essays, "Imitation and Gender Insubordination." It is important to remember that Butler's example does not mean to equate gender with drag as something one can put on or take off, but rather something constructed and not natural, as the identities and sexualities crafted at the border:

> If gender [national identity] is drag, and if it is an imitation that regularly produces the idea it attempts to approximate, then gender [national identity] is a performance that produces the *illusion* of an inner sex or essence or psychic gender core; it produces on the skin, through the gesture, the move, the gait (the array of corporeal theatrics understood as gender [national identity] presentation) the illusion of an inner depth. In effect, one way that gender [national identity] gets naturalized is through being constructed as an inner psychic or physical *necessity*. And yet, it is always a surface sign, a signification on and with the public body that produces this illusion of an inner depth, necessity or essence that is somehow magically, causally expressed. (187-88)

My proposal now is to rewrite the theoretic scripts long imposed to the cross-dressed, transvestite, or transsexual and to allow them a discursive space; since, on both sides of the United States-Mexican border the totalizing projects that sustain both nations—that is, heterosexuality and national identity—seem to start to crumble.

NOTES

1. I would like to thank Dr. Wolf for sharing her work with me as well for her encouragement and mentoring. Mary Ellen Wolf is the Women's Studies Program director at New Mexico State University, where she is also an associate professor of French. She is the author of *Eros under Glass: Psychoanalysis and Mallarmé's "Herodiade"* (1987). "Stand Like a Woman," her first photo essay, appeared in *Puerto del Sol* (1995). "Out of Frame: Border(line) Images" appeared in *Critical Inquiry* 23 (1997): 494-508.

Lesbians of Aztlan
Reclamation, Resistance, and Liberation
Trino Sandoval

> *Cada vez que veo a un grupo de hombres, se me hunde*
> *el corazón hasta los pies, cada vez que de repente oigo*
> *ruidos, choques, gritos masculinos o aun, su mera risa,*
> *me encojo por dentro, rehuyo hasta las paredes de mi*
> *alma, busco un lugar donde esconderme. Naomi*
> *Littlebear*[1]
>
> —quoted in Moraga and Castillo, Esta puente 32

Throughout history, feminism has tried to confront a series of social problems. A prominent example is the fight for civil rights, among others. However, it wasn't until the 1970s that white feminists began to emphasize that oppression was based on gender and started to confront this agenda. The white feminists' movement, however, failed to incorporate the interests of women of color in the U.S. in their agenda. This was due, among other things, to the fact that white women were not direct objects of racism like women of color[2].

At the end of the 1970s, Moraga tells us that there wasn't even a viable movement of feminists of color in the United States with which one could identify, much less one that focused on Chicana lesbians (*Esta puente mi espalda* 2). When they were not included in white feminism, women of color started to combat the sexism found inside a society dominated by white men. It was then that a movement emerged based on the union of voices of women of color who were and are experiencing oppression based on race, class, and sex.

In the 1980s activists of color put aside the fight against the war in Vietnam and the struggles that united Third World activists and started

a fight against racist America. More specifically Chicanas and Chicana
lesbians had been obliged to put aside their fight of liberation against
the oppressive forces of the white colonizer and the Chicano Machismo
in the name of Aztlan, in order to back the Chicano movement that
emerged in the latter part of the 1960s. However, for many of these
Chicanas like Cherríe Moraga: "Aztlan gave language to a nameless
anhelo inside me. To me, it was never a masculine notion" (Moraga,
"Queer Aztlán" 152). These women were conscious of the sexism that
was found in all movements including the Chicano, but even so, they
put aside their preoccupation as women and were obliged to chose their
identity as people of color over their identity as women. This resulted
in the emergence of a Chicana feminist movement in which many of
the first women of color who identified with such a movement were
lesbians. Moraga believes that their own lesbian identity made it
impossible to postpone their interests as women. They were women
that, due to their sexual difference, did not find a place in any of the
Third World movements (*Esta* 3).

   Alicia Gaspar de Alba tells us that with the publication of *This
Bridge Called My Back*, published originally in English in 1981 by
Cherríe Moraga and Gloria Anzaldúa, the voices of a politically active
Third World feminism started to be heard in action and reaction.
(Gaspar de Alba 957). This gives a start to a cultural production by
Chicanas in the U.S., many of them lesbians, that no longer emphasized
the traditional Chicano struggle, nor the recurrent rural themes present
in the canonized writers of the 1960s and 1970s. The new women
writers of the 1980s began to develop and politicize a new Chicana
feminist movement.

LANGUAGE, IDENTITY, SEXUALITY, AND BORDERS

*Deslenguadas. Somos los del español deficiente. We are
your linguistic nightmare, your linguistic aberration,
your linguistic mestizaje, the subject of your burla.
Because we speak with tongues of fire we are culturally
crucified. Racially, culturally, and linguistically somos
huérfanos—we speak an orphan tongue.*
                                        —Gloria Anzaldúa, *Borderlands* 58

   The new Chicano feminist movement, headed by Chicanas and
Chicana lesbians, resulted a proliferation of works. Those of Gloria

Anzaldúa, Cherríe Moraga, Sandra Cisneros, Ana Castillo, Juanita Ramos, and Carla Trujillo, among others, underscore and raise consciousness about the position of Chicana feminism, and with it, the problematics of language, identity, and sexuality in a series of spaces called borders.[3]

Many of these writers go beyond cultural nationalism and dogmatism to create a particular socio-historical and ethnic identity, consequently "modifying and reshaping female history, myths, and ultimately personal and collective identity" (Ordóñez 19). These same writers, according to Elizabeth Ordóñez, try to create a revitalization of feminine ethnicity in a broader context. They also believe in a need to break with the rules of the game imposed by one player (the man) resulting in the production of texts by Chicanas that consequently implies the existence of a Chicana community and a political Chicana feminist movement.

An integral part of the revision of this negative postulate is the reevaluation of Spanish as spoken by Chicanos. Regarding this point, Gloria Anzaldúa in her critical essay "Linguistic terrorism" confronts the internalization of a Chicano complex (*Borderlands* 53). According to Anzaldúa, the internalization of the belief that Chicano Spanish is an illegitimate bastard language is due to the insistence of its being seen as such not only by the dominant culture but also by the recent immigrants from Latin American and Spain. The dominant culture has historically censored Spanish in school for example; those who spoke Spanish were punished for doing so. Today, there exist movements from the political right to make English the official language in the U.S., resulting in a direct and constant threat to Spanish-speaking people in this country. The problem intensifies when taking into consideration that people of color are not immune to colonizing and/or marginalizing their own. When studying the essay by Anzaldúa we can see that Latino and Spanish immigrants have contributed to Chicanos' low self-esteem. Anzaldúa writes:

> If a person, Chicana or Latina, has a low estimation of my native tongue, she also has a low estimation of me. Often with mexicanas y latinas we'll speak English as a neutral language. Even among Chicanas we tend to speak English at parties or conferences. Yet at the same time, we're afraid the other will think we are agringadas because we don't speak Chicana or Spanish. We oppress each other trying to out-Chicano each other. . . . (Castillo-Speed 252)

The marginalization of Chicanos due to language is obvious in the dominant culture and among new Spanish-speaking immigrants. Moraga says that recent immigrants

> have not had their self-esteem nor that of their parents and grandparents worn away by North American racism. For them the American dream still looms as a possibility on the horizon. Their Mexican pride sustains them through the daily assaults on their intelligence, integrity, and humanity. (Moraga, "Queer Aztlán" 155)

Another topic found in Chicana lesbian writing as part of a revisionist dimension is the idea of a new Chicana identity as Chicanas and Chicana lesbians define it. It is no longer understood that Chicana identity is only a Chicano nation conceived in a double rape—first, by the Spanish and then by the Gringo, but also a new identity where:

> Chicanos are an occupied nation with a nation, and women and women's sexuality are occupied within Chicano nation. If women's bodies and these of men and women who transgress their gender roles have been historically regarded as territories to be conquered, they are also territories to be liberated. Feminism has taught us this. The nationalism sought is one that de-colonized the brown and female body as it de-colonized the brown and female earth. (Moraga, "Queer Aztlán" 150)

This position of a community of Chicana lesbians colonized in a nation dominated by dominant Anglo culture and by the colonization that exists in the Chicano community dominated specially by machistas, is not found exclusively in the works by Chicanas like Moraga and Ana Castillo.

SEXUALITY: POLITICIZING CHICANA LESBIANISM

Cachapera,
Manflora,
Jota,
Rara,
Maricona,
Anormal,
Tortillera,
Lesbiana,
Marimacha,
Andrógina,
Hombrecito
y Más, y Más y Más
Lidia Tirado White[4]

—quoted in Trujillo, *Chicana Lesbians* 22

Sappho, The Amazons of North Africa, the Beguines, Aphra Behn, Queen Christina, Emily Dickinson, The ladies of Llangolle, Radclyffe Hall, Natalie Clifford Banrney, H.D. . . .., according to Karla Jay, form a list of universal lesbians writers who have been victims of government and religious institutions and who have also been denied their lesbian existence, have maintained their works out of circulation and out of print and/or have maintained their ideas far from sympathetic eyes. The above writers and their works, although containing a similar lesbian thematic, spans a long period of time. To this list of great names we could add contemporary writers identified as lesbians, but it's worthy of note that the latter enjoy a privilege perhaps never imagined by the first. According to Karla Jay and Joanne Glasgow in their text *Lesbians Texts and Context: Radical Revisions* (1990), the new texts by lesbians of color:

> . . .surface and thrive because they have something to say, because they shake things up. . . [F]ew are getting published by mainstream houses. A few, particularly the more radical and lesbian books, are produced by independents such as Kitchen Table/Women of Color Press, Allison, Spinters/Aunt Lute and Crossing. (16-17)

A number of texts written by Chicana women in the recent years testify to what Jay and Glasgow believe. Some examples include

Cherríe Moraga and Gloria Anzaldúa, *This Bridge Called My Back*
(1981); Lillian Castillo-Speed, *Latinas. Women's Voices from the
Borderlands* (1995); Norma Alarcón et al., *Third Woman: The
Sexuality of Latinas* (1989); Alma Luz Villanueva, *Naked Ladies*
(1994); Alvina Quintana, *Home Girls* (1996); Carla Trujillo, *Chicana
Lesbians: The Girls Our Mothers Warned Us About* (1991); Ana
Castillo, *Massacre of the Dreamers* (1994); and Juanita Ramos,
Compañeras: Latina Lesbians (1987). The fact that some of these
works, such as *This Bridge Called My Back* and *Third Woman. The
Sexuality of Latinas* have been reprinted and in some cases translated to
other languages, is another example of their success. However,
limitations still exist in the publication of texts by Chicana lesbians, due
not only to the monopoly controlled by the publishing industry but also
to the limitations even in traditionally liberal centers such as
universities. For example, in nine of the university campuses of the
University of California, 36 percent of the faculty surveyed by Jay and
Glasgow refrained from doing research related to lesbian and gay topics
for fear of a negative response from colleagues. According to the
University of California Lesbian and Gay Intercampus Network
Appendix A, 41 percent of the faculty decided against including such
texts in their courses. Despite all the obstacles, lesbian material written
by Chicanas has prevailed and has influenced social norms, effecting a
revision of the social and political conventions of the status quo ruled
by a compulsory heterosexist, supremacist, capitalist, misogynist,
homophobic, imperialist, and machista United States society (Moraga
and Castillo 99). This lesbian position of writing against such strong
institutions puts writers that decide to do it in multipe dangers. Even so,
Cherríe Moraga, Gloria Anzaldúa and Naomi Littlebear Moreno, were
the first to articulate a Chicana feminism that included a radical
criticism centered in the woman and a sexuality which has resulted in
positive benefits to not only Chicana lesbians but Chicanas in general.

In *Massacre of the Dreamers* (1994), Ana Castillo talks about a
nonpoliticized Chicana lesbian, blaming strict social attitudes that reject
sexual openness and liberation. Castillo affirms that lesbians in Chicano
culture have not politicized their sexual desires nor have they openly
declared it as a way of life. She also believes that lesbians of color,
suppressing their own lesbianism, have failed at a literary level to
produce works that function as models to practice a lesbianism that is
seen as something natural. However, we must also consider that to
other Chicana lesbians politicizing their lesbianism is already under-

way. Cherríe Moraga, for example, says that "my real politicization began, not through the Chicano movement, but through the bold recognition of my lesbianism" ("Queer Aztlán " 146).

Gaspar de Alba adds that Chicana lesbianism is not only a sexual identity but also a political and spiritual one (960). With the same belief, Castillo in her essay "La Macha" creates a woman who becomes the center of the world resulting in an interpretation of a Chicana feminist who is liberated from the Chicano in order to decide her own destiny as a "Macha." Such a position is not only to be taken from the semantic definition "Macha=lesbian," but also from the biological definition of the word "Macha=feminine," thereby enabling the choosing and/or defining of her own sexuality. Both positions allow us to apply the postcolonial, postfeminist, sociopolitical analysis presented by Cheryl Clarke in her article "Lesbianismo: un acto de resistencia."

According to Clarke, to be a lesbian is in itself an act of resistance that should be recognized by all the progressive forces, since we live in such an oppressive culture in the United States. Lesbianism is a form of rebellion against the enslaving lord that prostitutes her. This form of resistance is a dangerous act, since men of all privilege levels, social classes, and ethnic backgrounds hold the power to act legally, morally, and violently when they cannot colonize women nor limit them in their sexual, productive, reproductive, or energetic prerogatives. This multifaceted position of the lesbianism Clarke proposes is evident in the text by Chicana lesbian writers of recent years. In *Loving in the War Years: Lo que nunca paso por sus labios* (1983), Cherríe Moraga takes into account and defines the established dichotomy between a sexual alliance and sexual definition. This coincides with what David William Foster emphasizes when finding that such texts, including also Moraga's *Giving up the Ghost: Teatro in Two Acts* (1986), contain a distinction created between Anglo society's destructive lesbians— because above all, it is seen as a reduplication of the macho stereotype—and the beatific lesbianism of Chicana society where the Hispanic emphasis on dignity and sensitivity of interpersonal relationships counteracts the anglo society's unforgiving competitiveness. She reaffirms a strong and vibrant lesbian continuum in Hispanic culture, which gives resources in order to reconcile its own personality. ("Erótica" 59)

In other texts, such as Juanita Ramos' *Compañeras: Latina Lesbians*, and Gloria Anzaldúa's *Borderlands/La Frontera: The New Mestiza*, a mestiza consciousness is traced to include a radical,

historical, and sexual political consciousness. According to Gaspar de
Alba this consciousness "both literary and metaphorically, in the
geographical borderlands of the U.S.-Mexico frontera and extends into
the multilingual tricultural borderlands of Chicano-Mexicano culture
(958). To Anzaldúa, lesbianism or the choice to be queer implies an act
of self-empowerment and a self-definition and rebellion that opens a
way to a knowledge and learning of the history of the oppression of "La
Raza" or the people. Other important texts such as Alarcón et al.'s *Third
Woman: The Sexuality of Latinas*, and Anzaldúa's *Making Face,
Making Soul. Haciendo Caras: Creative and Critical Perspects by
Women of Color* offer a construction of a Chicana feminine identity
inside an oppressive society. Such an identity, according to Gaspar de
Alba, breaks disciplinary barriers, occupations, and orientations
through cultural, physical, and spiritual borders (958). Therefore, with
the texts mentioned and their contents, the patriarchal domination that
maintains the subjection of women through a compulsory
heterosexuality is reconsidered. Cherríe Moraga adds that "it is
historically evident that the female body, like the Chicano people, has
been colonized, and any movement to decolonize them must be
culturally and sexually specific" ("Queer Aztlán" 149). A lesbian
accepts the potential of the mutuality of a lesbian relationship and at the
same time, rejects a life of servitude that is implicit in heterosexual
relationships, and thus attacks the institution of heterosexuality and
through it, the institutions of a supremacist man that ensure their own
perpetuity and control over women.

QUEER THEORY AND CHICANA LESBIANISM

*La sexualidad es gran parte de la vida. No es la
sexualidad lo prohibido sino la sensualidad. Hay que
erotizar el cuerpo, por lo tanto hay que erotizar la vida
misma. Lidia Tirado White[5]*
                                                    —quoted in Trujillo 23

Years after the classic period of the Chicano movement, Cherríe
Moraga started to question the racism of the white feminist movement,
the elitism of the gay and lesbian movement, and the homophobia and
the sexism of the Chicano movement. She was also a witness to the
emergence of a Chicana national feminist consciousness connected to a
activism of the same level to support literature and art:

I've seen the growth of a lesbian-of-color-movement, the founding of
an independent national Latino/a lesbian and gay men's organization,
and the flourishing of Indigenous people's international campaigns
for human and land rights. A quarter of century after those school
walk-outs in 1968. (Moraga "Queer Aztlán" 147)

Moraga adds that the Chicana lesbian and the Chicano gay not only
desire to be included in the Chicano nation, but also in a nation strong
enough to embrace a broad space of racial, as well as sexual, diversity.
But the reality is something else. Chicana lesbians and Chicano gays
lament their exclusion from the Chicano movement and from the white
lesbian and gay movements. An explanation of this exclusion is due to
the reaction of the Chicano men against Anglo America. Chicano men
adopted a machista attitude taking the most patriarchal aspects of their
Mexican heritage through the process of emasculation to oppose the
dominant culture. They took the worst of Mexican machismo, including
some of the most oppressive idealizations of what it meant to be a
traditional Mexican woman through a nationalist notion conceived by
the Chicano in the name of cultural integrity. Moraga develops this idea
in "Queer Aztlán":

> They subscribe to a machistas view of women, based on the
> centuries-old virgin-whore paradigm of la Virgen de Guadalupe and
> Malintzin Tenepal. Chicano politcos ensure that the patriarchal father
> figure remains in charge both in their private and political lives.
> Women were, at most allowed to serve as modern day "Adelitas,"
> performing "the three F's" as a Chicana colleague calls them:
> "feeding, fighting, and fucking." (158)

Another explanation is due to the limitations of "Queer Nation"
whose leather-jacketed, shaved-headed white radicals and accom-
panying anglo-centricity were an alien nation to most lesbians and gay
men of color. Also, the Chicano nationalism never openly accepted
Chicana lesbians and Chicano gays. For these reasons, to arrive at a
consciousness of being a Chicana lesbian was a way of leaving behind
an oppressive patriarchal society and enjoying her own sexual
orientation/preference. It can be seen that an intent to understand and
accept the loss of "familia" caused by their sexual preference emerged
along with the desire to win a new "familia". Moraga adds that "in
order to understand and defend our lovers and our same-sex loving,

lesbians and gay men must come to terms with how homophobia, gender roles, and sexuality are learned and expressed in Chicano Culture" ("Queer Aztlán" 159).

The concept of identity as an ensemble of unstable and multiple positions from the point of view of queer theory contends to the formulation of sexuality as a personal agenda (Hennessy 965). Sexuality can no longer be seen as a simple marginalization in relation to the dominant, thus a new form is established. According to David William Foster, the priority of the reference to the body grasps the emphasis of queer thought on erotic pleasure and on confrontation of social traditions that repudiate it. But in addition to this, it reinstates, not the authority of the body to confirm social and historical knowledge, but the centralization of an investigation about what is social and what is historical that embraces the project to define the body and ponder the relations between the body as perceived by the subject and the horizons of social and historical experiences ("Producción" 3).

The principal objective of queer theory is to write a political culture founded in the categories gay and lesbian in order to produce another discursive horizon and other ways of thinking about the sexual which include the discovery of new uses for the body, thus defying patriarchal economics and refuting the circumscribed utilization that are assigned by it to the body (4).

Queer theorists agree that resistance is a form of reclaiming an erotized, desired, and ambivalent identity, but not without evaluating the social order from the point of view of the oppressed, including a way of understanding the reality that could be understood for each one of us. According to Rosemary Hennessy, the lesbian is the only concept that goes beyond the sexual categories (woman/man), because the lesbian subject is not a woman as far as political, ideological, and economic terms are concerned (968). For this reason, to be a lesbian means to deny the power of men in a patriarchal society, a point very evident in the writing of Chicana lesbian writers.

CONCLUSIONS

We [Chicana lesbians and Chicano gays] have formed circles of support and survival, often drawing from the more egalitarian models of Indigenous communities.
—Cherríe Moraga, "Queer Aztlán" 165

The vision Cherríe Moraga formulates protests the exclusion of Chicana lesbians and Chicano gays from the movement. Even though they have all contributed to the Chicano cause, they have not been recognized. The cultural production by Chicana lesbians and their contributions to the betterment of the situation of women of color is proof of their capacity to be an important force in the movement. Their exclusion or lack of recognition by the Chicano movement as part of a bronze continent only delayed their rebirth, their success, and their impact until the 1980s and 1990s. During these years, Chicana feminists forced and continue to force a serious critique of Chicanismo. Along with Cherríe Moraga, new Chicana writers—some lesbians—are conscious and dedicated to the preservation of a Chicana culture, but at the same time know that that Chicano culture will not survive rape, incest, drug abuse, alcoholism, domestic violence, AIDS, and the marginalization of their lesbians sisters and gay brothers (Moraga, "Queer Aztlán" 159). The import of a new revisionist consciousness stirred by writers like Cherríe Moraga, Gloria Anzaldúa, Ana Castillo, Lillian Castillo-Speed, Juanita Ramos, and Carla Trujillo, among others, who are the most renowned Chicana critics of sexism in the Chicano movement, is already evident. Such evidence is found not only in their cultural production, but also in their acts of benevolence and liberation. Moraga adds that some of the most impassioned activism in the area of Chicana liberation, including work on sexual abuse, domestic violence, immigrant rights, indigenous women's issues, and health care, and have been advanced by lesbians (Moraga, "Queer Aztlán" 160). In the criticism found in the works of the authors mentioned, we can also see the dissolution of an active Chicano movement. For Moraga,

> El movimiento has never been a thing of the past, it has retreated into subterranean uncontaminated soils waiting resurrection in a "queer" more feminist generation. What was right about Chicano nationalism was its commitment to preserving the integrity of the Chicano people. A generation ago, there were cultural, economic, and political programs to develop Chicano consciousness, autonomy, and self-determination. What was wrong about Chicano Nationalism was its institutionalized heterosexism, its inbred machismo, and its lack of cohesive national political strategy. (Moraga, "Queer Aztlán" 148)

Along the lines of what Moraga says, with or without the heterosexual acknowledgment, Chicana lesbians and gay Chicanos have redefined and continue to redefine the significance of family, culture, and community. Chicana lesbians, in order to defend their women lovers, have had to confront and understand the roots of homophobia, sexual roles, and sexuality as expressed in Chicano culture. In addition to this, a redefinition and criticism of the conventional ideologies and practices is in order. But we must remember a Chicana who confronts such conventions in a heterosexist, supremacist, capitalist, misogynist, homophobic, imperialist, and machista society and still chooses to be a lesbian lives dangerously.

NOTES

1. Whenever I see a crowd of men, my heart sinks to my feet, whenever I hear sudden noises, sudden crashing, anger, male noises, their very laughter is abrasive to my ears. I shrink inside, walk close to the walls of my soul, I look for a place to hide.

2. The term women of color will be used here as used by Cherríe Moraga and Gloria Anzaldúa to reclaim by women of Asian, Latin-American and North-American indigenous and African descent a political identity and to distinguish themselves from the dominant culture.

3. "Borders" is understood as a traced history of a mestiza consiousness and a politicized racial, historical, and sexual awareness. This awareness begins, both literally and metaphorically, in the geographical borderlands of the United Stares and Mexico and it extends metaphorically into the borderlands of a multilingual and tricultural Chicano/Mexicano culture.

4. It is virtually impossible to translate each word of this inventory: they are all synonyms for "lesbian," "dyke," and "queer."

5. Sexuality is a big part of my life. It is not sexuality that is prohibited, but sensuality. We must eroticize the body; therefore, we must eroticize life itself.

Memories of Girlhood
Chicana Lesbian Fictions
Catrióna Rueda Esquibel

> *To link families with four sisters who would be friends
> longer than their lifetimes, through children who would
> bond them at baptismal rites. Comadres. We would
> become intimate friends, sharing coffee, gossip, and
> heartaches. We would endure the female life-cycle—
> adolescence, marriage, menopause, death, and even
> divorce, before or after menopause, before or after
> death.*
>> *I had not come for that. I had come for her kiss.*
>> —Pérez, 13

In my research of Chicana literature, I have found a series of stories in which girlhood provides a space, however restrictive, for lesbian desire. Within the socially sanctioned system of *comadrazgo*, young Chicanas are encouraged to form lifelong female friendships, and it is the intimacy of these relationships that often provides the context for lesbian desire. Specifically, I consider the representation of girlhood friendships in four novel-length works by Chicana authors: Sandra Cisneros's *The House on Mango Street*, Denise Chávez's *The Last of the Menu Girls*, Terri de la Peña's *Margins*, and Emma Pérez's *Gulf Dreams*. Of these, only the lesbian-authored texts—those by de la Peña and Pérez—are generally perceived as "lesbian" fiction. By including *Mango Street* and *Menu Girls* in my study, I argue that they too are Chicana lesbian texts, not because the characters (or their authors) self-consciously claim a lesbian identity, but because the texts, in their

59

literary construction of such intense girlhood friendships, inscribe a
desire between girls that I name "lesbian."

In this, I participate in lesbian textual criticism, which has
discussed at length the question "What is a lesbian text?" Bertha Harris
has defined lesbian texts thus: "If in a woman writer's work a sentence
refuses to do what it is supposed to do, if there are strong images of
women and if there is a refusal to be linear, the result is innately lesbian
literature" (quoted in Smith 164). Such a definition seems to use lesbian
as a metaphor for "feminist" or "woman-identified." Barbara Smith
implicitly demonstrates the exceedingly broad scope of Harris's
definition when she applies it to Black women's writing. Indeed, Smith
argues that according to Harris's definition, the majority of Black
women's literature is lesbian, "not because the women are 'lovers,' but
because they are its central figures, are positively portrayed and have
pivotal relations with one another" (164). While I concur that such a
definition likewise encompasses most contemporary Chicana literature,
so defining all Chicana literature as lesbian would hardly enhance an
understanding of either Chicana literature in general or Chicana lesbian
literature in particular.

However, in her well-known reading of *Sula*, Smith gestures
toward a more nuanced description of lesbian fiction: "[*Sula*] works as
a lesbian novel not only because of the passionate friendship between
Sula and Nel, but because of [its] consistently critical stance toward the
heterosexual institutions of male/female relationships, marriage, and the
family. Consciously or not, Morrison's work poses both lesbian and
feminist questions about black women's autonomy and their impact
upon each other's lives" (165). Seemingly, Smith's use of the term
"lesbian" to describe a critique of heterosexual institutions is both
metaphoric and utopic.[1] Because she seems to use "lesbian" and
"lesbian feminist" interchangeably, both the passionate friendship and
the critique of institutionalized heterosexuality are necessary to her
definition of lesbian. However, if one applies Smith's description of
"both lesbian and feminist" *respectively* to the "passionate friendship"
and critique of heterosexual institutions, one comes closer to a usage of
lesbian that is neither metaphoric nor interchangeable with "feminist."
Thus the critique of heterosexual institutions makes *Sula* feminist (in an
nonheterocentric sense), while the "passionate friendship" invites a
lesbian reading.

It is important, I think, to differentiate "lesbian" from other
homosocial relations between women and from female desire in

general, lest the latter two erase the former, as has been the case with
many applications of Adrienne Rich's "Lesbian Continuum." In *The
Practice of Love*, Teresa de Lauretis unravels "lesbian" from its
metaphoric and political applications to define it in quite specific terms:

> Whatever other affective or social ties may be involved in a lesbian
> relationship—ties that may also exist in other relations between and
> among women, from friendship to rivalry, political sisterhood to class
> or racial antagonism, ambivalence to love, and so on—the term
> lesbian refers to a sexual relation, for better or for worse, and
> however broadly one may wish to define sexual. I use this term . . . to
> include centrally—beyond any performed or fantasized physical
> sexual act, whatever it may be—the conscious presence of desire in
> one woman for another. (284)

De Lauretis argues that "lesbian" is not equivalent to woman-identified
or feminist, but derives from desire, that is not simply female desire but
desire in one woman (or girl) for another. I feel that Smith was
invoking just such an understanding of desire between women in her
discussion of Sula and Nel's "passionate friendship," which Lorraine
Bethel has characterized as expressing "a certain sensuality in their
interactions" (quoted in Smith 166).

Yet, extending de Lauretis's definition to girlhood raises other
interpretive questions, for what constitutes "the conscious presence of
desire" in girlhood stories? As Bonnie Zimmerman has noted, "Lesbian
writers of retrospective narratives often claim to have felt themselves to
be lesbian from birth or age two, or certainly from puberty and thus
always to have had a lesbian perspective" ("Perverse Reading," 136).
Thus, as retrospectives, girlhood stories in particular are "products of
the very perspective that they purport to explain." By this logic,
"lesbian" girlhood stories are those that retroactively construct adult
lesbian identity,[2] but this too is a subjective definition; "for example, a
woman might focus on the fact that she was intimate friends with Sally
at age six and fail to note that so were a dozen other girls, none of
whom became lesbians" (136). In the interplay between reader and text,
it occurs to me that this retroactive construction might work both ways:
a story of being "intimate friends with Sally" might appear to some
readers to be a simple girlhood story, with no implications about
sexuality outside of gender identity, while to others it would be a
specifically lesbian girlhood story. Thus for many readers, *The House*

on Mango Street, and *The Last of the Menu Girls* would constitute lesbian girlhood stories because the readers identify with the protagonist and her feelings of loss for her friend, while other readers, approaching these stories from a heteronormative stance, would emphatically refute such a reading for precisely the same reasons.

Zimmerman claims that "if a text lends itself to a lesbian reading, then no amount of . . . 'proof' ought to be necessary to establish it as a lesbian text," ("What Has Never Been" 39). As I undertake a lesbian reading of all four of these texts, I hope that my readers, while they may hold themselves unconvinced, will yet acknowledge that I am not "demanding a plot . . . that the writer has not chosen to create" but am "picking up on hints and possibilities that the author, consciously or not, has strewn in the text" ("Perverse Reading" 144). While both Cisneros and Chávez depict the cultural structures of institutionalized heterosexuality, neither fixes a heterosexual ending for her protagonist, who is alone at the end of the text, with many possibilities open to her.

In Chicana/o literature, tales of girlhood and adolescence provide a glimpse into the construction of sexual identity when "the girls come . . . face to face with . . . their prescribed roles" in Chicana/o (hetero)sexual economies (Saldívar, *Chicano Narrative* 184). The stories show how and what the young female characters learn about sexuality and the sense they make of it. *Las chamacas* are frequently perceived as asexual, since they are not sexually active, or more specifically, not (yet) heterosexually active. They are discouraged—by mothers, family, community, and religion—from recognizing or exploring their sexuality. At the same time, the cultural role of *comadres*, which raises lifelong friendships to the status of kinship, is both encouraged and recognized. In this essay, I focus on the representation of desire as it develops between girlhood friends and on the ways in which that desire, and any explicitly sexual perception of it, is masked by the presumed sexlessness of adolescent girls.[3]

In *The House on Mango Street, The Last of the Menu Girls, Margins*, and *Gulf Dreams*, girlhood friendships have a very specific relationship to institutionalized heterosexuality. These texts critique the limited and heterosexual roles open and indeed prescribed to young Chicanas, as well as the ways in which female friendships are less valued than heterosexual relationships. However, I have chosen these texts neither for their critique of heterosexual institutions nor for their depiction of the role of girlhood friendships within their respective Chicano communities, but because they locate certain erotic elements in girlhood friendships.[4] Chicana/o literary criticism has not yet discussed these texts in terms of lesbian sexuality.[5] While more scholarship on Chicana lesbian literature is being produced, most criticism focuses on the two best-known Chicana lesbian writers, Cherríe Moraga and Gloria Anzaldúa. As the coeditors of the 1981 anthology *This Bridge Called My Back: Writings by Radical Women of Color*, Moraga and Anzaldúa were instrumental in the circulation of writings by lesbians of color. Many of their subsequent individual works have been widely anthologized, often several times over. While both have taken pains to develop and promote the work of other writers—through editing, teaching, and workshopping—they are often taken as representative of Chicana lesbians in general and thus are published in lieu of other Chicana lesbian writers. Because of the prominence of these two authors, criticism on Chicana lesbian writers has focused mainly on the genres of drama and nonfiction prose. In looking at girlhood friendships, I hope to broaden the scope of Chicana lesbian literary criticism, both by bringing attention to less well-known writings and authors and by reevaluating Cisneros's and Chávez's works in light of the explicit representation of lesbian desire in girlhood in the novels of de la Peña and Pérez, and thus to expand Chicana lesbian literature beyond the writings of lesbian-identified authors. In my readings, I dwell on the "passionate friendships" between girls that other scholars have been at pains to ignore, rationalize, or misrepresent.

THE HOUSE ON MANGO STREET

Sandra Cisneros's *The House on Mango Street* was first published in 1984 by Arte Público, a small press out of the University of Houston featuring the works of Latino writers in English and Spanish. In 1991, the third edition was published by Vintage and has been an international best-seller. It is frequently referred to as a "novel-in-stories"; it is, in fact, a series of forty-four vignettes that feature the same narrative voice and cast of characters. Alvina Quintana takes exception to the tendency to classify *Mango Street* as a novel, which she sees as a means of incorporating Cisneros's work into traditional forms: "Cisneros defined a distinctive Chicana literary space—oh so gently she flung down the gauntlet, challenging, at the least, accepted literary form, gender inequities, and the cultural and economic subordination of minorities. Theoretically speaking, this little text subverts traditional form and content in a way that demonstrates how conventional applications of literary genre and the social construction of gender undermine a feminist aesthetic" (55). Ironically, in spite of its being classified as a novel, critical discussions of *Mango Street* (Herrera-Sobek; Saldívar, *Chicano Narrative*) often approach it as a collection of separate stories, with little effort to appreciate the complex relationships among the characters as they develop throughout the work. As a departure, then, I examine one relationship as it is developed in five of the vignettes: "Sally," "What Sally Said," "The Monkey Garden," "Red Clowns," and "Linoleum Roses." These stories focus on the developing relationships between Esperanza, the narrator, and Sally, with whom she shares a particular friendship.

All the stories (or vignettes) in *Mango Street* are told by the adolescent Esperanza in first person. She discusses the other inhabitants of Mango Street, at some times giving her own views on people, at others repeating what she has been told. Most of the secondary characters are also girls: her younger sister Nenny; her friends across the street, Lucy and Rachel; the older girls in the neighborhood, Marin, Alicia, and Sally. In this community an adult woman is one who has a house, and women are classified by whether they have a husband or whether their husband has died or has left them. Women are viewed primarily in relation to men, in heterosexual terms. The narrator begins describing herself by explaining her name "Esperanza," which means both "hope" and "waiting." She does not want to wait for a man to change her life; she wants to write her own changes. Esperanza seeks an alternative to the options presented to her: options proscribed by sexism and institutionalized heterosexuality. One of Esperanza's dilemmas is how to reconcile her desires with her opportunities. She looks forward to having her own house, without a husband to lock her in or leave her lonely. Such a thing is unheard of on Mango Street, where women are confined to the home, where a woman is alone not by her choice but by necessity or by a man's choice. Thus Esperanza, who looks for something more, must look beyond Mango Street.

Ramón Saldívar, in *Chicano Narrative*, discusses *Mango Street* at length in his chapter "Gender and Difference in Ríos, Cisneros and Moraga." Like many other critics, including Olivares, Quintana, and Rosaldo, he focuses on the space of Mango Street, the houses, gender roles, and the confinement of women. Ironically, while addressing the limited roles made available by the patriarchal structure, he becomes caught up in its discourse, defining women in relation to men, and thus missing the significant relationships between girls that occur in the novel. Saldívar places the intense friendship Esperanza feels for her friend Sally solely in the realm of emulation or shared experience and does not differentiate it from Esperanza's other friendships, such as those with Rachel and Lucy, who are nearer her own age, or the significant but less charged older-girl/younger-girl friendships she enjoys with Marin and Alicia.

For Esperanza and for her world, adulthood—that is, womanhood—is defined by men. In "The Family of Little Feet," Esperanza, Lucy, and Rachel are given three pairs of fancy high-heeled shoes by a neighbor lady.[6] They practice walking and running up and down the street with them, and then

> Down to the corner where the men can't take their eyes off us . . .
>
> Mr. Benny at the corner grocery puts down his important cigar:
> Your mother know you got shoes like that? Who give you those?
>
> Nobody.
>
> Them are dangerous, he says. You girls too young to be wearing shoes like that. Take them shoes off before I call the cops, but we just ran. (40–41)

The shoes enact one transformation on the girls and the men another. On the one hand, the shoes make the girls into desirable objects; they see their own legs becoming long and shapely because of the high heels: "the truth is it is scary to look down at your foot that is no longer yours and see attached a long long leg" (40). On the other, the men, through their desiring gaze, make the girls into women: here, clearly, to be a woman is to be an object of desire to heterosexual men. The male attention places the girls in the adult world; they are solicited by the men and finally run away home to hide the shoes for another day because they "are tired of being beautiful." But that other day never comes, and they leave the shoes hidden, to be thrown away later by a cleaning mother.

"The Family of Little Feet" is a good example of the ways in which Esperanza keeps coming up against adulthood, womanhood, which actually means adult heterosexuality, and her resistance to that change. At the same time, Esperanza distinguishes herself from her younger sister Nenny, who is firmly in the realm of childhood. In "Hips," Esperanza, Lucy, and Rachel are discussing their desire to grow hips, what hips mean, and what they are for. As they jump rope, each girl makes up a rhyme about hips. Nenny does not understand the conversation: "Everybody is getting into it now except Nenny who is still humming *not a girl, not a boy, just a little baby*. She's like that" (51).[7] Instead of making up her own song about hips, Nenny uses standard jumping rhymes, like "Engine, engine number nine" and "My mother and your mother were washing clothes," even when the other girls tell her she's not playing right. In contrast to both Nenny, who is a child, and Esperanza, Lucy, and Rachel, who are adolescents, the older teenage girls in the stories are constantly circulating in the male sexual realm. Whether under the control of their fathers, meeting with boys at dances, fulfilling the roles of absent mothers, or marrying and being confined to the house, Marin, Sally, and Alicia are clearly situated within adult heterosexuality. While Esperanza is friends with most of these older girls, one in particular—Sally—has a transformative effect on her. Esperanza admires Sally, and desires her, although that desire is not explicitly sexual. Through Sally, Esperanza comes to understand the value system in which female friendships are relegated to childhood, while adulthood is reserved for heterosexuality.

"Sally," the first of the stories to depict Sally and Esperanza's relationship, introduces "the girl with eyes like Egypt and nylons the color of smoke" (81). Esperanza describes Sally first as Sally's father perceives her—"to be this beautiful is trouble,"—and then as Esperanza's mother sees her—"to wear black so young is dangerous,"—both parents implying that Sally's sexual desirability will bring her grief. Indeed this is already the case, as she has no best friend, "not since [Cheryl] called you that name" (82), that is, presumably, since Cheryl labeled her as sexually dirty. While it attracts males, Sally's sensuality creates a barrier between herself and other girls. She is judged to be fast or dirty or ill-fated and is thus left alone. Furthermore, Sally seems afraid to go home and attempts to "clean herself up" before entering her house: "You pull your skirt straight, you rub the blue paint off your eyelids. You don't laugh, Sally. You look at your feet and walk fast to the house you can't come out from" (82). Both Saldívar and Quintana look at the story "Sally" as being primarily about the danger of sexuality. Yet they do not contextualize this story with the other Sally stories, but see it as one of a series of introductions, not as part of a larger narrative about this one character. Cisneros introduces Sally between "Rafaela Who Drinks Coconut & Papaya Juice on Tuesdays," a view of a young married woman locked up in her house, and "Minerva Writes Poems," the story of a friend "only a little bit older than me but already she has two kids and a husband who left"

(84). The Sally stories are unique within *Mango Street* because they are not isolated vignettes but chart the development of the character Sally and her relationship with Esperanza. The stories dealing with Lucy and Rachel, for example, could be read in any order, whereas the Sally stories chronicle the growing intimacy between Esperanza and Sally, the ending of that intimacy, and the subsequent distance from which Esperanza perceives Sally.

Saldívar argues that "Esperanza wishes to be like Sally, wishes to learn to flick her hair when she laughs, to 'paint [her] eyes like Cleopatra,' and to wear black suede shoes and matching nylons as Sally does" (185). Yet Esperanza's desire to be taught how to paint her eyes "like Egypt" is less about being *like* Sally than it is about being *with* Sally.[8] It is intertwined with the desire to lean against the fence with Sally and share her hairbrush, to hear Sally's dreams. Esperanza then goes on to articulate a world for Sally—like Esperanza's own dreams for a "real" house, far away from the barrio and the limits of Mango Street—a world where Sally keeps walking to a quiet, middle-class neighborhood, where she can dream her dreams, where her desire for desire is innocent and not damning, and where her desire for love is not "crazy" but the most normal thing in the world.

Quintana is most interested in the way the depiction of Sally and her desires "illuminates the contradictions in an ideology whose primary objective is masculine gratification" (69). The negative opinions of Sally, such as those voiced by Esperanza's mother and Sally's father, and "the stories the boys tell in the cloakroom" are clear evidence of the contradiction that women face: they must reproduce themselves for a desiring male gaze, but in doing so, they incur censure. Although she labels this ideology "heterosexist" (69), Quintana does not herself go beyond a heterosexual framework, and in my view she fails to fully appreciate Sally the character and her significance for Esperanza. Esperanza's descriptions of Sally are poetic and appreciative, although when she describes Sally as pretty she does so in reference to male approval: "The boys at school think she's beautiful because her hair is shiny black like raven feathers and when she laughs, she flicks her hair back like a satin shawl over her shoulders and laughs" (81). In her own mind she poses questions to Sally, in a bantering, flirting tone quite unlike Esperanza's usual form of address: "Sally, who taught you to paint your eyes like Cleopatra? And if I roll the little brush with my tongue . . . will you teach me?" Here she goes on to articulate a desire to be like Sally, to have shoes and nylons like hers, but again her means of expressing this point out how much it is Sally she desires. Precisely because they do read "Sally" in conjunction with the other four Sally stories, Quintana and Saldívar miss the development of Esperanza and Sally's relationship throughout the book. Perhaps they see no reason to privilege female friendships or to consider lesbian desire in their critique of the gender limitations within *Mango Street*. Instead, they see "Sally" as merely one of a sequence of character introductions, between Rafaela and Minerva.

Of all the characters, however, it is Sally that Esperanza desires, and it is Sally who betrays her. In "The Monkey Garden," Esperanza is torn between running with the children and talking to the boys with Sally. "Play with the kids if you want to," Sally says, from the circle of a boy's arms, "I'm staying here" (96). In their sexual banter, the boys take Sally's keys and refuse to return them unless she gives each of them a kiss, and the group enters the garden to accomplish this:

> One of the boys invented the rules. One of Tito's friends said you can't get the keys back unless you kiss us and Sally pretended to be mad at first but she said yes. . . .
>
> I don't know why, but something inside me wanted to throw a stick. Something wanted to say no when I watched Sally going into the garden with Tito's buddies all grinning. It was just a kiss, that's all. A kiss for each one. So what, she said.
>
> Only how come I felt angry inside. Like something wasn't right. (97)

Esperanza is incensed at this manipulation of her friend. Confused by Sally's compliance, she interprets it as passivity and attempts to interfere with the male coercion. She first complains to the mother of one of the boys, who tells her, in effect, that boys will be boys. Frustrated, Esperanza decides she has the responsibility to rescue Sally.

> I . . . ran back down the three flights to the garden where Sally needed to be saved. I took three big sticks and a brick and figured this was enough.
>
> But when I got there Sally said go home. Those boys said leave us alone. I felt stupid with my brick. They all looked at me as if *I* was the one that was crazy and made me feel ashamed. (97)

Esperanza is shown that her assistance is neither required nor desired. In fact, her aggression, if you will, her refusal to accept this male sexual barter as "justo y necesario"[9] is precisely what marks Esperanza as "childish" rather than "womanly." Furthermore, Sally not only demonstrates that she thinks Esperanza is childish for resisting, but she is quite clear in expressing her preference for Tito's company over Esperanza's. Sally, articulating her adult sexuality (heterosexuality), mocks Esperanza and signifies her as infantile both for her active role (attempting to rescue the seemingly passive Sally) and for her perception of male sexuality and heterosexuality as dangerous. It is this rejection by Sally that affects Esperanza so strongly that she feels sick and angry and "wrong." She hides herself in the monkey garden, weeping and praying for death: "I wanted to will my blood to stop, my heart to quit its pumping. I wanted to be dead, to turn into the rain, my eyes to melt into the ground like two black snails. I wished and wished. I closed my eyes and willed it, but when I got up my dress was green and I had a headache" (97–98). The violence of her reaction demonstrates the depth of her feeling for Sally and the pain of betrayal. Yet her feelings, her love, are clearly of little value in comparison to male attention. Although Esperanza frequently expresses feelings of rebellion and resistance toward the limited gender roles available to girls, in this instance, she resents heteronormativity, as well as sexism because it limits not only what she can do, but who she can love and how. Sexuality—heterosexuality—however it is naturalized, defined, and promoted, remains outside the realm of Esperanza's understanding. "They were laughing. She was too. It was a joke I didn't get" (96). For Sally and Tito and the other boys, the joke is heterosexuality: it's fun, it's funny, it's a game they all know. And yet, like Nenny singing her childish rhyme, oblivious to the advantages of hips, Esperanza lives in a world that does not accommodate such things. Heterosexuality is, throughout the novel, a brutal intrusion into the world of girls.

In Chicana contexts, girlhood is a space and time before the imposition of normative heterosexuality and, as such, provides a site for texts to stage lesbian desires, such as those of Esperanza, whose feelings for Sally go beyond those of simple friendship. According to the institutions of heterosexuality, Esperanza's reluctance to enter into (hetero)sexuality is both validated by and a symptom of her sexual immaturity. Because she is a child, she is repulsed by the mature reality of heterosexuality. When she is older, she will get the joke. Yet, throughout *The House on Mango Street*, Esperanza resists this forced heterosexualization. In "Red Clowns," she is violently initiated into heterosexuality by a boy who says "I love you, Spanish girl." She and Sally are at a carnival, and it is while she is waiting for Sally, who has gone off with another boy, that she is forced into sex. She cries out against the act, which is not like the stories of her girlfriends, or the songs, or the movies, but is painful and unpleasant and a manifestation of male desire that has little to do with her as a person. Esperanza's resistance constitutes what Smith would describe as the text's "critical stance toward the heterosexual institutions of male/female relationships, marriage and the family" (165). And yet, what moves *Mango Street* into the realm of lesbian text is Esperanza crying out to Sally. "Sally Sally a hundred times" (100). As in "The Monkey Garden," Sally chooses male company over Esperanza, leaving the latter confused and vulnerable. Esperanza very clearly voices her desire for Sally and the ways in which she perceives it to differ from male desire: "And anyway I don't like carnivals. I went to be with you because you laugh on the tilt-a-whirl, you throw your head back and laugh. I hold your change, wave, count how many times you go by. Those boys that look at you because you're pretty. I like to be with you, Sally" (99). Esperanza is attempting to articulate a desire for Sally that she differentiates from the mere physical attraction of "those boys that look at you because you're pretty." She is, however unable to find words to express that differentiation and thus falls back on the acceptable description of female intimacy: "You're my friend." Saldívar misses the nuances of this story, stating only, "Waiting to meet Sally at an amusement park, Esperanza is assaulted by three white boys" (186).[10] Esperanza's love for Sally and Sally's preference for a boy are precisely what has placed Esperanza in this vulnerable position; Sally's action represents not merely "complicity in embroidering a fairy-tale-like mist around sex" (Herrera-Sobek, 178), but the further betrayal of Esperanza's love for her.

What stands out about both "Red Clowns" and "The Monkey Garden" are the ways in which Esperanza relates to heterosexuality, not through boys, but through Sally. Sally desires male attention, while Esperanza desires Sally's attention. She wants to be Sally's friend and confidante, to stand by her when others do not. Instead she is rejected and left waiting while Sally chooses to kiss the boys. It is Esperanza's desire for Sally, both in the way that it differs from her friendships with Lucy and Rachel and in the way that it pushes Esperanza into heterosexuality, that makes this a lesbian girlhood story. I do not mean that Esperanza chooses heterosexuality, but merely that she is violently initiated into it because of her desire to be with Sally, who does not prefer to be with her. "Linoleum Roses," which follows "Red Clowns," effectively brings Sally's narrative, and Esperanza's involvement in her life, to a close. Sally is married and locked away in a man's house. Although he is prone to violence, Sally says her new husband is "okay. Except he won't let her talk on the telephone. And he doesn't let her look out the window. And he doesn't like her friends" (101-2). Thus Sally is lost to Esperanza, who is not allowed "to visit her unless he is working." Not even able to gaze at roses outside the window, Sally can only view those printed on her linoleum floor.

The Sally stories, and "the Monkey Garden" and "Red Clowns" in particular, have a transformative effect on both the narrator and the text. They are situated near the end of the collection[11] and suggest "a change in Esperanza's attitude" (Quintana 65). In these stories Esperanza passes out of adolescence, not in the patriarchal sense of "being made a woman" through intercourse with a man, but because she is passed over in favor of a male and then subsequently used for male pleasure. These traumatic events are marked off, as is Esperanza's perception of her self: "I looked at my feet in their white socks and their ugly round shoes. They seemed far away. They didn't seem to be my feet anymore. And the garden that had been such a good place to play didn't seem mine either" (98). Esperanza's world, her self, and the way she views everything have dramatically shifted as a result of the loss of Sally's friendship. However, while the world in which Esperanza moves is exclusively heterosexual, she is not recuperated by heterosexuality at the end of the book. The ending, in fact, raises more questions about Esperanza's future than it answers.

> Friends and neighbors will say, What happened to that Esperanza? Where did she go with all those books and paper? Why did she march so far away?
>
> They will not know I have gone away to come back. For the ones I left behind. For the ones who cannot come out. (110)[12]

Perhaps Esperanza will come back one day for Sally, the one "who cannot come out."

THE LAST OF THE MENU GIRLS

Denise Chávez's 1987 work, *The Last of the Menu Girls*, has enjoyed moderate success for a small press book. Like *The House on Mango Street*, *The Last of the Menu Girls* is a series of interrelated stories about an adolescent female character negotiating her womanhood. Also like Cisneros's work, *Menu Girls* resists easy classification. While the seven stories are distinct, their depiction of Rocío Esquibel, the primary narrator, demonstrates the depth and movement of her character. Several of the stories were originally published individually, yet as a collection the stories achieve a certain unity that informs the minor aspects of the individual stories.[13] However, Rocío's world is very different from Esperanza's: women are not defined by men or dependent on them for identity or support. Rocío herself comes from a household of women, although traces of her mother's two husbands can be found in dusty corners.

The stories are set in the area of Las Cruces, New Mexico, which borders El Paso, Texas, which in turn borders Ciudad Juárez, Mexico. They are generally told from the perspective of Rocío, who lives with her younger sister, Mercy, and their mother, Nieves, a schoolteacher. Her father, Salvador, has deserted the family and is working up north, and Ronelia, her elder sister, has left home to marry. Although she is looking back on her adolescence and captures the bluntness of that period, Rocío clearly speaks as an adult through most of the stories. In *The Last of the Menu Girls*, I am primarily interested in Chávez's portrayals of the relationships among girls and between girls and women, and in the way that Rocío's eroticism and desire focus on women. Chávez is quite frank in depicting the sensual dynamics of these relationships, and in fact it is the sensual dimension that causes Rocío to question herself continually. Rocío is a challenging narrator, for unlike Esperanza of *Mango Street*, who holds little back, Rocío is often coy and evasive, providing only hints of her true feelings.

The book begins with the title story, which describes Rocío's first job, delivering menus to patients at the local hospital. Being in the presence of the "sick and dying" reminds her of caring for her dying great aunt Eutilia four years earlier. Following a multitude of visceral images of Eutilia's illness, Rocío recalls dancing "around her bed in my dreams, naked, smiling, jubilant. It was an exultant adolescent dance for my dying aunt. It was necessary, compulsive. It was a primitive dance, a full moon offering that led me slithering into her room with

breasts naked and oily at thirteen" (14). This "full moon offering,"
charged with imagery of female sexuality, is not solely self-expression.
In her mind, Rocío performs not merely in the presence of Eutilia, but
for Eutilia:

> Down the steps I leaped into Eutilia's faded and foggy consciousness
> where I whirled and danced and sang . . . Eutilia stared at me. I turned
> away.
> I danced around Eutilia's bed. I hugged the screen door, my
> breasts indented in the meshed wire. In the darkness Eutilia moaned,
> my body wet, her body dry. Steamy we were, and full of prayers. (15)

While one could perhaps read this scene as solely a fantastic healing
ritual, it seems clear that Rocío herself sees it as distinctly sexual.
Renato Rosaldo describes this dance in terms of "sexuality and danger"
and acknowledges a "bodily sexual connection" between Rocío and
Eutilia, but does so, perversely, without considering the implications of
that "sexual" connection being between women. Instead he reads it
exclusively as an aspect of her familial ties to generations of women
(89-90).[14] However, this fantasy of Rocío offering her own oiled
breasts, pressing them against the screen door that separates her from
Eutilia, the contrast of "my body wet, her body dry," Eutilia's stare—
which simultaneously draws Rocío and drives her away—and Eutilia's
moans mark this not merely as female sexuality but as sexuality
between women.

Throughout the stories Rocío's sexuality is expressed most
profoundly in relation to other women. Although Rocío does not
identify as a lesbian—and she does know lesbians—she repeatedly
expresses complex desires for other female characters. For example,
Rocío describes a significant week:

> When Arlene took a short vacation to the Luray Caverns, I became
> the official menu girl. That week was the happiest of my entire
> summer.
> That week I fell in love.
> ELIZABETH RAINEY (26)

The name Elizabeth Rainey marks a section break within the story. The
previous sentence, "That week I fell in love," sets up an expectation
that Rocío will tell of her first boyfriend, perhaps of an awkward

courtship, or a romantic one. Instead, she describes Elizabeth Rainey, an elegant young Anglo patient at the hospital, who impresses Rocío with her beauty and sorrow.

> I ran out, frightened by her pain, yet excited somehow. She was so beautiful and so alone. I wanted in my little girl's way to hold her, hold her tight and in my woman's way never to feel her pain, ever, whatever it was. (27)

> It was this woman in her solitary anguish who touched me the most deeply. How could I, at age seventeen, not knowing love, how could I presume to reach out to this young woman in her sorrow, touch her and say, "I know, I understand." (27)

Elizabeth Rainey has an aura of sexuality, for she "was in for a D and C. I didn't know what [that] was, but I knew it was mysterious, and to me, of course, this meant it had to do with sex" (26). This is another example of the difference from *Mango Street*, where, although girls may marry before high school or leave home because of pregnancy, they do not get abortions.[15]

Elizabeth Rainey is indeed marked by sexuality but not treated kindly by it: "She looked fragile, and yet her face betrayed a harsh indelicate bitterness" (26). Although her hospital room is full of flowers, there is no tender lover to greet her, to inquire anxiously how she is feeling. Instead there is only a seventeen-year-old menu girl fascinated and yearning, but unable to act: "As long as I live I will carry Elizabeth Rainey's image with me: in a creme-colored gown she is propped up, her hair fanning pillows in a room full of deep sweet acrid and overspent flowers. Oh, I may have been that summer girl, but yes, I knew. I understood. I would have danced for her . . . had I but dared" (28). Yet in spite of foreshadowing the week of Elizabeth Rainey as "the week I fell in love," Rocío avoids actually saying that she has fallen in love with Elizabeth. Rather, she articulates those qualities that attract her to Elizabeth Rainey—her beauty, her pain—and then her own inability to reach out, to give the comfort or understanding expected of the Florence Nightingales of the hospital. Although she expresses her desire in terms of nurturing, she also dwells on her desire to dance naked for Elizabeth Rainey as she dreamed of doing for Eutilia. Yet, while she was able to fantasize quite explicitly about that dance for Eutilia, something—perhaps the fact that Elizabeth Rainey is marked by sexuality—keeps Rocío from actively fantasizing that dance for her: instead she regrets her lack of daring.

Here and elsewhere in *Menu Girls*, Rocío attempts to explain her desire away in terms of identification. "I shrank back into myself and trembled behind the door. I never went back in her room. How could I? It was too terrible a vision, *for in her I saw myself*, all life, all suffering. What I saw both chilled and burned me. I stood long in that darkened doorway, confused in the presence of human pain. I wanted to reach out . . . I wanted to . . . But *how*?" (27; ellipses in original, first emphasis added). However, as Judith Butler argues, "it is important to consider that identification and desire can coexist, and that their formulation in terms of mutually exclusive oppositions serves a heterosexual matrix" ("Imitation and Gender Insubordination" 26). One need not choose either to identify with a person or to desire that person (see Butler, *Bodies That Matter* 99). Such an argument seems to refute the distinction de Lauretis makes between (lesbian) desire for a woman and" 'intrafeminine' self-directed, narcissistic 'fascinations'" (*The Practice of Love* 120), which she sees as "quintessentially heterosexual." However, within the cultural contexts of both *Mango Street* and *Menu Girls*, the narrators are unable to articulate desire for females except through socially acceptable identification.

Unlike *Mango Street*, which does not include the possibility for women-loving women, Rocío's world is inhabited by lesbians. Quite a few lesbians, in fact, such as "the Nurses González and González—Esperanza, male, and Bertha, female" (28).[16] "Esperanza the dyke" is the head nurse of the surgical floor (32). She is bossy, prejudiced against immigrant Mexicans, and wholly unsympathetic, in stark contrast to the feminine women to whom Rocío is attracted. Far from identifying with this lesbian character, Rocío seems quite repulsed by this "Esperanza of no esperanzas" (32), who is "without hope" both because of her own aggressive belligerence and because, looking back from the future, Rocío knows of her early death in a car accident: "Later when Esperanza was killed my aunt said, 'How nice. In the paper they call her lover her sister. How nice!'" (32). This incident marks both the visibility and invisibility of lesbian relationships. Everyone knows that Esperanza and Bertha are lovers. The author of the newspaper obituary recognizes the significance of that relationship by claiming Bertha as "sister," that is, as the closest legitimate female kin. Yet that same claim simultaneously erases their lesbianism by conflating it with the nonsexual blood ties. Anyone not personally acquainted with González and González will merely see that a woman has died in a car accident and was survived by her sister. Meanwhile, the ending of the story links Rocío back to Esperanza the dyke because her summer also ends with a car accident, although not a fatal one. Like Elizabeth Rainey, she is installed in a hospital room full of flowers, and she curses her own stupidity, which has brought her to such a pass. While Chávez thus creates a chain of signification from Esperanza to Rocío and back to Elizabeth Rainey, Rocío is at pains to distance herself from Esperanza, and thus from lesbianism. The subsections of this story are named for the characters who are most prominent in them (Mr. Smith, Arlene Rutshman, Elizabeth Rainey, and Dolores Casaus): this section should logically be named "Esperanza González." Instead, it is named for a rather minor character, Juan María—an undocumented Mexican worker disfigured in a barroom brawl—as if Rocío is afraid to put too much emphasis on "Esperanza the dyke." In the stories dealing with Rocío's desires for women, Chávez repeatedly invokes lesbian figures who stand simultaneously for lesbian potential and the denial of that potential. The lesbian serves as a marker, as if to say, "Something queer is going on here" and yet, because of her unsympathetic portrayal, that queerness is never claimed for Rocío. Instead, the narrator chooses to rearticulate that desire for women as an identification.

  "Shooting Stars," the third story of the collection, deals at length with Rocío's relationship to other girls, specifically her friend Eloisa, who is sixteen and "already a woman" in comparison to the still girlish Rocío. During her annual summer visit with relatives in Texas, Rocío discovers that Eloisa is a cousin, of sorts: "Her aunt wore men's shirts and pants and bound her breasts with rags. One day I found that Eloisa's mother and aunt (half men to me), were relatives! This made Eloisa, too, part of my mother's family. Most of them were a queer, unbalanced lot" (55). Eloisa's nameless "aunt" is clearly a butch lesbian. The earlier euphemistic representation of González and González as sisters provides a certain ambiguity as to whether Eloisa's mother is the "aunt's" lover rather than her sister. That Eloisa's mother is included in the designation "half men to me" seems to support the possibility that the two women are lovers. These queer women serve to introduce Rocío's relationship with Eloisa, whose "womanliness" or her maturity makes her desirable to Rocío and at the same time contains the rejection of that desire. "How I admired Eloisa! How grateful I was for allowing me into her magical woman's world. Eloisa and I were bright girls, mature girls . . . .Later, after the nightly watermelon, I would fall asleep under the stars thinking about Eloisa. She was Venus, I myself was a shooting star. The two of us were really one. We were beautiful girls, bright beautiful girls spitting out watermelon seeds. We were coyotes calling out to the moon" (56). Representing Eloisa as Venus, the bright planet and also the goddess of love, Rocío again emphasizes identification with her: "The two of us were really one." Yet the title, "Shooting Stars," emphasizes the ephemeral quality of their relationship.

Rocío's love for Eloisa, like Esperanza's for Sally in *Mango Street*, eventually comes up against socially sanctioned heterosexual relationships. Rocío's reverential love for Eloisa is destroyed when she sees her at a movie theater, smoking lasciviously and allowing some faceless man to paw her. Eloisa, then, implicitly rejects Rocío's love through her desire for a man, and Rocío retaliates by withdrawing entirely and curtailing their rambling walks together. This new image of Eloisa as fast, as wanton and decidedly heterosexual, produces a physical revulsion in Rocío who feels "sick with nicotine, faint with its smell . . . sick to my heart . . . faint with disappointment" (56), just as Esperanza was sick in the Monkey Garden. Even after her return to New Mexico, Texas and Eloisa continue to haunt Rocío, taunting her to make sense of her feelings and her memories: "To me, Texas signified queer days, querulous wanderings, bloody fairy tales, hot moon-filled nights. . . . Texas was women to me: my fading grandmother, my aunt dying of cancer, my mother's hunchbacked aunt and Eloisa. All laughing, laughing . . . . When I lay in the solemn shade of my father's study, I thought of myself, of Eloisa, of all women. The thoughts swirled around like the rusty blades of our swamp cooler. . . . Perhaps someday when I grow older, I thought, maybe then I can recollect and recount the real significance of things in a past as elusive as clouds passing" (57). Rocío specifically expresses her desire for women, always placing it in the context of exploring womanliness. Thus as she conjures up images of women she has loved from the patterns in the stucco walls, she wonders, "What did it mean to be a woman? To be beautiful, complete? Was beauty a physical or a spiritual thing, was it strength of emotion, resolve, a willingness to love? What was it then that made women lovely?" (53).

Rocío's next "crush" is on Diana, an occasional domestic worker in the Esquibel household. She cleans and acts as older sister for Rocío, whose sister Ronelia left home to marry. Diana is a beautiful innocent,

"unlike her Texas counterpart," and for Rocío she was "first and
foremost: a friend who could never betray, no never. Nor could she see
the possibility of betrayal. In this assumption of hers and mine lies all
the tragedy of young womankind" (58). Diana's loyalty clearly
constitutes one part of Rocío's attraction: she is still smarting from
Eloisa's betrayal. She attempts to articulate what it was about Diana
that attracted her, whether it was her beauty, her body, her laughter,
which "crossed the fields and fogged all consciousness" (58). She then
swiftly sidesteps any suggestion of lesbianism by asserting that "in
observing Diana, I observed myself" (58). This is in spite of the fact
that Diana and Rocío are not otherwise represented as similar. Diana is
not a fully formed character nor yet a fully formed person. Her speech,
always formal and polite, always yielding gracefully, nevertheless takes
the form of "monosyllabic utterings of someone dependent upon the
repetitious motions of work, the body and its order." When she speaks
she is "naive, a little girl" (58). Her "weakness of spirit" separates her
from Rocío, as she marries, has children, and is neglected by her
straying husband. She thus ultimately accomplishes another kind of
betrayal—a betrayal of Rocío's image of her, Rocío's hopes for her.
When she becomes a good wife to a bad husband, Diana's youth, her
beauty, and her laughter fade to a yellowed shell. Rocío cannot even
recognize "Diana the huntress" in the wrinkled, whiskered woman with
sad eyes whom her mother points out at church. She feels a strong
sense of loss for the beautiful Diana.

The perceived betrayals by Eloisa and Diana, and Rocío's
subsequent rejection of them are ultimately refigured as their
unsuitability as "role models." In actuality, of course, within the
cultural constraints of institutionalized heterosexuality, they are
unsuitable objects of desire. Thus Rocío tells herself to "let them go."
She thinks about "*loving* women. Their beauty and their doubts, their
sure sweet clarity. Their unfathomable depths, their flesh and souls
aligned in mystery" (63). However, given the apparent fact that women
are destined for heterosexual relations, Rocío sternly puts this thought
from her mind, supplanting it with the image of her sister Ronelia, a
more suitable (heterosexual) role model. Yet, inevitably the thought of
them comes back to her: "Women. Women with firm, sure flesh of that
age in time. In dreams. Let them go . . . They were clouds, soft bright
hopes. Just as quickly as they were formed, they dissolved into vast
pillows. Their vague outlines touched the earth and then moved on"
(65). This passage from the end of "Shooting Stars" articulates very

carefully that one should not love women precisely because of an inherent flaw: their propensity for betrayal. This awareness is charged with regret and nostalgia, for Rocío, as if to say: Who can help loving women, even if there is no future to it?

The final story, "Compadre," demonstrates the different ways in which Rocío expresses desire toward women and toward men. Her repulsion for the large daughters of Regino Suárez (her mother's compadre) clearly does not extend to all members of the family: "The car was being driven by Eleiterio, Regino's only son. Handsome, handsome young man, with Regino's dark skin and bright eyes, he was the embodiment of whatever passion there was in the union between Braulia and Regino" (150). Later, Rocío thinks she has seen Eleiterio cruising Main Street, pachuco-like, but convinces herself that she has not: "I imagined things. Almost always imagined things, and only once or twice with Eleiterio. *Su apá era adventista*"[17] (159). While Rocío is conscious of a desire for Eleiterio, she speaks of him very briefly. His younger sister Zianna, however, draws Rocío's sustained attention during an unplanned visit to the Suárez family. Unlike her sisters, Zianna is slender and attractive.

> Zianna, the darkest, loveliest flower in the Suárez garden. A hose in hand, fingers laced over the hose head, Zianna watered the roses that grew near the street side of the house. She stood between the tame and the untamed worlds, that of her father's constant laborings and that of her mother's rampant, uncontrollable life.
>
> Zianna's face, lovely as a dark brown, dusky rose, was lit with natural highlights. Her neck was long, her small proud head balanced by a full, fleshed mouth. Her luminescent eyes shielded themselves against the elements and luxuriated in the absence of explanations.
>
> Full, lush and firm, her breasts were carefully rounded swells of female flesh, flowerets full of awakening fragrance. Zianna stood straight, her face in the direction of her thirsty charges. Her feet were planted firmly on the grateful grass. (154)

Rocío dwells on the "lush" curves of Zianna's body as the girl stands in the garden watering flowers. After the scene in which Rocío thought she had seen Eleiterio cruising, she fantasizes about Zianna:

> Ssssmmosh. MMMMmmmmm. Patter, patter, patter, patter. Black bird, blackbird, *what are you thinking*? Zianna stood nearby, a part of

the landscape. She was too wild for the garden's cultivation, yet too
refined for the wildness of the Suárez home. She was a small, silent
black bird on the nearest branch.
    Sssmooosh. Mmmmmmmm. Patter, patter, patter . . .
    I imagined Zianna standing in the grass, watering wearing [my]
squash dress. That dress will be hers. Dark girl in the sunshine,
seeking shade. (159, emphasis and ellipses as in the original)

The language used to describe Zianna, in direct contrast to that used for
Eleiterio, is wholly unrestrained and exults in Zianna's physical beauty,
her flesh, and the eroticism she inspires in Rocío. Rocío imagines
Zianna in her own dress (the Esquibels generally give their old clothes
to Zianna's family) and dwells on how well it will suit her and on the
visual pleasure of Zianna: "Zianna would get her dress wet; she never
wore pants like the other girls. She stood on the grass barefooted, with
no shoes on and in a wet dress and never caught cold" (158).
    While critics such as Rosaldo are quite vocal about the sexual
energy of *Menu Girls*, and even direct attention to many of the same
examples I draw from the text, they completely avoid the possibility
that Rocío actually desires these women. Rosaldo recognizes the
"bodily, sexual connection" with other women but considers only the
context of female desire without respect to its object. Quintana does not
examine the intimate relationships between Rocío and the different
women: she sees them (as she did in *Mango Street)* as merely "a
catalogue of female characters . . . a variety of female options for
solving the riddle of female self-fashioning" (104). Such themes are
certainly present in the book, and even Rocío herself offers them as
explanations for her interest in women, but they are not the whole story.
Although Rocío is attracted occasionally to men her most passionate,
sexual desire is directed toward a series of feminine women. It is that
desire I name "lesbian."

MARGINS

Terri de la Peña's 1992 novel, *Margins,* is sometimes incorrectly
identified as "the first Chicana lesbian novel." If this means a Chicana
lesbian-authored text with Chicana lesbian characters, then that honor
more properly belongs to Sheila Ortiz Taylor's *Faultline.* However
Ortiz Taylor, de la Peña, and Pérez all prepared their manuscripts for
publication conscious of the scarcity of fiction focusing on Chicana

lesbians. De la Peña initially published a series of short stories imagining a community of Chicana lesbians from the West Los Angeles area, while at the same time creating an audience for the novel to come.[18] Like *Margins* itself, the majority of these stories were published in mainstream lesbian anthologies and journals and are concerned with positive representation of Chicana lesbians in relationships with one another.[19] *Margins* is primarily a coming-out novel, emphasizing lesbian identity, coming out to family, and adult relationships with lesbian-identified women.[20] I concentrate on how this novel deals with the subject of lesbian girlhood, as it recalls the first lesbian love relationship of the main character, Veronica Melendez.

The novel opens as Veronica is recovering from an automobile accident that killed her "best friend," Joanna Nuñez. Veronica and Joanna had been best friends since girlhood, and their relationship had become sexual during adolescence. They lived together as "roommates" throughout their college years and lived a closeted life, without participating in a lesbian community or referring to themselves as lesbians outside of their relationship. And yet throughout their girlhood, adolescence, high school, and college years, both their families were accepting of their "particular friendship" without perceiving the possibility of sexuality or homosexuality. That Veronica and Joanna could carry on a sexual relationship for over ten years without anyone else noticing demonstrates both the cultural validation of same-sex friendships for girls and the heterosexual structure within which those relationships are presumed to exist. When Isabel, Joanna's mother, explains her own oblivion to the sexual aspect of the relationship, she dwells on the perceived sexlessness of girlhood friendship:

"Roni, I'm not sure *I* understand. I had favorite girlfriends too. We just never—"

"Joanna and I were so close that loving each other came easily, too."

"I remember how you girls could practically read each other's minds. . . . I thought that was friendship, nothing else. . . . I never thought of you two—that way. I knew Joanna and you were always together, and had been for years, but I thought she was close to you because she didn't have a sister. . . . All the time you girls were growing up, I was always glad Joanna had you for a friend. You're such a good student, a nice quiet girl—never in trouble."

"You have to watch those quiet ones," Veronica quipped.
Isabel ignored that modest attempt at levity. "I thought you were
a good influence on her." (111–13)

Although she comes to accept the truth, Isabel initially insists on a
perceived "innocence" of the girls' friendship, echoing literary critics
discussions of *Mango Street* and *Menu Girls*. She later tries to
reestablish this narrative of innocence when Steve, a young teenage
boy, begins displaying pornographic pictures of lesbian sex and telling
both Isabel's younger sons and Veronica's nephew Phil that Veronica
and Joanna used to "do that." Isabel exclaims, "Oh, Roni. It isn't your
fault. You and Joanna loved each other in an innocent way. It wasn't
like—in that magazine" (180). This narrative is further developed by
other family members, including Veronica's older sister Lucy, a
Carmelite nun: "You're the baby of the family. I think Mama wanted to
keep you inocente as long as she could. . . . You loved Joanna from the
day you met her in kindergarten. Everyone knew that. We just never
looked beyond the friendship" (248). Veronica's relatives rely on the
idea that there is an innocence, a sexlessness, to young Chicanas that by
definition precludes the possibility of homosexuality. This becomes
clearly marked in the novel when rumors of the sexual aspect of
Veronica and Joanna's relationship begin to spread. When Phil is asked
to explain to his grandparents his argument with the boy who showed
him the magazine, he does not reveal the discussion of lesbianism:
instead, the topic of conversation becomes his own (hetero)sexuality:

"And what were you y Steve arguing about?"
"Some girl," Phil murmured.
"Ay, que muchachos! You're too young for that, Philly."
"Sara, he's old enough to shave." Joe offered his grandson a
conspiratorial smile. "Just be careful next time, Phil." (146)

This "boys will be boys" discussion makes it clear that, while the
fourteen-year-old boy is perceived as a sexual being, his twenty-four-
year-old aunt is not. The issue of female sexuality is further
complicated because there are no women in the family, other than
Veronica, who claim an active sexuality. Her mother, Sara, clearly
thinks of sex as dirty, and her sister Lucy has taken a vow of celibacy.[21]
While Veronica blames her parents for the family's silence around
sexuality, Lucy argues "Es la cultura" (248). This is a very different

world from Cisneros's *Mango Street* and Chávez's *Menu Girls*, in
which female heterosexuality is an explicit force to be reckoned with. It
is precisely because of this erasure of all female sexuality that Joanna's
family attempts to produce Veronica as the "living lesbian" who
seduced their innocent Joanna. Threatened by the attack on Joanna's
"honor," they react first by denying that the two women had a lesbian
relationship; then, when Veronica begins living openly as a lesbian,
they refigure her as their daughter's seducer.

Veronica attempts to displace this narrative of "innocent girlhood,"
arguing for an active lesbian girlhood. For Veronica, same-sex play is a
natural (physical) extension of the emotional intimacy of girlhood
bonds, one which does not change the nature of that relationship, but
extends it significantly.

> "Joanna and I were so close that loving each other came easily, too."
>
> " . . . Joanna wasn't interested in a men in a sexual way. How
> could anything compete with what we had?"
>
> " . . . At first, we thought we were going through a phase,
> experimenting with each other before getting involved with men. We
> both tried dating, but we realized right away we were much more
> comfortable with each other." (111)

She argues against being cast as the "lesbian seducer" by stressing the
mutuality of their relationship and again by attempting to show that for
both girls it followed a natural progression from friendship to sexual
intimacy:

> "Well, no one stays innocent for long. Joanna and I started playing
> around when we were in grammar school. I still can't believe no one
> caught on." (248)

> "Joanna and I used to spy on you [and your boyfriend]. Afterwards
> we'd go to her house and practice kissing." (264)

Both of these examples are from a conversation Veronica has with
Lucy. She emphasizes the sexual precocity of her relationship with
Joanna: how early they started "playing around." When she reveals that
she and Joanna used to spy on Lucy, she is talking about a time before
Lucy entered the convent, which took place when Veronica was

thirteen. Veronica is articulating a specific model of lesbian identity, the "born lesbian" who never has voluntary sex with men. Although Lucy does not respond directly, she accepts Veronica's explanation, perhaps because she believes that homosexuality is innate, and therefore not a "choice."[22] While she can accept Veronica's homosexual feelings, she cautions Veronica against claiming a lesbian identity without Joanna. To some extent, then, the ground conceded in the natural extension of particular friendship is taken back by arguing that, with the end of that girlhood friendship, lesbianism need not be embraced.[23] Implied is the idea that this lesbian adolescence must come to an end, must be replaced by adult heterosexuality.

Because of Joanna's early death, de la Peña avoids the question of betrayal of a "passionate friendship" in the sense that we have seen, albeit in less explicit form, between Esperanza and Sally and between Rocío and Eloisa in the two earlier books. Veronica is, to some extent, betrayed in adulthood when her affair with her initially heterosexual neighbor Siena ends abruptly and Siena begins sleeping with a man. The characterization of Siena is caught up in the question of coming out. Siena is explicitly criticized by the other lesbian characters in the novel for not being "out" as a lesbian, bisexual, or a woman-loving woman. This is in marked contrast to their acceptance of Veronica, who is not criticized for being closeted in her ten-year relationship with Joanna, although Siena has been sexual with a woman for less than a week. This double standard is tied to the representation of the Chicano community: to be close to their families, to be within the culture, Veronica and Joanna needed to be closeted. However, the same argument is in no way held valid for Siena, an Italian American from a Catholic background no less conservative than Veronica's. Like Elizabeth Rainey in *Menu Girls*, Siena is recovering from the aftereffects of an abortion. Thus she, too, is "marked" by sexuality but, in the new context of lesbian identity, she is also marked as untrustworthy. Her sexual desire for Veronica is invalidated by her inability to claim a lesbian identity and trivialized by the other lesbian characters. The novel privileges the "born lesbian," viewing women who have been heterosexually active with suspicion.

Ironically, Veronica herself sets aside her relationships with Joanna, just as the Esperanza's and Rocío's "passionate friendships" are expected to be set aside. In this case, however, the relationship is not superseded by institutions of heterosexuality but is replaced by Veronica's new lesbian identity and lesbian relation. Joanna is relegated to the past and to the "innocence" of girlhood as the novel turns toward Veronica's mature, adult relationship with Chicana lesbian René Talamantes. The novel ends with Veronica giving a public reading from her short story collection, a "fictional recreation of Joanna" (328). As she reads, Veronica looks to René for encouragement, and to the multiethnic audience at Sisterhood bookstore for affirmation. Because of its emphasis on lesbian identity, and in particular because the novel privileges identity over desire, *Margins* reinforces the division between (innocent) girlhood friendships and adult sexual relationships portrayed in both *The House on Mango Street* and *The Last of the Menu Girls*, with the significant difference that in this case adult relationships are not exclusively heterosexual.

GULF DREAMS

Emma Pérez's 1996 novel *Gulf Dreams* first appeared in short story form in the anthology *Chicana Lesbians: The Girls Our Mothers Warned Us About* (Trujillo). The novel is ambitious in both range and style as it addresses socialization and sexuality in the fictional Texas Gulf town of El Pueblo. The novel has a loose chronological structure that is abruptly contested by a competing narrative of memory, which is violent, fragmented, and often cinematic in the ways in which it evokes images. We see the narrator meet and fall in love with a young woman, the sister of her sister's best friend. Their relationship is extremely passionate although, at least initially, the actual sexual activity is limited to that between the young woman and her first boyfriend, which she describes to the narrator in detail. Eventually, the two women enroll in a nearby junior college, where the young woman begins dating Pelón, a male pre-law student from the university. The two women become more intimate while their relationship is entangled with that between the young woman and Pelón, and with physical and emotional violence. Although we are not told the details of the young woman's childhood history, Pérez makes it clear that she has been emotionally scarred by violence from those she loves. According to the narrator, the young woman thus seeks out violence along with love, first going from Pelón, who abuses her, to the narrator, who comforts her, and later verbally abusing the narrator until she too marks the young woman with bruises. The narrator then leaves Texas for California; the novel reveals little about her life there, except that she hides in anonymous sex and perhaps makes a living as a sex worker. After her departure, the young woman marries Pelón.

The narrator returns to El Pueblo some years later, after she reads a newspaper account of a gang rape in the town: Ermila, a young Chicana, is picked up and raped by five Chicanos. Pelón is the defense attorney for the offenders; he builds his case on the negative representation of Chicanos by the Anglo media—completely erasing Ermila as a Chicana as well as the violence done to her—and on the premise that, as the type of woman "who says yes," Ermila did not have the option of saying no. The narrator stays for the trial and verdict, seeing the young woman again and resuming their relationship, from which she has never truly been free. Four of the five rapists are acquitted. The fifth, the ringleader, is convicted and receives a thirty-year sentence. The narrator leaves before the appeal and returns to Los Angeles.[24]

Having given a very basic sketch of the novel, I now focus specifically on the relationship between the narrator and the young woman. The two girls are brought together when the narrator is fifteen by their sisters who are best friends, *comadres*. In the passage that I have taken as my epigraph, Pérez introduces their relationship, contextualizing the expectations for close female friendships within this Chicano community:

> To link families with four sisters who would be friends longer than their lifetimes, through children who would bond them at baptismal rites. *Comadres.* We would become intimate friends, sharing coffee, gossip, and heartaches. We would endure the female life-cycle—adolescence, marriage, menopause, death, and even divorce, before or after menopause, before or after death.
>   I had not come for that. I had come for her kiss. (13)

Pérez is referring here to the cultural system of *comadrazgo*. The masculine term, *compadrazgo*, refers to the relationship between the father and godfather, or the parents and godparents, of a child. The baptismal ceremony unites these people, raising their friendship to the level of kinship in recognition and mutual commitment. Thus their relationship is extended beyond the present through the lives of their children. The terms *compadre* and *comadre* are also used more informally to refer to friendship relationships that are as close as family and to specify the relationship between the parents of married children.

Compadrear, the verb formed from the masculine noun compadre, means to be on familiar terms with another person. Pérez is talking specifically about the relationship between women, *comadrazgo*. The verb *comadrear*, however, has a slightly different meaning—to gossip,—which she acknowledges with the phrase "sharing coffee, gossip, and heartaches" and by stressing the verbal aspect of the relationship—the telling, the sharing, the speaking. Notice that men are not essential to *comadrazgo* and that this relationship extends beyond that of the heterosexual marriage through which it is evoked. Withstanding "even divorce, before or after menopause, before or after death," *comadrazgo* emphasizes the permanence of women's relationships, over the temporality of men. *Comadrazgo* itself, then, is constructed paradoxically: women are simultaneously central and marginal in each other's lives. They are central because their friendship, their intimacy, will outlast the passion, the trauma, the infidelity, or the demise of heterosexual relationships. And yet they are marginal because these friendships function as a constant prop to the heterosexual structure—maintaining and always yielding precedence to heterosexuality or, in effect, to the male.

Pérez ruptures these narratives—both of the "female life-cycle," which is, by definition, heterosexually proscribed, and that of the "platonic intimacy" achieved by *comadrazgo*—by foregrounding the sexual desire of the narrator for the young woman: "I had not come for that. I had come for her kiss." She does not want a platonic intimacy with other heterosexual women, but rather a sexual union of the flesh. Precisely because of its built-in deference to the male and to heterosexuality, the narrator attempts to avoid the pattern of *comadrazgo*: "The promise of female rituals enraged me" (15). Here it may be enlightening to think back on Esperanza's relationship to Sally, particularly in "Red Clowns." where Sally, who is forbidden to associate with boys, is allowed to go to the carnival with Esperanza. Their friendship provides the opportunity for her heterosexual rendezvous, ultimately at Esperanza's expense.

The narrator's desire is created and inspired by the young woman. Although she says "I met her in the summer of restless dreams" (11), it becomes clear that the restless dreams are brought on by their first meeting, when, with a glance, the young woman "caressed a part of me I never knew existed." For weeks after their brief meeting, the narrator is haunted by dreams of the young woman's erotic touch: "I dreamt of her fingers brushing my skin, lightly smoothing over breasts, neck, back, all that ached for her. A fifteen-year-old body ached from loneliness and desire, so unsure of the certainties her body felt" (12). The early part of the novel focuses on this lesbian desire, awakened by the young woman, and on the frustration of that desire both by the heterosexual limits of female friendship within the community and by the young woman's flirtatious rejection of the narrator. The desire between the two girls is tangible and even articulated, but only as mediated by the young woman's relationships with men: "That day under the shaded tree, she had spoken about a young boy. She craved his delicious, expert mouth, she said. She told me he had sucked her nipples. He was careful not to hurt her or impregnate her. Instead he licked her moistness. . . . I revered the lips that relived desire for him" (14). The young woman seduces the narrator emotionally, by verbalizing her sexual experiences. By describing her erotic activities, she gives form to what the narrator, with her more limited sexual experience, has not yet imagined that she would like to do with the young woman. Because the young woman's desire is described through her sexual behavior with the boy, the narrator's fantasies in relation to the young woman become heterosexually marked. No longer visited in her dreams by the young woman alone, instead she sees at night the scenes described under the shaded tree, sees him pleasuring the young woman in the ways she has described.

The young woman is clearly aware of the narrator's susceptibility: "She longed for someone to arouse her. Each time she dared to look directly into my eyes, she quickly averted hers. She alerted the passion, repressed it immediately" (14–15). The very structure of girlhood friendship allows the young woman to solicit the narrator's desire. Because the two girls do become "intimate friends, sharing coffee, gossip, and heartaches," the young woman can tell the narrator of her sexual activities, continuously drawing her in closer, so that she becomes both voyeur and participant in the young woman's sexual relationships: "She confessed details, delightfully. She told me how she shook with pleasure from the strokes of a ravenous tongue. I listened, opening to her seductive words, wanting more particulars to bond us intimately" (52). The narrator attempts to resist the "promise of female rituals," albeit unsuccessfully. The *comadrazgo* she sought to escape is precisely what creates and aggravates lesbian desire in this situation. Desire exists—is created—in the telling. Although she resents its inevitable frustration, the narrator cannot resist the telling: "Intimacies of the flesh achieved through words. That was our affair. Years later, I rediscovered my compulsion to consummate intimacy through dialogue—to make love with a tongue that spewed desire, that pleaded for more words, acid droplets on my skin. With her, I learned to make love to women without a touch. I craved intimate, erotic dialogue. I was addicted to words and she had spawned the addiction" (52). Ironically, then, the young woman, who is not identified as lesbian, instructs the lesbian narrator, teaching her how to make love to a woman with her tongue, literally and figuratively, by narrating eroticism. She speaks of the pleasure she receives and in doing so gains pleasure and inspires it in the narrator.

While the narrator attempts to resist this sexually heightened *comadrazgo*, she is unable to do so precisely because of the level of eroticism it contains: "She half-expected me. Took my hand, led me to her bedroom, shoved me playfully on her twin bed next to her. She spoke reasonably. She had missed me. Why had I stopped coming? Why had I stayed away? She relied on my friendship, a passionate friendship, she called it. Mute, I looked away, paralyzed, embarrassed, hurt. She played at my emotions under the guise of friendship" (17). The narrator's words bring to mind both Smith's discussion of *Sula*—which works as a lesbian novel in part "because of the passionate friendship between Sula and Nel" (Smith, 165)—and Esperanza's inability to fully articulate her desire for Sally—"those boys that look at you because you're pretty. I like to be with you, Sally. You're my friend" (99). Yet for the narrator, the young woman's words are harsh, an insult, a blatant denial of her own active participation in this sexual game. However, the young woman uses the "guise of friendship" not only to incite the narrator's desire but to supplement her own heterosexual relations: "We became enraptured, entrapped, addicted to each other's eroticism. A kiss on the cheek inflamed me for hours. I witnessed her greed. Teasing reached new heights. . . . The desire to desire her—my weakness. . . . Her boyfriend grew more threatened each time I appeared. . . . She and I, trapped in social circumstances. Propriety kept us apart" (28). The boyfriend's antagonism is one of the early signs that the narrator's participation in the young woman's relationships with men is not limited to voyeurism: "After rushing to him, he would oblige her by hurting her, then she would come to me. I rescued her, then resented my duty to her. And so we played this deceitful game, angry because we didn't know how to quit" (29). In a sense, then, the narrator is the conventional *comadre*, in that she provides support for the young woman in the latter's heterosexual relationship; in addition, she acts as a sort of lesbian supplement to heterosexuality, providing a love and a level of eroticism that balances the inadequacies (for the young woman) of the heterosexual relationship and helps to maintain it.

Gulf Dreams contrasts with de la Peña's *Margins* in the way it shows female friendships to be represented within the community. Because neither Joanna nor Veronica dates or is sexual with men, both are, in the eyes of the community, sexually infantilized, which provides a screen behind which they explore their sexuality together. They are, in effect, good girls, and as Veronica wryly explains to Joanna's mother, "You have to watch those quiet ones." Ironically, their hidden lesbianism is what earns them the classification of "good girls." In the world of *Gulf Dreams*, the luxury to be a "good girl" is rather limited. Both the narrator and the young woman are introduced to sex before they are old enough to make such choices for themselves. The young woman seeks out strong men to protect her from the caresses of her stepfather, and the narrator chooses a quiet boy from Alabama, whose demands are easy to put down. But because the young woman is actively and visibly sexual, her relationship with the narrator is also more visibly marked as "queer": her first boyfriend, who has evidence enough of her heterosexuality, complains of her relationship with the narrator and finally uses it as an excuse to break up with her, saying he wants only her and "not some lezzy and a pet dog" (53). As with so many other aspects of sexuality in the novel, the young woman's heterosexual activity simultaneously masks and promotes her own "lesbianism."

Sexism and heterosexism are pernicious in the Pérez novel to a degree unseen even in *Mango Street*. Within El Pueblo, the potential for male sexual violence is omnipresent. As a two- or three-year-old child, the narrator is molested by a group of adolescent and pre-adolescent boys. As a nine-year-old she is sexually harassed publicly by a thirteen-year-old, to the extent that she no longer feels safe, and yet she is told to accept it, while the boy is never disciplined or even discouraged. Packs of boys roam the railroad tracks and, catching up with the narrator and her younger brother, force kisses on her, leaving her smeared with saliva. In the schoolyard, a group of boys will chase a younger girl and pull down her underwear. All of these images build up to the gang rape in El Pueblo, which becomes notable because the woman in question, Ermila, refuses to accept predatory male sexual violence and refuses to see herself as merely a tool for male sexual use.

This is an atmosphere in which male sexual violence is normalized and female sexual assertion is punished with more sexual violence. Lesbian desire, while clearly present, is not only circumscribed but often violently policed. In fact, at one point, the young woman claims that her husband's domestic abuse was not a result of his personality or behavior but a consequence of her relationship with the narrator. While the narrator is justifiably suspicious of such an argument, which displaces the responsibility for the husband's violent behavior onto her, the possibility that lesbian relationships would be policed in an even more violent fashion is real enough. The possibilities for a public lesbian identity under such circumstances are severely limited. As in *Mango Street*, the text foregrounds the restrictions imposed by normative heterosexuality, as the young woman is confined to her house after her marriage, staring at the linoleum, just as Sally does after her marriage in *Mango Street*.: "She stood in the middle of her kitchen, gaping at her floor, absorbed in the linoleum's stain, a muddy brown stain in the same corner of the kitchen. For years she had tried chemicals of every brand . . . .But the floor covering only looked thinner and paler and the dirty film reminded her that her world was imperfect" (47). Unlike Veronica in *Margins*, the narrator of *Gulf Dreams* does not write herself a happy ending. Instead, she writes herself out, writes the young woman out, writes everything out of her own narrative. She writes the young woman out of the story by obfuscating how much she exists independently and how much she is merely the narrator's creation: "With phrases I create you. I create you here in text. You don't exist. I never wanted you to exist. I only wanted to invent you like this, in fragments through text where the memory of you inhabits those who read this. You have no name. To name you would limit you, fetter you from all you embody. I give you your identities. I switch them when it's convenient. I make you who I want you to be. And in all my invention, no matter how much I try, you don't have the skill to love, to love me as I am" (138-39). For the narrator, there is no ultimate resolution, no utopia to be gained in lesbian identity. The girlhood friendship, so casually glossed over in the criticism on *Mango Street* and *Menu Girls*, so easily recuperated in the narrative of an adult lesbian relationship in *Margins* is here revealed as the most important relationship of the narrator's life, the one for which all others are pale substitutes.

CONCLUSION

The House on Mango Street, *The Last of the Menu Girls*, *Margins*, and *Gulf Dreams* construct images of intense emotional attachment and erotic attractions between girls and women. They contribute to the representation of Chicana lesbianism by providing images of intimacy and intensity beyond that considered appropriate for proper heterosexual girls. While such friendships are initially encouraged, especially over heterosexual relations that might result in premature sexual activity and pregnancy, the girls are expected to relinquish the primacy of these friendships as they become part of the grown-up heterosexual world. Within these fictional Chicano communities in Chicago, New Mexico, Southern California, and Texas, the female protagonists are confronted by limited options for women. Both Esperanza and Rocío leave or will leave their communities of origin so that they can make different lives for themselves. The narrator of *Gulf Dreams* also leaves her community but finds no solace in the outside world. Certainly, within the Chicano communities depicted in these four works, there are no women actively claiming a Chicana lesbian identity, in spite of how they form love relationships with other females. The exception here is René Talamantes of *Margins*, who lives as a lesbian with her mother in the barrio, and whose relationship with Veronica Melendez gives the latter a sense of deep connection to her cultural heritage. Veronica makes this move to cultural identification, although it is fraught with tension with regard to her family, but prefers not to live within Chicano neighborhoods. Additionally, the Los Angeles of *Margins* is both more "multicultural" than the rural or barrio worlds in which the characters of the other three books live— thus escaping a rigid Anglo/Chicano or Anglo/Latino dichotomy—and more permeable, so that Veronica can move to a different part of the city. She clearly has more options than the other women.

The representation of Chicano families is significant in all four of the works studied, and particularly in *Mango Street* and *Gulf Dreams*, which deal with domestic violence and sexual abuse. While all of the protagonists come from families free of abuse, they are constantly confronted by the reality that the same does not hold true for many of their friends; Esperanza and the narrator of *Gulf Dreams* are also aware that even their families are not enough to protect them from harm. These families, too, provide mixed messages about sexuality: daughters are protected but restricted; daughters are kept ignorant of sex to preserve their innocence; daughters are expected to fulfill the roles of mother and wife.

Throughout these stories, intimate girlhood friendships are predetermined to end in loss. Esperanza loses Sally, who prefers male sexual play to Esperanza's childishness. Rocío, while not rejected by Eloisa, is nevertheless disillusioned when she sees her friend enjoying lascivious male attention. Veronica loses Joanna to an automobile accident, but Joanna's death begins to take on the aspect of a natural progression, necessary in order for Veronica to live openly as a lesbian and to enjoy an "adult" relationship with René. Pérez's narrator alone does not "lose" her young woman, but she does not "keep" her either, nor can she successfully negotiate adult relationships because of the scars she carries both from childhood sexual abuse and from the emotional dynamics of her obsessive relationship with the young woman.

Mango Street, Menu Girls, and *Gulf Dreams* all show that these girls' behaviors, identities, and their desires are mediated by the heteronormativity of the worlds in which they live. Love and desire are constituted in relation to heterosexuality: Esperanza knows that the way she likes Sally is different from the way boys look at Sally, even as it is different from her platonic girlhood friendships. While Eloisa does not explicitly choose a boy over Rocío, Rocío sees Eloisa's heterosexual behavior as contaminating the "brightness" of their relationship. Her perception of the inevitability of heterosexuality leads her to perceive of the "brightness" of the desire between girls as that of a shooting star, intense and fleeting.

The ways in which female friendships are socially perceived and encouraged provide a space, however restrictive, for lesbian desire in these texts. The intimacy itself provides the context for lesbian desire. Because they are intimate friends, the young woman in *Gulf Dreams* will tell the narrator of her sexual pleasures, knowingly exciting the narrator, and deriving pleasure from that knowledge. On a less overtly sexual level, Esperanza can be close to Sally, hold her hairbrush, and wave to her on the tilt-a-whirl, because they are close friends. That intimacy provides a space for Esperanza's feelings of love to grow, feelings that are distinct from the male desire based on Sally's appearance. Esperanza's desire is based on Sally's self, the way she laughs, her pleasure in a carnival ride, her own desire to be loved. In *Margins* this space for lesbian desire is much more literal: their very intimacy provides Joanna and Veronica with a "good girl" image, which in turn gives them the freedom to develop a lesbian relationship. This freedom is quite material: both Veronica's and Joanna's parents are paying the rent on an apartment for their two "good girls" while they are in college.

In *Gulf Dreams*, female friendship is articulated in terms of comadrazgo, a friendship and commitment that is perceived as being stronger than the heterosexual marriage around which it is constituted. At the same time, the women's relationship is a supplemental component of the heterosexual marriage, providing constancy and support alongside the fluctuations of heterosexuality. Because they require deference to heterosexuality, such female friendships are undesirable to the narrator; because they provide intimacy, they are also irresistible. While Rocío consciously makes a decision to "let them go," Pérez's narrator cannot do so and instead strikes back at one of the forces that has imposed heterosexuality on her world, with a violence which equals the violence done to her.

All of these fictions represent same-sex love and desire at approximately that moment at which girls are expected to set aside female friendships in favor of heterosexual relations. Within these texts is a recognition that however privileged heterosexual desire may be, it is in no way more natural or innate than homosexual desire. Indeed, I would argue that, with one exception, these works depict a fluid and dynamic notion of female sexuality. Only in *Margins* is sexuality explicitly tied to claiming a lesbian identity. Pérez, while perhaps privileging her lesbian narrator (who has had both positive and negative relationships with men), complicates binary heterosexual/homosexual models of female sexuality through her portrayal of the young woman. Ostensibly a "heterosexual" teenager, she teaches her "lesbian" best friend about teasing, eroticism, making love through words alone, as well as the mechanics and pleasures of oral sex. The stories that *Gulf Dream*'s narrator weaves for the young woman, of an idyllic future where she has a good husband, children, and secret male and female lovers, combine what the young woman needs socially (a good husband as equivalent to a stable family) with what she desires (children, passion, variety, and secrets).

Finally, although the lesbian content of *Mango Street* and *Menu Girls* has been ignored by literary critics, I have tried to show how that very erasure constitutes part of the representation of lesbianism. That is to say, like the social perceptions of female friendships within the four books, this very silence about the possibility of lesbianism has nevertheless provided a space for lesbian reading.

NOTES

1.   See also Farwell, who promotes a metaphoric usage of "lesbian," and de Lauretis, who critiques such a usage at length in "The Seductions of Lesbianism," chapter 4 of *The Practice of Love*. By utopic, I am referring to texts that invoke the idea of lesbianism as an escape from the problems, inequalities, and power dynamics of heterosexual relationships, as if lesbian relationships would somehow be free of problems, inequalities, and power dynamics (not to mention passion). Such a romanticization of "lesbian" is curiously akin to fantasies about the convent as just such an escape. See, for example, Alma Luz Villanueva's *Weeping Woman: La Llorona and other Stories*, particularly "El alma/The Soul, Three" (151-56), and Denise Chávez's *The Face of an Angel*. In the latter, the fantasies of the convent and lesbianism as escapes from heterosexuality are united in the figure of Sister Lizzie (439–46).

2.   An excellent case in point is Becky Birtha's "Johnnieruth," in which the eponymous heroine, a fourteen-year-old African American girl, constantly resists the gender expectations put on her by her mother and her neighborhood. While walking to church one day she sees "this lady...She ain't nobody's mama—I'm sure," who is not all dressed up and on her way to church, but who (like Johnnieruth) is dressed comfortably, pleasing nobody but herself. As Johnnieruth turns to watch her walk by, the woman eyes her in recognition (73). Near the end of the story, Johnnieruth sees two women kissing "for a whole long time" (75). Again, they seem to recognize her and she them, and as she bicycles home, thinking about them kissing and then looking at her, she finds herself laughing "for no reason at all" (76).

3.   I wish to reiterate that I discuss Chicana lesbian fictions within a Chicana literary context: I do not attempt either a history or a sociological study of Chicana girlhood friendships. Nor do I position these representations of Chicana girlhood friendships within a universal, and thus problematic, construction of "lesbian" and/or homosocial relations between women, which would merely inscribe Chicana lesbian fiction within a largely Anglo American, Northern European "tradition." While the characters or the texts themselves often construct Chicana sexuality against Mexicana and Anglo American sexuality, with the former seen as more restrictive, and the latter as less restrictive (see nn. 15, 21), I urge the reader to avoid a slippage from the literary to the sociological: These texts represent stories Chicanas tell about

themselves and their communities that may or may not have anything to do with the material social conditions of (sexual) lives. Indeed, any sociological statement about Chicana (or Mexicana, or Anglo) sexuality per se would flatten the heterogenous, historically embedded, and conflictive ways in which sexuality is constructed in diverse Chicano/a communities. However, I should acknowledge that the stories themselves become part of the material social conditions, so that even while arguing against slippage I acknowledge the overlap.

4. I have deliberately chosen not to include comparable works that focus exclusively on adult friendships or adult sexual relationships, such as Estela Portillo's *The Day of the Swallows*, Sheila Ortiz Taylor's *Faultline*, Ana Castillo's *The Mixquiahuala Letters*, and Jeanne Córdova's *Kicking the Habit*, to name but a few. Laura del Fuego's novel *Maravilla* could easily be included in the current study, as could short stories by Alma Luz Villanueva and Helena María Viramontes, which I hope to discuss in the future.

5. Rebolledo mentions de la Peña only briefly: "The 1990's has brought forth a variety of lesbian novels and other creative materials about lesbian consciousness, including *Margins* by Terri de la Peña" (199). To date, *Margins* and *Gulf Dreams* have been discussed only in book reviews. (On *Margins*, see Daly, *Publishers Weekly*; Robinson; and Wolverton. On *Gulf Dreams* see de Lauretis "Closing the Gulf Between Us.")

6. Rosaldo mistakenly identifies Esperanza's mother as supplying the shoes.

7. Emphasis in the original. "Not a girl, not a boy, just a little baby" is one of the jump rope rhymes Nenny chants.

8. This is not to imply that wanting to be *like* Sally is wholly divorced from wanting to be *with* Sally. I develop this more in relation to Rocío in *The Last of the Menu Girls*, below.

9. "justo y necesario" comes from the Catholic mass in Spanish. In English, it would be equivalent to just, right, or righteous and needful, although in the English language mass the equivalent of "Es justo y necesario" is "It is right."

10. See also María Herrera-Sobek, who recognizes that Esperanza's lament "is directed not only against Sally the silent interlocutor but at the community of women" (178). Because Herrera-Sobek is discussing "Red Clowns" without reference to the other Sally stories, she minimizes the significance of Esperanza's relationship to Sally.

11. "Sally," "What Sally Said," "the Monkey Garden," "Red Clowns," and "Linoleum Roses" appear as numbers 32, 37, 38, 39, and 40, respectively.

12.   The line actually reads "For the ones I left behind. For the ones who cannot out." Yvonne Yarbro-Bejarano, reading from the first edition, gives the last line as "For the ones I left behind. For the ones who cannot get out" ("Chicana Literature" 143). One could interpret "For the ones who cannot out," which appears in the second revised edition (Arte Público, 1988), to be a printing error, with the verb accidentally omitted. However, it seems likely that such an error would have been caught in the 1991 Vintage/Random House edition. I prefer to believe that Cisneros intentionally changed the line when she revised the manuscript in 1988, leaving the gap to be bridged by the reader.

13.   "Willow Game" appeared in *Nuestro* (1982), "Evening in Paris" in *Nuestro* (1981), "The Closet" in *The Americas Review* (1986), and "Space is Solid" in *Puerto del Sol* (1986).

14.   Rosaldo's term for this connection is *matrimony*, used here as the female equivalent of *patrimony*, and thus matrilineal heritage. By choosing a term which already signifies the institution of heterosexual marriage, Rosaldo embeds a heteronormative understanding of women in general and of Rocío in particular (see Warner xi, xxi-xxv).

15.   There is an implication, however, that in Rocío's community Chicanas do not get abortions either.

16.   Interestingly, Bertha, the "female" lesbian, never appears, although "Esperanza the dyke" (32) figures prominently in the ninth and eleventh sections of the story.

17.   "His father was a [Seventh Day] Adventist" (my translation). That is, being from a strict religious background, he is unlikely to do such things as Rocío imagines.

18.   The Los Angeles stories are "Beyond El Camino Real," "Blue," "Desert Quartet," "Labrys" "Mariposa," "La Maya," "Mujeres Morenas" "Once a Friend," "A Saturday in August," and "Tortilleras." Indeed, many of the characters from these stories and those from *Margins* appear in a community scene at the end of de la Peña's second novel, *Latin Satins* (250).

19.   These works draw certain essentialized notions of identity and race in their idealized depictions of Chicana/Chicana relations. This is somewhat self-consciously done, since de la Peña is working in a publishing realm in which the majority of representations are of Anglo/Anglo lesbian couples, or more infrequently, an Anglo woman with a woman of color. Indeed, a favorable but rather uninformed review of *Margins* in the *Advocate* explains that "the spectrum of lesbian literature includes so few Latina voices" because of "the dominance of the Catholic church" (Wolverton 40).

20.   Closeted lesbians and bisexuals alike are represented as unhealthy partners.

21.   Veronica's married (heterosexual) sister, Angela, does not appear in the novel. Like Joanna, Veronica's sister-in-law Connie died young, and thus has assumed the sexual innocence of "an angel." This sexual innocence is limited to Chicanas, for Veronica's new sister-in-law Joyce, an Anglo, is demonstrably passionate with her husband.

22.   A view to which Veronica, Lucy, and indeed the Catholic church subscribe.

23.   Lucy may again be echoing the Catholic church's judgment that while one does not choose to be a homosexual, one can—and should—refrain from acting on homosexual impulses.

24.   This is the most basic outline of the novel. Structurally, there is also a second narrative, of memory, which produces abrupt images of sexual abuse and sexually motivated violence directed against the narrator, as well as images of her turning violence against herself.

The Quest for Freedom
The Process of Female Sexual Liberation in Alma Luz Villanueva's *Naked Ladies*
Daniel Enrique Pérez

> *Until we can all present ourselves to the world in*
> *our completeness, as fully and beautifully as we see*
> *ourselves naked in our bedrooms, we are not free.*
> —Merle Woo, "Letter to Ma"

Homoerotic writing in Chicano/Chicana texts has been considerably limited by both the quantity of authors who partake in its cultural production and the identity of the authors themselves. John Rechy, a self-identified gay author, has been virtually the only Chicano author to produce homoerotic texts, and the majority of these texts have been realized in subaltern spaces outside of a Chicano cultural context. Most of what has been revealed about homosexuality within a Chicano cultural context has been from the writings of self-identified Chicana lesbian writers like Cherríe Moraga and Gloria Anzaldúa and Chicano gay writer Francisco Alarcón. The boundaries that confine homoerotic writing in Chicano/Chicana texts have traditionally been that it occurs in subaltern spaces and/or that it be created by the few, self-identified gay and lesbian Chicano/Chicana authors. It is not only the scarcity of homoeroticism in Chicano/Chicana texts that lead David William Foster, in his essay, "Homoerotic Writing and Chicano Authors" to question "to what extent there is even any legitimacy in speaking of the homoerotic in Chicano/Chicana writing" (55), but more importantly, "what aspects of Chicano/Chicana homoeroticism coincide with an agenda defined from within Chicano/Chicana culture and what aspects constitute homologies with general American and international priorities" (49). I posit that in her latest novel, Alma Luz Villanueva transcends the boundaries that have limited the cultural production of homoerotic texts by creating a text that includes interracial homoeroticism in a Chicano/Chicana cultural context and that is produced by a nongay writer. Villanueva, who is married, has a child and has not identified herself as a lesbian, becomes the first nongay, overtly identified Chicano/Chicana to incorporate homoeroticism in this manner with the publication of *Naked Ladies* (1994).

Naked Ladies is a remarkable exploration of interracial, heterosexual, and homosexual relationships. The protagonist, Alta, is a young Chicana mother of two struggling to complete her education, raise a family, and save a broken marriage. Her husband, Hugh, is Anglo-American, a construction worker and a closeted homosexual who wanders from home over the weekends to indulge in man-to-man sex. In the novel, Alta evolves through three different stages of sexual development: confinement, exploration, and liberation. These three stages are paralleled by the three stages of Alta's own personal development: repression, exploration, and independence. The concomitance of her sexual and her personal development is what allows her to solidify her personal independence and sexual liberation by the end of the novel.

The first stage of Alta's development is identified by the repression she suffers from men and her confinement in her husband's queer sexual desires. Every woman in the novel suffers from some form of physical and psychological abuse by men, including incest and rape. Alta's repression began at the age of eight, when she was raped: "'If you scream I'll kill you,' he said. The man. The boy. The man. The boy. She never screamed. She never even cried" (34). Alta's sexual confinement is manifested by her need to fulfill her husband's sexual fantasies. This need results in Alta's digression from the compulsory heterosexual norm and simultaneously stifles the gender roles that she assumes when she participates in sexual intercourse with her husband. This includes her playing a dominant, active role during sex, as well as her performing what can be construed as nonnormative heterosexual practices that can be interpreted as typical man-to-man sexual activities:

> She kissed his neck, then lowering herself, she licked and sucked his nipples. "Do you? I couldn't stand it if you didn't love me." Tears came to her eyes, and they fell on his belly. He continued to keep his hands to his sides. He thought of his lover and let her suck him. She

was trying so hard. She licked the inside of his shaft with the flat of her tongue. (45)

For the purposes of this paper, I will use the terms passive and active in the traditional sense of their antithetical meanings (passive referring to the submissive, inactive receptor and active referring the nonstative, effective, dominant insertor). With this in mind, it becomes apparent that Alta is *forced* to assume both passive and active sexual roles when she engages in sex with Hugh, while Hugh, on the other hand, *chooses* to assume both passive and active sexual roles. The catalysts that nurture this difference between force and choice in this stage of their relationship are: Alta's passivity (even when she's playing active sexual roles because she does not enjoy them), her financial dependence on her husband, her cultural background and her low self-esteem, as well as Hugh's closeted homosexuality. Sex between Alta and Hugh often includes her actively making love to him by placing herself on top of him, performing fellatio, and/or playing the passive role in anal intercourse. The insight that the reader has due to the fact that the story is presented by an omniscient narrator uncovers Hugh's homosexual desires during sexual intercourse with his wife. The revelation that he was thinking "of his lover" while Alta assumed the role of fellator, leads the reader to suspect what is revealed shortly thereafter—Hugh's "lover" is a man. This presents an entire different set of circumstances surrounding Hugh's sexual object choice versus his sexual aim and the roles he assumes during sexual intercourse.

Utilizing Freud's distinction between sexual object choice and sexual aim, as described in the "Three Essays on the Theory of Sexuality" (sexual object choice is the biological sex of the person toward whom sexual activity is directed and sexual aim is the act one wants to perform with another person) it becomes evident that Hugh's sexual object choice, Alta, can only be realized if his sexual aim is Alta as a young boy or Alta as his male lover. This sexual aim equates to nonnormative heterosexual practices between a man and a woman that can unquestionably be deemed homosexual. The fact that this occurs between an interracial couple presents an entirely new set of circumstances regarding miscegenation and homosexuality as a result of "abnormal" sexual object choice.

In his essay, "Scientific Racism and the Invention of the Homosexual Body," Siobhan Somerville claims that: "While gender insubordination offers a powerful explanatory model for the 'invention' of homosexuality, ideologies of gender also, of course, shaped and were shaped by dominant constructions of race" (242). Hugh's construction of race is a paradigm that has transitioned from generation to generation and it is one that Alta is very much aware of. The novel presents several examples of Hugh's racism and the conflicts that it produces: "Alta was thinking about the times Hugh would talk like his father, about not wanting spics and niggers in the Ironworkers. She'd remind him, "I *am* a spic, remember?" (21). Hugh's dominant racial ideologies combined with his homosexual ideologies are the constructors of Alta's gender roles. Issues of race and sexuality are dispersed throughout the novel. Somerville claims that these issues can overlap and perhaps shape one another "through models of interracial and homosexual desire. Specifically, two tabooed sexualities—miscegenation and homosexuality—[become] linked in sexological and psychological discourse through the model of 'abnormal' sexual object choice" (251).

Hugh's homosexual desires result in a complete deconstruction, as well as reconstruction of his compulsory heterosexuality. His participation in sexual intercourse with his wife includes him taking on a passive, subservient role, which is also the case when he has sex with a man. When Hugh and his lover, Bill, are having sex, Hugh refers to Bill as "Daddy," and when Bill remarks, "Daddy needs to love you, " Hugh becomes the passive receiver:

> "I love you, too, Hugh. I love you, too. Now bend over here," Bill said, placing Hugh carefully over his worktable, chest down. "Daddy needs to love you too. Daddy needs to love you . . . " Why is the first thrust the best? Bill wondered with a violent shudder. Like piercing the cosmos, dead center, it is. Yes, it is. Yes. But first Bill placed a rubber on his penis. He only trusted his steady lover. You never know what you might catch from these young guys, he thought as he fumbled with it.
> "Forget the rubber, I don't care," Hugh moaned. (78)

Taking into consideration Alta's cultural background, we can analyze Hugh's social behavior in a Latin American context to demarcate how Alta's culture may influence the way she interprets Hugh's sexual activities. If we compare Hugh's sexual behavior to the way many Latin American men behave in order to avoid being stigmatized as gay by participating in solely active roles during sex, it is obvious that Hugh has adopted what Tomás Almaguer describes as

"North American homosexual patterns" by incorporating both passive and active sexual roles into his sexual behavior.

Alta's financial dependence on Hugh is another factor in the role that she plays during the first stage of her development. For Hugh, payday means taking his check and escaping for the weekend. For Alta, payday means not seeing Hugh for a few days and trying to maintain the household on the little he has left over from his escapades: "Alta remembered dismally that the next day was payday. It was an automatic reminder as though a built-in panic button were being pushed. Payday. His payday" (43).

Her financial dependence on Hugh and her lack of self esteem contribute to her repression and her confinement: "How many times can I back down and just let him fuck me to get it over with?" (44). When her twelve-year-old daughter, April, asks, "Do you like being a woman and everything, Mom?" Alta replies, "You know, April, sometimes I have trouble liking myself, just who I am" (59).

With Alta in a racially mixed marriage, her cultural background plays a significant role in her relationship with her husband. Her Chicana identity is an important factor that contributes to her oppression. It is evident that she is hesitant to violate the rigid structure of the family which she learned growing up in a Chicano family. This structure traditionally places value on the patriarch at the expense of all women in the household, who are only there to serve him. Alta also struggles with what Cherríe Moraga describes as an internalized racism that has been formed by the Anglo society in which she was raised:

> I have internalized a racism and classism, where the object of oppression is not only someone outside of my skin, but the someone inside my skin. In fact, to a large degree, the real battle with such oppression for all of us, begins under the skin. I have had to confront the fact that much of what I value about being Chicana, about my family, has been subverted by anglo culture and my own cooperation with it. (30)

Furthermore, by the evidence presented thus far, it becomes evident that Alta has become more than Hugh's sexual object choice, she has in fact become his property by being financially dependent on him and by remaining submissive. She has fallen into what Kathleen Barry has termed "female sexual slavery":

Female sexual slavery is present in ALL situations where women or girls cannot change the conditions of their existence; where regardless of how they got into those conditions, e.g., social pressure, economic hardship, misplaced trust or the longing for affection, they cannot get out; and where they are subject to sexual violence and exploitation. (33)

This type of slavery is suffered by every woman in the novel despite race or class, but Patricia Williams argues in her essay "On Being the Object of Property" that much of what women who find themselves in this position lack is "will-fulness":

As I reflected on all this, I realized that one of the things passed on from slavery, which continues in the oppression of people of color, is a belief structure rooted in a concept of black (or brown, or red) anti-will, the antithetical embodiment of pure will. We live in a society in which the closest equivalent of nobility is the display or unremittingly controlled will-fulness. To be perceived as unremittingly will-less is to be imbued with an almost lethal trait. (157)

In the second stage of Alta's development, we begin to see the deconstruction of the family structure, as well as of Alta's internalized repression, and, more importantly, a gain in her "will-fulness" to escape the reigns of enslavement and make substantial strides in gaining her independence.

Alta's personal quest toward freedom depends largely on her ability to control the household finances and gain financial independence. Her first step is to control Hugh's frivolous spending. She begins by picking up Hugh's check at work on Fridays, before he can get to it. She cashes the check and leaves Hugh a bit of spending money: "The rest was in her wallet, safe and sound. She'd make out money orders for bills Monday" (62).

Although she manages to control some aspect of the household finances, Alta remains confined to her sexual role with Hugh until the night that he tries to rape her. For the first time, Alta refuses to have sex with Hugh after a family quarrel. She responds to his request for her to have oral intercourse: "You know, Hugh, if you just want someone to suck you off, why don't you pay someone to do it" (97). Evidence that Alta's financial dependence continues to contribute to her repression is revealed in Hugh's response, which he makes as he attempts to rape her: "I pay you every Friday, remember?" This time Alta does not submit to Hugh. She hits him in the face and then again in the groin area. Hugh punches her in the face, and then the children stop the fight. Alta threatens to kill him if he stays the night in the house and she throws him out. Her dedication to changing her situation is evident when April asks her if she was really going to kill her dad: "If he ever touched me like this again, yes. I think I have to leave your father, April. Do you understand?" (99).

Alta's second stage of development is also identified by her sexual and personal exploration. Alta begins to experiment with her own sexuality. She learns about her sexuality when her friend Katie, who subsequently dies of breast cancer, reveals that her first lover was a woman and then asks her if she has ever made love to a woman while the two are alone in bed. Katie teaches Alta about woman-to-woman sex: "It's like making love to your mother, finally. And it's like making love to yourself, in a way, discovering the taste and feel of yourself in another woman. The taboo breasts, Mom's nipples" (128). Katie and Alta do not participate fully in woman-to-woman sex, but Alta is enlightened by her response to Katie's revelation:

> Katie's revelation about her woman lover had taken her by surprise. But hadn't Katie been one of those beautiful women she'd always been drawn to? Alta thought. Katie's long, thick, red hair grazing her full, soft-looking breasts, her once limber walk, the sway of her hips. "Bird of paradise," Alta murmured, "you were so beautiful. So goddamned beautiful." (131)

During this time, Hugh also reveals to Alta, immediately following making love to her, that he is homosexual and that Bill, his partner of several years, has AIDS. Hugh assures her that he has tested negatively for AIDS. These two events are the catalysts for Alta to begin her sexual and personal exploration. It is important to note that Alta does not condemn Hugh for being gay. Alta would probably have responded the same way had Hugh revealed that he was having an affair with another woman. Her angst is a result of Hugh's infidelity and his endangering her life by exposing her to AIDS. Her indifference to Hugh's homosexuality leaves the door open for her to begin to experiment with the same type of sexual behavior. Her first experiment with woman-to-woman sex is with her friend Jackie. The experience is

Alta's first sexual encounter that excludes man or any type of male role:

> They came in circles of sorrow, in circles of joy—crying, then laughing together. Circles of ecstasy electrified their bodies from head to foot, and they came again: mouth to cunt, tongue to clitoris, soul to soul, woman to woman. Without man. They died, slowly, into swirling pools of utter pleasure. They remembered a woman's selfish, hungry, howling, singing pleasure to be food, to be fed. Without man. They searched for the hot, life-giving, creative, and golden sun. Without man. (157)

This woman-centered eroticism that renders both women completely satisfied poses a threat, and, in effect, downsizes the importance of the male phallus by making it virtually obsolete. The result is the construction of the female phallus which possesses an equitable amount of power that is traditionally and automatically granted to men. Utilizing Judith Butler's theory on the lesbian phallus, it becomes evident that the conversion of the tongue to a phallus "both recalls and displaces" masculinity and simultaneously becomes a female figure of power:

> When the phallus is lesbian, then it is and is not a masculinist figure of power; the signifier is significantly split, for it both recalls and displaces the masculinism by which it is impelled. And insofar as it operates at the site of anatomy, the phallus (re)produces the spectre of the penis only to enact its vanishing, to reiterate and exploit its perpetual vanishing as the very occasion of the phallus. This opens up anatomy—and sexual difference itself—as a site of proliferative resignifications. (*Bodies That Matter* 89)

It is not the construction of a lesbian phallus, but the pleasure that Alta receives from her participation in homoerotic exploration with Jackie that provides her with the tools necessary to deconstruct and reconstruct her normative sexuality. The lesbian phallus becomes a symbol for female power, whereas the power itself emerges, as Butler describes, from "erotegenic pleasure":

> For what is needed is not a new body part, as it were, but a displacement of the hegemonic symbolic of (heterosexist) sexual

differences and the critical release or alternative imaginary schemas
for constituting sites of erotegenic pleasure. (91)

Alta's empowerment during this exploratory stage, allows her to
assume whichever roles she *chooses*. She begins to demolish the
compulsory heterosexual, as well as homosexual models of sexuality
that have been instilled in her by both a patriarchal society and her
husband's queerness, and begins to construct her own normative
sexuality. This new normative sexuality for Alta is one that no longer
maintains Alta as a female sexual slave. In her proceeding sexual
encounters, gender roles are obfuscated by inverting sexual roles, as we
witness when she makes love to Doug, who is left a widower by Katie's
death:

> Ripples and ripples of unending pleasure flowed between them as she
> raised and lowered herself, watching his cock disappear; and he, for a
> moment, becoming a woman like herself; and she, with his hardness,
> for a moment, becoming a man; and then she utterly feminine, being
> penetrated; and then he utterly masculine, penetrating; and then
> peace. And then they fucked again. This was the comfort of the
> living. Woman to man. Cock to cunt. (172)

The sexual relationship she encounters with Doug is obviously woman-
to-man sex, but there exist no boundaries regarding who's the woman
and who's the man or who's active and who's passive. Alta is in touch
with her femininity and her masculinity and she can assume the role she
chooses.

Another factor that contributes to Alta's empowerment during this
stage of her development is the female bonding that takes place. Each
bond that she forms and reinforces with various women in the novel
provides a means of support for battling the abuse suffered by a
hegemonic patriarchal society. Virtually all men in the novel make a
concerted effort to rupture the bonds that these women form because
they threaten the chains of oppression that they maintain. Alexander
Doty's comment: "This story of straight male hysteria breeding
misogyny and homophobia in order to undermine close bonds between
women is depressingly familiar" (39) provides a comparable depiction
of what occurs in the novel. Fortunately, the rampant male hysteria is
met by a heightened, innovative formulation of female bonds. Adrienne
Rich's term "lesbian continuum" can be used to suggest that the term

"lesbian" can be expanded to include a wide range and degree of female experience and emotion:

> I mean the term lesbian continuum to include a range . . . of woman-identified experience; not simply the fact that a woman has had or consciously desired genital sexual experience with another woman. If we expand it to embrace many more forms of primary intensity between and among women, including tyranny, the giving and receiving of practical and political support . . . we begin to grasp breadths of female history and psychology that have lain out of reach as a consequence of limited, mostly clinical, definitions of "lesbianism." (192)

This expanded definition of lesbianism to include various aspects of female bonding combined with Alta's ongoing reconstruction of her normative sexuality, that by this time de-emphasizes whether or not she is participating in heterosexual or homosexual activities and places the emphasis on Alta's personal satisfaction, produces the naturalization of her newly constructed normative sexuality. According to Judith Butler, the concept of construction is "a return to the notion of matter, not as site or surface, but as a process of materialization that stabilizes over time to produce the effect of boundary, fixity, and surface we call matter" (*Bodies That Matter* 9). Butler further contends that this process of materialization occurs through the reiteration of norms which creates an influx of instabilities as it approaches stabilization:

> Crucially, then, construction is neither a single act nor a causal process initiated by a subject and culminating in a set of fixed effects. Construction not only takes place *in* time, but is itself a temporal process which operates through the reiteration of norms; sex is both produced and destabilized in the course of this reiteration. As a sedimented effect of a reiterative or ritual practice, sex acquires its naturalized effect, and, yet, it is also by virtue of this reiteration that gaps and fissures are opened up as the constitutive instabilities in such constructions, as that which escapes or exceeds the norm, as that which cannot be wholly defined or fixed by the repetitive labor of that norm. This instability is the *de*constituting possibility in the very process of repetition, the power that undoes the very effects by which "sex" is stabilized, the possibility to put the consolidation of the norms of "sex" into a potentially productive crisis. (10)

The stabilization of Alta's newly constructed normative sexuality is not materialized until the end of the novel. It is in this latter part of the novel that Alta's personal independence and sexual liberation are realized. The novel skips approximately five years. By this time Hugh dies of AIDS, and Alta has completed her counseling degree and is teaching at the university. Her complete financial independence and her overall autonomy foster her freedom. She falls in love with her female Asian student, Jade, and does not keep her relationship with her student secretive. She admits to her male lover, Michael, that she loves both of them, but at the same time she does not make any commitments to either. Her true liberation is manifested in her encounter with both of her lovers simultaneously:

> Michael's lips were on hers, pressing gently. Then Jade was stroking her breasts and moaning, and Michael's tongue was inside her mouth exploring her, and it all felt new, so new, as though she'd never made love before. A small fraction, a very small fraction, of herself began to censor this unbelievable, almost unbearable, pleasure these two people who she loved were giving her. No, it was unbearable, and she felt like thrashing and screaming and rolling into the hot, living fire, but she contained herself, and she simply stopped listening to that small fraction of herself that always said NO. That said, No one loves you and you love no one. (259)

It is evident that by this final stage in her development, Alta has materialized a personal normalized sexuality that she is very comfortable with. She has constructed what I will refer to as a *nonnormative normative* sexuality (i.e., it has become her norm to participate in nonnormative activities). It is important to refrain from making any attempt at classifying her sexuality in any way. Alta does not assume a lesbian nor a heterosexual identity. The identity she has constructed is strictly Alta's despite her sexual object choice. It is also evident that Alta's sexual aim has become her own personal satisfaction and nothing else. We must get away from the system of classification that Annamarie Jagose claims categorizes sexual orientation by sexual object choice:

> The increasingly organised articulation of the identities of lesbians and gays of colour destabilised the notion of a unitary gay identity. The assumptions that structured the core of the ethnic model of gay

identity were similarly challenged and critiqued by non-normative
sexualities. The ethnic model uncritically accepted dominant
understandings of sexuality, figuring the sexual field through the
binary opposition of heterosexuality and homosexuality. This is, it
assumed it to be both self-evident and logical that sexual orientation
is determined principally or even solely by the gender of one's sexual
object choice. (*Queer Theory*)63)

Eve Kosofsky Sedgwick also argues against the naturalization of
this system of classification:

It is a rather amazing fact that, of the very many dimensions along
which the genital activity of one person can be differentiated from
that of another (dimensions that include preferences for certain acts,
certain zones or sensation, certain physical types, a certain frequency,
certain symbolic investments, certain relations of age or power, a
certain species, a certain number of participants, etc. etc. etc.),
precisely one, the gender of object choice, emerged from the turn of
the century, and has remained, as *the* dimension denoted by the now
ubiquitous category of "sexual orientation." (8)

Alta's "sexual orientation" has, in effect, become her sexual
*dis*orientation which allows her to engage in *nonnormative normative*
sexual practices. Alta has become successful at deconstructing the rigid
heterosexual, and even homosexual (as inscribed by her husband),
normative models of gender and reconstructing her own model. As
Jagose mentions in her comment on Butler's *Gender Trouble*, this
becomes necessary in order to legitimate "lesbian and gay subject-
positions":

Although *Gender Trouble* is framed most prominently in terms of
feminism, one of its most influential achievements is to specify how
gender operates as a regulatory construct that privileges
heterosexuality and, furthermore, how the deconstruction of
normative models of gender legitimates lesbian and gay subject-
positions. (*Queer Theory* 83)

Taking this legitimization a step further, we can argue that the
deconstruction of normative heterosexuality, and even homosexuality,
also legitimates interracial and multiple subject positions. Furthermore,

we can take Butler's theory on gender performativity which allows the reinvention and resignification of gender (while it remains an "ongoing discursive practice") to demonstrate how Alta has reconstructed her gender identity. Jagose comments:

> Like Foucault, who foregrounds the importance of discursive strategies and their revisionist potential, Butler identifies gender as 'an ongoing discursive practice . . . open to intervention and resignification.' Her strategic resignification of normative gender models and heterosexuality is achieved by staging gender in ways that emphasise the manner in which 'the "unity" of gender is the effect of a regulatory practice that seeks to render gender identity uniform through a compulsory heterosexuality.' (*Queer Theory* 84)

Alta has created her own gender identity around her *nonnormative normative* sexuality. Alta becomes, as her name signifies "tall," perhaps the tallest of all of the "naked ladies" (referring to the wild flower from which the title of the novel is derived) that remains resilient despite the harsh realities of the world. In the novel, "naked ladies" are described as having "a long, dark, mauve stalk with a delicate pink flower on its tip. The pink [is] the color of the most tender, innermost flesh: of womb or heart. Or soul" (39). This is clearly representative of Alta in the final stage of her development. Despite the name, the gender of the wild flower is ambiguous. It is powerful and intimate. It is male and female. It is multicolored. Alta has truly gained her freedom by allowing the world to see her in her completeness and in her nakedness.

Alma Luz Villanueva has transcended the boundaries that have marginalized homoerotic Chicano/Chicana texts. By incorporating interracial homoeroticism within a Chicano/Chicana cultural context, Villanueva has broken the silence that Teresa de Lauretis claims limits the production of writings by lesbians and gay men of color:

> Thus an equally troubling question in the burgeoning field of "gay and lesbian studies" concerns the discursive constructions and constructed silences around the relations of race to identity and subjectivity in the practices of homosexualities and the representations of same-sex desire. (*Queer Theory* viii)

As Teresa de Lauretis claims, dealing with interracial relationships in same-sex desire is analogous with opening a Pandora's box:

> One of the constructed silences in the discourse of homosexuality as
> same-sex desire is around interracial relationships, fraught as they are
> with erotic, economic, social, and emotional stakes. (x)

The fact that Villanueva herself is not gay or lesbian identified, and that
she produced a novel that addresses issues of racism in a homoerotic
context renders her contribution to Chicano/Chicana literature even
more significant. Villanueva has opened the door for new voices in
Chicano/Chicana literature. The limitations that have been traditionally
placed on the production of homoerotic texts by writers of color (i.e.,
restricted access to higher education and publishing houses, and the
marginalization of gay and lesbian writers of color) have ebbed. We no
longer have an excuse to, nor can we allow a misogynist, racist,
homophobic society to dictate parameters on our cultural production.

Feminine Desire and Homoerotic Representation in Two Latin American Films

Danzón and *La Bella Del Alhambra*

Juana Suárez

The advent of the Cuban film *Fresa y chocolate* (*Strawberry and Chocolate*; Tomás Gutiérrez Alea 1993) provided a space to reconsider the representation of homosexuality in Latin American film. This is not the first film screened in the United States dealing with the treatment of homosexuality in a repressive Latin American political system,[1] but since it has obviously solicited a good deal of attention, one cannot detach its appeal from the ongoing political debate between the two countries (Cuba and United States).[2]

In spite of the space opened by Gutiérrez Alea's film, there is still the need for a more general account and analysis of the representation of homosexuality in Latin American cinema, especially one that places particular emphasis on Latin American cultural diversity, different cultural backgrounds, cultural heritage, and socio-political contexts. My study is designed to make visible the presence of two supporting gay[3] characters in two films in which homosexuality is not the preliminary agenda: *Danzón* (María Novaro, México, 1991) a feminist Bildungsroman; and *La Bella del Alhambra* (The Beauty of the Alhambra, Enrique Pineda Barnet, Cuba, 1995), which tells the story of the survival of an actress during the Cuban Belle Époque, and the later annihilation of her artistic career, which fails both because of patriarchal domination and the character's direct involvement in political issues.

113

Although they are placed in different times (Mexico in the 1980s and Cuba in the 1930s, respectively) the films share common issues: patriarchy, women's search for identities, and friendship with gay characters that enables them to direct the gaze toward themselves. The true friendships that the women in both films establish with gay men contrast with the impossibility of building a trusting relationship with their love partners. It is important, though, to analyze them individually in order to have a better understanding of why these movies call for finding ways to make visible the participation of their gay characters, why these gay characters are supporting roles, and what contribution these two films make to the configuration of a corpus of Latin American queer cinema.

LE ROUGE ET LE NOIR IN *DANZÓN*

As stated before, *Danzón* is a film version of a feminist Bildungsroman: Julia, the protagonist, sets out on a trip encouraged by a love affair. She is determined to find the man she believes she is in love with. This trip becomes a discovery of her inner self, and thanks to Susy—her new transvestite friend—an encounter with and sublimation of her desire. The question becomes: how does the transvestite character facilitate the shift toward her encounter?

Radical feminists like Janice Raymond attack the legitimacy of the transvestite by arguing that their representation "depends upon the assimilation of stereotypical femininity" or upon "exaggerating femininity as a birthright" (216). Commenting on cases like those of RuPaul and Boy George, prototypes of show business drag queens, Raymond regrets that this kind of woman "looks and acts so much like the woman of man-made femininity" (217).[4]

This critique of the exaggeration of the construction of femininity is not different for Latin American drag queens. The inspirational model ranges from—according to the time and generation—the cabaret artist to the American pop Diva. She either masters Cuban rhythms such as mambo, cha-cha, rumba, and danzon, or mimics the great singers or actresses. Celia Cruz's clothes, dances, and energy; Pimpinela's histrionics; and Madonna—a universal symbol—are some of the most frequently copied icons.

The transvestite construction of identity embraces a double opposition: the object of women's envy and moral repulsion. A good example of the above are the mixed feelings of Doña Ti (Julia's temporary landlady in Veracruz) for the transvestite: feelings of jealousy and morality. She possesses a talented voice for singing but has never been an artist. Her *lack* surfaces as frustration and manifests itself by her calling Susy and her friends *chotos*, a Mexicanism for "crippled." It is ironical, though, that she condemns transvestism but permits prostitution at her hostel, does not care anymore about frequent scenes of violence against women, and admits to having been involved with at least twenty men herself.

Doña Ti's reaction—to consider homosexuality (as apparently manifested by drag) either a limitation or an aberration—is closely related to the high moralism imposed by traditional Catholicism, social taboo, and a history of misinformation on gender issues and homosexuality studies in Latin America. On the surface of this religiously grounded morality, the shocking aspect of transvestism and/or cross-dressing, is the fact that the transvestite "man" has appropriated feminine garments, gestures, and sensibility, and the fact that this "man" may overtly flirt with another man (and with an audience).

In the movie, Susy asks Julia: "Are you afraid of looking like a whore or of men liking you?" Such a question, which may represent an ambivalence for a Mexican working-class woman (like Julia), is already resolved for the transvestite. The exaggeration of the feminine, and limitless coquetry is an appropriation, naturalization, and reidealization of the feminine that has already overcome the fear of that dilemma. In this construction of the feminine, there is an obvious questioning of the radical feminist postulate that argues that women should give up high heels, make up, and other stereotypical elements of femininity (as a construct supposedly intended to please masculine desire) to prove strength and/or oppose patriarchal order.

Given the fact that most current queer theories are either European or American, a problem of method of analysis emerges in the applicability of those theories to the realities of Latin America. That is a question that I will come back to toward the end of this paper. However, some of Judith Butler's remarks (*Bodies That Matter*) on the appropriation of clothes, in her chapter "Gender Performativity and Drag" might be useful to explain Susy's behavior and function in the film.

Constructing another sexuality involves certain ideals of femininity and masculinity that are related to the idealization of heterosexual limits (231-32). The transvestite, aware that the transformation is built for a performance, is not afraid to transgress those limits. The appropriation of the feminine is facilitated by the free experimentation of tips from magazines such as *Glamour, Mademoiselle, Vogue* and in the case of the Spanish speaking world, *Vanidades, Cosmopolitan, Hola,* (among others) and the conviction that the fantasy portrayed in these magazines may become true. I am in no position here to examine and vindicate or condemn this kind of reading as the assertive or wrong one for women. I am merely contextualizing an important fact in the construction of the transvestite image in Latin America, and, therefore, its representation. Somehow, these two transformation acts, experimentation and conviction, equate to the "publicization of theatrical agency" that, according to Butler, exercises great influence in the emergence of drag. As many women look at these magazines only as spectators, and dump in them their desire of what they could be or become "to please their men," the transvestite truly dares "to carry out that fantasy."

In *Danzón,* Susy uses all her drag-queen knowledge in order to help Julia liberate her desire. Her instructions repeat advice she has learned from magazines. Susy suggests Julia should wear black "if you are feeling very aggressive," and red, a color that as social construct is identified with passion, because Julia is "an autumn woman." Those two colors translate into two feelings missing in Julia's life until then: bravery and passion. Susy is the one who makes Julia address her gaze to the mirror, and it is at that moment that she can interrogate herself on the reasons for her fears: looking like a "whore," as Susy states it, or acknowledging that men like her.

By contrast, Susy asks Julia to teach her how to dance *danzón.* Afraid of breaking the social conventions of this dance, Susy emphasizes that one should not look straight into the partner's eyes: "the gaze should be directed to the sides, so that it has to be guessed." That sentence summarizes what Julia's life has been until meeting Susy: the art of suggestion and evasion. When she finally comes back to Mexico City, now wearing a black dress, she re-encounters her phantasmagoric love and dance partner, Carmelo. Julia is a new woman: by breaking the same social conventions of *danzón,* the ballroom dance that has brought them together, she finally dares to look into his eyes, as Susy has suggested. She is finally able to consolidate her identity, to make real her fantasies. In other words, she is able to name herself. On the surface, the role of the friendship with the transvestite may be simply understood as an element to underline women's stereotypes that relate to beauty, but it is this friendship that sponsors a new articulation and redefinition of the roles of men and women. *Danzón*, as a dance space, becomes the arena to examine such roles by breaking with tradition. The film potentially conveys a powerful feminist message that advocates a new order.

But if Julia finds redemption and the ability to name herself, another issue to discuss is how to name and designate Susy. Given the grammatical gender *différance* in the Spanish language, naming poses another problem. At no moment in the film narrative does Julia question the sexuality of her friend, in spite of her awareness that genetically Susy is a man. However, when Julia is preparing a farewell note for him, the camera does a close-up of the adding of a line to convert the letter *o*—a grammatical word ending for masculine gender words—into an *a* for the feminine.[5] This act of writing, performed in solitude and in silence, represents an acceptance of Susy's being and existence with no need to question his/her sexuality and gender orientation. For Julia, acceptance of Susy's sexual orientation is a genuine and true act of sealing an alliance. Not even upon her return to Mexico does she gossip or comment about the sexuality of Susy with her friends, which could be a normal cultural reaction to expect as a result of either fascination or voyeurism. Besides the neutrality with which she accepts Susy and her friends' transvestism, she acknowledges them as "artists" when interrogated by her friends on Susy's profession.

THE BEAUTY AND ADOLFITO

Set in the Cuban Belle Époque (the 1930s), the topic of the film allows for the representation of different acts of dressing and transvestitism that reflect both colonialism and desire. As is the case with *Danzón*, in *La Bella del Alhambra* the female protagonist seems trapped in love relationships with men who, in spite of their weak characters, easily dominate women. In this film, Rachel—the main character—moves from her first love, Eusebio, a man unable to overcome his Oedipal dependance on his mother, to the love of Federico, an artistic patron for whom Rachel is just an acquisition and an object to exhibit. Her last lover is Pedro, who puts the same pressure on her Eusebio did: she must make a decision between love and theater. Her final decision is to detach from them and seclude herself.

It is only her gay friend Adolfito who opposes the common dominant traits of the other three men. He not only stands by her every

time that she goes through a personal crisis, but also teaches her acting
tricks, and supports her in every artistic enterprise she undertakes. In
contrast to Susy in *Danzón*, Adolfo's dream to become a star does not
come true. Therefore, he sublimates and transfers his desire into facilitating fame for Rachel.

In a film that from the opening scene suggests the act of dressing
and cross-dressing, there are many times in which Rachel has to face
the mirror in the search for patterns to construct her own (artistic)
subject. I will only examine two examples here: one that stands for
Rachel's struggle in a dominated world, and one that conveys the idea
of annihilation of both the dissident woman and the gay character. In
the first example, Rachel must dress as a man so that she can attend a
performance in La Alhambra, the most important cabaret-theater in
Havana in the 1930s. She does so motivated by a voyeuristic curiosity
about what men might feel when attending shows there. Her attire is
reminiscent of films like *Tootsie, Victor Victoria* and *Some Like It Hot*
which are, as Judith Butler points out: "forms of drag that heterosexual
culture produces for itself" (*Bodies* 126). Since the Cuban cabaret of
those times was intended mainly to sublimate male desire, Rachel's
failure to bear in mind the costume she is wearing, and her explicit
displays of friendly affection for Adolfito, produce an uncomfortable
situation for the rest of the audience. Therefore, transvestism in such
scenes is not subversive but pleasing, and as Butler posits it: "these are
films which produce and contain the homosexual excess of any given
drag performance, the fear that an apparent heterosexual contact might
be made before non-apparent homosexuality" (*Bodies* 126).

In the second scene, Adolfito has made plans to attend a costume
ball so that Rachel will meet Federico, the famous patron of the arts.
For this occasion, Adolfito dresses as Dracula, a costume that opposes
the nature of his personality. He is not the one who "sucks the blood of
people;" rather he is the one gets annihilated as Rachel climbs up
artistically and socially. But his annihilation will eventually generate
Rachel's fall.

But if Adolfito is the one who clears the road for Rachel, he is also
the one who exposes Rachel to the mirror after Federico has brutally
beaten her. The possibility of reconciling the relationship between the
entity and the identity fails here. In *Danzón,* Susy places Julia in front
of the mirror and succeeds in making her recognize her imago. After
that, she gets a sense of what is missing in her life and can go forward
as a reassured woman. Something completely different happens in *La*

bella del Alhambra: Rachel faces the mirror and then drops it. Her image disintegrates. There is an impossibility for the consolidation of her image since the establishment of a relationship between the organism and the identity does not happen. Metaphorically speaking, redemption for her, as well as for Adolfito, is impossible.

As was the case in *Danzón*, the interpolation of elements of popular culture such as songs and dances emphasizes Rachel's struggle to survive in a male's world. Adolfo's lessons on classic theater enter in direct opposition to Rachel's fascination for popular dances like "El vacunao," a Cuban dance of African origin in which, as the word suggests, the man attempts "to vaccinate" the woman. As explained by Yvonne Daniel in *Rumba, Dance and Social Change in Contemporary Cuba*, the goal of this dance is to confront male sexual domination with feminine sensuality:

> this word came from the Spanish verb vacunar, meaning primarily "to vaccinate." Cubans coined it to signify this erotic pelvis gesture, the object of male pursuit and female flight that is the aim of dance. Sometimes it was not the pelvis or hips but a foot, a hand, even a scarf, that made the male's symbolic vaccination of the female. No matter what body part was used, the dancers reveled in mounting the attack and in preparing a defense. (4)

By using a counterpoint of visual images, the movie always places Rachel as a female character in constant search of her artistic identity, often reflected in mirrors, and fluctuating in a world highly marked by forms of male domination and colonization.

Music plays an important role in both films. *Danzón* derives its name from a Cuban rhythm that became very popular in the east coast of Mexico, mainly in Veracruz (where most of the movie takes place). The lyrics of the *danzones* and *boleros* chosen for the soundtrack are usually synchronized and reinforced with the specific content of an image, such is the case of "Viajera" (Traveler), which is danced by a solitary woman as Julia contemplates her before setting off on her trip. It is also the case of "Lágrimas negras" (Mourning Tears), played as Julia strolls by the deck analyzing the names of the boats. The song talks about someone wanting to die out of love, and later deciding to stay alive in order to see *the other* suffering. The very last song, "Mujer perjura" (a woman who breaks a promise), supports Julia's resignation to keep being a weak woman and to depend on a nonexistent relationship.

In a similar way, *La bella del Alhambra* interpolates dressing scenes with specific songs. Such is the case of the song interpreted by Rachel when La Mexicana (her artistic rival) shows up in the theater. Rachel is dressed as a soldier and sings a song that slightly ridicules the military order, but in fact dramatizes the artistic war between the two vedettes.

For the performance of "The Island of the Parrots," Rachel must play "La señorita de Maupin." The carnivalesque atmosphere of the play goes from *danzón* to opera, and from tango to rhumba. The musical chaos encompasses a masquerade that Rachel must resolve for the audience. Rachel, dressing as a man, kisses her lover and an operatic voice screams: "two men kissing? How awful, in my country, we call them faggots." The hysteria that the scene produces in the audience urges Rachel to prove that in fact there is a woman under the costume. Rachel exhibits her breast as all the men clap and scream in extasy. Back on the stage, Adolfito cries for the masquerade.

In *Danzón*, music and dance taken from popular culture help Julia to reaffirm her position in her social circles; in *La bella del Alhambra*, they force Rachel to back away from them. In the closing scene of *Danzón*, Julia, as a woman in control, dancing to the lyrics of the danzon "Mujer perjura" (the one who breaks a promise), leaves the spectator feeling good. In *La bella del Alhambra*, the avoidance of Cuban songs and the closing scene, edited to orchestrated music, emphasize Rachel's consequent alienation from society.

The ending of the movie, the assassination of Adolfito in an attempt on the life of Federico, and the later condemnation of Rachel for her overt participation in plays of political content, may be read here as a metaphor for the impossibility of women and gays to be a part of the map of power. Adolfito's assassination is the act that makes Rachel reconsider the impossibility of succeeding and finding a space for her desire. Suffocated by feelings of guilt, Rachel is forced to disappear from the public scene.

In *La bella del Alhambra*, the ending forecasts disappearance for both the woman and gay male character. I have repeatedly quoted Judith Butler's *Bodies That Matter*; however, the explanation that she offers for the disappearance of Venus Xtravaganza (a Latin drag queen in *Paris is Burning*) would be useful to explain Adolfito's death (and Rachel's marginalization), if it were not for Butler's scornful tone.

Venus Xtravaganza, as analyzed and sufficed by Octavia St. Laurent—
another drag queen from Livingston's documentary—just wants "to be
a rich somebody." According to Butler,

> her death testifies to a tragic misreading of the social map of power, a
> misreading orchestrated by that very map according to which the sites
> of a phantasmatic self-overcoming are constantly resolved into
> disappointment. (131)

Framed in these words, it seems like Venus Xtravaganza's tragedy
is more of a punishment than the result of a failed attempt to fit into
"the rearticulation of kinship" (as Butler herself calls it), and the
inability to find a representative space within the same. Venus's death
has to do more with her inability to participate in a world that, although
shaped into a domestic order (the ball preparation and its extreme
emphasis on household chores such as sewing, ironing, and others),
must produce entertainment for capitalistic systems. The same
circumstances appear to remain for Rachel and Adolfito in *La bella del
Alhambra.*
    The plot develops from Rachel's direct involvement in the
production of "The Island of the Parrots." This show criticizes the
earlier attempts of the American intervention in Cuba, and the massive
investment of capital for the construction of American casinos, hotels,
and similar business in Havana. The polemics generated by Rachel's
participation results in her condemnation as an actress by her audience,
and as a woman by Pedro. It also eventuates in Adolfito's disappearance
in an attempt to kill Pedro. In this way, the elimination of two marginal
characters (the woman and the gay male character) allows the
consolidation and reaffirmation of hegemonic power, where patriarchal
order prevails.

AND FOR THE DRAG QUEEN AND THE GAY?
REDEMPTION OR ANNIHILATION?

The appearance of a transvestite character and a gay friend in these two
movies may be compared to the presence of a fairy in children's tales of
the Nordic tradition: they show up, rescue the protagonist, make their
wishes come true, and then disappear. But do they disappear, or are
they made to disappear? Adolfito's death and its political context
somehow remind us of Molina's death in *Kiss of the Spider Woman.*

They are different, however, in that Adolfito dies so that Pedro, Prince Charming, can survive.

But in relating *Kiss of the Spider Woman*'s ending to that of *La bella del Alhambra,* a coincidence surfaces: homosexuality is killed. In the other two movies I have mentioned here, Diego in *Fresa y chocolate* decides to leave Cuba in exile, and in *Danzón*, the last appearance of Susy is blurred by the camera and the spectator never finds out what happens to her.

In addition, another coincidence surfaces: three of these four movies are based on literary pieces. *Strawberry and Chocolate* is based on Senel Paz's short story: "The Wolf, the Woods and the New Man" (Paz also wrote the script for the movie); *La bella del Alhambra* is the film version of Miguel Barnet's novel *Canción de Rachel* (Miguel Barnet is a cousin of Enrique Pineda, director and producer of the movie); and *Kiss of the Spider Woman* is a version of Manuel Puig's novel.[6]

Those four movies intend to make *visible* the issue of homosexuality in Latin America (i.e., being marginal within the marginal), but as an apparent corollary, they all provide an invisible end to the gay/transvestite character. Disappearance in these movies is not made in a critical way, but rather in a reiterative fashion. Though these cultural productions finally dare to speak up about something silent, the treatment of the queer characters suggests the need to move the queer issue from a supporting role to a protagonistic one. In a way, they call for a construction of a Latin American queer space of representation in which homosexuality does not have to disappear, leave in exile, and/or be killed. They also advocate for plot sources where queer cinema does not necessarily have to refer to/or originate from literary pieces.

In the construction of that space, another question must be resolved. I have intentionally showed certain lenience to over-incorporate queer theory in the analysis of these two films. As shown, I still have many reservations towards some of Butler's comments and concerns about the criticism of Raymond. A model that proves degrading for drag queens in London might mean vindication in some Third World contexts. So, will current American and European queer theories be the most appropriate to construct or frame that space of representation? or, as Chicano feminist scholar Gloria Anzaldúa proposes in the case of Chicano studies:

> Necesitamos teorías/ we need theories that will help us rewrite history
> using class, gender and ethnicity as categories of analysis, theories
> that cross borders, that blur boundaries—new kinds of theories with
> new theorizing methods. (*Making Face, Making Soul* xxv)

To which I would add, "we need to construct those theories," as well as to continue the already exisiting articulations of queer theories in "Third Worlds" that understand that there is not just one Third World to represent. If it is true that Latin American countries share a lot of similarities, the concept of Third World applies differently and moves in various maps in each one of them. The visibility of homosexuality in each country would be more effective if special attention is given to each specific context, rather than the assumption and enforcement of theories that emerged in order to explain the circumstances of other realities.

Theories that deal with gender issues in specific Latin American contexts must consider the different relations to regimes of power and visibility resulting from being gay, lesbian, transgendered, somewhat camp, a sometime cross-dresser, and a preoperative transsexual. In both, *Danzón* and *La bella del Alhambra*, the transgendered figure (whose sexuality may or may not be *sous rature*) functions as a pedagogical force in relation to a genetic woman, avoiding vicious competition between them. Nonetheless, the two films (as well as the increasing amount of films on queer issues) demand a specific definition of what is gay within the Latin American contexts to determine if there is a specificity to the transgender dimension and/or if cross-dressing is simply read as metonymic of gayness. With that as a start, we might take on a new reading of the inclusion of homoeroticism in Latin American cinema as well as literature.

NOTES

1. *Kiss of the Spider Woman* (1985) is a movie usually associated with Latin American representation of homosexuality under repressive systems. The movie is based on the novel by the Argentinean writer Manuel Puig; it stars Raúl Juliá and William Hurt and it is an American production, although directed by Héctor Babenco, who is an Argentine working in Brazil.

2. After the screening of *Fresa y chocolate* in the United States, special films on homosexuality in Cuba have been sponsored by American filmakers. Among these films are *Mariposa en el andamio* and *Gay Cuba* (1995).

Although their contribution is valuable, they immediately relate gay representation to American patterns. The first one, for example, follows the documentary model established by *Paris Is Burning* in order to portray the daily routine and the artistic life of a group of transvestites in La Guinera neighborhood in Havana. The second one closes with a parade in which a representation of the Cuban gay community exhibits the rainbow flag, a harbinger for American gay communities, to portray the image of Cuban gay alliance.

    Fresa y chocolate merited even more attention than documentaries like *Conducta impropia* (*Improper Conduct*; 1984), produced by Néstor Almendros, a Spanish cinematographer who had adopted Cuba as homeland and left three years after the Revolution. As Paul Julian Smith claims: "exile, homosexuality and early death from the effects of AIDS" (59) are similarities and differences between Almendros's production and Reinaldo Arenas's autobiographical text *Before Night Falls*.

    3. The use of the word "gay" by no means intends to reduce the difference between gay, lesbian, bisexual, transgendered and/or crossgendered individuals. It is used mainly to solve a problem of designation, and is also derived from the fact that the word "gay" is the term often used in Latin American countries to refer to homosexuality.

    4. It is important to keep in mind that Judith Butler's *Bodies That Matter* originated as a response to interpretations given to her former book *Gender Trouble*. Some of her answers reply to extremely radical comments precisely from feminists like Raymond. One of Butler's phrases that might posit the issues of this debate is: "I never did think that gender was like clothes, or that clothes makes the woman" (231). In fact, in the construction of queer theories for Latin America, special attention should be given to women's (and men's) particular interest in dressing up.

    5. Julia writes: "para tí que has sido tan buen*o*" (for you who've been so good [masculine]), and immediately marks the difference by adding a slash to the *o* so that it reads: "para tí que has sido tan buen*a*" (for you who've been so good [feminine]).

    6. Based on literary pieces, there are obviously many differences between the short story, the novels, and the scripts for the movie. One worth emphasizing is the treatment of Adolfo and Rachel's friendship in *La canción de Rachel* as a fraternal friendship. In the movie it seems as if Adolfito were in love with Rachel but unable to express his love due to his sexual orientation.

A Scene from
Deporting the Divas; A Play
Guillermo Reyes

(Brief Summary: Michael J. Gonzalez, a young Mexican-American border patrolman, attends a Spanish-language class. His wife has left him, he's begun to question his sexual identity, and while on duty he's recently stumbled into a gay wedding of migrant workers in the middle of the desert which has left him especially disconcerted.)

MICHAEL: (*to audience*) San Diego . . . city college . . . Beginning Spanish for Pochos. (*The Teacher approaches.*)

TEACHER: Roll those r's, dammit! (*Michael valiantly tries the "r" exercise.*)

MICHAEL: "Que rapido corren los ferrocarriles en los rieles del. . ."

TEACHER: You are an embarrassment to your people, Miguel. (*Teacher exits.*)

MICHAEL: (*to audience*) And that night, I met him. (*Sedicio comes in. A light shines on him. It's a very important, attitudinal entrance as he wears sun-glasses, a dark sports coat, black pants and a t-shirt with a spiderweb drawn on it which will become noticeable when he takes it off. It's his "Black Widow" motif. He approaches Michael.*)

MICHAEL: There he was, ready to utter the words that would forever change my life.

SEDICIO: I'm talking to you, is that seat taken?

MICHAEL: Ah, no.

SEDICIO: Let me through then, move it. (*squeezes past him, then settles down on his seat*) Am I late? Did I miss something?

MICHAEL: Only the whole first week.

125

SEDICIO: What? You mean the class started last w. . . . I didn't read the enrollment form carefully enough? Now wait a sec, haven't I met you before?

MICHAEL: I don't think so.

SEDICIO: Sure. You're that INS officer. You deported my cousin Javier and his wife last year.

MICHAEL: Nothing personal.

SEDICIO: I would have done the same. I can't stand my cousins either. Especially Javier who's such a homophobe.

MICHAEL: Excuse me?

SEDICIO: Oh, I'm openly gay and he doesn't approve, but I'll have you know they slipped in a few weeks afterwards just by driving through the border.

MICHAEL: They drove through just like that?

SEDICIO: My mom brought them in for a family funeral. Old aunt died of heartbreak and spinsterhood. They stayed to help with the farm. We exploit them, but they're family.

MICHAEL: Right.

SEDICIO: That was a joke.

MICHAEL: Oh?

SEDICIO: I'm actually a fiery advocate of immigrant rights myself, but a joke is an attempt to find a comfortable middle ground with someone like you who represents the Enemy.

MICHAEL: I am no one's "enemy."

SEDICIO: And don't tell me you're here to learn Spanish, too, border man?

MICHAEL: Just don't make fun of me please, that teacher's been hounding me.

SEDICIO: (*meaning Teacher*) Oh, here he comes.

TEACHER: Para los estudiantes nuevos, yo soy el profesor Serrat, yo soy de Barcelona.

SEDICIO: Good, a real Spaniard.

TEACHER: Excuse me, I'm not a Spaniard, I'm a Catalonian. (*Teacher withdraws, insulted.*)

SEDICIO: Oooops! Sorry.

MICHAEL: Last week he was a Puerto Rican from New York.

SEDICIO: I don't get it. (*Sedicio's left looking confused and self-conscious.*)

MICHAEL: (*to audience*) The next couple of weeks, we sit next to each other, not saying much, staring at each other until one night, he thanks me. (*to Sedicio*) Thank me for what?

SEDICIO: For not laughing at me that first day like the rest of the class did.

MICHAEL: Were they laughing? I don't think they were. . . .

SEDICIO: Mocking me, all of them! I was feeling very, very Richie Valenz that day, sensing the turbulence of my private life, the aftermath of a bad one-night stand with a Marine, but you don't need to hear all that. And that teacher, I insulted him without meaning to. You're a real doll, thanks, I owe you.

MICHAEL: Ok, you do. (*to audience*) After class, I ask him out for. . . (*to Sedicio*). . . Coffee?

SEDICIO: Coffee?

MICHAEL: No?

SEDICIO: Yes! Ah. . . Quel Fromage Coffee House on Fifth and University. Separate cars, street parking should be doable.

MICHAEL: No, why take two cars? Let's ride together, you show me the way. I have an Isuzu Hombre, of course.

SEDICIO: Of course. (*Transition to coffee house*)

MICHAEL: (*to audience*) Coffee house. Hillcrest. He seems to know everyone. (*Jazz music plays, lending ambience to the place.*)

SEDICIO: (*acting bohemian and talking Italian to other customers*) Francesca, come va? Ciao, Rinaldi. Tutto bene, caro, tutto bene. This here is Michele (*pronounced Mee-kay-lay.*)

MICHAEL: Ciao, I guess.

SEDICIO: Rinaldi and I go way back. He and I still get together occassionally to . . . you know. . . .

MICHAEL: (*a little titilated*) To what?

SEDICIO: To discuss Derrida's theory on poetic discourse, of course.

MICHAEL: Of course.

SEDICIO: Not that he knows anything about it. He's way too Susan Sontag.

MICHAEL: I read Ayn Rand once.

SEDICIO: Don't even try it. Well, what should I get?

MICHAEL: (*to audience*) I order. . . . (*ordering to imaginary waiter*) Just regular coffee of the day, please.

SEDICIO: For me, double cappuccino with non-fat milk, cinammon on top, twist of lemon on the side, two packs of nutra-sweet, one of those long spoons for mixing and a job application. Thanks, doll.

MICHAEL: (*to audience*) Espresso goes to his head. He gets to the point.

SEDICIO: Are you a top or a bottom?

MICHAEL: What? (*to audience*) What the hell was he talking about?

SEDICIO: One of my surveys: do you take it or do you give it? (*to audience*) He'd either punch me or take me.

MICHAEL: (*to audience*) He couldn't have been this gay.

SEDICIO: (*to audience*) He couldn't have been this straight.

MICHAEL: Now wait a second, this is my story, I am the narrator here.

SEDICIO: This first person narrative can be very patriarchal and oppressive.

MICHAEL: What is that supposed to mean?

SEDICIO: Share your narrative, Michael. (*Michael sits down like a kid who's been scolded by his mother.*)

SEDICIO: Let's get something straight right now, Michael! I don't have time for closeted men. I want to marry a man by the time I'm 25, and I think I'm already past that but who's counting really. Either you're interested or you're not. I need an answer and I need it now! (*to audience*) I am getting good at this! (*turning back to Michael*) So. . . Michael? Miguel? Michele? (*Michael looks away, feeling a little troubled, "tuned out."*)

SEDICIO: (*bragging*) Some revelation had dawned upon him, I have that effect on men.

MICHAEL: I'm just a little. . .

SEDICIO: Married?

MICHAEL: What?

SEDICIO: You're wearing the ring.

MICHAEL: Oh. And that didn't stop you from flirting, did it?

SEDICIO: You asked me out. I figured, don't ask, don't tell.

MICHAEL: Yes. As you can see, I'm going through some personal changes.

SEDICIO: And you work for the INS . . . you're a real mess, aren't you?

MICHAEL: Excuse me?

SEDICIO: I wasn't passing judgment, I was just observing: Mexican-American borderpatrolman who doesn't speak Spanish and is also in the closet. You've got a lot of "issues" and I like that in a man. I'm issue-challenged myself. I just got a BA in Italian Literature and what am I doing with my life? I'm filling out job applications to dole out cappuccino to a bunch of FAILED POETS! And look, there goes my UC professor: Signora Sabatini! She sold me on the humanities. FUCK THE HUMANITIES, lady! Vaffanculo! Vaffanculo!

MICHAEL: Just calm down!

SEDICIO: Sorry. How has your week been?

MICHAEL: Like you wouldn't believe . . . especially that damn wedding.

SEDICIO: Breeder concepts!

MICHAEL: No, this was a gay wedding.

SEDICIO: Oooooh, do tell.

MICHAEL: Two Mexican boys. No, one was Mexican-American . . . out in the desert, dancing the "quebradita," it was a very strange sight, never seen nothing like that. At first, I just thought they were a buncha illegals, or undocumented workers, excuse me. So I raided the place and, well, it wasn't what I thought. They were just "getting married" and I disturbed their wedding, and now I'm the laughing stock of the department. We're not supposed to go after weddings, no matter how illegal.

SEDICIO: You were left traumatized by a gay wedding?

MICHAEL: No, it just left me wondering, I guess.

SEDICIO: Wondering what?

MICHAEL: I just had to get out of the house and enroll in a Spanish class.

SEDICIO: Really? I'm taking it only because I need to meet a husband.

MICHAEL: In class?

SEDICIO: I'm attracted to Latino men who speak lousy Spanish.

MICHAEL: Well, that would be me.

SEDICIO: My grammar always needs reviewing anyway, so I keep taking the same class with these loser teachers. It's like a fetish really. I think it's lovable for a Latin boy to speak such awful Spanish as you do. It's cute, it's macho.

MICHAEL: Then I'm "macho."

SEDICIO: I'll be the judge of that.

MICHAEL: So, ah. . . ah, when do we cut to the chase and do what you gay men do?

SEDICIO: What?

MICHAEL: I don't know how you folks proceed in mating rituals and all, but I read it in "Newsweek," about how promiscuous you all are, let's get to that.

SEDICIO: Whatever happened to candlelights, music, and a substantial dinner?

MICHAEL: Don't you back down now! You wanted an answer and you wanted it now so here you are. My wife left me for a reason, to test

me perhaps, to see how far I'd go, and now here I am with you. I
need to know what I feel and why I feel it, whether this is the right
thing for me or not and you've practically volunteered, so you can't
take it back. You flirted with me and now you're stuck. So when do
we get to it? Give me a time and a place 'cause I need some big
changes in my life and I need them soon, preferably now!

SEDICIO: (*intimidated*) But I'm into dating.

MICHAEL: What about that Marine?

SEDICIO: That was a very sordid one-night stand!

MICHAEL: That's what I need then!

SEDICIO: I won't do that again.

MICHAEL: Great, now you say that!

SEDICIO: I have rules about all this. I'm gonna be a teacher one day,
and I believe in establishing the rules right upfront. Three dates
might get you a hickey.

MICHAEL: Does this count as a date?

SEDICIO: I should say not

MICHAEL: I think it does! We'll go out tomorrow, and the day after
and that's it. You live close, don't you?

SEDICIO: Near the Gay Center on Normal Street.

MICHAEL: Within walking distance, huh?

SEDICIO: Yes, why?

MICHAEL: Well, because. . . (*backing down a bit, trying a new tactic*)
Look, I have a lot of studying to do. My promotion actually
depends on me learning better Spanish. How would you like to
tutor me? I'll come over.

SEDICIO: I'm not comfortable with this, Michael. It borders on sleaze.

MICHAEL: Then here's my card. Need a ride?

SEDICIO: Not right now.

MICHAEL: Suit yourself. But now at least you know where to find me.
(*Michael exits*)

SEDICIO: Goodness. (*to audience*)
What have I done? A marine, a border patrolman, I'm being used by the
sexually repressed right-wing of this country!

END OF EXCERPT

(The entire script is available from Guillermo Reyes, Theatre Department, Arizona State University, Tempe, AZ 85287-2002.)

Hybrid Identities
and the Emergence of
Dislocated Consciousness
Deporting The Divas By Guillermo Reyes
Beatriz Cortez

Guillermo Reyes is a United States citizen born in Chile. He is
therefore part of the great masses of immigrants and exiles of our times.
As a playwright, he has negotiated a space that allows him to be part of
different communities. He is a Latin American playwright in the United
States who writes mainly in English, and his plays deal with the
identity of both the Latin American immigrant communities and the
Latino communities in the United States. And yet they also explore gay
identity inside and outside those communities. This has made it
difficult to classify Reyes as a Latino playwright, or as a gay playwright, or even as a Latin American playwright. His work questions the
different identities that both the center and the subaltern communities
have undertaken to create and maintain in the United States. This
traditional concept of identity as a cohesive and complete definition of
the individual becomes a limitation when we read Reyes's plays. His
position is that

> in the new age of e-mail, cellular phones, faxes and satellites, the
> modern writer may belong everywhere at once, his words and his
> message crowding a universe awash in sensations not always verbal
> and yet ever in need of writers to bring it together and punctuate
> meaning on the runaway run-on sentences of modern satellite culture.
> The writer therefore could belong to all his groups, his subgroups,

and yet be universally American or Americanly universal. ("The Latin American Writer" 113)

My proposal is that *Deporting the Divas* questions the alienating tendency to classify individuals according to their sexual preferences, ethnic backgrounds, economic positions, or professions. It questions this type of cohesive identity because they are ideological constructs that are falsely represented as able to encompass a large number of individuals and/or communities. In *Divas*, what we find is an alternative to this type of identity. Through a game of shifting stereotypes, nationalities, immigration status, gender, and sexual orientation, the characters, far from being forced into a defining category, are able to negotiate a flowing hybrid identity that makes it possible for them to simultaneously belong to a variety of spaces of difference and/or to shift from one space to the other. In this sense, the play also opposes the concept of identity as a permanent trait of the individual, allowing its characters to constantly transform and shift from one identity to the next. With regards to transvestism, Marjorie Garber argues that "one of the most important aspects of cross-dressing is the way in which it offers a challenge to easy notions of binarity, putting into question the categories of 'female' and 'male,' whether they are considered essential or constructed, biological or cultural" (10). This game of transformation, which in the play extends itself beyond the limits of gender, is a sort of drag performance within the performance that allows for the denaturalization of all categories.

The option for a hybrid identity in contrast to the violence that the imposition of a cohesive identity poses on the individual, has been widely supported by postcolonialists, Gayatri Spivak, among them. In her well known article, "Can the Subaltern Speak?," Spivak finds an ideological problem in the position taken by Western intellectuals as the latter analyze what they conceive to be the Third World. Spivak points out that what these intellectuals achieve is to assign and construct a cohesive identity of that Other which, for her, is nothing but a reflection of their First World Selves. She then chooses to return to Marx, because in opposition to other Western intellectuals, Marx was not attempting to construct a cohesive subject, but rather what Spivak calls a subject with a "dislocated and incoherent consciousness" (276). In other words, class conscience, political affiliation, or any other type of positioning in society become sources for the emergence of the subject that do not operate in a cohesive way. The subject, therefore, cannot be a continuous, cohesive entity. Spivak points out that for Marx, "in so far as millions of families live under economic conditions of existence that separate their mode of life . . . *they form a class.* In so far as . . . the identity of their interests fails to produce a feeling of community . . . *they do not form a class*" (277). For her, these propositions are evidence of Marx's respect for the subject's agency, both at an individual and at a collective level. In the case of Latinos in the United States, the subject's different, and often contradictory, affiliations, be they political, ethnic, religious, cultural, or sexual, prevent the formation of a cohesive identity and provide for the construction of a dislocated subject.

Homi Bhabha has also positioned himself against the categorization of individuals from a single perspective in order to construct and speak about their subjectivity as a whole. He proposes that

> what is theoretically innovative, and politically crucial, is the need to think beyond narratives of originary and initial subjectivities and to focus on those moments or processes that are produced in the articulation of cultural differences. These 'in-between' spaces provide the terrain for elaborating strategies of selfhood—singular or communal—that initiate new signs of identity, and innovative sites of collaboration, and contestation, in the act of defining the idea of society itself. (1-2)

Deporting the Divas presents a range of possibilities for the negotiation of a hybrid identity through which an individual can be part of different spaces at the same time, even spaces that are contradictory or incompatible among themselves. In this interstice, difference can not only coexist, but also overlap. This is the case of Sedicio, who, among other things, is a gay Latino illegal immigrant, and Michael, a bisexual Latino border patrol officer. None of the subaltern categories (Latino/gay/illegal immigrant/bisexual border patrol officer) are able to completely describe any of the characters in the play. They only describe certain aspects of one individual or group of individuals. From the perspective of the center, many of these are despicable identities. At the same time, from the perspective of the different subaltern communities, the other marginal identities might be despicable as well. This is exemplified by Michael's behavior: he is the Latino character whose job is to deport Latin American immigrants, that is, potential members of his own community. And it is also exemplified, from the perspective of the center, by Marge McCarthy's character, who points out that "having a gay son these days is not as tragic as having an immigrant in the family" (2). This remark is a recognition of the possibility of the white/U.S. citizen center to be intercepted by the gay community. But it is also a reassurance that this white center can try to avoid being part of the Latino community, it can even allow itself to doubt whether Latinos are really U.S. citizens (just as Miss Fresno points out in the play: "most people in the U.S. don't know Chicanos are, like, U.S. Citizens"), and it can know that it will never be part of the illegal-immigrant community. Therefore the different categories of the subaltern are arranged in a hierarchy depending on one's point of view. This can also be perceived as we analyze the traditional gay identity's allegiance to the center, white, middle class American (to which we might add U.S. citizen). Even when this has significantly changed in recent years, for a very long time the gay community in the United States was mostly insensitive to issues of sexuality (in its exclusion of the lesbian, bisexual, and transgender perspectives), class (in its exclusion of the lower-class gay experience), and ethnicity (in its exclusion of minority perspectives about the construction of gay identity). Annamarie Jagose argues that even when the gay and lesbian identity was constructed based on the ethnic model, it perceived sexual preference as the defining characteristic of the individual, and therefore, it relegated other type of allegiances to a secondary level (*Queer Theory* 63). Due to this, for a long time, the identification of an individual as a member of the gay and lesbian community went against this individual's identification as a member of other ethnic and cultural communities. Jagose points out that

> ironically, given its origins in a race-based politics, the ethnic model's gay and lesbian subject was white. It was not simply that the lesbian and gay community described by the ethnic model happened to be predominantly white. Rather, in describing that community as organised by a single defining feature—sexual orientation—the ethnic model could theorise race only as an insubstantial or, at best, additional category of identification. Lesbians and gays of colour, frustrated by the assumption that they would have more in common with white lesbians and gay men than with their own ethnic or racial communities, began to critique both overt and covert racism in the mainstream gay community. (63)

In the same way, the Latino/Chicano communities in the United States constructed their identity by often turning to traditional cultural values that united them as a group of people. The cultural production of the Latino/Chicano communities shows a return to indigenous theological and cultural models in the search for a shared identity. This emphasized the importance of those aspects that contributed to the cohesion of the Latino identity. Therefore, it diminished the importance given to gender and sexual preference issues or any other issues that could divert attention from the most pressing matter: the construction of the Latino identity in order to survive, to meet needs, and to obtain rights that were denied to the whole community. Cherríe Moraga speaks of her experience finding a place where she felt that she belonged as a Chicana lesbian:

> When "El Plan Espiritual de Aztlán" [The Spiritual Plan of Aztlan]
> was conceived a generation ago, lesbians and gay men were not
> envisioned as members of the "house"; we were not recognized as the
> sister planting the seeds, the brother gathering the crops. We were not
> counted as members of the "bronze continent." . . . In the last decade,
> through the efforts of Chicana feministas, Chicanismo has undergone
> a serious critique. Feminist critics are committed to the preservation
> of Chicano culture, but we know that our culture will not survive
> marital rape, battering, incest, drug and alcohol abuse, AIDS, and the
> marginalization of lesbian daughters and gay sons. ("Queer Aztlán"
> 298)

Concomitantly, Latin American societies have often denied the existence of gay members in their societies and actively persecuted those who publically embraced such identities. Military regimes that have plagued Latin American history for a great part of the twentieth century have distinguished themselves for their homophobia and machismo. David William Foster argues that "hispanic machismo, which derives only part of its ideological capital from Catholicism, must necessarily defend a variety of masculine supremacy that excludes the gender-role transformations that are integral, if not thoroughly coextensive, with gay identity" (88). On the other hand, the Latin American liberation movements associated with the political left failed to recognize the emergence of gay communities within their own political organizations. Historically, the guerrilla movements in Latin America have been directed mostly by men—although in the 1970s and

80s, women's participation in popular movements gained significance. The men in the early guerrilla movements reinstitutionalized the same machismo ideology that characterized their societies. In fact, Diana Taylor, in her introduction to *Negotiating Performance* points out that

> Liberation movements in Latin America have tended to be revolutionary ones organized around class conflict and "communist/capitalist" tensions. In part, too, the resistance to accepting feminist and gay/lesbian liberation movements is seen as displacing male intellectuals and leaders from center stage. The glorification of the revolutionary hero (in the tradition of Che Guevara, for example) casts the powerful (even *macho*) male as leader in the struggle for self-determination and relegates women to supportive but subservient roles. All of a sudden, then, this virile hero is stripped of his status as revolutionary leader of the oppressed and becomes seen instead as the oppressor of other oppressed groups— women, gays, and lesbians. ("Opening Remarks" 8-9)

Moreover, gay and lesbian identities were rejected within left-wing movements because they were associated with U.S. capitalism, ultra-right-wing politics, and in recent years, neoliberalism. Foster points out that

> the inability of dogmatic Marxism to see in gay culture anything other than one of bourgeois capitalism's many diseased faces, and its failure to distinguish between homosexuality . . . as part of the corrupt market system and gay identity as a dimension of personal liberation, provided a potent substratum for the homophobia of the Castro revolution, which itself had its origins in one of the great subsystems of machismo, the armed forces. (88)

Furthermore, the concept of homosexuality could not/cannot be transplanted from the North American and European models into Latin America. For instance, with regard to male homosexuality, Foster points out that in Latin America it may be understood "in terms of the Euro-American medico-criminal discourse where any sexual commerce between individuals of the same sex makes them both homosexual" (3) or it may be understood from the perspective of patriarchy, "in terms of a disjunction between the insertor, who never loses his alignment with establishment masculinity, and the insertee, to whom alone a deviant sexual persona is attributed" (3). This patriarchal model allows for the social marginalization of both women and *maricones/culeros* (male insertees), while it reaffirms the masculine identity of the insertor regardless of his sexual preference. On the other hand, in most Latin American cultures, there is a clear distinction between proscribed behavior in public spaces and permitted or desired behavior in the private space. As a result, homosexual acts can take place within the secure environment of private space. Yet, the process of their appearance in public within most Latin American urban spaces has been slow and problematic, to say the least.

The above issues have made an impact on the emergence of a gay identity within the Latino communities in the United States. Throughout the process of construction of this identity, gay and lesbian Latinos in the United States have negotiated between their identities as Latinos, their identities as gays and lesbians, and their identities as members of American society as a whole. Furthermore, as Bhabha emphasizes, "the shadow of the nation falls on the condition of the exile" (141). Therefore, Latin Americans in the United States have also had to negotiate their identities as Latin Americans in exile. *Deporting the Divas* performs the negotiation of their hybrid identities through the diverse experiences of the Latino/gay/illegal immigrant characters. Bhabha, talking about the interstices, or what he defines as "the overlap and displacement of domains of difference," asks:

> How are subjects formed 'in-between', or in excess of, the sum of the 'parts' of difference (usually intoned as race/class/gender, etc.)? How do strategies of representation or empowerment come to be formulated in the competing claims of communities where, despite shared histories of deprivation and discrimination, the exchange of values, meanings and priorities may not always be collaborative and dialogical, but may be profoundly antagonistic, conflictual and even incommensurable? (2)

In *Deporting the Divas* Reyes offers an answer to these questions.

The play displaces the concept of "foreign" from its traditional role as a defining term for immigrants, to other spaces of difference, especially that of sexual dissent. In this sense, Miss Fresno, who is self-identified as a foreigner, is a foreigner because she is an immigrant from Guatemala, as well as a foreigner because she is played by a male actor. Even Marge, who is not "openly" an immigrant, is described as "a real woman played by a man" (2). Once we are aware of the fluidity of these two spaces of difference, and once we hear that the teacher has previously taught a course titled "Embracing Your Inner Foreigner," we just have to wonder about Marge's origin. In her analysis of gender construction, Judith Butler argues that

> drag constitutes the mundane way in which genders are appropriated, theatricalized, worn, and done; it implies that all gendering is a kind of impersonation and approximation. If this is true, it seems, there is no original or primary gender that drag imitates, *but gender is a kind of imitation for which there is no original*. ("Imitation" 185)

Therefore, drag, as an appropriation that denaturalizes the compulsory performance of gender, functions here as a tool that unmasks gender as what it is: a cultural construction imposed by the dominant ideology of compulsory heterosexuality. If the concept of "foreign" can be applied both to a sexual outlaw and to an undocumented immigrant, drag can also unmask and denaturalize the center in all of its meanings (the construction of gender, the heterosexual imperative, the U.S. citizen's primacy) as a cultural construct.

One of the issues that the play problematizes is the construction and reproduction of stereotypes. The play itself reproduces numerous stereotypes, and the spectator—who can only view the play from his/her own positioning in the social text—is part of the same game. Yet, it is significant that these stereotypes do not remain as permanent traits of any one character throughout the play, but rather transform themselves as the characters' identities change. In this sense, stereotypes lose their permanence and become another sort of drag performance.

But it is through the use of stereotypes—our ideological baggage— that we are able to make sense of the text. And as the various realms of difference interact, it is through ideology that they read and interpret each other. Mas'ud Zavarzadeh defines ideology as "the structure of (mis)representation that explains away social contradictions in the interest of a particular class" (92-93). He points out that "ideology participates in the construction of cultural reality by providing a (seemingly) coherent and integrated view of life and a sustained theory of reality for members of a culture" (92). Therefore, stereotypes, as part of ideology, engage in a process that results both in the creation of difference and in the stereotypical construction of a national identity. Bhabha points out that stereotype, "as a form of multiple and contradictory belief, gives knowledge of difference and simultaneously disavows or masks it" (77). In this process, the margins can negotiate a stereotypical identity within the boundaries of a specific time and space and with a specific purpose in mind, such as the survival of the community within a system of oppression. Therefore, stereotype, when consciously used by the margins, can function as a form of obstacle for the center to gain information and access to its space, as well as a point of departure from which to challenge the center. Yet, if it is imposed permanently by the community, it can also be detrimental, since for far too long the center has been assigning to the margins a stereotypical identity that keeps the margins where it is: outside the realm of discourse. As Butler points out,

> identity categories tend to be instruments of regulatory regimes, whether as the normalizing categories of oppressive structures or as the rallying points for a liberatory contestation of that very oppression. ("Imitation" 180)

In *Divas*, the characters both produce, displace, and break stereotypes. This allows them to multiply the possibilities for their hybrid identity. For instance, Miss Fresno, who, again, is represented by a male actor, is also a candidate for Miss California, an illegal immigrant, and a Guatemalan of German descent. Since this does not impress Michael, she adds:

MISS FRESNO: Look, pendejo, I'm hiding a lot more than my legal status, OK?
MICHAEL: Like what?
MISS FRESNO: What I really am is a. . . a. . . well, let me show you. (*Starts unbuttoning her dress*)
MICHAEL: (*More intimidated by this*) Wait! Maybe I don't want to know! (11)

Michael is a border patrol officer whose wife has abandoned him. He was looking for what he described as "something grand, and magnificent, almost unreal in [his] life—even if it just happens in [his] head" (14). Then one night, while working at the border, he finds something unexpected. He explains:

> I saw it here: the two grooms dancing the "quebradita" to the beat of
> "The Wedding Samba". . . yes, it was a gay wedding—a Mexican—
> make that a Mexican-American gay wedding—female priest, multi-
> layered cake, no-host bar, practical gifts: toaster ovens and Mary Kay
> products. (3)

Since that night, this image haunts him. It becomes a motif
throughout the play. As the play moves forward, Michael moves further
and further away from the passive role that he had consciously taken, a
role that performed the identity that others had constructed for him.
During a conversation, he explained to Miss Fresno the role that he had
assumed:

> I say, if they see you as Miss Fresno, why disappoint them? If they
> see me as Michael, average, beer-guzzling guy with the remote in my
> hand, mortgage, kids, basketball hoop in the driveway, let them have
> him. (12)

As Butler points out, the performance of gender, and in this case of
identity in general, is not so much a choice but a mandatory act. She
argues that "acting out of line with heterosexual norms brings with it
ostracism, punishment, and violence" ("Imitation" 187). Michael, when
he chooses to be what others want him to be, is avoiding the social
punishment that deviance brings with it, in the same way that the
characters who represent immigrants try to avoid the punishment that
comes with the discovery of their illegal alien status.

Another comparison that can be established in the play is that of
the individual's sexual identification and his/her nationality. Serrat, the
Spanish teacher, questions the naturalization of nationality as a
permanent trait. He goes from being a Puerto Rican, or rather, a
Nuyorican, to being a Catalonian (which he makes sure to point out that
it is not the same as being a Spaniard), to being an illegal immigrant.
From our previous comparison, we can conclude that one's sexuality
(as in the case of one's nationality) does not need to be defined
permanently: it can flow, it can transform itself. Therefore, Serrat's
national identity can be seen as a premonition of Michael's sexual
identity, which also flows throughout the play from heterosexuality to
homosexuality to bisexuality.

Serrat needs to complement his pay check as a Spanish teacher for
assimilated Latinos at the City College. So he goes to the Immigration

Department to offer a course on "Self-Esteem for Immigrants." This course, he explains, will allow the deported immigrants to return to their respective countries with "the focus, the energy, and yes the self-esteem needed to make it in their own country" (7). Michael, who needs to improve his Spanish, and also because he is lonely and because he wants a promotion, enrolls in the classes for assimilated Latinos at the City College. That's where he meets Sedicio, a gay illegal alien who lives near Gay Center on Normal Street and who takes the class because he is attracted to Latinos who speak poor Spanish. Sedicio is attracted to Michael. Yet as an undocumented immigrant he is at odds with Michael's position as a border patrol officer. Nevertheless, he finds ways to negotiate with Michael. On one occasion, after telling Michael a joke, Sedicio explains to him:

> I'm actually a fiery advocate of immigrant rights myself but a joke is an attempt to find a comfortable middle ground with someone like you who represents the Enemy. (16)

This process repeats itself throughout the play. On another occasion, as Michael is telling him a story, Sedicio interrupts with his own input. Michael points out to him that this is *his* story and therefore that the only narrator here is *himself*. Yet Sedicio fights for a voice:

SEDICIO: This first person narrative can be very patriarchal and oppressive!
MICHAEL: What is that supposed to mean?
SEDICIO: Share your narrative, Michael. (19)

Michael is also forced to find a way to negotiate between his involvement with Sedicio and his position as a border patrol officer. He asks, "Would a man compromise all his values and duties for one moment of satisfaction?" (24), and then he quickly replies, "Oh, yeah!" (24). Yet later, it is this very point that creates a division between them. When Michael is assigned to deport Sedicio, he tells his boss that he is unable to deport him. Even more, he opens up to him and tells his boss, "I'M sleeping with him, Dean!" (58). Yet Dean sees this as just a passing phase in Michael's life. Michael, under all this pressure, is about to renounce to Sedicio's love, but once more, Sedicio is able to negotiate a solution with him. Michael decides to get back with his pregnant wife, Teresita. Yet he tells her about his relationship with Sedicio:

SEDICIO: What? She knows?
MICHAEL: It's as if she's known all along. Of course, now she's pregnant again, and that complicates things. . . The best I can do is . . . keep seeing you occasionally. Teresita understands. (70)

In the end, Michael and Sedicio find a space for themselves. It is a limited space representative of the compromises that they both have been able to make, and the compromises that neither of them has been able to make. Michael describes it: "I run into him occasionally—on weekends, when I drive into the city, he sees me, he spies on me all alone in a bar. I may flirt with a stranger, and I let him watch me do it. . . I don't have to say a word. That's how it is between us now" (71-72).

Throughout the process of their relationship, Michael and Sedicio challenge the stereotypical view of intimacy. Zavarzadeh argues that the perception of intimacy as a possibility for transparency and communion are ideological constructions aimed at hiding the opacity and lack of communication that separates all individuals. He points out that "private intimacy, which is postulated by dominant culture as the embodiment of similarity, transparency, closeness, and plenitude, is but an exemplary instance of difference, opacity, distance, scarcity, and gaps" (115-16); to him, "people in contemporary culture are not only incomprehensible to one another but also to themselves" (116). Due to the personal crisis that both Michael and Sedicio are experiencing, they are unable to buy into that idea of intimacy, nor to enter the space of the "intimate" without consciously analyzing their being there. Rather than buying into the illusion that they know and understand each other, that they have a permanent relationship, and that they are responsible for one another, throughout their time together each one of them is actively trying to understand himself. This is evident from the very beginning, when Michael states:

> I need to know what I feel and why I feel it, whether this is the right thing for me or not and you've practically volunteered, so you can't take it back. You flirted with me and now you're stuck. (21)

During their conversation at the coffee house, in the scene from *Divas* reproduced in this volume, Sedicio explains that his goal is to "marry a man by the time [he is] 25" (19). He is looking for romance and a meaningful relationship. Michael, on the other hand, wonders, "When do we cut to the chase and do what you gay men do?" (20) because he is hoping for a sexual encounter with Sedicio. There is even another position, that of Leonel, Sedicio's roommate, who, as Sedicio explains, chooses to be "unattached and promiscuous" (22). These different positions towards sexual relations in one way or another break with the patriarchal norm of monogamous, heterosexual, permanent relationships. Yet, Michael's and Sedicio's desires gradually evolve towards each other's original position. Therefore, as the play moves along, it is Michael who becomes more interested in meaningful relationships, while Sedicio wants to directly engage in sex. This is significant because it breaks with the idea that sexual desire is a permanent trait of the individual. In this sense, the characters in the play do not have to subscribe to any type of predetermined ideal of what a sexual encounter should be, and they are able to try different perspectives and to participate in different types of relationships.

Nevertheless, there is conflict among them. As Michael assumes his bisexuality, he is confronted by Sedicio, who clearly states: "I don't believe in bisexuals, I'm opposed to them" (37). Amanda Udis-Kessler analyzes the sources of both heterosexual and homosexual biphobia. She argues that for heterosexuals, the bisexual is just another version of the queer or the "homo" (243). Whereas for the gay and lesbian community, the bisexual represents a threat to everything that has been achieved throughout the long process of construction of that community. Udis-Kessler points out that

> when bisexuality equals constructionism, bisexuals become walking reminders of the potential crisis of meaning for lesbians and gay men, posing a threat to identity and community far greater than the one posed by heterosexuals. Lesbians and gay men have been able to define themselves as other than heterosexual; bisexuals challenge that definition regardless of our intention to do so. (245-46)

As we have already discussed above, the gay and lesbian identities have had to renew themselves and to find new ways to construct themselves in order to escape becoming a smaller version of the oppressive society that they were trying to escape in the first place. This has led to the emergence of 'open identities such as queer, which Alexander Doty defines as an interstitial space "related to any expression that can be marked as contra-, non-, or anti-straight" (xv). In that sense, queer identity becomes an option where bisexuals do not pose a threat to the gay and lesbian community. In the play, Sedicio eventually accepts Michael's bisexuality, and once more a comparison is established between Michael's bisexuality and his identity as a Chicano or a Mexican-American. As Sedicio points out that "the whole border is a joke anyway," (46) Michael replies:

MICHAEL: The border is still the law. You break it, you pay for it.
SEDICIO: It's more complex than that, you oughta know, you're bisexual.
MICHAEL: You don't need to call me that in public!
SEDICIO: You're a Chicano at least. Can you say that in public?
MICHAEL: Mexican-American. (46)

This is an interesting comparison, since the problematic reception of bisexuality both by the gay and the straight communities can be related to the situation of the Chicano/Mexican-American rejection by both the Anglo and the Mexican community. The space for the Chicano, just like the space for bisexuality, remains a threatening border for those who inhabit either side of it.

As part of his job as a border patrol officer, Michael is assigned to deport Silvano, a Salvadoran immigrant who has been infected with the AIDS virus. Silvano's character also breaks with stereotypes. Although undocumented, Silvano is not a member of the lower class, as the stereotypical idea of an illegal immigrant would have it. On the contrary, he comes from a family in a very good position within Salvadoran society and his economic situation is probably better than that of most of the other characters. Furthermore, Silvano does not adhere to the ethnic stereotypical identity of an illegal alien. Besides, his education level is higher than Michael's. In his dialogue with Michael, he points out that his situation is quite the opposite than what Michael expected:

SILVANO: It's not as if my family couldn't afford the price of a plane ticket. My father owns San Salvador!
MICHAEL: That's nice.
SILVANO: All of it!—Including the army, especially the army. When we want people to disappear, we make sure they do. Are you intimidated yet?

MICHAEL: I notice you're not packing.
SILVANO: I have everything I need back home! You thought I was just
  one of these Indian-looking peasants you're used to deporting,
  didn't? (53)

The treatment that undocumented immigrants receive from the
characters who are U.S. nationals leads me to one final comparison: just
as in the case of illegal aliens who are necessary for the maintenance of
the American economy, although they are never recognized for their
contributions to it, straight culture uses queers for economic benefit and
to produce pleasure, without ever recognizing the important role that
queerness really plays in popular and mass culture. In fact, Doty argues
that

> connotation has been the representational and interpretive closet of
> mass culture queerness for far too long . . . the concept of connotation
> allows straight culture to use queerness for pleasure and profit in
> mass culture without admitting to it. (xi-xii)

His proposal is to unmask this process of connotation that straight
culture uses to its advantage. Doty points out that "brought forward . . .
the queerness in and of mass culture might be used to challenge the
politics of denotation and connotation as it is traditionally deployed in
discussing texts and representation. In this way the closet of
connotation could be dismantled, rejected for the oppressive practice it
is" (xii). From the perspective of the comparison that we are
establishing, this can be seen as a possibility for the rejection of the
oppressive marginalization of immigrants in the United States while the
mainstream (U.S. citizen) culture profits from their work.

As a final word, *Divas* takes advantage of stereotypes and their
value as negotiating tools within a specific cultural and temporal space.
Through the use of these stereotypes and the continuous parallelism
between the various spaces of difference, it enables us the spectators to
critically read and to question the validity of cohesive and rigid identities which attempt to describe both the individual and the community.
Finally, it opens up new possibilities for the emergence of a dislocated
consciousness in its characters and for the construction of a hybrid
identity where difference—in its varied forms and combinations—can
coexist.

Incorporated Identities
The Subversion of Stigma
in the Performance Art of Luis Alfaro

Antonio Prieto

For the past decade or so, performance art has become a favorite vehicle used by subaltern artists for the articulation of their sociopolitical issues.[1] Due to its interdisciplinary approach and to its stress on the artist's body and personal history, performance art has usually been regarded as an elitist and narcissistic medium. However, both Latin American and U.S. Latino artists have found in its conceptual language a means of readdressing political issues, and the way these affect the lives and bodies of oppressed people.

The subaltern performance artist usually stages a personal experience, showing how it is linked to a collective plight, in a move derived from the feminist "the personal is political" argument. Thus, Cuban-American Coco Fusco presents a scene of sexual exploitation, or Chicano Luis Alfaro a scene of stigmatization, as personal dramas which, because of their collective resonance, have strong political implications.

In this paper I address Alfaro's work, focusing on the way this exceptional artist, educator, and social worker uses performance to resignify the social and bodily markers of stigma. My argument is that Alfaro transforms stigmatized signs into signs of resistance and affirmation by means of displaying a performative identity. By performative identity, I mean a relational, negotiated, self-reflexive, and processual identity, taking the cue from Judith Butler's understanding of this issue. In Alfaro's case, as a gay Chicano he finds himself in the complex position of negotiating both a sexual and an ethnic identity, as well as the communities that ascribe to them. In his work, he examines the problems that arise from navigating these communities while trying to create strategic allegiances among them. In doing this, I find that Alfaro posits himself between the essentialist and constructivist approaches to identity, in that he celebrates difference while advocating a critical self-examination of how identities are performed.[2] I'll refer to Alfaro's performance *El juego de la jotería* (The Game of Queerness), that he presented both in Los Angeles and Mexico City as part of the binational project "Danger Zone/Terreno Peligroso," in February 1995.[3] This example gives us the opportunity to examine the way his work is recontextualized across the Mexico/United State border, and the audience responses thereto.

But first, a word about Chicano art. The crucial role that visual arts and theater played within the Chicano movement is well known. They proved essential in the job of displaying and imagining the emergent community. In cases such as that of El Teatro Campesino, theater was initially used as a vehicle for denouncing the agro-industry's exploitation of the farmworkers, as well as parodying the oppressor. Within the Chicano community, both the visual and the narrative arts were seen as means of consolidating a coherent, stable and strong community. This was done by creating a clear dichotomy of us-oppressed/them-oppressors, and, as Bruce-Novoa maintains (*Chicano Poetry* 7-9), responding to the perceived chaos of gringo society with the imagined order of the Chicano world (within the space created in literature). This is why during the late 1960s and early 1970s stress was put on the display of positive images that would resist the negative stereotypes in mass media, text books, and publicity. The downside of this move was the creation of allegedly positive stereotypes that grossly simplified the community's complex social component. Men were macho heroes, women their faithful, enchilada-baking sidekicks, and gays simply did not exist. Apparently, the Mexican patriarchal "family values" structure was seen as a desirable element for the Chicanos in their striving to differentiate themselves from the dominant society. This, of course, spelled trouble for overtly queer literature such as that of John Rechy, whose groundbreaking 1963 novel *City of Night* was a best seller among the beatniks, but ignored by the Mexican Americans.

Attitudes began to change, fortunately, towards the early 1980s. The Chicano Movement's initial thrust had been lost due to internal ideological disagreements, and women activists and artists began aggressively to assert their presence. The new critical climate, made possible by the emergence of a new generation of University-educated, middle-class Chicanas/os, was open to internal difference, as well as to seeking allegiance with other oppressed communities. Artists began to work differently, not anymore as collectives that sought to impose political dogma, but as individuals who explore their identities and experiment with avant-garde forms such as conceptual and performance art. The earliest example of this move was the group ASCO, founded by Harry Gamboa Jr., Gronk, Patssi Valdez, and Willie Herrón in 1971. The group, based in Los Angeles, provoked internal debates within the Chicano art world because of its aggressive use of avant-garde styles. ASCO is credited with the first Chicano performance pieces, the "Walking Murals" that playfully juxtaposed Chicano and Anglo popular symbols such as the Virgin of Guadalupe and the Christmas tree.

Towards the late 1980s, performance art was taken up by several other artists who appreciated its transgressive potential as well as its focus on autobiography and the politicized body. In her essay on contemporary Chicana/o art, María Teresa Marrero observes that perhaps the most creative and politicized work is today done in the field of performance art, since it is an art "interested in deconstructing its own community's as well as the Other's stereotypical images of the Chicano/Latino, rather than creating images that are palatable to a mainstream paying audience." (147) The deconstructive drive of these new artists, however, is often met with skepticism or outright scorn because it apparently contradicts the essentialist identity discourses that are still dear to grassroots activism. A problem seems to be that *deconstruction* is confused with *destruction*. As we shall see, artists like Alfaro are highly critical of exclusionist identity discourses, but he still sees the affirmation of multiple, border-crossing identities as important for the community.

The title of Alfaro's performance, *El juego de la jotería*, refers to a popular Mexican game, a kind of lottery (*lotería*) where cards with symbolic images (the mermaid, the grim reaper, better known as *la muerte*, the cactus) are shown and the players must find the matching image on their boards, until one is filled and that player wins. When he evokes the game, Alfaro implies that queerness is a performative play of stereotypes, that is, of visual signifiers that are susceptible to stigmatization. However, within the frame of a performative game, these stereotypes can be resignified as markers of an affirmative identity.

In his UCLA presentation, Alfaro performed before a multiethnic
audience of mostly students. He began talking while seated among the
audience, dressed like anybody else, and he then moved towards the
stage, where he disrobed to reveal a feminine nightgown made of
elegant black silk. This coming *out of* and *to* the audience starts with
his gender identity, and proceeds with his ethnic identity, as he begins
to incorporate Spanish words into his mostly English-spoken text. As
Alfaro told me in an interview, his coming out of the audience has two
objectives:

> En mis *performances*, siempre empiezo saliendo del público. Lo hago
> por dos razones, uno, es una cosa técnica, yo no sé cómo se siente el
> público, tal vez están de mal humor y no quieren reir, *so* todo el
> tiempo estoy muy conciente de dónde vengo. Pero también lo que
> estoy tratando de decir, cuando hago eso, es que yo también vengo de
> ese grupo, y entonces eso cambia la posición de cómo te ven, porque
> entonces lo que estás diciendo es *is this real time, or is this fake time?*
> Hago la pregunta, sin palabras, ¿me estás tratando como algo real, o
> me estás tratando como un actor? Yo estoy cortando esa percepción
> de cómo te ven.[4] (Personal interview in Alfaro's office at the Mark
> Taper Forum, LA, February 24, 1997)

Alfaro thus questions the given conventions of audience viewing, the
idea that the performance is a representation of fiction and not of a real
person's issues, and a person who could be anybody in the audience.

His United States presentation relied primarily on the spoken word,
with a minimum of props and a few actions such as roller skating. The
text was full of cultural references easily identifiable by his young
audience, who responded with hearty laughs and applause. In Mexico
City, his performance was staged inside the main chapel of the former
convent of Sta. Teresa la Antigua, a colonial building that today houses
the Centro de Arte Alternativo Ex-Teresa, a government funded
facility. The former chapel, roofed with a high dome and still decorated
with religious murals, lent a religious atmosphere to the presentation.
Alfaro adapted his performance for the Mexican audience so that it had
more visual elements than text. In other cases, he attempted to involve
the audience by making some variations in the actions. For example, in
UCLA the skating action was limited to the stage, while in Ex-Teresa
he skated around the audience, speeding dangerously close to the lamps
and chairs. The image of a large, hairy man dressed in a nightgown,

rollerblades, and helmet was simultaneously funny and grotesque. Alfaro fell rather noisily several times, which at first made people laugh, but later made us wonder if he was really getting hurt. Throughout the skating, he seemed to be in a frantic argument with his father. Each time he cried "papá," he slipped and fell. The action adopted a pathos upon its depiction of what could be a commentary on father-son incommunication, or on physical self-abuse.

There are other moments in which Alfaro touches upon the double colonization—both physical and sociopolitical—that gay Chicanos are subjected to. In the Mexican version, slides were projected on the wall of pictures of his naked torso painted with the phrase "Yo soy gay" ("I'm gay"). One image showed his back painted with the words "Queer/Joto"; the diagonal line that separated the two words suggested the border that separates and unites two cultural ways of being gay. This is important since, as Chicano critic Tomás Almaguer maintains, homosexuality is lived differently in Mexico and the United States, and Chicanos must negotiate these sometimes conflicting worldviews. The fact that the words were painted on Afaro's back indicates that someone else wrote them as colonizing stigmas.

Stigma management is a basic theme of *El juego de la jotería*, and for that reason I now turn to Erving Goffman for some leads on how to approach this practice. According to Goffman, stigmas were originally cuts or burns made on the skin of criminals in ancient Greece in order to advertise their moral and legal status. Today, stigma is related to a complex interplay of ethnic, sexual, class, religious, and physical attributes. Visual markers are still heavily relied upon to classify the subject, whose identity—it is commonly believed—can be read on the body. When the marks of identity are not easily read (as with a light-skinned Chicano like Alfaro), Goffman says that the subject must manage the information that s/he gives on her/his identity in order to avoid discrimination. The subject might decide to "pass" as a "normal" person (which in some parts of the United States means as a WASP), or take the radically opposite direction: bring forth the stigmatized attributes as proud markers of a politicized alterity. This is the road Alfaro chooses in his performance, where markers of abjection are resignified as markers of defiance and pride.[5] Not an isolated, narcissistic pride, as we shall see, but an affirmative and relational one.

All attempts to transform a stigma into a vehicle of resistance are, however, subject to risks. A basic problem is that we all move in the context of a dominant society that has already established a language that places subaltern people at a disadvantage. Within this system, both the stigmatized (abject) and "normal" subjects share basically the same notions of what an identity is. And since the idea of identity has been shaped by the dominant society, then subaltern people are forced to demand acceptance and equal treatment. This process leaves the dominant systems of classification intact, and the "normal"/"deviant" binary firmly secured.

The deconstructive drive of recent performance art attempts to expose the arbitrariness of this binary construct, while at the same time seizing dominant language codes and using them for other ends. The project is thus simultaneously critical and creative, and can be traced to the writings of Cuban critic Roberto Fernández Retamar, whose 1974 essay *Calibán* takes the "savage" character of Shakespeare's *The Tempest* as a symbol of Latin American subversive appropriation of European language and culture.

In Alfaro's *juego*, identity is put forth as both metaphorically and metonymically associated with the stigma. Metaphorically, because a silk night gown worn by a man may suggest an alternative sexuality. Metonymically, because the words "queer/joto" written directly on the artist's skin make his body a parchment on which his identity may be read. Thus, stigma becomes a vehicle for both performing and *incorporating* a person's many identities.

Alfaro parodies the visual markers of gender identity by establishing a move from "normality" to "abnormality." In terms of Bakhtin, this transgression is done by moving from the "classic body" to the "grotesque body." According to Bakhtin, the classic body is a construct of Western behavior codes, usually asexual, odorless, and devoid of orifices. On the other hand, the grotesque body shamelessly displays its bodily functions, thus offering a "a particular conception of the body and its limits" (63). In Alfaro's performance, the progressive display of the grotesque helps to question the arbitrariness of dress codes (as does that of all drag queens). The black nightgown only accentuates his obesity and his body hair, aggressively subverting contemporary beauty standards. Throughout the performance, Alfaro engages in actions that accentuate the grotesque body and its social implications.

For example, there's a moment when he opens a small travel bag from which he produces industrial junk food of the Twinky Wonder sort. He literally stuffs his face with the cakes, as we hear his prerecorded voice telling the story of how his parents arrived in the

United States from Mexico with no money. He narrates the initial poverty they faced, and the consumerism that they soon fell prey to. Consumerism was a suffocating force, and Alfaro's mother underwent pressure from his father to slim down and conform to American standards of beauty. Her body, she was informed, was "too Mexican." Alfaro's action stresses the simultaneously tragic and absurd situation by depicting pathetic eating disorders. More importantly, he denounces the colonization of the body by means of the digestive systems and dominant beauty regimes. The compulsive eating at first appears as masochistic self-abuse, but can also be read as a desperate rebellion against colonizing aesthetic codes. In an interview, Alfaro explained the concerns that underlie this part of his performance:

> . . .si estoy tratando de cambiar algo, es cómo nos vemos. Para mí, eso se manifiesta en el cuerpo, qué pasa con este cuerpo gordito. Hablo del sida, de cómo cambia el cuerpo, de cómo se mueren mis amigos. Cuando me estoy comiendo los *Twinkies*, estoy comiendo "cultura", me estoy ahogando en la cultura, pero la cultura es algo tan dulce ¿que no?[6]

In the same vein as his colleague, Chicana performance artist Nao Bustamante, Alfaro is concerned with the obsession that U.S. society puts on physical appearance, an obsession that translates into the erasure of millions. Alfaro links this concern with his family's history, with their willing submission to the colonization of their bodies, and how those bodies carry the memory of a culture. In the story, the memory of a Mexican body is what his father wants to get rid of, subjecting his wife to a psychological pressure that nearly drove her to suicide:

> Mi papá veía a mi mamá como veía a México, algo muy romántico, algo de otro tiempo pasado. Vienen a los Estados Unidos, y él quiere que se vea más delgada, como son las mujeres americanas. Él lo hacía porque quería ser americano, olvidarse de México. Cuando se oye esa historia, estoy comiendo los pastelitos, y la pregunta es: ¿qué es lo perfecto? ¿qué pasa con ese cuerpo que no es el cuerpo *gay*? Porque si ves todos los *magazines* me dicen que este cuerpo mío no es *gay*, porque no es sexual. Entonces, ¿gente con este cuerpo no pueden ser *hot*? Gente con este cuerpo, ¿dónde caen en la comunidad? Si tú no tienes un cuerpo perfecto en una comunidad obsesionada con *beauty*

and youth, ¿qué pasa? [. . .] Yo quiero que el público que ve ese ritual
(el *performance*) se pregunte esas cosas.[7]

The patriarchal social pressure that his mother suffered in order to
conform to an ideal standard of beauty is likewise suffered by Alfaro.
His performance exposes the way people are forced to focus their self-
esteem and identity on an epidermic level in order to conform to the
fascist desire for all to be the same. Not equal, but the same—a
sameness that is deceiving, because it doesn't contemplate sociopolitical equality, while it shows disdain for signs of difference. And
difference is feared because it potentially leads to dissidence. Alfaro's
strategy is to get his audience's complicity by having them identify
with the anecdotes and personal stories he tells, narratives that manage
to chronicle ethnic and sexual difference while establishing human
bonds.

At one point in his UCLA presentation, Alfaro narrates the
relationship with his *abuelita* (grandmother). He tells of how he hated
her when he was a kid, of how he was disgusted when she sucked the
blood out of his wounded finger. Years later, he tells of how he again
cut his finger. This time, he was with his gay workmates, and of course
no one offered to perform his abuelita's house remedy. Fear of AIDS
may have played a part in their unwillingness to help. He then had to
suck out his own blood, remembering his grandmother, a memory that
makes him say:

> *I wish for an abuelita in this time of plague;*
> *I wish for an abuelita in this time of loss;*
> *I wish for an abuelita in this time of sorrow;*
> *I wish for an abuelita in this time of death;*
> *I wish for an abuelita in this time of mourning,*
> *I wish for an abuelita in this time,*
> *I wish, I wish,*
> *I, I, Ay, Ay. . ..*

In that last line, the personal pronoun is transformed into a very
Mexican lament, linking his memory and identity with his pain. It is
pain because of the loss of family, of caring. Pain because in times of
plague people are so unwilling to help. Alfaro seems to ask: in these
times of death and mourning, when one most needs trust and love,
where may these be found?

While his performance is full of humor, Alfaro pauses to implicitly ask these questions, and the beauty of his art is his suggestion that the answer lies in compassionate and brave community work. Indeed, he advocates a community that bridges ethnic and gender, differences in order to tackle very urgent issues.

The Mexican presentation of *El juego de la jotería* closes with a semi-ritualistic action that manages to involve the audience and create a fleeting sense of community. Alfaro walks around a circle of votive candles carrying a basket out of which he draws small pebbles that he holds up high while mentioning the name of a person, and than places the pebble next to a candle. After a while, he stops calling the names, but repeats the action. Spontaneously, random audience members called other names, and the act became a collective homage to the dead. We shared the certainty of living under the same crisis, and some may have reflected on the urgency to, so to speak, act up.

In order to create a space for identification, Alfaro evokes his personal recollections, thus coaxing the audience's memory of similar stories. In this sense, he deploys autobiography as an "ideology of the self" (Ramón Saldívar's term) that explores the links between the personal and the political. Saldívar maintains that Chicano narrative aims to *denaturalize* the official canon, that is, to expose the arbitrariness of discriminatory and oppressive practices that have been incorporated into the daily *habitus*, and thus pose as natural and necessary. According to Saldívar, Chicano autobiography reveals the "heterogeneous systems that resist the formation of a unitary base of truth," by dealing with issues of language, identity, and the laws that govern behavior (13). He further argues that the genre achieves this by presenting a "decentered" subject, one that negotiates bicultural and bilingual universes. We could thus say that Alfaro makes use of the strategies of Chicano autobiography, projecting his personal memory into the public sphere by means of his body-in-performance. This way, his body is the vehicle of a politicized memory.

In her discussion on the use of the body in militant art, Janet Wolff maintains that, while it can be a site of oppressive colonization, the body can also be a site of political intervention (122). In his work, Alfaro performs the double act of presenting his body as the subject of a discourse, and the oral narrative as susceptible of "incorporation." He likewise confronts the surveillance regime by denouncing the violence of stigmatization. In Wolff's terms, he articulates "politics as a gaze," that is, he displays his body as an object of scrutiny that nevertheless returns the gaze to claim agency. The agency he exerts stems from his reappropriation of a memory that is both personal and collective, and thus concerns us all. Towards the end of his UCLA presentation, Alfaro challenges his audience to become involved, when he directly asks "Are you friend or foe? We can accept no half enchiladas here!" And, according to him, the "whole enchilada" must include the issues of race, gender and class.

By the end of *El juego de la jotería*, Alfaro has transformed the stigmas value from a moral blemish into a vehicle for incorporating militant identities. I say militant because they question the dominant regime of classification and behavior. Indeed, to perform a Chicano gay identity is to engage in political action. But his performance is also about faith and compassion, and in this sense his management of stigma may recall the way Christian tradition sees those marks. Saint Francis of Assisi believed that the stigmata that appeared in the palms of his hand and feet signaled a spiritual merge with Christ. Alfaro's stigmas may likewise signal a merge, not necessarily with the divine, but with other humans that share the same struggles. Stigmas began as marks for the identification of criminals or diseased people. Through the ritual of Alfaro's performance, stigma is transformed into a badge of pride, and also a way for the body to incorporate a politicized identity.

NOTES

1. This is a reworked English version of my essay *Identidades incórporadas: el manejo del estigma en el performance art de Luis Alfaro*, which appeared in *Chasqui; revista de literatura latinoamericana* 26.2 (noviembre 1997): 72-83.

2. For a debate on the intersection of gay and ethnic identity politics, see Steven Epstein's illuminating essay "Gay Politics and Ethnic Identity: The Limits of Social Constructionism."

3. "Terreno Peligroso/Danger Zone" brought together five Mexican performance artists (Felipe Ehrenberg, César Martínez, Elvira Santamaría, Eugenia Vargas, and Lorena Wolffer) and five U.S. Latino performance artists (Guillermo Gómez-Peña, Elia Arce, Nao Bustamante, Luis Alfaro and Rubén Martínez). They performed two weeks in Los Angeles and two weeks in Mexico City.

4. In my performances, I always start coming out of the audience: I do this for two reasons: one, I don't know how the audience feels, maybe they are in a bad mood and don't want to laugh, so I'm always very sensitive to their

mood, to who I'm addressing. But also, what I'm trying to do with this is to say that I belong to this group, and that changes the way you are seen, because then what you're telling them is "is this real time, or is this fake time?" I implicitly ask: "are you treating me as something real, or as an actor?" I undercut that perception of how I'm seen.

5. In this vein, Butler has argued that "The public assertion of 'queerness' enacts performativity as citationality for the purposes of resignifying the abjection of homosexuality into defiance and legitimacy" (*Bodies That Matter* 21).

6. If I'm trying to change something, it's the way we look at ourselves. For me, that is revealed in the body, in the question of what happens to this fat body. I'm talking about AIDS, about how it changes the body, about how my friends die. When I'm eating the "Twinkies," I'm eating culture, I'm drowning in culture. But culture is so sweet, isn't it?

7. My father saw my mother as he saw Mexico, as a very romantic thing from the past. When they come to the U.S., he wants her to look thinner, like American women. He did that because he wanted to be American, to forget Mexico. When you hear this story (during the performance), I'm eating the little cakes, and the question is: what is perfect? What happens with this body that is not the "gay body"? Because if you notice, all the magazines say this body of mine is not gay, because it's not sexual. Then, people with this body cannot be hot? Where do people with this body fit in the community? If you don't have a perfect body in a community obsessed with beauty and youth, what happens? [. . .] I want people who see this ritual to ask themselves these questions.

The Poet as the Other

Francisco X. Alarcón

What would we call that moment in life in which the precarious nature of our existence without warning is exposed and suddenly everything we accept, believe, take for granted, seems to succumb to the unrelenting questioning of our mind? For some, these are symptoms of what is known as mid-life crisis. For me, these are just some of the very conditions in which poetry frequently comes to me. As a Chicano poet who also celebrates being gay, I have come to realize that I write *desde afuera del margen mismo de la sociedad* (from the outside of even the margin of society), and that for some, even my own *gente*, I represent the ultimate Other.

For me poetry is a necessity. Since I cannot separate poetry from life, I find poetry everywhere, or better, poetry comes to me unexpectedly, without much warning. Experience has taught me to respect these rare and mysterious poetic moments. Poetry comes quietly, unnoticed, freely, as morning dew, but also, at times, bursting in a fit of passion, hot-headed, ripping, fierce, as a thunderous storm. Yes, poetry is generous, whimsical, demanding, jealous, full of tenderness but also fury, just like any lover.

The feminist movement taught me that the personal is political, that even the most intimate experience—as that epiphany commonly dismissed as an orgasm—has social and political implications. This seems an easy proposition to accept and follow, but it takes more than courage to speak up the unspeakable, to say what has remained unsaid for so long. This lesson in courage and guts, in defiance and spirit, I learned from such a group of very strong women, most of them, Chicana lesbians like Gloria Anzaldúa, Cherríe Moraga, Carla Trujillo, Esther Hernández, among others.

Living in the Mission District in San Francisco, I came to know, appreciate, and learn from the poets from Central America committed to the struggle of liberation; they showed me the subversive possibility of bringing together poetics and politics, and that writing poetry could be indeed a dangerous undertaking that often led its practitioners to persecution, imprisonment, exile, disappearance, or death.

Since then, I personally have engaged in a process that sees poetry as an extension of life. We live in such critical times. Everyday we are witnesses to the annihilation everywhere of ancient and communal ways of life. Even our once strong oral tradition is being assaulted from many fronts and is now at stake. What is the role of the poet in front of these predicaments? Would the poet against all odds resolve to accept the role and duty of being a voice of the voiceless, of becoming the pestering conscience challenging the status quo, of keeping alive the collective memory of a group?

Sometimes I experience poetry as an unsolicited burden and feel I am condemned to be a poet with poetry as life-long sentence without the possibility of parole. How can we break the politics/poetics of exclusion and silence that have prevented the poetic expression of people like me? How can we empower others if we do not first empower ourselves? We have to empower ourselves by bringing together what has been disjointed, by recognizing ourselves in others, by accepting and celebrating who we are.

Being a Chicano gay poet who has crossed several social, cultural, linguistic, and sexual barriers, borders, and taboos, I have experienced a life full of contradictions and differences in that virtual space Gloria Anzaldúa calls the "Borderlands/La Frontera." I was born in Los Angeles, but my working-class family moved to Guadalajara when I was five years old, so I was raised in Mexico. We were really picked on by the other Mexican kids in our *barrio* for speaking *Pocho* Spanish. So, I got it both ways.

There is no moment in which I was struck by a special light that finally made sense out of my life. Since early age, I somehow suspected that I was somehow *different* from my four other brothers. Quoting again from Gloria Anzaldúa's text, I would reiterate: "If you are Mexican, you are born old." I knew I was *different*. I had some intuitions about the personal and social consequences of this fact. Acting on this *difference* essentially meant transgression.

There is a bitter sweet irony in that my "coming out" process as a gay Chicano, as a *joto*, did not take place in San Francisco, the gay

Mecca, where I had lived for many years in the late 1970s, but took place in the early 1980s in Mexico City where I had gone to spend a year as a Fulbright scholar to do research for my dissertation at Stanford University. A great Mexican poet became my true mentor in matters of poetry and sex: Elías Nandino. When he died on October 2, 1993, it was widely known that at 93 years old he was considered one of the youngest poets of Mexico. Elías Nandino was a great role model of a person who was openly gay and had a successful career both as a doctor and a poet/writer. We became more than friends, we became soulmates.

In 1983 Elías Nandino was given the highest literary prize in Mexico for a collection of homoerotic poetry, *Erotismo al rojo blanco/ Eroticism at a Burning White*. I remembered that I went with him to the National Palace in Mexico City where President López Portillo gave him a proclamation. Elías then went on to read from his collection of homoerotic poems. While this was going on, I just could not imagine an American president ever giving the highest literary honor to an openly gay poet in a public ceremony at the White House in Washington. This is one of Elías's poems:[1]

De veras

Abre la boca, dame la lengua,
adáptame tus labios
y yo te doy la mía. . .
Ahora olvidemos el cuerpo,
apaguemos los ojos
y vamos permitiendo
que ellas gocen a solas
sus revolcamientos
cambiando salivas.
Que punta con punta
cohabiten
como dos moluscos
en lucha agresiva,
hasta que se cansen,
hasta que se rindan,
hasta que se safen
y babeando regresen
a sus propias guaridas.

—Es que hay veces que valen
mucho más
que un coito completo;
porque son tan carnales,
de veras,
que nos dejan las bocas
con dolor de caderas.
Elías Nandino,
    Erotismo al rojo vivo (1983)

Truly

Open your mouth,
give me your tongue
fit your lips on mine,
I give you my tongue. . .
Now let's forget our bodies,
let's extinguish our eyes
and allow our tongues
alone to enjoy
their rollings,
exchanging saliva.
Let them make love
tip to tip
like two mollusks
in a life and death struggle,
until they tire,
until they surrender,
until they let go,
and slobbering, return
to their own dens.
—You see, there are kisses
that are worth much more
than an actual fuck
because they are so carnal
they truly
leave our mouths
aching like hips
(translated by Francisco X. Alarcón)

I want to bring up the question of why until very recently there was an almost complete lack of verbal articulation of the Chicano/Latino gay male experience when at the same time there has been a prolific booming of the verbal, critical, and literary articulation of the Chicana/Latina lesbian experience. I don't have any definite answer to this question. Without doubt this phenomenon is affected by the fact that Chicana lesbians and lesbians of color have found a resounding echo and solidarity in the Lesbian and Women of Color communities in particular and in the feminist movement over all. On the other hand, there is no comparable men of color consciousness or movement at this moment. Solidarity among men of color across ethnic boundaries or between White middle-class gay men and gay men of color is still not very common. Sexual and ethnic apartheid somehow still seems to rule supreme among males in this country.

I see my poetry both as a celebration of life and as a challenge to silence and death. The poems included here come from an unpublished manuscript I have titled *Canto hondo/Deep Song* that invokes the spirit of the *Poema del cante jondo/Poem of Deep Song* by Federico García Lorca, the great Spanish poet who wrote about the woeful fate and oppressive experience of the gypsies in southern Spain. Since the end of the Cold War, and with the disappearance of the Communist threat, I have come to realize that like the gypsies Chicanos, undocumented workers, and Latino immigrants seem to increasingly be given the role of society's scapegoats, the easy targets, the unwelcome outsiders, the internal enemies. Of course, AIDS has only made this process of singling out even more distressing to Chicano/Latino gay males. This is the life and death context of *Canto hondo/Deep Song* which is a collection comprising close to a hundred poems divided into four poetic sections: "Nuevo credo/New Creed," "Dialécica del amor/Dialectics of Love," "Para nosotros/For Us," and "Canto hondo/Deep Song."

NOTES

1. Alarcón publishes all of his poetry in bilingual versions. It is for this reason that translations are included in the main body of the text rather than, as in the case of other literary works cited in this volume, in the footnotes.

POETRY BY FRANCISCO X. ALARCÓN

From *Canto Hondo / Deep Song*
I. Nuevo credo / New Creed

Ecce Homo	**Ecce Homo**
enterrado	deep within
llevo	I carry
mi dolor	this grief
enterrado	of mine
como	like
espina	a thorn
me punza	it pierces
por dentro	me inside
si me río	if I laugh
mucho	too much
comienzo	I begin
a sangrar	to bleed

Sobreviviente	**Survivor**
he perdido	I've lost
todo menos	everything
la esperanza	but hope

Encuentro	**Encounter**
sin decir	without
nada	saying a word
nos decimos	we can say
tanto	so much
los golpes	the bruises
por dentro	no one sees
las noches	the endless
sin fin	nights
aunque	even apart
separados	we're already
ya estamos	embracing
abrazados	each other
somos	we are
espejo	mirror
memoria	memory
umbral	threshold
extraños	familiar
conocidos	strangers
que lo saben	who know all
todo a la vez	at once

Nuevo credo	**New Creed**
no	I don't
creo	believe
siento	I feel
toco	touch
lloro	cry
sangro	bleed
estoy	I am
vivo	alive

Nos/otros	**Us/Others**
al fin	at last
nos hemos	we shall
de hallar	find us
en otros	in others

Lengua de fuego	**Tongue of Fire**
muy	deep
adentro	inside
esta llama	this burning
viva	light
llamada	named
deseo	desire

II. Dialéctica del amor / Dialectics of Love

Dialéctica del amor	**Dialectics of Love**
para el mundo	to the world
no somos nada	we are nothing
pero aquí juntos	but here together
tú y yo	you and I
somos el mundo	are the world

Contigo	**With You**
no tengo	I don't have
casa	a house
tengo hogar	I have a home

Manejando a casa	**Driving Home**
comienzo	I'm starting
a pasarme	to run
semáforos	red lights

Noches frías	Cold Nights
sonríes	you smile
sonrío:	I smile—
innecesaria	no need
la calefacción	for a heater

Caliente	Horny
comienzas	you start
a apuntar	pointing
al cielo	to the sky

Mordiéndome	Biting
las orejas	my ears
me susurras:	you whisper:
"cálmala	*"take it easy*
tonto"	*you fool"*

Cigarros	Cigarettes
ardemos	we burn
cada uno	in each
en la boca	other's
del otro	mouth

Clímax	Climax
de pronto	suddenly
en la punta	on the tip
de la lengua	of our tongue
¡una galaxia!	a galaxy!

Talento natural	**Natural Talent**
"no soy	*"I'm not*
poeta"	*a poet"*
me cuentas	you tell me
después	after
de un gran	a great
poema vergón	fucking poem

Conocimiento común	**Common Knowledge**
yo sé	I know
tú sabes	you know
todos	everybody
saben	knows
y aún así	and yet
nadie	nobody
parece	seems
saber	to know

III. Para nosotros / For Us

Para nosotros	**For Us**
no hay	there are
palabras	no words
por eso	that's why
al encontrarnos	sometimes
a veces	when we meet
se nos hace	a knot
nudo	ties up
la garganta	our throat

Proscriptos	Outcasts
qué decir	what to say
ante	about
el silencio	silence
las páginas	the pages
que se quedan	left
sin escribir	unwritten
los libros	the books
en donde	in which
todavía	we are yet
ni somos	to be
ni estamos	appear
ni existimos	or exist
esta vida	this life
condenada	condemned
al olvido	to oblivion
aquí	here
nadie supo	nobody knew
sabrá	will know
del mar	of the sea
que llevamos	we carry
adentro	within us
del fuego	of the fire
que encendemos	we ignite
con el cuerpo	with our bodies
aquí seguimos:	here we remain—
proscriptos	outcasts
por vida	for life

Blues del SIDA	**AIDS Blues**
casi todos	almost all
nuestros amigos	our friends
de San Francisco	in San Francisco
ya se han ido	nowdays are gone
no más postales	no more cards
no más llamadas	no more calls
no más lágrimas	no more tears
no más risas	no more laughs
silencio y neblina	silence and fog
ahora oscurecen	now darken
nuestro antes asoleado	our once sunny
Distrito de la Misión	Mission District
dondequiera	everywhere
que ahora vamos	we now go
somos sólo un par	we're just a pair
de extraños	of strangers

Pro vida	**For Life**
dejas	you stop
de asistir	attending
a funerales	funerals
te rehúsas	you refuse
aceptar	to accept
la muerte	death
te pones	you start
a prender	lighting
veladoras	candles
para así	in order to
iluminar	illuminate
las vidas	the lives
de amigos	of friends
fallecidos	gone in
en plena flor	their prime

IV. Canto hondo / Deep Song

Grito	**Scream**
¡ay!	*ay!*
en	around
la esquina	the corner
lo mataron	they killed him
¡ay!	*ay!*
por	on
la espalda	his back
lo balearon	they shot him
¡ay!	*ay!*
gritan	the streets
las calles	of the *barrio*
del barrio	scream
¡ay!	*ay!*
¡qué roja	how red
la sangre	the blood
a los 16 años!	of a 16-year old!

Canto hondo
después que se aprobó la Propuesta 187 en California (1994)

¿por qué	¿qué papeles	puedes
me escupes	tiene	negarme
la cara?	el sol?	la escuela
¿qué mal	¿qué ley	echarme
te puedo	viola	la culpa
hacer yo	la noche?	de todo
por tener	¿qué crimen	construir
morena	cometen	otro muro
el alma?	los sueños?	de Berlín

¿por qué
me cierras
la puerta

¿qué ganas
con robarme
la calma?

pero
nunca
podrás

después
que pongo
la mesa

¿acaso
te alegra
mi dolor?

nunca
apagar
el fuego

y doblo
las últimas
sábanas?

¿te hace
más rico
mi pobreza?

la sed
la lucha
en mi corazón

Deep Song
after the passage of Proposition 187 in California (1994)

why do
you spit
on my face?

does the Sun
need
an I.D.?

you can
deny me
an education

what harm
can I ever
do to you

does the night
break
any laws?

blame
me for
everything

by having
a brown
soul?

have dreams
become
a crime?

build
another Berlin
wall

how come
you throw
me out

why do you
then steal
my calm?

but you
will never
ever

after
I've served
you dinner

does my grief
give you
joy?

be able
to extinguish
the fire

and folded
your last
white sheets?

does my poverty
make you
richer?

the thirst
the struggle
in my heart

Como puntita de pasto

mi color	ni trocaré
mi lengua	montañas por
mi tonal	sendero cruel
no me	para
los pueden	conseguir
quitar	mi corazón
rehúso	listos
renegar de	deben
mis antepasados	venir
beber	a sacarlo
de la copa	rajándome
pozoñosa	el pecho
no tomaré	a su paso
—repito—	como puntita
no tomaré	de pasto
el tren	me paro
rumbo	apuntando
a Auschwitz	a las estrellas

As a Blade of Grass

my color	leave
my tongue	the mountains
my soul	for a Trail of Tears
cannot	in order
be stripped	to get to
from me	my heart
I refuse	ready
to renounce	they must
my ancestors	come

to drink   to rip it
from the cup   right out
of poison   of my chest

I will not   on their path
—I repeat—   as a blade
I will not   of grass

take   I stand
the next train   pointing
to Auschwitz   to the stars

The Poetry of Francisco X. Alarcón
The Queer Project of Poetry
David William Foster

> *un beso*
> *is not just*
> *a kiss*
> *un beso is*
> *more dangerous*
> *sometimes*
> *even fatal*
>
> —Alarcón, *Body in Flames. Cuerpo en llamas* 49

> *we must chart the new coordinates of living*
> —Herrera, introduction to Alarcón, *No Golden Gate* v

Francisco X. Alarcón is a third-generation Chicano born in Wilmington, California in 1954. He went to school in California and Mexico as a child and did doctoral studies at Stanford University; as part of his doctoral studies, he held a Fulbright Fellowship in Mexico. Alarcón is considered one of the most original poetic voices in Chicano literature: certainly, he holds a secure place in the development of a specifically Chicano homoerotic writing, as exemplified by his major collections, *Body in Flames. Cuerpo en llamas* (1990), *Snake Poems; An Aztec Invocation* (1992), *No Golden Gate for Us* (1993), and especially by *De amor oscuro. Of Dark Love* (1991), modelled on the late gay poetry de Federico García Lorca written in 1935-36 just before his assassination (see Eisenberg *passim*). In addition to an extensive poetic production

175

dating from the mid-1980s, Alarcón has been deeply involved in barrio
activism and has worked tirelessly as a defender of gay rights.

Alarcón's writing is marked by a complex poetic voice (he is only
treated in passing by Arteaga, who does not include him in his chapter
on "Tricks of Gender Xing"; he is totally excluded from the chapters on
literature in volume 3 of *Handbook of Hispanic Cultures*). Although
there is an apparent superficial simplicity in his poetry, one can
immediately perceive the effort to construct a dense network of
meanings and feeling. Such is necessarily the case when dealing with
the representation of homoerotic desire (for an overview of Alarcón's
homoerotic writing, see Hernández-Gutiérrez). For, as complex as the
representation of heterosexual love must be, it depends always on
horizons of knowledge and experiences broadly shared and publicly
accepted and endorsed. Even the perversion of and deviation from what
is commonly "known" about heterosexual desire relies, at least in a first
instance, on such knowledge. However, in the case of homoerotic
desire, unless it is simply understood as an inversion of heterosexuality
(which it, of course, often is—i.e., where homoesexual identity mimics
heterosexual roles, particularly along the lines of the gender binary), the
poet must work from the assumption that there is no common ground of
readerly knowledge, not even among readers who themselves may be
gay-identified. This is so to the extent that the relative scarcity, even
now, of a public discourse of homoeroticism makes it difficult to lay
claim to shared knowledge. The function of the bilingual adjectival pair
oscuro/dark in both Alarcón's book and in Lorca's pre-text (*Sonetos del
amor oscuro*) is less to capture the shady attributions of homoeroticism
evoked by homophobic accounts and than to refer to the unknown, the
uncharted that characterizes homoerotic desire as a dark continent: cf.
the title of Winston Leyland's anthology of Latin American gay writing,
My Deep Dark Pain Is Love.

Alarcón works in general with short texts that feature short lines
and short strophes and stanzas, in addition to highly compact
languages. This affords his poems their deceptive simplicity. In a
certain sense, Alarcón is evoking ironically one facet of an interrelated
Anglo classism and racism: Chicano experience is taken to be simple
by nature—the simple experience of a simple person, blessed with a
simple soul and unfettered by the "profound" reactions of the more
sophisticated and worldly. Certainly, every human experience is
profound, but what is directly pertinent here is that life seen under the
purview of classism, racism, and, in Alarcón's case, homophobia as

well. Alarcón abets the condescension of the superficial reader by seeking to capture the specific resonances of daily Chicano life, of a life that is held in common rather than being privileged by the poetic voice of the outside. Precisely, Alarcón strives to place homoeroticism within the context of Chicano life, to see it as integral to shared experiences, and not as a marked deviance lived by someone who is outside of Chicano life, as an outcast from an ideology that perceives homoeroticism to be alien to Chicano culture and, indeed, even something induced by predatory and corrupting Anglo society. Alarcón has spoken of Chicano life as a mestizo phenomenon, where the mixing of cultures and the life of open and fluid borders allows for a human experience where everything is possible, including homoerotic identities (interview with Cabrera; essay in this volume).

Body in Flame. Cuerpo en llamas contains forty poems distributed among five sections. It is worth noting that the first three divisions each contain eleven poems; the fourth, six poems; while the fifth consists of a single text. The first of the main three parts consists primarily of references to Chicano culture and heritage; the second group deals essentially with marginality, while the third, an eloquent juxtaposition to the second, focuses on regenerative love. The fourth section evokes themes of love and spirituality, while the single text of the fifth division is titled in such a way as to look toward the future: "Carta a América/Letter to America." Several of the poems that make up this collection have appeared in other books by Alarcón, giving the impression that his poetry circulates freely from one collection to another as participating in a unified effort to construct a lyrical mosaic of Chicano life, one in which homoeroticism is as much a legitimate ocurrence as anything else.

Alarcón's poetry is, therefore, particularly attractive for the way in which the emphasis on details of barrio life underscores a collective social memory. The poem "En un barrio de Los Angeles" opens with the affirmation that "el español/lo aprendí/de mi abuela,"[1] which establishes from the outset a correlation between two primary values of Chicano life that interconnect all of Hispanic life. Language is crucial for individual identity. It consists of a structured network of signs by means of which one establishes a connection with and forges an interpretation of the world. In the process, one charts the borders between the language of the community to which one belongs and the borders of other communities, along with the multiple social variations that are bound up with the circumstances of linguistic use. Spoken language is also a cultural medium that allows individuals to accede to innumerable worlds of the discourse of poetry, songs, legends, sayings, not to mention, of course, an entire tradition of written literature.

The grandmother, in turn, possesses an iconic value in the sense of family and community tradition. Alarcón plays with the fact that, in Spanish, the concept of maternal language is grammatically feminine, allowing for all sorts of metaphors and personifications that mark the descent of language from the womb of the female. Therefore, the acquisition of language has its roots in a sustained contact with the feminine—here, the double-marked feminine space of the grandmother, the mother of the mother, who stands in for parents who are away at working in a cannery.

The bilingual poem "I Used to Be Much Darker"/"Yo antes era más moreno" shows Alarcón using skin color to characterize the degree, in an inverse form of racism, of his physical and emotional approximation to Chicano life. When his life was closely tied to the barrio he was much, much darker. But now "maybe I'm too / far up north,'[2] which prevents him from being as dark as he was before. This strategy of concentrating on mundane details of the body and on the space that one occupies, articulated in such a way as to provoke deep sentimental reactions toward Chicano life, is one of the most brilliant features of Alarcón's poetry.

The homoerotic dimensions of Alarcón's poetry are explicit, and they are particularly evident in *De amor oscuro* in the second part, which bears the title "El otro día encontré a García Lorca."[3] As many commentators have noted, it has been difficult for Chicano society to accept homoeroticism, and the subject is either passed over in silence (as is the case in the four-volume *Handbook of Hispanic Cultures in the United States*) or it is denounced as a deleterious influence of Anglo mores (the best treatment remains Almaguer's essay, although it is in need of serious revision). This is as much true of lesbianism as it is of gay male relations. In the case of the latter, the practice has been to consider the appearances that are detected and acknowledged to exist as a violation of a proper healthful, heterosexual masculinity that, it is insisted, serves as a bulwark against a dominant and exploitative society. In the case of women, homoerotic relations are viewed as a violation of the male-female couple and the chastity of women who ought, rightfully, to be disciples of the Virgin of Guadalupe (see Moraga, "Queer Aztlán"). Such positions ignore the intense man-man relationship that exists in Mexican and Mexican-American society (*compadrazgo*) and the virtually exclusive world of women who engage in the Marian cult (*comadrazgo*). This does not mean that such homosocial models are necessarily homoerotically based, but only that they provide in barrio culture an alternative to the predatory heterosexism commonly associated with the Anglo world.

The particular emphasis of Alarcón's poetry is the representation of a society in which erotic relations with persons of the same sex incite profound and refreshing resources of love and affection which are a relief against what is claimed to be the dehumanization of the Anglo world. Certainly, Alarcón looks toward sexual acts and not merely a free-floating and disembodied amorous sensation. For example, he speaks of being kissed on the mouth by García Lorca, which serves to prefigure other intimate contacts. But what is of greater significance is the legitimation of homoerotic love that flows from the intense emotions sparked by Chicano life in general, where any sense of shame is banned with regard to feeling and the expression of forbidden and intimate interpersonal experience that are completely meaningless from the point of view of dominant Anglo society. That is, what is viewed by some as the cheap emotionalism of barrio life is reinterpreted by Alarcón as the privileged realm of profound feelings that cannot help but include love between men. Finally, the very title of the collection puts into motion provocative images concerning the materiality of the body (as does also the title *Body in Flames. Cuerpo en llamas*), which in turn transgresses systematically the taboos of a traditional Hispanic society that proscribes the display of the body, whether masculine or feminine. Indeed, even in a modernist context in which women's bodies may be displayed, male bodies are still off limits, which in part explains the repudiation within the Chicano community of the Pachuco phenomenon and its modern-day equivalents (cf. the plays of Luis Valdez).

Alarcón's poetry, as should now be evident, is openly sentimental. Sentimentality is a double-edged phenomenon. On the one hand, it can be taken as a facile emotion that works to effect a distraction from the cruel realities of life: cry crocodile tears and you will be able to avoid face the real facts of the suffering at issue. The result is no adequate attention to the root causes of that suffering, and social structures go unchallenged and unchanged. But there is another face to sentimentality, one where it can serve as a therapeutic response to suffering, as a recovery as much as an insistence on the deep emotions experienced in the face of a social structure that would deny any legitimation to such emotions. The denial of human sentimentality in order to effect the "serious work" of life, which may often mean its ongoing exploitation, is in the end a negation of basic humanity. A poetry that stimulates such a sentimentality, that promotes unrestrained feeling in the prizing of what a conventional ethos sees as uncontrollable and therefore threatening, although the threat may come from a directly unconcealed homoeroticism, is necessarily beneficent.

Alarcón attempts to elaborate a mosaic of themes that provoke and animate an emotional and sentimental response in the reader. Some of his texts focus on icons of barrio life, on symbols and elements that provide instant points of reference. They may be elements of language or they may be elements of decor, such as the sounds and smells of the barrio. Other texts seem more arcane, and a reader might well wonder what they have exactly to do with the context of barrio life. Nevertheless, literature, and especially poetry typically involve an attempt to establish a connection, even when it is not immediately apparent, that proposes networks of meaning that stretch the imagination of the reader toward forms of shared experience. Alarcón writes with a language marked by the queer, and he does so with a vocabulary that is markedly colloquial and accessible, which results in an expression of intense poetic quality. By the same token, the depiction of homoerotic desire within the context of what is colloquial and immediately recognizable serves to naturalize it within the boundaries of Chicano life: the effect is to naturalize what must ostensibly be repudiated as alien to the barrio.

I would like now to examine in closer detail a few of Alarcón's poems that I have mentioned in passing. "En un barrio de Los Angeles" is from the 1990 collection *Body in Flames. Cuerpo en llamas*:

el español
lo aprendí
de mi abuela

mihijo
no llores me decía

en las mañanas
cuando salían
mis padres

a trabajar
en las canerías
de pescado

mi abuela
platicaba
con las sillas

les cantaba
canciones
antiguas

les bailaba
valses en
la cocina
cuando decía
niño barrigón
se reía

con mi abuela
aprendí
a contar nubes

a reconocer
en las macetas
la yerbabuena

mi abuela
llevaba lunas
en el vestido

la montaña
el desierto
el mar de México

en sus ojos
yo los veía
en sus trenzas

yo los tocaba
con su voz
yo los olía

un día
me dijeron:
se fue muy lejos

pero yo aún
la siento
conmigo

diciéndome
quedito al oído
mijito (11-12)[4]

Alarcón establishes a privileged realm of meaning dominated by
the figure of the grandmother. It is not so much that this realm is
juxtaposed to an intervening parental realm that may be problematical
as it is an antithesis or an antagonist to the space of the grandmother.
The parents are merely absent, and their only active presence is to
express euphemistically the fact that the grandmother has died. But this
information is treated as an inconsequential parenthesis, because it is
grounded in a meaning outside the one that has been created in the
privileged space of the grandmother's influence: the fact that she may
have physically died does not affect her presence or her influence, and
her importance for the narrator—as still-child of the poem—endures in
a timeless fashion. This fact is captured by the grammatical detail that
the description of the realm of the grandmother's influence is rendered
via verbs in the imperfect tense, one of whose semantic functions is to
capture a past durative meaning. By contrast, the information about her
death is presented in the two preterite verbs "un día/me *dijeron:*/se *fue*
muy lejos," which constitutes a circumstantial parenthesis in the series
of imperfect verbs used to characterize the grandmother's presence and
her influence. The other preterite verb, the *aprendí* of the opening
stanza precedes the litany on the grandmother and functions to relate
the present moment of the existence of the poem to the childhood of the
narrator. Indeed, what that verb describes is what permits the poem,
since the point of having learned Spanish from the grandmother is what
enables the poet, precisely, to write a poem in Spanish.

As I have already stated, the issue of retaining Spanish, of the ordered transmission of the language from one generation to another (as opposed to the often deeply humiliating experience of studying it in school, often with teachers who may not speak Chicano Spanish,[5] who may encourage the acquisition of a "standard" sociolect, or who may even disparage and ridicule the student's use of the langauge) is an important sociolcultural issue for Chicano culture in general, and it bears remarking that now at the end of the 1990s, poetry is the one genre of Chicano literary production that still retains a vigorous commitment to the use of Spanish.

The use of Spanish in a Chicano context, as in the case of the imperative to maintain ethnic preserves in general in the United States, is an intertwined question of both the nostalgia for roots and the view that the non-English language protects against the destruction of identity as exercised by the homogenizing effect of English. This is a fairly recognized and accepted principle of Chicano culture. However, where Alarcón makes it into a distinctive practice is in the representation of the world that his grandmother evokes for him via the Spanish language.

"Magical realism" is a term that, when applied to Hispanic culture, especially Latin American literature, has become quite debased, especially when it is used in such a way as to imply, if not to affirm, that, by contrast to U.S. and Western European societies, Latin America is essentially premodern, nonrationalistic, spiritual, and, indeed, prelapsarian as regard the belief in the fantastic, the otherworldly, and, in a word, the magical. Since marketing campaigns of publishers and, in fact, even quite a number of scholarly careers are grounded on such beliefs, one makes little headway in denouncing such characterizations as grounded in ethnocentric characterizations of Hispanic culture.

For this reason, I would want to avoid characterizing the realm of the grandmother as a magical-realist antithesis to a supposed ordinary world out there where English is spoken and one's parents have (presumably) grim employment in a fish cannery. The point of Alarcón's characterization is, rather, not so much a generalized magic that his grandmother evokes, but the difference of Spanish, the difference of her guiding love toward him, a love that survives her death as though the latter never really mattered at all, and the difference of his remaining forever someone who is a *mijito* ("my little son") to someone else. The circumstance of difference rather than the texture of the realm in which that difference is produced, even though the latter is lovingly evoked, is the structuring principle of the poem. It is the experience of inhabiting this realm of difference that legitimates the individual's sense of being different, of being able to retain a fundamental element of that difference, which is the privilege of having someone whisper *mijito* in his ear.

Alarcón's gay poetry underscores the beauty of the grandmother, the charm of her ways, and the poetry of the world she creates. It is, of course, not a gay world or a queer world or a homoerotic world; it is not even an erotic world in any evident way, although its sensorial qualities (voice, sounds, smells, appearances) can, without too much effort, be recodified as sensual, especially with the mixture of the literal and the synaesthesic in seeing geographic features in the grandmother's eyes, but also seeing them in her braids; or, in a different reading of the flow of the stanzas, touching them in her braids and smelling them in her voice. Such a disruption of what would be considered the normal distribution of sensory reactions underscores a difference of perception that becomes a prepoetic privilege, and like language, it serves subsequently to enable the poetic act itself.

A poem like "En un barrio de Los Angeles" cannot, therefore, be read only as legitimating any particular concept of identity, whether linguistic, sociocultural, or, given the body of texts in which it is embedded, any specific interpretation of the body and its sexuality. Rather, it confirms the importance to the poet of a radical difference, of a spiritual and emotional space that is marked as privileged because of the unique satisfactions that it provides him with. One could argue that the homoerotic does not require legitimation, no matter how much it is denied legitimacy by the force of homophobia from which children and adolescents must be protected. A discourse of legitimation, however, will not overcome homophobia, any more than a discourse of racial equality handily overcomes racism. Consequently, one does not look in the poetry of a writer like Alarcón for a discourse of legitimation, even when there may be an attention to the destructive, indeed, murderous nature of homophobia.

What "En un barrio de Los Angeles" images instead is the creation for the poet of an opportunity for the perception of difference and, more important, of the conditions for a poetic voice that is the embodiment of that difference. Because of the emphatic position it occupies at the end of the poem, the description of the everlasting whispering in the poet's ear of the term of endearment of his grandmother can be interpreted as his primary *flatuus poeticus*, the essential source of his inspiration for a poetry dedicated to recounting the same sense of marvelous admiration for the possibilities of life that the poet sees in the person, in the physical attributes, and the actions of his grandmother. Such a marvelous admiration is, to be sure, not in itself essentially gay. But one variety of gay experience may be the experiencing of a privileged sense of difference, privileged precisely because it is an alternative to the grimness of the surrounding reality. The fact that Alarcón expresses this in terms of the juxtaposition of the outside world versus his grandmother's kitchen and in terms of the juxtaposition between English and Spanish recirculates the privilege of Spanish for the Chicano and for a Chicano creative expression. And like Cherríe Moraga in *Giving Up the Ghost*, Alarcón would also seem to be seeing in the Spanish of the Chicano between a hegemonic heterosexism of English and the Anglo world it articulates and an opening toward a recuperative queerness in the domain of meaning spoken through Spanish (see Foster, "El lesbianismo multidimensional").

Also from *Body in Flames. Cuerpo en llamas*, "El otro día me encontré a García Lorca" is one of Alarcón's more specifically gay-marked texts. Where the majority of the texts in this collection speak rather of enabling conditions for a poet who is publicly gay—cultural parameters, privileged experiences, the difference of Spanish—"El otro día" avails itself of a series of overt indicators of homoerotic desire:

lo reconocí
por el moño
los labios
los ojos
olivos

lloraban
guitarras
y bailaba
flamenco
la tarde

de pronto
se paró
vino
directo
a mi mesa

y me plantó
un beso
como sol
andaluz
en la boca (50)[6]

Lorca has become an international symbol for gay culture, just as
much as he has always been a symbol for the senseless slaughter of the
Spanish Civil War (Gibson). In fact, Lorca is a particularly powerful
figure, not only because of the degree to which his writing in all genres
lends itself so comfortably to the identification of explicit homoerotic
motifs, but also the ease with which it has been possible profitably to
interface his work as a whole with a queer reading of cultural production. Morevoer, the particular interest of Lorca for an agenda of
gay/queer studies has been the extent to which criticism on his work,
much of it institutionalized in concert with the monumentalization of
Lorca as a symbol of fascist/Franquista brutalities, has studiously
avoided any identification of Lorca as a gay man or of the homoerotic
elements in his poetry. If it is only after the death of Franco that Lorca's
Sonetos del amor oscuro, written 1935-36 immediately before his
death, can be published in Spain (the first edition was in a marginal
format in Buenos Aires after the return to constitutional democracy and
the demise of the homophobic military dictatorship), international
criticism, uncircumscribed by the censorship existing in Spain until
1975, is only occasional willing to mention the hypothesis that Lorca's
death was either motivated by homophobic persecution and/or the
vengence of a powerful spurned lover. Virtually no mention is made to
specific textual features of his writing that can be related to dimensions
of homoerotic desire. Only recently, has there begun to be a body of
scholarship that addresses forthrightly Lorca's identity as a gay writer,
the pertinent details of his public persona, the specifically homoerotic
themes, motifs, and allusions of poetry and the latter's queer interpretations of human experience, as well as what the sources and relations
might be between these elements and the traditions of sexuality of his
native Andalusia. Precisely because there are so many interlocking gay
and queer aspects of Lorca's poetry, he has become such an integral
part of an international gay canon.

Alarcón's poem plays off of a more specific detail of Lorca's
prominence as a gay writer, and that is the public images of him. As
part of a proper constitution of Lorca as standing at the core of a

modern gay cultural tradition, there has been an interest in recovering a Lorquian imagery that underscores the publicness of his gay persona during the entre-guerre period in Europe in which one finds such a remarkable concentration of gay-marked culture (indeed, part of Alarcón's essential cultural formation was, during his Fulbright tenure in Mexico, to establish contact with what remained of the Contemporáneos poets—he speaks with special fondness of Elías Nandino (1903-?)—which was a group of writers many of whom were associated with an urban homoerotic culture in Mexico and had contacts with Lorca, who, however, never visited Mexico; he is supposed to have had a ticket for such a visit when he was assassinated). Many recently published images catch Lorca in what would be called stereotypically gay poses (see the cover of Binding).

Specifically, Alarcón evokes Lorca via three metonymies of physical attributes, one part of his dress (the signature bow-tie that appears in so many photographs) and fetishized bodily details that are crucial to sexual attraction and erotic engagement. Alarcón continues with an evocation of metonymies, with typical cultural icons associated with the culture of Andalusia, especially its erotic dimensions: both the guitar and flamenco are recurring motifs in Lorca's poetry, and they both serve for many readers as seductive cultural allusions, especially as regards the display of the body in flamenco and its homoerotic dimensions (see Jaime Chávarri's 1989 film on the flamenco star Hugo Molina, *Las cosas de querer*, which stresses the homoerotic associations of both the dancer and his performances).

But what is of particular interest in "El otro día" is the question of gay visibility. Although visibility has been an integral part of the international gay movement, it is important to stress that, in Hispanic culture, whether in Spain, Latin America, or among Latino groups in the United States, the visibility of the homoerotic is the violation of the greatest taboo: what can be accepted as one's private life cannot be tolerated when it becomes part of the public record, and commonly it is asserted that a public display of the homoerotic, whether in dress, behavior, speech, or contact with another person, is an invasion of the privacy, if not the morals, of the onlooker (on gay visibility in Latin America, see Foster, "El homoerotismo y la lucha por el espacio en Buenos Aires"). What Alarcón's poetic voice describes, then, is not only the seeing of Lorca in a public space (and, to be sure, Lorca here may be read as a cover term for anyone who is identified as a gay man, as though he were like Lorca by virtue of the metonymies of

recognition that are listed), but an overt homoerotic act in concert with
him. Same-sex kissing remains an unbreachable proscription in most
public spaces of American society, Chicano or otherwise, and the
representation of "Lorca" as rising from his table and purposefully and
deliberately going over to kiss another man in public describes a degree
of visibility that can only be interpreted as stridently transgressive.

That the agent of this transgressive act is Lorca is certainly the
vocation of a gay icon. However, it is also an allusion to the danger of
such transgressions, since one interpretation of García Lorca's death is
that his openly assertive homosexuality was the cause of his torture and
assassination at the hands of the Guardia Civil, particularly so in view
of the fact that other Spanish gay writers were not assassinated at that
time, despite their subsequent victimization by the homophobia of the
Franquista regime. Thus, Lorca is both an icon of gay visibility, as well
as an icon of homophobic murder because of the high-stakes
transgressiveness of that visibility. Alarcón's poem further underscores
the importance of the transgressive act of public sex by tying its
performance to the two physical metonymies mentioned at the
beginning of the poem: Lorca's eyes seek out the narrator of the poem,
and his lips are the organs of the sexual act. Too, the kiss is described
in terms that reference back to the metonymies of Andalusian culture.

It is interesting to note that "El otro día" also turns on an issue of
privilege: the narrator attributes to himself the privilege of seeing
Lorca, having Lorca see him, and experiencing the sexual attentions
Lorca dispenses. This detail, however, introduces an ambiguity in the
text that cannnot be ignored or argued away, and that is the sex of the
poetic voice. My commentary has assumed that it is masculine, since,
of course, there would be nothing particularly transgressive about the
surprise kiss if the receiver were a woman (excluding those categories
of women for whom it would be transgressive: a nun, a little girl, an
older woman, or even another woman accompanied by another man).
Were the poem written in the third person—that is, were the receiver of
the kiss someone other than the poem's narrator—it could be difficult to
avoid marking the gender of that person. Of course, speaking in the first
person does not make it much easier to avoid gender marking, but first-
person references are less likely to be gender-marked than are third-
person ones—that is, first-person pronouns are not marked for gender
(marking is traced in predicate nominals and predicate adjectives), but
at least the third-person direct object pronouns are. In any event, it is an
act of interpretation to assume that the poetic voice of "El otro día" is

masculine rather than feminine. One might argue that the poem would not have much of a point if it were being articulated by a woman, precisely because the possibility of transgression being involved is significantly lower. Or, to put it differently, the reader assumes the speaker to be masculine, not because the poem is signed by Alarcón (a trivial but nondeterminate detail of biographical criticism), but because since the interest of the text turns on the assumption that the culmination of what is described is an act of transgression, it could only be a transgression meaningfully associated with the name of Lorca were the poetic narrator to be a man.

Alarcón's collection *De amor oscuro. Of Dark Love* is, as I have said, explicitly inspired by Lorca's *Sonetos del amor oscuro*. Indeed, the English translations of Alarcón's poems in this text are the work of Francisco Aragón, who has published verse translation of Lorca's *Sonetos* (acknowledgement is also made to Adrienne Rich for earlier versions). Alarcón roughly observes the classic sonnet form in Spanish,[7] although he presents fourteen sonnets, rather than Lorca's eleven: the latter odd number gives the impression that Lorca, who wrote his sonnets shortly before his death, left the collection unfinished, while the number fourteen, the same number as the amount of lines in each sonnet, bespeaks Alarcón's freedom from the oppression of Lorca's Spain in the mid-1930s. Like Lorca, Alarcón makes use of the sonnet, a poetic form typically associated with highly personal love poetry, to address the lover and the lover's body. It should also be noted that Alarcón, like Lorca, surely recognizes the privilege of the sonnet form in homoerotic poetry, given the fact that the bulk of Shakespeare's sonnets are addressed to men.

Sonnet II continues Alarcón's metapoetic interest in treating the conditions of poetic expression:

> tus brazos desarmaron mi tristeza,
> bastó que se extendieran como ramas
> de olmo por la noche para que luego
> salieran las estrellas en el techo
>
> ya no estamos en el macizo piso
> de una sala de apartamento pobre,
> ni forman nuestra cama dos colchas
> encimadas, ni nos cubren cobijas

estamos abrazados a la tierra
cálida, la noche nos arrulla
descubierta, muy cerca canta un río

yo sigo tu voz como quien sigue
una antorcha en lo oscuro del monte
lejos, todos duermen en sus alcobas. (n.p.)[8]

The first thing to be noted is that the poem is not specifically
marked as homoerotic. Neither the speaker nor the addressee are
grammatically marked for gender, and the predicate adjective in the
first line of the first tercet refers as much to a combination of masculine
and feminine as it does to two men. Thus, since only an equivalence
between author and narrator and between unmarked addressee and
specifically marked male addressee of other sonnets allow the reader to
perceive the sonnet as homoerotic in nature I would discount any
attempt to argue that the imagery of the poem is essentially homoerotic,
since only a sexist convention of love poetry could deny to woman the
attributions made here. While the other poems only barely refer
specifically to a homoerotic gaze (Sonnet VII: "qué suerte . . . /
la del cristo que cuelga / de una cadena entre tus pectorales"[9]) and never
directly to a homoerotic coupling, Soneto II is one of several poems
fundamentally interested in the enabling of poetry by the erotic effects
of the lover.

Like "En un barrio de Los Angeles," Soneto II is constructed in
terms of a privileged space and a power that inspires and enables poetic
expression. The space described here is that of the *alcoba* (bedroom),
itself a commonplace as the typically specific domain of love—from a
heterosexist point of view, it is, for the legally constituted couple who
practices love in a legally sanctioned fashion, the inviolable space of
their state-sanctioned coupling. Significantly, the room, prior to the
effects induced by the presence of the beloved (understood by the
reader, because of the poem's contextualization, to be a homoerotic
partner) is characterized as shabby and dreary. Indeed, it is not even a
bedroom, but the hard floor of a living room of a poor apartment, and
the bed consists of two quilts, one on top of each other to form a thin
mattress. In addition to signalling the misery of the destitute poet, this
characterization might also be read as portraying the misery of heterosexist love, erotically impoverished (at least, in its legal, reproductive

sanctions) and terrifying (for what it excludes and persecutes as a deviation from its priority).

However, the presence of the beloved reconstucts this impoverished space, and for the reader who understands the poem as homoerotic, he is seen to transform into an exuberant bower: "tierra cálida," "noche [que] arrulla," "canta un río." This transformation juxtaposes the grim misery of the apartment into a privileged realm of nature, confirming the transition from what is oppressive (because miserable) into what is enabling (because marked by the poetic *topoi* of love that occurs in an Arcadian space). Thus, the outside (the dreary world of which the poor apartment is a continuation)/inside (the *alcoba*) is inverted, and what was inside (the miserable makeshift bedroom) becomes part of a utopian outside (the privileged Arcadian bower of satisfying love). This same inversion underlies the poem discussed earlier, "En un barrio de Los Angeles," because if the grandmother's kitchen is a privileged inside against the outside of the Anglo world, the world of fish canneries, the poetic legacy of the grandmother allows the poet to attain a privileged utopia of poetically created space where he will always hear his grandmother's whispered endearment. Here, the transformation brought by the lover's presence also endows the poet with a voice to be followed. In turn the lover's voice, it is implied by the irregular syntax of the final line, is powerful enough to affect all those asleep in their bedrooms, as though it provided an erotic illumination (one might wish here to interpret *antorcha* as specifically homoerotic, an allusion to the erect, burning member of the beloved) in the way in which, in the metaphoric system of Baroque mystical poetry, God the beloved provides a light to find oneself through the forest of the night of the fallen soul. Here any dark forest, any fallen soul, would be that not only of those who are without love, without a lover, but also the dreary world of compulsory heterosexuality from which lovers such as this one save us.

The present-tense verbs of Alarcón's poem lend a durative quality to what is being described, and as was also the case with the characterization of the grandmother's whisper, the voice of the lover is what the poet is (always) following: since it changes his reality, disarming his sadness, and bestows him with an idyllic realm of love, it also enables his poetic voice: the articulation of the poem becomes possible by virtue of the voice the poet adheres to. In this and other poems, Alarcón not only describes the beneficent effects of love, and specifically, of homoerotic love, but he is particularly concerned to forge a relationship between that love and the ability to work poetry on the basis of it:

desde que escuché el rumor de tu voz,
las demás palabras se me hacen huecas,
inútiles, estorbosas, hechizas (Soneto XI)[10]

This stanza reaffirms Alarcón's perception of the enabling voices of those who are beloved, whether out of family affection of homoerotic desire, and he goes on to say in the next stanza: "por eso ya no quiero escribir poemas / sino vivirlos contigo,"[11] which expands the scope of poetry from a verbal creation to a life's project. Moreover, his poetry elaborates an interpretation of the spaces within which poetry and its enabling force takes place, thereby charting the frontiers between privileged, utopian domains that serve to exclude worlds the poet considers oppressive, most notably an Anglo world of oppressive heterosexism. And even though Alarcón has published virtually all of his poetry in bilingual editions, it is clear that access to the privileged, utopian domains comes via the the worlds that the Spanish language figures. Whether or not, from a sociological point of view, one can rightly say that the access Alarcón imagines Spanish to have to a resistance to an Anglo world of homophobic oppression, the utopian power he attributes to it through the voice of those who enable his poetry and through his own poetic voice constitutes a powerful cultural vision.

NOTES

1. "I learned / Spanish / from my grandma"; I quote first from the first-page language of the text and footnote the language used on the facing page.
2. "quizá yo estoy muy / lejos al norte"
3. "The Other Day I Ran into García Lorca"
4. I learned
Spanish
from my grandma

mijito
don't cry
she'd tell me

on the mornings
my parents
would leave

to work
at the fish canneries

my grandma
would chat
with chairs

sing them
old
songs

dance
waltzes with them
in the kitchen

when she'd say
niño barrigón
she'd laugh

with my grandma
I learned
to count clouds

to point out
in flowerpots
mint leaves

my grandma
wore moons
on her dress

Mexico's mountains
deserts
ocean

in her eyes
I'd see them
in her braids

I'd touch them
in her voice
smell them

one day
I was told:
she went far away

but still
I feel her with me

whispering
in my ear
mijito

5.   It should be noted that Alarcón's poetry makes use of what one could
call standard literary Mexican Spanish, although Chicano regionalisms are to be
found, such as the use of *canería* (cannery) in this poem.
6.   I recognized him
     by the slim bow tie
     his lips
     his eyes
     olive-colored

     guitars
     wept and
     the afternoon
     danced
     flamenco

     suddenly
     he stood
     walked
     directly
     to my table

and planted
a kiss
like an Andalusian
sun
on my lips

7. Two quatrains followed by two tercets, with hendecasyllabic lines with major tonic stress on the tenth syllable and a semantic shift between the two quatrains and the two tercets. Alarcón, however, deviates from the requirement that each line have a minor tonic stress on the fourth and/or sixth syllable, that the quatrains have a consonantal ABBA rhyme, and that the tercets also have at least two different consonantal rhymes (various patterns are possible).

8. your arms disarmed my sorrow
    by stretching like boughs
    of elm in the night, they made
    stars shine on the ceiling

    we are no longer on the hard floor
    of a poor apartment's living room,
    nor do two quilts form our bed,
    nor do we hide beneath covers

    we are embracing on the warm earth,
    the night lulls us, uncovered,
    very nearby a river sings

    I follow your voice as one follows
    a torch in the dark mountainside,
    far off, all are asleep in their bedrooms

9. "how lucky! . . . / the crucifix that hangs / from a chain on your chest!"
10. ever since I heard the rumor of your voice,
    all other words ring hollow to me—
    useless, cumbersome, bewitching

11. "this is why I no longer want to write poems / but live them with you"

1898 and the History of a Queer Puerto Rican Century
Imperialism, Diaspora, and Social Transformation
Larry La Fountain-Stokes

It is commonly known that when Spanish and other European explorers arrived in what we now refer to as the Americas, the indigenous populations practiced sexualities contrary to those deemed acceptable in the Old World.[1] Colonial documents and narrations show how countless efforts were engaged in by both clerical and political authorities hell-bent on eradicating such "barbarous" customs as homosexual sex, referred to as sodomy, practiced by the native inhabitants of these continents.[2] Documents of the Inquisition have also shown how Europeans and Africans were accused of these proscribed activities in the Americas during the period of the colony, while nineteenth- and early twentieth-century medical and criminal records have been useful for scholars studying countries as diverse as Argentina and Cuba in their attempt to reconstruct and analyze discourses and technologies for the control of sexuality of those years.[3]

There has been little or no research, to my knowledge, of homosexualities in Puerto Rico during the period of Spanish domination, which goes from 1509 to 1898.[4] This, of course, should not suggest an absence of same-sex sexual practices, but rather is indicative of how scholars have traditionally dealt with the subject, which is by totally ignoring it. The question of how homosexualities manifested themselves before 1898 in Puerto Rico is thus a ripe field of inquiry awaiting its own discoverers. The same, unfortunately, also holds true for much of post-1898 gay and lesbian Puerto Rican history, which is to

say, that of the period under United States domination.[5] This essay
forms part of a broader attempt to remedy such a lack.[6]

What were the effects of the United States invasion of Puerto Rico
in 1898 on homosexual practices and on the formation of subjectivities
on the island and in the diaspora? One almost immediate and clearly
identifiable result was the criminalization of sodomy in Puerto Rico for
the first time in 1902 (Braulio 33).[7] How has the U.S. occupation
affected current identities up to our days? And to ask the question in
reverse: What have the effects of Puerto Rican homosexualities been on
the United States? The answers to these questions are complex and
have traditionally been fraught with ideological underpinnings, the
likes of which I will attempt to map out.

Theories of Importation

In Puerto Rico, there is, or has historically been, a division
regarding valorizations of U.S. influence: on the one hand, general
distrust among leftists or independentistas of social transformations
whose origins are in the United States, be they direct governmental
policies or reflections of particular groups or individuals, and, on the
other hand, general enthusiasm from those eager to embrace Americanization, particularly among annexationist sectors.[8] There are also those
who try to divorce strict political-status considerations from such social
considerations, in an attempt to be more "objective."

Cultural nationalists have generally understood that American
social structures (which are seen as monolithic) are contrary to the
"essential" values of Puerto Ricans (who are, in turn, also seen as a
cohesive and unitary group), and that any and all influence is a threat.
While there is ample justification for this fear in the light of policies of
colonial domination,[9] it unfortunately clouds the reception of progressive, liberatory influences that might challenge oppressive, antidemo-
cratic, sexist, classist, racist, and homophobic elements of Puerto Rican
society.

A particularly noteworthy case of such a reception is René
Marqués's vitriolic attacks against the changing roles and rights of
women in society, expressed in his 1960 essay "The Docile Puerto
Rican" and carefully studied by Agnes Lugo-Ortiz (1997). Marqués's
posture regarding women had already been anticipated in 1934 by
Antonio S. Pedreira in his essay *Insularismo* (Insularism), in which
(middle-class) women were criticized for not being adequate home-
makers and for participating in politics, changes which were intensified

after 1898. This tendency of attributing any social transformation deemed inappropriate to a foreign influence is reminiscent of the situation in other countries, such as turn-of-the-century Argentina, where, as Jorge Salessi has shown, homosexuality was presented as an Italian working-class import, ignoring historical evidence of authochthonous practices, and slighting the fact that local Argentinean activists were profoundly knowledgeable of and inspired by German activists' struggle for acceptance in Europe.

Even when the foreign influence is acknowledged as good, it is still deemed problematic and seen with suspicion. Debates which reflect this occur often in Latin America, for example those concerning what is seen as the recent "importation" of the North American "gay" or "equal partners" model for male homosexuality, which displaces more traditional dichotomized paradigms of relations between "masculine" and "effeminate" men. This confrontation has resulted in lexical struggles regarding the use of the term "gay" and other variants such as "moderno" or "internacional" employed to reflect the North American type of identity or sexual/gender attitude.[10] It becomes difficult for people to distinguish between different types of North American cultural influences, since they are all grouped together and lumped as cultural imperialism.

In an article on racism and sexism recently published in Puerto Rico in the socialist weekly *Claridad*, the Reverend Margarita Sánchez de León made the following comment: "Recientemente hemos recibido a través del cable una comedia cuya protagonista, Helen (sic), es una mujer lesbiana. Nuevamente el modelo nos llega vía Estados Unidos" (32).[11] This article was accompanied by a photograph of Ellen De Generes and her girlfriend, Hollywood actress Anne Heche, alongside which the passage in question was reproduced in large type. Sánchez's contribution appeared in a section entitled "human@s[12] y con derechos" [Human and with rights], a column dedicated to gay and lesbian political concerns which began to appear roughly around the same time as the LLEGO (National Latino/a Lesbian and Gay Organization) 1997 Conference, held in San Juan in October of that year. This conference was a landmark event in which island activists came together with Latino activists from across the United States for the first time in Puerto Rico in an event of such magnitude; it received substantial, mostly positive press coverage.[13] Public and official reception differed dramatically from the debacle which surrounded the 1995 GOAL (Gay Officer's Action League)'s convention, in which gay

American police men and women visitors to the island were harrassed by Puerto Rican officers during a raid at Cups Bar in Santurce.[14]

Before proceeding further, it is important to understand the importance and singularity of Margarita Sánchez. She is a self-identified black, Protestant, partially deaf, lesbian Puerto Rican, co-pastor of the Iglesia Cristo Sanador (Christ the Healer Church), a branch of the Metropolitan Community Church in Santurce, who achieved national recognition when she demanded to be arrested for violating Article 103 (regarding sodomy) of Puerto Rico's Penal Code. Article 103 reads: "Toda persona que sostuviere relaciones sexuales con una persona de su mismo sexo o cometiere el crimen contra natura con un ser humano será sancionado con pena de reclusión por un término fijo de diez (10) años" (Lugo-Ortiz 1995, 118).[15] Authorities refused to jail Sánchez, claiming that she could not be prosecuted because she lacked a "virile member." Sánchez's act is part of a much broader civic effort led by her to have the law stricken off the criminal code as unconstitutional.

Claridad's decision to publish the aforementioned quote to accompany the article's photograph can be understood as responding to the column's general mission: to provide a space for the debate of lesbian and gay politics in Puerto Rico. It is no small sign of how the times have changed that this weekly newspaper, traditionally associated with the homophobic independence movement, prints such a column. The article itself, however, does not focus on North American influence in Puerto Rican activists' struggle, but rather on racial discrimination and on the repression of feminists and lesbians, tracing a history of their political involvement. What is, then, the purpose and effect of the photograph and highlighted passage?

While the image of Ellen might serve to immediately and easily alert readers that this column is about lesbians, a word that oddly does not appear in the article's title, I believe the photograph unnecessarily distracts from the central argument of the piece: that is, that Puerto Rico is a racist, sexist, and homophobic society in dire need of transformation. The article's presentation of Ellen is meant as a critique of the absence of positive representations of lesbianism in the Puerto Rican media, yet it unfortunately reads as a complaint against yet one more form of colonization. Ironically, while the example set by Margarita Sánchez is one of an authochthonous radical activism, it becomes caught up in a much more mediated and foreign framework— that of U.S. television. The analysis of the implications of Sánchez's religious vocation as the pastor of a gay and lesbian U.S. Protestant church in Puerto Rico and of the impact of an American gay and lesbian Latino conference (organized with island activists) also merits further attention. I will now comment only briefly on the first.

U.S. Protestantism has been used in Puerto Rico not only as a vehicle for some of the most liberatory currents, such as exemplified by Sánchez, but also to defend the most repressive and rabidly homophobic ideologies. A case in point is that of Reverend Jorge Rasche and of Milton Picón, leader of Morality in Media. Rasche and Picón are among the most powerful foes of the lesbian and gay rights movement on the island, and have organized countless protests and boycotts in his effort to stymie any social or political advance. These include protests against a gay and lesbian literature class taught at the Colegio Universitario de Cayey by José (Keke) Rosado, and against the work of Puerto Rico CONCRA, an AIDS-services organization. This pattern is reproduced in the diaspora: in New York, the Puerto Rican Protestant Reverend Rubén Díaz is one of the greatest enemies of the North American gay and lesbian rights movement.[16]

On the other hand, Protestant groups such as the Movimiento Ecuménico Nacional (MENPRI) (National Eucumenical Movement), Centro Cristiano Otras Ovejas del Rebaño (Other Sheep of the Herd), and the Iglesia Comunidad Metropolitana Cristo Sanador, have been some of the most vocal advocates of social tolerance and political reform in Puerto Rico. Joined by progressive Catholic groups and diverse nonsectarian human rights, political, social, and cultural groups, they form the backbone of the actual lesbian and gay movement on the island.

A much more serious yet opposite blurring of American influence on the island occurs in Frances Negrón-Muntaner's 1994 film *Brincando el charco: Portrait of a Puerto Rican*, in which a character called Maritza, who is the narrator of a segment showing documentary footage from the first Lesbian and Gay Pride March in Puerto Rico, held in 1991, wonders if lesbian and gay liberation necessarily comes from the United States and, in fact, if English is the language of gay liberation.[17] In response to this "provocation,"[18] Claudia Marín, the film's protagonist, replies "yes, the debt is obvious" and "no, there are so many other debts."[19] What these other debts might be is not discussed; the visual image, which presents Juanita Ramos leading a chant in Spanish, suggests that this might have to do with the tradition of leftist, independentista gay and lesbian activism in the island and the diaspora. Yet, since both Maritza's and Claudia's thoughts are presented as voice-over, it is difficult to tell them apart; spectators are led to think that both women basically think in a similar way.

In the film, Cristina Hayworth, a Nuyorican transsexual who originated the parade and who until only recently was one of the better known spokespersons and activists on the island, is incorrectly identified by Maritza as an "American drag queen" (or "una travesti americana"), accidentally discounting her Puerto Rican heritage principally on the basis of the language she speaks, while also misidentifying her transgender status.[20] This mistake is never clarified in the film.[21] Negrón Muntaner's unfortunate blunder is, of course, all too common in Puerto Rico, where nationality is often reduced to language, where return migrants are many times subjected to harassment, and where there isn't a highly developed consciousness regarding transgender distinctions. Ironically enough, Negrón Muntaner devotes an important segment of the film to criticizing the very same problem of language as nationality that she then inadvertently goes on to commit; in her scholarly articles, she has also been one of the biggest defenders of transgender activism in the movement.

Negrón Muntaner's mistake or lack of clarity is worrisome given her position as arguably the most important and perhaps the most prolific scholar of the gay and lesbian movement on the island, as well as an important commentator of gay and lesbian Latino issues in the United States.[22] In addition to her films on the subject, including *AIDS in the Barrio*, she has published the only account of early organizational efforts which took place in Puerto Rico in the 1970s. In that lengthy, ground-breaking article, titled "Echoing Stonewall and Other Dilemmas: The Organizational Beginnings of a Gay and Lesbian Agenda in Puerto Rico, 1972-1977," Negrón Muntaner argues that the most important men's group from the early 1970s on the island, the *Comunidad de Orgullo Gay*, failed largely because it was subservient to a white North American organizational model which was not responsive to the specific need of its Puerto Rican constituency. The class and race origin of the group's leadership also did not facilitate a broad incorporation of new members, and alienated black, working class, and female individuals.[23] In this case, it would seem, U.S. influence was both the origin and downfall of that group; failure stemmed not simply from Puerto Rico's relationship to the United States, but from the very divisions which plague Puerto Rican society as a whole. "Speaking English" (that is to say, following American paradigms) was the problem and not the solution. The narrator of *Brincando el charco*, oblivious of this earlier analysis, privileges American influence (and the English language) in her discourse, underplaying other complex issues that the very same director had addressed in scholarly and community journals. It is no surprise to learn that Negrón-Muntaner has recently gone on to become part of the "Estadidad Radical" or Radical Statehood movement, having been one of the original signers of the Manifesto presented by a number of academics last year which defends statehood for Puerto Rico as a means of joining what is presented as a multicultural, Latinized, and socially progressive United States.[24]

WHEN IN TROUBLE, JUMP OVERBOARD: THE CASE OF EMIGRATION AND HOMOSEXUALITY

Readers of Magali García Ramis's 1986 novel *Happy Days, Uncle Sergio* will recall what happens to gay and lesbian Puerto Ricans who don't move to New York out of their own self-accord: they get shipped out, the farther the better, to places like California. Such is the fate of Tati Almeyda's son, a minor character only mentioned in purely anecdotal fashion:

> —¡QUE BARBARIDAD!
> —Qué barbaridad, tan guapo-decía Nati.
> —Sí, hombre, pato, le salió pato ese muchacho a la pobre Tati Almeyda. Ajá, pero ya lo mandó para Estados Unidos, allá lejos, a California que dicen que allá es que los están mandando a todos. (30-31)[25]

Throughout the book it is also suggested that Uncle Sergio, the character of the novel's title, leaves Puerto Rico because of his homosexuality. It is no surprise that Lidia, the proto-lesbian protagonist of the novel, will in turn dream of leaving, of being (even if only at an unconscious level) just like her Uncle Sergio and Tati Almeyda's son, and going to Italy or New York, purportedly to meet and/or live with Sophia Loren.[26]

Literary sources have, for a long time, documented how emigration has served both as a regulatory measure and a liberatory strategy in Puerto Rico with regards to nonnormative sexualities; at the very least, having narratives set outside of Puerto Rico seems to facilitate certain

types of representation. Bernardo Vega's memoirs, as it has been amply
noted, mention his throwing his watch overboard as he arrived in NY
for fear of being considered "effeminate."[27] As early as the 1920s, José
I. de Diego Padró presented a Cuban bisexual sadist in New York in his
monolithic novel *En babia*.[28] Pedro Juan Soto's celebrated book of
short stories *Spiks* (1956) opens with a story, "La cautiva," about a
young woman who is sent to New York by her family after they
discover that she is romantically involved with her brother-in-law.
Another anthology of migration stories, Vivas Maldonado's *A vellón las
esperanzas o Melania* (Hopes for Only a Nickel or Melania; 1971),
includes a story, "La última la paga el diablo" (the devil pays for the
last one), about a young Puerto Rican male who turns to hustling out of
desperation and financial necessity. Emilio Díaz Varcárcel's *Harlem
todos los días* (Harlem Every Day), in turn, includes an American
transvestite among its other assorted and occasionally sordid characters.
Luis Rafael Sánchez's well-known essay "La guagua aérea" (The Air
Bus) makes mention of Víctor Fragoso's mother, flying to New York to
visit her son who is dying of AIDS.[29]

It is not until openly self-identified gay and lesbian cultural producers begin to document and explore their migration, or "(s)exile," as
sexual-based migration has been termed, that more insightful, contestatory voices become heard.[30] Perhaps the two paradigmatic figures of
this are Luz María Umpierre and the now deceased Manuel Ramos
Otero, lost to AIDS in 1990.[31] In their work, albeit in very different
ways, both explore the experience of first-generation migrants who
confront traditional Puerto Rican values and foreign realities in the
United States. Umpierre does this through her poetry, in which she
freely switches from Spanish to English; Ramos Otero's poetry and
narrative always remained in Spanish. Numerous literary critics have
devoted copious pages to studying the work of both of these artists,
neglecting to some extent that of others authors who write in Spanish
such as Nemir Matos Cintrón, Víctor Fragoso, and Alfredo Villanueva-
Collado. English-language writers have also received scant attention,
except for rare cases, such as Arnaldo Cruz-Malavé's important article,
"What a Tangled Web!," where he analyzes works by Pedro Pietri, Piri
Thomas, and Miguel Piñero.[32] Finally, in addition to new cohorts of
first-generation migrants, there are now a healthy number of second-
generation gay and lesbian Nuyoricans, such as playwright Janis Astor
del Valle, dancer/choreographer Arthur Avilés, and poet Emanuel

Xavier, whose work reflects the dramatically different experience of being born and raised Puerto Rican in the United States.[33]

Yet the realm of the literary is perhaps not the most representative of the profound mark or effect that queer Puerto Ricans have made on U.S. society. Five Puerto Rican figures who have played a crucial role in North American gay and lesbian history and culture include Stonewall veteran Ray "Sylvia" Rivera, Warhol Factory superstar Holly Woodlawn (née Harold Ajzenberg), activist and scholar Juanita Ramos, activist and politician Margarita López, and the young actor Wilson Cruz.

As Martin Duberman and others have widely documented, the anger and frustration which crystallized on a prophetic evening of June, 1969 (igniting the Stonewall riots now widely considered to be the cornerstone of the modern North American gay and lesbian liberation movement) had at their root the fury and bravery of the Latina and African-American drag queens who were the regulars of the Mafia- and police-controlled businesses in Greenwich Village.[34] Ray "Sylvia" Rivera, a U.S.-born Latino of Puerto Rican extraction, is one of the five figures that Duberman chose in his book as emblematic of the different perspectives and positionalities that came together at that time and in the years immediately following and that helped organize and cement the enthusiasm and activist diligence of thousands of individuals no longer willing to hide their sexual preference or live as second-class citizens on its account.

In addition to participating in the riots, Sylvia, along with Marsha P. Johnson, founded STAR (Street Transvestite Action Revolutionaries), an organization which aimed to provide homeless gay and transgender youth with a place to live.[35] Ray also played a central role in some of the most notorious actions associated with the Gay Liberation Front, including a protest on Forty-Second Street which received widespread media coverage. Sylvia's participation in the Stonewall riots was recently fictionalized in the major-budget independent film *Stonewall*, where the character La Miranda plays the pivotal role.

Revolutionary in a different kind of way, Holly Woodlawn joined Andy Warhol's factory after a failed attempt to steal a camera using Warhol's name and a fortuitous interview in which she posed as a Factory member for the press. She became notorious after starring in the Paul Morrisey-directed film *Trash*; later performances would include appearing in *Women In Revolt*.[36] Born in Puerto Rico in 1946 to a Puerto Rican mother and an American father, Holly (then known as Harold) moved first to the Bronx and then to Miami Beach with her parents, later running away to New York, where she made her debut into stardom. While it can be argued (as she suggests) that she was exploited by the Warhol Factory and in fact received next to no financial remuneration for her work, she did contribute a Jewish Puerto Rican sensibility and perspective to their oeuvre. Her story is brilliantly captured in her autobiography, *A Low Life in High Heels.*

Juanita Ramos, best known for her work as editor of *Compañeras: Latina Lesbians*, a collection of essays, poems, short stories, drawings, and oral histories, is also the co-founder of the Latina Lesbian History Project and currently a professor at SUNY, Binghamton. Born in Puerto Rico to a working-class family, she came to the United States in 1961 when she was eight and has ever since been a frequent traveller back and forth to the island. Her biography is sketched in her essay "Bayamón, Brooklyn, y yo" (Bayamón, Brooklyn, and Me) which forms part of *Compañeras.*

Ramos describes the enormous difficulties encountered in putting the volume together in the preface. Ramos initially founded the Colectiva Lesbiana Latinoamericana in 1980 along with Digna Landrove de la O with the intent of publishing such a book. Contributions were initially not forthcoming, so she began to recollect oral histories, a fundamental element of the present text. As she describes, "The change in focus from written to oral history took place because I realized that it was not just that Latina lesbians did not want to write for the book but that coming from an †oral history' they preferred to tell their stories" (xvi-xvii).

Compañeras remains to this day one of the most ambitious and comprehensive anthologies of its kind; a fundamental text along with other classics of Latina/Third World North American feminism such as Gloria Anzaldúa's and Cherríe Moraga's *This Bridge Called My Back*, Anzaldúa's *Haciendo caras/Making Faces*, and Carla Trujuillo's *Chicana Lesbians: The Girls Our Mothers Warned Us About.*

Margarita López, the first openly lesbian Latina elected to public office in the United States, won a seat on the New York City Council in 1997 as representative of the Lower East Side, a position formerly held by another gay Puerto Rican, conservative Antonio Pagán.[37] She was born in Río Piedras to working-class parents in 1950, and attended the University of Puerto Rico. Her life-long work as a community activist was summarized in the Chicago monthly *En la vida (voces de lesbianas, gays, bisexuales y transgéneros latinos)* as follows:

> A graduate of the Victory Foundation Training Institute with a long (more than 20 years) and distinguished history of community and political activism, López has organized thousands of tenants against unfair attempts to deregulate public and private housing. As Chair of the Joint Planning Council, López fought for rent regulations that would encourage entrepreneurs, pushed for development plans that provided rental space for small businesses, and organized a campaign to promote local merchants. As a social worker, she worked for more than 10 years at Project Reachout, a program that helps the homeless mentally ill find clothes, jobs, and places to live. (Englebrecht, 6)

López's run was particularly notable in that she obtained the support of distinct constituencies in her district, including Latino, Jewish, gay and lesbian, and young and elderly voters.[38] In spite of an initial miscount of the primary votes, López beat the Democratic machine-endorsed candidate, Judy Rapfogel, and went on to form part of City Council in January of 1998.[39]

Wilson Cruz was born on December 27, 1973 in Brooklyn, New York, and is the eldest of three sons of Puerto Rican truck driver Wilson Echevarría and Puerto Rican office manager Iris Cruz.[40] The family moved to southern California when Cruz was ten years old; his parents believed that they could offer better opportunities for their children there.[41] Wilson, however, saw the move in different terms: "I was overweight, Puerto Rican in an area where there weren't many Puerto Ricans, and I was discovering I was gay—all of this added up to a loser" (quoted by Liskow); "I was this Puerto Rican kid in complete culture shock out here" (quoted by Farr).

After acting in high school and enrolling for a major in theater in Cal State-San Bernadino (where his family lived), he landed the role of Rickie Vásquez on the ABC series "My So Called Life," a critically acclaimed but unfortunately short-lived program, which was cancelled after 19 episodes in the 1994-95 session.[42] His "bi-racial,"[43] "sexually confused" character has been described as follows:

> Rickie Vásquez, a Puerto Rican and black student at fictional Liberty High, is a trusted confidant of both Angela Chase, the 15-

year-old focal character [played by Claire Danes], and her free-
spirited alter-ego Rayanne Graff [A.J. Langer]. Rickie is the only boy
at Liberty who can get away with following his female friends into
the girl's bathroom, though the school jocks don't always let him get
away with his preference for eyeliner and dangly earrings. (Jones)

In a notable episode that aired shortly before Christmas 1994,
Rickie is beaten up by the uncle he lives with and then thrown of the
house. The storyline was based on Wilson's own experiences—his
father kicked him out on Christmas Eve 1993 when he learned that his
son was gay, shortly before taping of the show began.[44] Wilson lived
for two-and-a-half months in a car and crashed at the houses of his
friends. He is now reconciled with his father, but often talks during
public appearances of the serious problems gay and lesbian youth face.
As Wilson often repeats, "Twenty-six percent of gay teens are kicked
out of their homes every year because they tell their parents they're
gay" (Graham). He has also travelled extensively around the country,
speaking at colleges (over thirty in the 1995-1997 period) about the
situation of gay adolescents; he often gets letters from teenagers who
turn to him for advice and solace. As a victim of high school peer
violence, he observes:

There seems to be such an indifference to our youth. Our schools
either don't know that this is a problem or it is not something they
feel comfortable dealing with. The freedom we are searching for will
be found only if schools show more compassion for people who are
different. (quoted in Liskow)

In addition to small roles in several films (*Johns, All Over Me,* and
currently *Supernova*) and other television programs (including guest
appearances on Phil Donahue and on Fox Network's "Ally McBeal"),
Wilson has appeared in the Los Angeles and New York productions of
the enormously popular rock musical *Rent,* in which he plays Angel, a
young drag queen dying from AIDS.[45] Wilson is not troubled by the
fact that all of the roles he has had so far follow the same model, but he
hopes to also be able to represent different types of characters in the
future.[46]

As should be evident by now, not only have Puerto Ricans been
affected by the colonial relationship between the island and the United
States, but in a truly dialectical process, the colonial subjects have

affected the imperial power. There is no such thing as "the American gay model" independent of the contributions of Puerto Ricans like Sylvia Rivera, Holly Woodlawn, Juanita Ramos, Margarita López, and Wilson Cruz. Marginalized as they might be, they are an essential component of this movement's history.[47]

The development of a liberatory struggle in the island, in turn, is intimately caught up with the imperial power that dominates it: because of significant American (white) gay migration to the island;[48] because of the prevalence of North American educational and media resources; because thousands of Puerto Ricans have gone (or been forced to go) to the United States and have often come back, many of them with new perspectives (those that can be only gained away from home, wherever that may be) and with organizational skills gained by participating in the North American struggle; and because of the prevalence of air travel associated to the AIDS epidemic.[49] Regardless of what the future may hold, Puerto Rican homosexualities have been intricately tied up in the colonial and diasporic reality of its people.

NOTES

1. See Jonathan Goldberg, *Sodometries: Renaissance Texts, Modern Sexualities*.

2. The Brazilian historian Luiz Mott has done extraordinary work in rescuing the history of homosexuality in Brazil during this period. Also see João Silverio Trevisan's *Devassos no paraíso* (translated as *Perverts in Paradise*).

3. I am thinking in particular of Jorge Salessi, *Médicos maleantes y maricas* (Doctors Miscreants and Queers) and Oscar Montero, *Erotismo y representación en Julián del Casal* (Eroticism and Representation in Julián del Casal).

4. Among the little information available is the following observation by Daniel Torres: "Puerto Rican literature has been dealing with gay issues since closet cases like Santiago Vidarte with his gay nineteenth-century masturbatory poem 'Insomnio' or the lesbian overtones of Lola Rodríguez de Tió, who like George Sand used to dress as a man" (179).

5. The independent scholar and book collector José Olmo Olmo, who resides in New York City, has a series of interesting documents which he has discovered but not published to date. These include two articles from the 1920s on cross-dressing men (Mario Operidel and Ramón Tirado) which appeared in *Puerto Rico Ilustrado* with numerous photographs of their arrests and

subsequent forced transformation to masculine appearance ("Estrena de sainete—hombre que se transforma en mujer" [Opening of a melodrama—a man is transformed into a woman] and "Otro curioso descubrimiento...25 años vestido de mujer" [Another strange discovery . . . 25 years dressed as a woman). Talk at Latino Gay Men of New York meeting, 5 June 1998, Gay and Lesbian Community Services Center, New York City.

6. An important contribution in the field of literary studies are the twenty-three bio-bibliographical entries on Puerto Rican authors (including two born elsewhere but currently residing on the island) who have written on the subject and which appear in David William Foster's *Latin American Writers on Gay and Lesbian Themes*. These are (in alphabetical order): Moisés Agosto, Rane Arroyo, Victor Fernández-Fragoso, Magali García Ramis, Abniel Marat, Nemir Matos-Cintrón, William Mena Santiago, Nicholasa Mohr, Carmen de Monteflores, Mayra Montero, Frances Negrón-Muntaner, Manuel Ramos Otero, Carlos Rodríguez Matos, Rafael Rodríguez Matos, Edgardo Sanabria Santaliz, Luis Rafael Sánchez, Alberto Sandoval Sánchez, Iván Silén, Piri Thomas, Luz María Umpierre-Herrera, Carlos Varo, Ana Lydia Vega, and Alfredo Villanueva. No entries appear for René Marqués, Mayra Santos Febres, or Daniel Torres, although the latter did contribute to the volume.

7. See Lugo-Ortiz ("Community" 118) for difference in wording of sodomy article before and after the 1974 Penal Code reform.

8. I should clarify that, at least at the current moment, dominant annexationist sectors favor an "estadidad jíbara," or creole statehood, in which key cultural elements, such as the Spanish language, would be preserved. These annexationists also espouse extremely conservative values similar to those of Republicans regarding fiscal spending and neo-liberalization programs. These sectors differ from the posture of other groups which have traditionally favored annexation, such as blacks and some segments of the working class, who see U.S. race and labor laws and customs as more progressive.

9. The most dramatic example of policies of Americanization were those followed in the educational system, as have been analyzed by Aida Negrón de Montilla in *Americanization in Puerto Rico and the Public School System 1900-1930*.

10. See, for example, Stephen O. Murray and Manuel Arboleda G.'s analysis.

11. We have recently received through cable tv a comedy whose protagonist, Helen (sic), is a lesbian. Once again, the model comes to us via the United States. Translation is my own.

12. The @ sign is used to suspend the conventional obligatory gender designation in Spanish as it refers to human subjects: @ may be either masculine or feminine or both.

13. Articles which appeared in the period immediately before and during the conference include a major, front-cover segment in *El nuevo día*, the island's most important newspaper, as well as articles in *El vocero* and *The San Juan Star*. See the front cover of *El vocero de Puerto Rico*, (San Juan, PR) 11 Oct. 1997 and coverage by Mario Alegre Barrios, Jesús Dávila, Mimi Ortiz, Lillian Rivas, and Marisol Seda.

14. See documents prepared by Del Toro and Santana, Attorneys and Counselors at Law, regarding Dr. Rosalina Ramos Padró et al., v. Commonwealth of Puerto Rico et al., Civil No. 95-1770 (HL). Dr. Ramos Padró, the owner of Cups Bar in Santurce, sued the police over their harassment of customers in her business establishment during the early morning of Saturday, February 11, 1995. For press coverage, see Peggy Ann Bliss, Lorraine Blasor, Karl Ross, and the articles "Puerto Rico Police Accused of Harassing a Gay Group" and "Toledo Orders Investigation of Raid at Santurce Gay Bar."

15. "Any person engaging in same-sex sexual relations, or who commits the crime against nature with a human being, will be condemned to jail for a fixed term of ten (10) years" (Lugo-Ortiz 1995, 118). Also see Braulio 33.

16. See, for example, the recent controversy regarding domestic partner rights, as reported on by Mike Allen.

17. Maritza's letter, presented in voice-over, reads: "Todo el proceso me hizo cuestionarme si un organizador del patio hubiera podido iniciarlo. Tal vez nuestra liberación es una donde primero se habla inglés y después se traduce" (*Brincando el charco* [The whole process made me wonder if a local organizer would have been able to start it. Perhaps our liberation is one where at first we speak English and then translate]).

18. Negrón Muntaner has stated in interviews that she meant the film as a provocation, to cause discussions among her spectators. That is certainly the reaction an assertion such as the one made by Maritza provokes. The only critic to specifically address this segment, Dorian Lugo Bertrán, has publicly stated his agreement with Maritza: "En esta última parte, Frances de veras hace gala de observaciones muy sutiles a manera de 'voice over' sobre el problema—o supuesto problema—de plantearse la homosexualidad y el lesbianismo puertorriqueños en conceptos `importados': `[para efectos de la discusión gay en PR] primero se habla en inglés y después se traduce'. Frances no emite juicio sobre esta alternativa puertorriqueña, y hace bien. Volvemos: ser o no ser. Es decir, o se es homosexual en inglés o no se es nada. That is the

question. Todavía mejor—otro momento de gracia en la película—es cuando una amiga de Claudia en esta misma parte le atribuye el éxito de la parada gay puertorriqueña a una mezcla de 'ay, bendito' y 'constitución americana'. Estoy completamente de acuerdo. No tengo nada más que decir" (137-40). "In this last part, Francis really makes a series of very subtle observations in voice-over regarding the probem—or supposed problem—of thinking of Puerto Rican homosexuality and lesbianism as imported concepts: 'as for gay discussion in Puerto Rico) at first we speak English and then translate.' Francis does not judge this Puerto Rican alternative, and she does well not to. Once again: to be or not to be. That it, you are either a homosexual in English or you are nothing. That is the question. Even better—another funny moment in the movie—is when a friend of Claudia in this same part claims that the success of the Puerto Rican gay parade is due to a combination of 'y, bendito' (oh, you poor thing) and the American constitution. I agree whole-heartedly. I have nothing to add."

19. Claudia's voice-over text is as follows: "Is the language of liberation English? Does it then get translated and transformed only later, after layers of mediations? Yes, the debt is obvious. [images of march and of blender with two different types of beans]. No, there are so many other debts" (*Brincando el charco*).

20. See Rubén Ríos Avila's interview with Cristina, titled "El show de Cristina." Island activists have expressed to me in private conversation that it was difficult to work with Cristina because she insisted on speaking English and was not inclusive of women. Yet without Cristina, the parade would have never ocurred—island activists generally thought Puerto Ricans "were not ready" for such a public display in 1991. By the next year, parade leadership was assumed by a new organization, the Comunidad de Orgullo Arcoiris, and Cristina marched by herself in protest to what she referred to as the "commercialization" and "carnivalization" of the parade.

21. Negrón-Muntaner has explained to me that she did not have time to interview Cristina in person and relied on the information she received from sources on the island. Most people on the island in fact think that Cristina is "una americana."

22. I make a distinction here between scholars who comment on social processes and those who predominantly address cultural (and especially literary) representations of homosexuality. Important scholars who have addressed social formations of homosexuality on the island and in the diaspora include Mildred Braulio, Hilda Hidalgo, Juanita Ramos, Luis Aponte-Parés, Manuel Guzmán, Jorge Merced, and Alberto Sandoval. Literary scholars include Jossianna Arroyo, Arnaldo Cruz Malavé, Juan Gelpí, Agnes Lugo-

Ortiz, Rubén Ríos Avila, José (Keke) Rosado, and Mayra Santos Febres, among others.

23. Also see Negrón-Muntaner's interview with Luis "Popo" Santiago.

24. See Ramón Grosfoguel's essay, "The Divorce of Nationalist Discourses from the Puerto Rican People: A Sociohistorical Perspective," for a more substantial elaboration of this position.

25. The English translation offered by Carmen C. Esteves is markedly less dramatic and coloquial: "'How terrible! . . . How awful. Such a handsome kid,' said Nati. 'Yes, my dear, queer. That kid turned out queer on poor Tati Almeyda. Yes, she sent him to the Uniteds State, far away to California. That's where people say they're all sent'" (43).

26. I am at present writing an article on Lidia as a lesbian character. To my knowledge, Luis Felipe Díaz is the only other scholar who has suggested as much. He does so in "Ideología y sexualidad en *Felices días, tío Sergio* de Magali García Ramis." Frances Negrón-Muntaner hints at this position in her interview with Magali García Ramis.

27. See Carlos Gil, "Bernardo Vega: un reloj echado al mar y una falsa ruptura," in *El orden del tiempo*, 55-79.

28. See Pedro Juan Soto, *En busca de J.I. de Diego Padró*.

29. On Sánchez and air travel, see Alberto Sandoval Sánchez, "Puerto Rican Identity Up in the Air: Air Migration, Its Cultural Representations, and Me 'Cruzando el Charco.'"

30. In a footnote, Manuel Guzmán claims authorship of the term: "A *sexile* is a neologism of mine that refers to the exile of of those who have had to leave their nations of origins on account of their sexual orientation" (227). I first heard Frances Negrón Muntaner employ the term, and am also familiar with Venezuelan filmmaker Irene Sosa's use. I am not able to ascertain Guzmán's role.

31. Luz María Umpierre's fundamental text continues to be *The Margarita Poems*. Manuel Ramos Otero's oeuvre was mostly centered on questions of homosexuality. See *Cuentos de buena tinta, Invitación al polvo, El libro de la muerte, La novelabingo*, and *Página en blanco y staccato*.

32. Also see his "Towards an Art of Transvestism: Colonialism and Homosexuality in Puerto Rican Literature."

33. Others include Samantha Martínez and Charles Rice-González.

34. In addition to Duberman, see Sylvia's interview with Eric Marcus, "The Drag Queen: Rey 'Sylvia Lee' Rivera," and Michael Musto's article, "Lost in Yonkers."

35. See Marsha Johnson's interview with Karla Jay and Allen Young for more details on STAR.

36. See Maurice Yakowar, *The Films of Paul Morrissey*.

37. For a description of Margarita López's platform, see her statement in *1997 Primary Voter Guide*. On the controversial Antonio Pagán, see his statement in *1997 Primary Voter Guide*, as well as Andrew Jacobs, "Natural Allies? Guess Again" and "Loved and Hated, He Wants To Be Borough President." For a comparison between López and Pagán, see Andrew Praschak, "P.R. Candidates in N.Y. Vie to End Stereotypes."

38. See Richard Goldstein, "Crossover Dreams: Two Gay Candidates Win Where They Weren't Supposed To—In the Barrios."

39. Regarding the primary campaign and vote miscount, see "Race for City Hall" series and articles by Frank Lombardi and Ed Shanahan.

40. Wilson has stated that the reason he uses his mother's maiden name (Cruz) as opposed to his father's Echevarría is that he was afraid to embarrass his father by public disclosure. "Like the closeted homosexual I was, I didn't want to embarrass him. I would have changed my name no matter what, because I knew I would come out to him. For me, it took a few years to come to terms with it. I cannot expect him to be immediately understanding" (quoted in Shister "*My So-Called Life*"). It is interesting, however, to consider his change of name as a refusal of patriarchal authority.

41. See Liskow.

42. See Allan Johnson and "We'll Always Wonder. . ." on the cancellation of the program.

43. Allan Johnson describes the character as "half-black/half Puerto Rican." By "black" one can only assume he means African-American.

44. See Graham, Littlefield, Mendoza, Shister (1994).

45. See Dunning for analysis of *Rent* role.

46. See Shister ("*Rent* Standout"). See Mark Huisman for an insightful analysis of the problem of minority characters vs. white lead stars in Hollywood.

47. In this respect, Luis Aponte-Parés's important contribution to the historiography of Latino gay movements in New York reminds us of the profound difficulties Latinos have had as members of the wider gay and lesbian community.

48. Many of the businesses which comprise the gay and lesbian economic sector in Puerto Rico are owned by Americans. A notable example is *Puerto Rico Breeze*, the only weekly gay newspaper in circulation, founded and owned by Tom Koontz.

49. A significant number of HIV-positive and AIDS-diagnosed individuals travel back and forth from the island to the United States (and vice-versa) for treatment and personal/family reasons. This has led to the establishment of

programs such as "Puente aéreo" or "Air Bridge" to facilitate the process. Moisés Agosto, a national AIDS leader in the United States, comments on this travel (including the arrival of AIDS activism and ACT-UP in Puerto Rico) in *Brincando el charco*.

The Last of the Boricuas
The Conventions of Porn: A Classical Experience
Sandra Quinn

As part of the research for this paper I examined the structural difference between straight and gay pornographic videos. I did a shot-by-shot comparison of two-person penetrative sex scenes from each type of video. The straight scene was from a recent, commercially produced straight porn film, *Latex* (Excalibur, 1995), and the gay scene was from The *Last of the Boricuas* (*Latin Connection* 1994), a gay porn film produced in New York City outside of the regular porn industry.

I counted the four types of shots that were used in both of these films to construct a sex scene. These are: the close-up, the extreme close-up, the medium, and the long shot. I was surprised to find that the percentages of each type of shot were about the same in each film. Although two cases aren't enough to comprise a "scientific" measure, they do have a common sense kind of validity. The result suggests that gay porn and straight porn may be more alike than different, although my purpose was to find ways in which gay and straight porn are unique.

THE GENRE FILM

That genres are identified by their conventions is a commonplace that predates Aristotle and corresponds to a curiosity about what kinds of things there might be in this world. Thomas Sobchack calls the genre film experience a classical experience because of its predictable effects. The particulars of a genre might change, but the structure, characters, and ending remain the same. The genre film retells an old story from a stable of standard plots. The genre film is an imitation, not of life, but of previous films of the same genre.

Pornography, no less than the Western, is manufactured according to an established formula, and it produces its effects as reliably as *Oedipus Rex*. Pornography corresponds to the classics in its concerns with form, the use of well-known plot structures, and of familiar character types. The classical experience reassures the viewer of an ordered world, and this is profoundly important to pornography. Sexuality, with its insistent demands, seems always to threaten to spin out of control. In pornography, a hierarchical narrative formal arrangement brings sexuality into control. This contradicts conventional thinking about porn, because porn is usually disparaged for its weak narrative. But Dyer suggests that pornography is all about narrative, that the male orgasm is in fact the original narrative (*Only Entertainment* 125). Indeed, a graph of the male orgasm, with its gradual ascension, peak and quick descent, is certainly what a graph of the classical drama, or the modern narrative, looks like. Its concern is with a beginning, a middle, and an end; tension, climax, and release.

PORNOGRAPHY AS A FILM GENRE

Richard Dyer avoids defining pornography as a genre, preferring to identify it by its effects rather than its conventions (*Only Entertainment* 121). Still, a definition in terms of formal conventions is useful. The phrase "the conventions of pornography" is tossed around in intellectual and art circles as if those conventions were so obvious they don't need explication, except to the most innocent among us. But I proceed on the assumption that pornographic material, however commonplace, is not everywhere in the environment. For the most part, one still must seek out pornographic products, and therefore the conventions of pornography are not so obvious. I thought of the conventions of pornography as nonrepresentational signs that convey a utopian meaning. I asked how the specific nonrepresentational signs of the genre made me feel. But first, I had to figure out what the conventions are.

THE CONVENTIONS OF PORNOGRAPHY

Parody, what Peter Lehman calls "the importance of fleeting moments of humor in porn," is certainly a staple in the titles of porn vehicles (Lehman 3). Titles in porn often lampoon popular mainstream titles from cinema, television, literature, and pop music. This selection of titles from gay porn is illustrative; *A Subway Named Desire, Spanish*

Harlem Knights, Super Barrio Brothers, Latin Instinct, and *The Last of the Boricuas,* a parody on *The Last of the Mohicans.*

The porn narrative, such as it is, is often a transgressive, parodic (and not in the postmodern, Jamesonian sense of nostalgic, blank parody, but in the sense of parody that remains clearly enough connected an original to suggest something the original leaves out), interpretation of a well-known film or television show. The difficulties of integrating sex scenes into narratives, outside the narrative model of the male orgasm itself, are not that easily worked out. Consequently, it's also a commonplace of porn to give up the parodic tone fairly soon, and allow the viewer to lapse into what Frederic Jameson calls the "rapt, mindless fascination" of the visual, which, he says, is inherently pornographic (1).

In terms of *structure,* it's quite a challenge to think of a single orthodoxy that is true for gay porn that isn't true for straight porn. Obviously, gay porn is about men having sex with men, but the rigid binary of hetero/homo is routinely broken down in straight porn aimed at the male spectator, as well as gay porn. Woman-to-woman sex, as a fetish of masculine desire, has long been a staple of straight porn, and in newer porn it's no longer unheard of for male-to-male sex to be present, though it's not widespread. The very fact that the sexual participants themselves are treated as interchangeable commodities makes the maintenance of rigidly defined and mutually exclusive sexualities difficult.

Commercially produced porn has at least four sex scenes that last a total of an hour. Different actors are featured in each of the sex scenes. When a featured actor is used more than once, the group of actors around him changes from scene to scene.

Linda Williams pointed out the similarities between the film musical and the porn film. The film musical offers musical numbers as interludes that are structurally complete and separate from the narrative. The narrative stops when the musical number begins. Sex in a porn film operates the same as song and dance in a musical, stopping the narrative, such as it may be, to provide an elaborately choreographed sex romp, accompanied with famously bad music, and often with "natural" sounds.

In *Entertainment and Utopia,* Richard Dyer discusses the correspondence between the film musical and a utopian tradition in "Western thought" (Dyer 23). This is another way in which the porn film resembles the musical. The utopias of entertainments provide a vision of what utopia feels like rather than a blueprint of how to make one. They present a sense of how things ought feel, not a representation of how things are. Pornography offers a release from the restrictions and difficulties involved in having sex in real life, and at the same time reassures us that sex, although not for good and all, can be put back where it came from.

Another way pornography is similar to the film musical is in the practice of producing compilation tapes. These are collections of a star's, or a category's, or producer's best sex scenes. Nothing like this really corresponds in mainstream filmmaking. We don't see compilations of John Wayne shootouts, or Bruce Lee kick-fighting. But there are films that are compilations of musical numbers from film musicals, such as the films *That's Entertainment!* (1974), *That's Entertainment, Part II* (1976), and *That's Entertainment! III* (1994).

Linda Williams says that in pornography the problem is sex, and the answer is more sex, but it's sex contained within the classical form. It's also utopian in its displays of sex as an abundance, the consumption of which will make want go away. It has been theorized that consumption as spectacle is the situation that precedes utopia. So the mere existence of pornography suggests that in real life sex is something less than utopian, that it is not the transcendent, spiritual, sacred act it is held out to be.

Simians, Cyborgs, and Porn Stars: Commercially produced pornography in general, and certainly gay pornography in particular, has developed a practice of casting people so shaved, so buffed, so sculpted by silicone and steroids, that they look more the like Disney characters from *Beauty and the Beast* or *Pocahantas* than real people. Beauty's Gastón, in fact, looks more like a gay porn star than any juvenile male lead in a film musical. In the porn industry, he would be called an "A" type; he's drop-dead gorgeous, someone who photographs well, has a big dick, acts "straight," and looks like a "movie star," however problematic that may be considering that the movie star look we're talking about is itself a pure signifier. In order to get a respectable release, there must be at least one "A" person in a porn film. And lots of big dicks. This may be a good place to suggest that, in the manner of a return of the repressed, the prevalence of these cartoon-looking porn stars might contribute to the demand for "amateur" porn, which seldom has "A" people.

It's very common for female porn stars to have breast implants. Buffed, shaved, and surgically sculpted, these female cyborgs are manufactured sex robots. Just like big breasts in straight porn, the big dick is the important staple in gay porn. As Susan Faludi notes, though, other than by circumcision, however, the penis isn't something that can usually be altered by surgical implants, exercise, or make-up. Examples of mechanically improved penises don't abound, but John Wayne Bobbit, with his foray into porn, is probably the closest thing in porn to a truly cyborg male.

Almost all male porn performers, whether in gay or straight porn, act straight. A gay sex performer's stock rises according to his ability to be "straight" acting, on the theory that all gay men are attracted to "straight" men. The corollary to this is that some performers, like Jeff Stryker, a gay porn idol who also crosses over to straight films, must also *act* straight, and act straight when it counts. Acting as the straight "top" is so much of the Stryker mystique that Faludi's discussion of Stryker's masculinity as a divisible "image" for reproduction and resale as commodities (Jeff Stryker's Realistic is the number one selling specialty sex toy) ignores the mystique that was developed for Stryker's gay audiences. Stryker was known in that market for having never performed fellatio, nor having ever been the receptive partner in penetrative anal sex on film. In this phase of late capitalism, such reputations are made in order to be broken down for profit, and Stryker did eventually make a gay porn film in which he did both, and it was a highly anticipated, though disappointing effort. It was disappointing to his fans because the masculine mystique broke down. Stryker's erotic power was diminished. Had he performed fellatio more enthusiastically, had he been penetrated by a bigger dick and "taken it like a man," the masculinity, the acting straight would have remained seamless and coherent. As it was, he seemed timid in the face of mutual male-to-male sex.

Transgression is the secret of porn's power to subvert the dominant order. Straight, let alone gay, porn rarely depicts sex in the context of the heterosexual nuclear family, monogamy, or reproduction.

Sex is distributed through a porn film according to a hierarchy of transgression. The first sex scene is often a one-person jerk-off scene. The next scene is often a two-person oral scene. This may be followed by scenes that introduce toys, or more people, and begin to include penetrative sex.

Although transgressive sex is the norm, scenes that combine violence and penetrative sex are popularly and legally thought to be dangerous, and most commercial producers of sexual entertainment comply with the taboo of combining violence and sex.

In thinking about what this transgressive hierarchy might mean, the words "husbandry" and "parsimony" come to mind. Another way of looking at the hierarchy of transgression is as husbandry—the parceling out of the commodity of sex. This suggests that sex is manageable, rather than dangerous.

The *money shot* and its professional significance is explained by Susan Faludi in her *New Yorker* essay on the porn industry. Quoting: "The on-command male orgasm is the central convention of the industry: all porn scenes should end with a visible ejaculation. . .it is a money shot for all concerned: for the distributors and filmmakers, who believe the largely male audience wants to see what Ira Levine sarcastically calls "the triumph of the dick"; and for the male actors themselves, who are usually paid by "the scene." . . .[But] getting it up isn't the kind of work in which industry guarantees rewards. Quite the contrary, by choosing an erection as the proof of male utility, the male performer has hung his usefulness on the organ that is, as Jonathan Morgan observed, "the one muscle on our body we can't flex." The man must wait for an erection to happen—the agony known in the business as waiting for wood" (Faludi 70).

Linda Williams *suggests that the utopian world of porn is "dissolved" by the insatiable female in straight porn, and the sign for this is the decreasing importance of the money shot in straight porn. I doubt this is true of commercially produced porn; certainly not of gay porn. The money shot is irrefutable *proof* that nothing has been faked, suggesting that the "straight" men having "gay" sex really happened.

The seventh convention, the most obvious convention of pornography, is the use of *pseudonyms*, which are often double entendres. People who are in or who work on porn films, skate on the edge of legality, and have certainly gone over the edge of bourgeois respectability. It is the better part of wisdom for porn workers to use aliases in credits, and in the furtherance of their star system. It is an exquisite irony that the placement, size, and overall treatment of these aliases in the credits are often just as contentious and significant as in mainstream filmmaking.

ANALYSIS OF *THE LAST OF THE BORICUAS*

The Last of the Boricuas both conforms to and deviates from these conventions. Starting with the title, the film "parodies" by troping a title from American frontier literature, although the inspiration came I'm sure from the release of the Daniel Day Lewis film adaptation of *The Last of the Mohicans*, which was released before *The Last of the Boricuas* was made. This film also parodies the ethnographic nature film by the recurring motif of an authoritarian voice-over narrator, and by locating the instinctive, natural man right in the middle of the world's most cosmopolitan city. This film is making a case that the natural state for the natural man is man-to-man sex.

The film opens with a dedication that reads: "This movie is dedicated to all the Boricuas who have the courage to leave Puerto Rico and brave a new life in New York City." Then we see a montage of maps of the Caribbean and Manhattan and hear a voice-over make a parallel between native Boricuas living on a wild island paradise, and the Boricuas who left Puerto Rico for the asphalt jungle island of Manhattan. The voice-over tells us that "neighborhood inbreeding means there will be fewer Boricuas." Logical internal coherence in the framing narrative isn't the strong suit in most porn, so the fact that this statement doesn't make sense is unimportant. It will probably be overlooked, made fun of, or scanned by most viewers. And, although the statement doesn't make ordinary sense, it does make sense as an imprecise reference to "inbreeding" as man-to-man sex (strongly suggesting that all men are brothers), to the practice in queer culture of referring to heterosexual people who have children as "breeders," and to the condition of "ghettoizing" the Other(s) in contemporary cities.

Although the film says that the problem of the Boricuas in Manhattan is that there are fewer of them, the problem of the Boricuas depicted in the film is to find a place to stay after being released from prison. This film suggests that the barrio is a place where gangs are the equivalent of native tribes, and imprisonment by the colonizer is part of the routine complex of problems. Sex is a way to situate a utopia of sex, but also of brotherly love, right in the middle of the barrio.

Strong gang presence combined with the Latino cultural/sexual mores scuttles any attempt to read this film strictly for its gay cultural signifiers. In Latino culture a man may penetrate another man he feminizes, and not identify himself as gay. In this film, however, male-to-male sex takes place between Latino men of equal social power without either man being marked or identified in any way as gay. As Comacho says, "I love sex, man," without distinguishing the sex of the partners with whom he loves to have sex.

It is possibly a felicitous coincidence for the makers of this film that the tough youth is a stereotype of gay erotic fantasy. All the performers in this film are "rough," and one street tough, blurring the boundaries between fiction and real life, identifies himself as a gang member, and displays his signifiers, including a Latin King tattoo on his chest. But all of the performers, whether read as gang members or not, are tough.

This film offers a bizarre utopianism, in that it doesn't invite outsiders to participate (there are no seductive looks directed at the camera), but only to observe the intensity of the feeling these boys have for each other.

The first sex scene in the film is a four-person circle jerk and takes place in an abandoned school building. The performers largely ignore each other, paying more attention to the straight porn magazines they're looking at. The magazines let you know that these guys are straight. Being straight liberates them to be more affectionate with each other than is often seen in gay porn. All of the guys in this film are uncircumcised and their bodies are unshaved. They were all clearly selected for their penis sizes, however.

"Wild Sound" is a term used in film production for "natural" sounds that are not designed to be part of a film's sync-sound strategy. It refers to any of the sounds that are heard in the general environment in which a scene takes place.

The sound track for this scene and the next one is wild sound from the streets! In most porn, when sex starts, music starts. The sync-sound track is also often mixed in for the slurps and sighs, but wild sound, the sounds of a neighborhood, that's distinctive. Children playing, dogs barking, whistles, horns, auto-engines, moms calling, (basket)balls bouncing over close-ups of penetration—are not the usual sounds of porn.

There is an establishing sequence that starts with a long shot of the Roosevelt Island cable car coming into the station. The gangmember gets on this car and looks at another guy on the car. This sequence lasts for several minutes, and is shot from the inside of the cable car. After the characters are established, the footage shows what is seen from the moving car. It's reminiscent of one of the crane shots from Wem Wenders's *Wings of Desire* (1987). The camera tracks over a billboard advertising DKNY, a traffic jam on the freeway, well-kept parks and apartment buildings, and a sailboat on a river. But what makes this effect so much like *Wings of Desire* is the sound track. The sounds of people inside the cable car are used throughout this sequence, and the effect is like the undifferentiated mass of human voices the angels hear when they swoop over human congregations in *Wings of Desire*. You can't even tell what language is being spoken.

After the car arrives at the station, the street tough follows the other guy and asks him, "Don't I know you from prison?" The two go to the street tough's sister's house to "chill out" and have sex. This scene is in Spanish and English, and uses an excellent original musical score, written for the film by a group called Barrio Beat.

Two things are highly unusual in this film. First, the character of the street tough is quite memorable. In all the scenes where he appears he speaks Spanish and English. He has an intense dramatic quality that is produced by the combination of good looks, a sad expression of serious concern, and this use of language that seems to exhort his friends to hold on to their culture. If you look closely, you can see that his front teeth are missing. He doesn't smile through the entire movie. He can act a little, and improvise pretty well, and he alone of the ten performers gamely maintains the Boricua theme throughout his performance.

Improvisation is mixed in this film with scripted dialogue, and the improvisation works out by far the best. Through improvisation, individual characteristics emerge more than is usually the case in pornography, where the rule, even in complicated plots, is that actors represent stereotypes, not characters. After all, the biggest acting challenge to a porn actor is usually just acting straight.

The music in this film is far and away superior to the music used in most porn films. The entire sound mix, whether containing music or not, evidences a carefully elaborated aural aesthetic. Even where only natural sound is used, it's never just the camera sync-sound. The street sounds and other nondialogue tracks are not cut with the picture, which means that a sound track was designed for those scenes even where music isn't used.

The third sex scene is a one-person jerk-off scene shot with a new character in studio limbo. This scene's primary connection with the Boricua/Puerto Rican theme is achieved by someone who walks into the scene with a Puerto Rican flag (to signify that he is a new immigrant), challenges the feature performer to prove how sexy he is, and then exits. The music used in this scene is more original "Barrio Beat" music.

The subsequent sex scene is also a one-person jerk-off scene with a warehouse guard, who comes back in the next scene as a prison guard. The segue to the next sex scene is a musical interlude. Three "Boricuas" sit on a cot in jail cell. A guard watches them. They break out in a beautiful three-part harmony.

Next, the street tough picks up someone on the street. They go to the sister's house and look at gay porn magazines. Pornography is often used in this film, but this is the only scene where it is gay porn. The pickup asks the street tough "what's that on your tit," and is told "that's my Latin Kings' earring." The two-person scene that follows is scored with what sounds like the Barrio Beat doing Japanese music. Aside from the unexpected music, this scene is noteworthy for a "docking" scene, which is a sexual practice that isn't often seen in U.S. porn. In docking, each partner pulls his foreskin over the head of the other's penis.

Another jerk-off scene follows. This guy is supposedly thinking about having sex with some woman he just spoke to on the phone. The scene starts out with natural sound, but gives way to Barrio Beat music that is scored to match the scene's mood of regret rather than the action of the scene. Highly unusual.

It would be an interesting to explore further the ways in which Latino men of equal social power engage in male-to-male sex without being "queer" identified, and also how that creates a contradiction for the filmmakers who must position this film commercially. While gay and straight porn may have a lot in common, they are not so much alike that they can fail to fit into one of these larger categories in the porn boutique. It is surely an unintended irony that what is represented as "natural," unrepressed human sexuality (that just happens to be between virile young men), and which is surely a more true depiction of sexuality in Latino culture than an expressly gay film would be, must be mislabeled for the anglicized sex market.

The film ends with a reprise of all the sex cut to excellent Barrio Beat music. When the ending credits begin there's a take of the director and the street tough standing together on the cable car, arm in arm. The grinning director wears the T-shirt the street tough wore in his last scene; the street tough summons a rather sad closed-mouth smile, and flashes a peace sign.

Despite achieving high degress of individualism, the characters in the film are also stereotypical. They are unintentionally so, yet at the same time it's possible the Latin Connection are taking advantage of this stereotype to achieve some benefit from commodity culture, to which they have restricted access. This assumes the intended market for the film is those (white people) who fetishize the young street tough, dark skin or both.

In the film's diegesis, white people don't exist at all. White viewers are not invited to participate in this film through an easily achieved identification with any of its characters. Few white people are represented in the film. This is an underworld where few white people exist (except for *some* drag queens, and even then only as decorative excess). Manhattan becomes a city of Latin brotherly love.

Yet white people do exist here in an odious way, in an overworld, which is amply represented symbolically. The great projects of patriarchy—the public transportation systems, river navigation, the buildings and billboards—are the works and possessions of powerful others. Projects that have outlived their purposes have been abandoned to the rats, the ravages, and the Ricans.

Still, the film deftly negotiates several cultures and stereotypes. In order to be any kind of success at all, the film had to be marketed, and was, through the well-established distribution system for pornography. That means the film couldn't be marketed exclusively "for" Latinos. Part of its appeal had to be consciously made to American white gay male culture, and its marketing took place through the existing systems of commerce in pornography.

Within the film, white gay male homosexuality doesn't even exist. What does exist is brotherly love, almost incestuous brotherly love, as the film's voice over clumsily explains in the very beginning of the film. The only sexuality is heterosexuality. In identifying transgressive sex as one of the conventions of pornography, the irony of the heterosexual presumption is exquisite. Not only are all the players in this gay film heterosexual, but they wind themselves up for their transgressive sexual encounters by looking at pictures or videotapes of one man and one woman having regular old missionary style sex. Man-to-man sex appears to be a release of an excess of masculinity. These boys are too much man for mere women, and must requite their voracious sexual appetites with men. Only a man is man enough for the intensity of sex these men demand.

The Last of the Boricuas creates a space in which these boys are free to show extraordinary affection, love, and tenderness towards each other. Love is not represented in pornography with enough frequency to amount to much. Few films would lend themselves to it as easily as this one does. As survivors of oppressive control systems, these characters have a common bond of struggle that allows their affections to grow unbounded, unobserved, and unremarked upon. Their mutual commitment is itself transgressive in this world.

Living within traditional gay male culture is, as John Waters says, as oppressive as living in heterosexual culture (Delaup). Gay culture is a bubbling cauldron of expectations and oppressions, because it is a political culture with a very intense and important agenda. Even though many gay porn films provide some release from the intensity of gay community through fugues of sex, the codes of gay culture are still apparent in most gay porn films, both intentionally and unintentionally. Very often a character in gay porn will represent a "straight" man, and very often the acting fails utterly, as an unintentional coding mishap. In *The Last of the Boricuas* the characters succeed at "straight" acting because they don't belong to a culturally defined sexually "other" category.

In "The Role of Stereotypes" Richard Dyer makes a distinction between the representation in narrative of social types and stereotypes. Social types are those who belong within a culture; social types are "us." Stereotypes are outcasts; stereotypes are "them." While the deployment of stereotypes is a convenient shorthand for "reading" an Other, what is important is who gets to define the stereotype. It's also important to consider how the stereotype of the Latino street tough is being used. *The Last of the Boricuas* defies the stereotype of the Latino street tough by depicting genuine brotherly affection. Whether this defiance has any effect is a function of how much it can actually challenge received definitions of the stereotype of the Latino male youth. Like genre, the stereotype offers a dramatic device with enormous potential for subversion, as Dyer says, by constructing the character as a stereotype "at the level of dress, performance, etc." But giving the character a "narrative function that is not implicit in the stereotype. . .[throws] into question the assumptions signaled by the stereotypical iconography" (Images 15). This film does emphatically take on the dominant definition of the stereotype. That begs the question of whether the porn film is an effective platform for making this challenge. This seems to me a problem that many deeply subversive works face. The larger mainstream culture will of course ignore or handily minimize critiques of it.

Given the power of gay culture itself, and its influence on mainstream culture, it's tempting to suppose that the gay porn film is an effective way to make this kind of statement. The critique of stereotype made in *The Last of the Boricuas* is not difficult to read, and surely any viewer who sees it will understand it. If that's so, it has more actual power to influence thought than the Unabomber Manifesto, for example, which is a subversive text that poses some very pressing concerns, yet few people have actually read it because it has been effectively repressed by our collective, and mediated, horror at the crimes of Ted Kaczinski. At least gays can be depended upon to support their local porn shops.

Also, I don't want to rhapsodize the deployment of stereotypes in *The Last of the Boricuas* because while the film is subversive, its representation of heterosexuality as naturally superior is problematic. In this respect, *The Last of the Boricuas* isn't very far from *Midnight Cowboy*, except that "queers, fags, and homos" exist in the Manhattan of *Midnight Cowboy*. They don't even exist as outcasts by the outcasts in *The Last of the Boricuas*. Gay people don't exist any more than white people do. Maybe that's a statement in itself, though. After all, it is useless to distinguish these polar sexualities "when in reality both heterosexual and homosexual responses and behavior are to some extent experienced by everybody in their life" (16). And traditional gay culture is, as already said, as oppressive as, and complicit with dominant white male heterosexual mainstream culture.

Pornography is, by its very nature, by its preference for depicting transgressive sex, itself transgressive, if not political. But it is transgressive at the same time that it reinscribes patriarchal values. While it transcends the rules about who may have sex with whom and how, it glorifies power, though not always in the body of the male.

The dynamic of power and pleasure is intricate, and implicated in what makes sex erotic. S & M practices recognize this. So does Foucault. Patriarchal authorities he says, function with the double impetus of pleasure and power:

> The pleasure that comes of exercising a power that questions, monitors, watches, spies, searches out, palpates, brings to light; and on the other hand, the pleasure that kindles at having to evade this power, flee from it, fool it, or travesty it. The power that lets itself be

invaded by the pleasure it is pursuing; and opposite it, power asserting itself in the pleasure of showing off, scandalizing, or resisting. (45)

Looked at this way, it is obvious that in the commitment to transgression, we do nothing more than engage patriarchy in an endless erotic *pas de deux*. Perhaps the true binary poles of erotics are not heterosexual and homosexual, but power and resistance. Maybe it is what my shot-by-shot analysis showed, after all. An old friend once rebuked me when I expressed shock that he was having sex with men and women indifferently. "What's the problem?" he said, "sex is sex."

Queering the Mexican Stage
Theatrical Strategies in Xavier Villaurrutia
Kanishka Sen

*The deviant culture of homosexuality has ways of making
fun of the "normative" culture around it, by virtue of its
normative characteristics. Then normality bercomes
strang and invites ridicule. To call a straight person
a "vanilla het" is a double insult. But more disturbing
is to refuse the preferred labels of either. This is an
inherently political challenge.*

—Tisdale 74

Xavier Villaurrutia (1903-50) is one of the foremost representatives of
experimental theater in Mexico, and his plays rely on different
strategies to locate subversive themes within an antiestablishment
framework with a tendency to create ambiguities and multiple interpretations. He is outstanding in his pioneering efforts to address issues that
are "illegitimate" and "invisible" in the official discourse propagated by
post-revolutionary governments of Mexico.

This paper focuses on reappropriating monolithic straight
narratives in *Invitación a la muerte* (Invitation to Death; 1940) which
have been categorized by critics as complex, abstract, and strange. I
will analyze the dramatic text and suggest a wide range of possibilities
for subversion, resistance, or resignification. Queer theory is particularly relevant here, as it provides a firm base to highlight the different
antistraight manifestations that take exception to the customary
"normal" expectations of patriarchal society.

One of my concerns in this paper is to challenge normalizing and
universalizing tendencies that conventional critics have asserted over

the last two decades in analyzing *Invitación a la muerte*. Concomitantly it would be only appropriate to incorporate legitimization of any "deviance," sexual or nonsexual, to create a tradition of resistance within the official discourse Alexander Doty explains so eloquently: "Queer texts/textual elements, then, are those discussed with reference to a range of network of nonstraight ideas. The queerness in these cases might combine the lesbian, the gay, and the bisexual, or it might be a textual queerness not accurately described even by a combination of these labels" (xviii). It is this built-in flexibility of queer theory that can destabilize the monolithic narratives and provide a chance to create alternative interpretations of straight texts.

It isn't necessary to believe every word published by the expert critics on how Villaurrutia's theatrical production is so tragic or abstract—adjectives that indicate the fossilized presumptions such critics have. Almost every critical analysis produced by established intellectuals would predictably rely on conventional heterosexual norms. The reluctance towards a queer interpretation of any cultural text is quite evident from the fact that such interpretations are still considered morally disruptive and are taken up by the patriarchal power structures only gingerly (one cannot but remember that even TV channels like Public Broadcasting Service (PBS), which takes pride in running greater risks in programming shows "politically dangerous" documentaries only at "certain hours" at night).

Even well known critics like Frank Dauster have adopted a decontextualized and superficial approach. There have been few attempts to question the fixed hierarchies of identities or highlight the nuances of the subtexts in the play. The critics have engaged in a perfunctory analysis of the tragic theatrical roles of the characters, while the play has been marked as a "provocative adaptation of Hamlet" (77). While Dauster makes various careful observations on the "strange" and "tormented" character of Alberto, he avoids making any investment in the homoerotic relation between Alberto and Horacio. It is not my intention to prove that Villaurrutia offers a creative and unalienated space for the gay characters in this play—far from it. The critical point here is to expose the invisible texts that provide a space for representation of the "unspeakable" queer desire, and problematize it through a series of textual strategies that we shall discuss in the following pages.

Invitación a la muerte was first staged in 1947 in the Palacio de Bellas Artes, Mexico, but it was never a commercial success. In addition, it was dismissed by critics as a complex and metaphysical piece of work that was ahead of its time. In the play, Alberto owns a funeral home. Horacio (who had been employed before as a tailor) works for him, while sharing with him an intimate emotional relationship. Alberto is a frail, sensitive, and pale young man who spends most of his time in complete solitude, trying to communicate with the father who abandoned him many years before. Aurelia is the daughter of an old employee in the funeral home and is supposedly Alberto's fiancée. Alberto lives with his mother, but he does not have an amicable relationship with her because she is having an affair with a man. The play is full of insinuations, and it catalogues selective actions and codified gestures, thus offering problematic images of subversive erotic desires, without trying to portray any explicit gay sexuality.

One of the key points of this paper is to create legitimacy for a set of representations of antistraight discourses. In order to create contestatorial positions, we must question the relationship between Alberto, Aurelia, and Horacio, because it is the constant negotiating between these characters that provides the basic framework of our analysis. It is necessary to interrogate the form and content of the visible narratives as represented by these characters to enunciate the invisible subtexts that surface in the "master narratives."

My objective is to create a framework that differs from previous forms of cultural critique because of the ways in which it seeks to recover the invisible subtexts and to problematize the so-called homogenous affiliations of the characters. In *Invitación a la muerte*, Villaurrutia locates queer images of the two male characters through specific dynamics basic to experimental theater (for example, the elaborate sets, curtains, and effective use of light and shadow), in order to emphasize an increasing bonding between Alberto and Horacio from the very outset. Their friendship has no trappings of an explicit gay relationship based on specific genital acts, but it is a relationship that on the one hand prioritizes an intimate emotional bonding between them, while on the other hand interrogates and even neglects the "legitimate" heterosexual relationship between Alberto and Aurelia.

In a world where any antistraight manifestation, either sexual or nonsexual, is a reason for exclusion, ridicule, and persecution from compulsory heterosexual institutions, Alberto's preference for Horacio can be considered as a threat to the patriarchy by producing a certain discomfort in the straight audience, as Horacio dares to express his intense feelings for Alberto. Alberto is spontaneous and emotional every time he meets Horacio alone, whereas his reaction to Aurelia can be surmised as a rather cold, formal, and unwanted desire. Aurelia, on the other hand, prefers to be in the company of both Horacio and Alberto, although she doesn't hide her displeasure at the intimate trust that they share. Dauster talks about the "amorphous state of nonbeing" (82) experienced by Alberto in the absence of Horacio, but fails to suggest that it is likely because of his secret erotic desire for Horacio and his disinterest in Aurelia.

The play focuses on the problem of visibility of queer desire that can exist only as a marginalized and oppressed element through furtive glances, gestures, and formalized rituals like spying. Chipping away at the repeated act of spying practiced both by Horacio and Alberto, the play offers a strategy for an erotic reinscription of pleasurable and problematic desires. The very act of spying constitutes an act of transgression that legitimizes the representation of the male body, as both Horacio and Alberto can construct, project, and fantasize their object of desire through secret glances. Alberto is categorized as a strange, pathetic individual who suffers from some unknown problem that is inexplicable and unspeakable. On the one hand, the relationship between Alberto and Aurelia is unsuccessful, as it does not achieve any harmony in terms of romance, intimacy, or pleasure. Thus, it repudiates the universalistic notion of compulsory heterosexuality that legitimizes only a relation between a man and a woman as "successful." On the other hand, the relationship between Horacio and Alberto is dismissed as a vain attempt, a defect, a doomed project. Alberto is forced to represent a pale, alienated individual, and although not overtly represented as a homosexual, he has all the trappings of a stereotypical homosexual character constructed as a hysterical and emotionally unstable individual. Nicholas de Jongh notes: "For it was one of the controlling myths about homosexuality, retailed for most of this century, that emotionalism and nervousness were stereotypical signs of homosexuality, while emotion repressed or denied approvingly was reckoned a sign of the ideal male" (28).

According to Nicholas de Jongh: "In the period 1925-58, since homosexuality is reckoned as the archetype of evil, the triumphalism of the Christian ethic, so beloved of the commercial theater, is ensured. Suicide, alcoholism, murder, mental breakdown, death, imprisonment, ostracism, blackmail, or mere misery are the ends to which homosexuals are brought at a play's lysis. Most of the protagonists are victims of negative emotions engendered by shame, fear, guilt, bewilderment, depression or hysteria" (3). Villaurrutia seems to have been forced to present a similar representation in Alberto who confesses to experiencing "un deseo de huir de todo y de todo, una sed que seca las palabras, paraliza los gestos" (365),[1] and thus offers internal exile as the only possible space where he can survive and reinvent himself. He is projected as a jealous individual who suffers from hysterical bouts, which make him susceptible to be categorized as strange. The family doctor observes that "Y esto es lo que me inquieta en el caso de Alberto; no poder hallar su punto vulnerable: los nervios, el corazón, qué sé yo" (368).[2] It is a strategy that locates Alberto within a framework that refuses to be categorized, and through a series of irregular patterns and behavior, it creates new sets of associations or impressions. As such, it provides a vantage point for Alberto to reinvent himself, through manipulation of the oppressive medical and juridical discourses. To be sure, there is a series of elements that posit separation, loss, and displacement between Horacio and Alberto. Yet at the same time, there is also an affirmation of homoerotic desire, as we find Horacio expressing his desire for Alberto in these terms: "siento algo así como un placer nuevo, como un calosfrío" (378).[3] The furtive glances of Alberto constitute acts of transgression and are means by which he can recognize his object of desire and can reconstitute himself. The male characters have access to a sexual looking that legitimizes same-sex desire, hinting tantalizingly at the possible erotic union between the two characters.

The frequent allusion to the act of spying behind the curtains problematizes the visibility of a gay character who is forced to reside within a framework of exile and seclusion: "Una cortina logra que estés en un lugar sin estar visible, envuelto en una pared delgada, blanda y buena conductora de la voz" (378).[4] Elsewhere we are presented with a detailed description of the mysterious atmosphere that prevails over the scene of action: "Se oye perceptiblemente el ruido de la puerta del fondo. Entra alguien que se mueve con cautela. La sombra del fondo impide ver quién es el que con toda clase de precauciones se desliza y se adelanta hasta el primer término" (366).[5]

Richard Dyer explains the idea of authorship and legitimacy in a lesbian/gay text: "They are about claiming the right to speak as lesbian/ gay, claiming a special authority for their image of lesbianism/gayness because it is produced by people who are themselves lesbian/gay. They do this in different ways; their doing so reintroduces the problem of the social construction of homosexuality; and they also often indicate that they know something of the problem" ("Believing in Fairies" 196). Villaurrutia stresses on the marginality of the gay male subject reappropriating the in-built ambiguities of straight language that is expressed explicitly in Horacio's discourse: "Yo no tengo culpa de que nuestro idioma se preste a estas lamentables confusiones" (354).[6] By refusing to marry Aurelia, and by refusing to comply with his mother's wishes of leading a compulsory heterosexual life, Alberto steps out of the realm of meaningless degradation and the conventional responsibilities of heterosexist society.

In scene VI of the second act, Alberto expresses his frustration and despair at being marginalized, as well as the necessity of being alone to reinvent himself for survival: "porque desde pequeño he tenido que ir descorriendo con mis propias manos las cortinas que se interponen siempre entre la realidad y yo, entre la verdad y yo; pero sucede, Horacio, que, las más de las veces, al descorrer una cortina encuentro que delante de mí, se presenta otra y otra, y que la duda sigue y que la verdad parece huir delante de mis pasos que se fatigan" (377).[7]

The funeral home operates to contextualize the "unspeakable" desire that Alberto nurtures for Horacio. First of all, it provides a basic space where the gay character can survive as an individual, though censored and stigmatized. The whole atmosphere of death, alienation and strangeness heightens and confronts the homophobia of dominant straight discourse. It also offers a cultural space that problematizes same-sex desire while focusing on the viewer's attention on the tyranny of the so-called center, the patriarchy.

In scene VIII of the Second Act, Aurelia enters the stage looking for Alberto, and to her utter disappointment, finds him in the company of Horacio. She is visibly upset as she observes, "Buenas tardes, Horacio. No esperaba encontrarlo aquí a estas horas, pero al entrar en el vestíbulo me salió al encuentro el gato y al acariciarlo saltó sobre la mesa y cayó, precisamente como si lo hubiera hecho exprofeso, sobre un abrigo y un sombrero que reconocí en seguida como suyos" (379-80).[8]

The visual allusion to a cat (and her ironical reference to the intentions of the cat) by Aurelia is the context for her biased straight vision, which questions any intimacy between the two men. She fails to understand why two men should be sharing their sentiments at "ciertas horas," which exposes the kind of baggage and preconceptions that the straight audiences apply when interpreting such texts. At this very moment the two men share a quick glance that provides them with an empowering experience. By the same token their erotic desire is symbolically represented through the prolonged embrace that is but one part of homoerotic representation. To Aurelia, far from representing any emotional expression, the embrace is simply incomprehensible: "El abrazo de los jóvenes se prolonga. Aurelia no comprende" (381).[9] What is at issue here is that both Alberto and Horacio are claiming a special authority for their gayness through gestures and eye contact that focuses the viewer's attention on the problem of the social construction of homoerotic desire.

All of these suggestive and oblique references to the relationship between Horacio and Alberto offer a space for heightening queer desire and representations. Horacio openly confesses his desire for Alberto: "¿Sabes Alberto? No te imaginas cómo a tu lado dejo de ser yo mismo; . . .y me siento arrastrado por tus palabras, cediendo a la invitación de tu pensamiento, abandonándome a una corriente cuyo rumbo desconozo" (378).[10] Nevertheless, for the most part, the narrative structures, far from celebrating union, offer a sense of culpability, separation, and total alienation. Alberto and Horacio fail to establish any kind of legitimate family, as opposed to the conventional heterosexual concept of family, while Horacio sums up the problematics of any kind of emotional bonding in a homophobic society as follows: "Estamos condenados a una prisión perpetua." (402).[11] This kind of fatalist attitude can perhaps be explained in the words of David William Foster:

> We have the impression that Latin American writers have accepted various contemporary hypotheses concerning sexuality and the many dimensions of homosexuality as one form the expression of sexuality may take, while their commentators continue to be tied to a patronizing view of the subject as an unfortunately acute form of psychological and social deviance that can only result in tragic or grotesque emplotments. (*Gay and Lesbian Themes* 3)

In *Invitación a la muerte*, homoerotic desire is both absent and present: absent as in the biased monolithic vision of the doctor, of the mother, or of Aurelia, for the gay subject seems invisible and is assumed not to exist. Yet the gay subject is also present, in the sense that its physicality is cloaked in various narrative strategies and ambiguities that for nongay constituencies might seem to be an adjunct of marginality. Alberto is unable to express his emotions overtly and must reinvent himself through internal exile and solitude while trying to displace the straight notions of the world in which he lives. Central to the representation of queer desire is the funeral home that provides a space where transgression of heterosexual definitions is encouraged through clandestine manifestations like spying. Nevertheless, the protagonists of this alternative homoerotic desire, unlike their hetero counterparts, do not end up coming together. In the words of Thomas Waugh, they "just wander off looking horny, solitary, sad or dead." (145) Alberto still feels guilty and sick: "contagio como un leproso con mi roce, y más aún con mi sola presencia" (378).[12] The implications of this culpability is that he must reside only within a framework of alienation: "Sólo entonces comprenderán por qué busco la compañía de este lugar, de este ambiente, de estas cajas llenas de vacío, que no tienen más objeto que encerrar para siempre el silencio de todos" (366).[13]

Invitación a la muerte is about claiming the right to speak in terms of queer structures of feeling. The ambiguity ingrained in Villaurrutia's text helps the male characters to express their homoerotic desire on a solid ground. The queerness of these characters, while on an external and visible level they seem to project a pathetic sensibility of homoerotic desire, subverts the heterosexist obsession for categorizing desire in terms of easy, safe constructs that often prove to be a source of false expectations and disillusionment. On the one hand, we are aware of the heterosexist oppression that attempts to catalogue queer desire in terms of absurd and pathetic medical categories, and on the other, we see how Alberto fights oppression by trying to form a community with Horacio. Thus, there is an articulation of queer presence forged through resistance to heterosexist society. What we have here is a set of cultural strategies of survival for homoerotic desire. Issues of sexual gaze, fetishism, and melancholia arise in the depiction of intimacy between the male protagonists.

But the play does not simply indulge the pleasure of looking; it problematizes such pleasure by questioning the "visible" and "normal" expectations and positions of the straight audience, thus focusing on the dialectic of seeing and being seen. The world that emerges from dispersed desire is one in which desire and despair run together, and how desire can often entail rituals of mourning. Villaurrutia forces us to take exception to a world of ready-made meanings by obscuring homoerotic desire, by inflicting fissures in the dramatic text and shattering the "normal" bourgeois expectations.

By projecting Alberto as a personality difficult to perceive in terms of monolithic medical categorizations, Villaurrutia creates a cultural category resistant to compulsory heterosexual conventions because abstract characterizations represent defiance toward speaking reasonably and logically that the straight audience would demand and expect in their analysis. What *Invitación a la muerte* showcases is an agenda of energetic opposition to mainstream straight culture. Homophobia and heterosexism are exposed through the deliberate alienation of Alberto and Horacio while there is a conspicuous absence of any coming-out theme.

In conclusion, one can say that *Invitación a la muerte* traces moments when dissident subjects disrupt the social hegemonic text as well as attempts to identify legitimate homoerotic agendas that confront the diverse configurations of "forms of life" that are considered "natural." Considering the homophobic attitude of the Mexican society that prevailed during the entire lifetime of Villaurrutia (and is still very much conspicuous in contemporary Mexico) and Villaurrutia's own conflicts with his sexuality, it is no surprise that we do not find an explicit characterization of homoerotic desire. Nevertheless, *Invitación a la muerte* succeeds in providing a space for suppressed discourses of gay male characters, which, in their struggle for interpretive power, achieve considerable visibility.

NOTES

1. A desire to flee from everything, a thirst that dries up words and paralyzes gestures.

2. And this is what leaves me perplexed in Alberto's case; not being able to locate his vulnerablility: his nerves, his heart, I just don't understand.

3. I can feel a new kind of pleasure, it gives me goose-flesh.

4. A curtain allows you to remain invisible, wrapped up in a thin, soft wall that serves as a good conductor of voice.

5. A rumble so soft is heard near the inner door. Somebody enters and moves with caution. The inner shadows makes any recognition of the stranger impossible, who slips through and moves well inside.

6. I am not to be blamed for such unfortunate confusions that our language suffers.

7. Because ever since my childhood I have had to draw back curtains that come in between the reality and myself, between the truth

and myself; but, nevertheless, every time I draw a curtain only to find yet another one, and the doubt keeps bothering me; the truth seems to be eluding form me, leaving me fatigued.

8. Good evening, Horacio. I was not expecting you here at these hours, but as I was passing through the hallway, the cat bumped into me and as I caressed it, it jumped on to the table and fell quite intentionally on a coat and a hat. I could tell immediately they were yours.

9. The young men remain embraced for quite some time. Aurelia does not understand.

10. You know what Alberto, you cannot imagine how I am not myself when you are with me. I feel myself being dragged into your words, surrendering myself to your thoughts, drifting away towards a current of unknown destination.

11. We are condemned to an eternal prison house.

12. I infect others like a leper, with my touch, even with my mere presence.

13. Only then will you understand why I look forward to be in this place, seek refuge in this setting among these empty coffins that only serve to bury the silence forever.

The Dialectics of Homoeroticism in Cuban Narrative

José B. Alvarez IV
Translated by Christina A. Buckley

El poder siempre busca un antagonismo con algún estrato de la sociedad. El homosexual es una persona que cuestiona el medio donde vive.[1]

—Guillermo Cabrera Infante

How oppressed people and minorities are treated is a meassure of a society.

—Marvin Leinier

Por lo visto, un buen marxista, además de saberse El Capital, *tiene que exhibir un impecable sistema endocrino. Al Partido se pertenece en cuerpo y alma. Lo del cuerpo incluye los genitales y el orificio excretorio.*[2]

—Carlos Montaner

REVOLUTIONARY CONSCIENCE

The arrival of what in retrospect we can designate as the ideological Cuban revolutionary process is much more than a mere political reorganization—from a rightist government to a leftist one; from a politico-economic dependence upon U.S. capitalism to a dependence upon Marxist-Leninist socialism, dominated by the Soviet Union; from

a community based on strong family ties to the catastrophic separation
caused by the exile of thousands of citizens. Fundamentally, for each
individual who decided to stay, or had no other option but to stay on the
Island and, consequently, for all those who were born in the following
years, January 1, 1959 marks the beginning of a new identity. I am not
referring here to the Cuban nation as a totalizing entity, but rather we
want to bring the concept of *identity* to an individual and personal level,
where each citizen must accept diverse roles but always under the
official rubric of "revolutionary," one which takes on different shades
and nuances with the passing of time in accordance with the specific
historical period to which the term is applied. The social parameters
that the State establishes, oftentimes by enacting laws and legal codes,
indicate that the Cuban citizen cannot assume his or her own *conscience*, as the Hebrew theorist Tzvi Medin would say. The ideological
apparatus that will rule over the Cuban people after 1959 had already
begun to take shape with the guerrilla wars in the Sierra Maestra. As is
well known, in those initial years of insurgence, formal indoctrination
tactics, particularly of the Marxist-Leninist type, did not exist, yet a
practical dialectic did: agrarian reform for the campesino, improvement
of the quality of life, literacy, and public health programs, all part of the
possibility of achieving real change that for the first time would benefit
the marginalized economic classes.

Even after Fidel Castro taook power, there existed no rigorous
government plan nor established ideology in Cuba, but rather the notion
that the path would be established "en plena marcha" [along the way].
It is for this reason that in 1961, after only two years and four months
of revolutionary power, without consultation with the people and
without any previous historical precedence, the construction of a new
socialist identity was hastily decided; that is, "la construcción de lo que
no existe, o que aún no tiene existencia predominante en la sociedad
civil" (Fleites-Lear y Patterson 55).[3] With reason Fleites-Lear and
Patterson ask themselves:

> ¿Cómo puede cambiarse en realidad la historia de golpe y porrazo?,
> ¿cómo puede uno acostarse convencido de que ha defendido una
> revolución democrática para levantarse a defender el comunismo que
> ni siquiera conoce? (55)[4]

To bring the previous observations to the specific theme of
revolutionary conscience and identity with which we are concerned, we

could ask ourselves: how is it possible that all of a sudden the people, by means of unilateral mandate, must conform to adopting a new conscience and a new identity, both in a communal and individual sense. This mandate is accompanied by a system of state entities that were put into operation to mold the identity of and to control the Cuban citizens. The task that the Revolution proposes is monumental; in effect it aims to eliminate and replace prerevolutionary "cancers"—for instance, parochial schools in which thousands of children were educated under the watchful eye of the Catholic Church were replaced by a comprehensive education system controlled by the state—in order to, in turn, establish a new culture based on Marxist-Leninist precepts.[5] Cuban leaders utilized pedagogical strategies to foster the development of a new revolutionary conscience. From early on various entities are created in order to put into practice the ideological conceptualization of the moment: the Institute of Art and Cinema (ICAIC), which produces and brings didactic documentaries, newsreels, and other films to the masses were created on March 24, 1959; the Organization of Pioneers and the system of educational scholarships for students of all ages, from young children to University students, was established; the Committee for the Defense of the Revolution (CDR) was founded to function at the block level, organizing the community in small sections in order to better control the population,[6] and with the specific capacity to invade the private space of each citizen; the Literacy Campaign was organized in 1960 and was initiated one year later with the dispersion of the newly trained Volunteer Teachers to the most remote areas of the island with the dual purpose of teaching reading and facilitating the inculcation of the new ideological thought; the Armed Forces (FAR) and the National Military were organized in 1960, replacing the previous military regime and the troops of the 26th of July Movement with young people trained under the new regime.

At the level of mass media, Radio Rebelde was inaugurated, a radio station that during the years of the Sierra Maestra guerrilla served clandestinely to report insurgent activity; the print press was officially organized under the shadow of the Journalism of the Revolutionary Front in March of 1961, along with the closing before June of 1960 of the newspapers *Diario de la marina, Prensa libre, El país*, and *Diario nacional y Excélsior*, all associated with the incumbent government, in order to make room for the dailies *Hoy, Revolución*, and later *Verde olivo, Trabajadores*, and *Granma*, among others. All of these mechanisms of ideological indoctrination yielded positive results in the first ten years of the Revolution. However, beginning in the 1970s, the previous propaganda became intensified and was accompanied as well by a greater degree of repression and censorship. In *Cuba: The Shaping of Revolutionary Consciousness* (1990), Tzvi Medin explains that the revolutionary government understood perfectly that different measures needed to be taken in order to supplant the initial and transitory euphoria, and thus the formulation and implementation of a new revolutionary conscience was indispensable:

> Castro conceived his political power in terms of strengthening the base of popular power, and he understood the need to perpetuate the base by developing a revolutionary consciousness in the masses to take place of merely transitory enthusiasm. (9)

By means of the diverse methods enumerated above, the Cuban government decrees from the outset what it means to be a *good revolutionary*, a concept to which all Cuban citizens would have to adhere in order to avoid any type of alienation or repression. The strategy of the government, ironically imposed from the official pulpit, was based on the notion that each citizen should feel included in the decision-making process of the country: the revolutionary conscience was based on the conceptualization that "we" (together) are working towards the future of the nation, and thus the achievements or failures of the country were in the hands of the people rather than in those of the autocracy, who in reality were the ones who were making all of the resolutions without democratic consensus. This, along with the different coercive methods that always existed and that increased with time (such as the distinct levels of censorship: institutional, direct, indirect, self-censorship, labor sanctions, "acts of repudiation" in work, and study centers),[7] are all preponderant factors in the acceptance, for lack of another option, of the newly established politics by the majority of the Cuban population.

GAYS IN THE REVOLUTION

We have thus established that one of the explicit goals of the new government from the time of its inauguration in 1959 was to inculcate in all of its subjects a new system of thought, of action, of responding, and this we have designated on the cognitive level as *the* revolutionary conscience. As the explicit purpose of this essay is to explore gay themes in Cuban literature, first we must attempt to respond to two basic questions, one of a general character, and one that pertains particularly to gays in Cuba. Let us first consider what we understand by gay identity in general, and secondly, establish how the gay individual fits into the new rigorous parameters established by the Revolution and demanded of all citizens through revolutionary decree.[8]

I believe it is possible to argue that we human beings are in an evolutionary process in which, as Jane Gallop asserts, identity "must be continually assumed and continually called into question" (cited in Weeks 69). In the specific terms of sexual identity, the power that the hegemonic heterosexual society exerts upon society as a whole assumes that its own standards are constants and that "normal" behavior is heterosexual, and thus, if an individual identifies him or herself publicly as homosexual, he or she runs the risk of being classified as an individual who deviates from the "norm," of being perverse or perverted. This entire game of power—of highly homophobic roots— holds as its purpose "[to] obscure a real sexual diversity with the myth of a sexual destiny" (Weeks 74), and succeeds in limiting and compartmentalizing the individual vis-à-vis a theoretical basis of a theological, biological, and juridical nature. By preventing a group from recognizing itself and being accepted under the rubric of a union which defies the norm of sexual identity imposed upon society as a whole, the patriarchal hegemony successfully debilitates the unified resistance that a gay movement could exert. Moreover, a participant in gay resistance activism does not necessarily consider him or herself homosexual, but rather may identify with any group that is politically or ideologically oppressed by the majority in power. The gay resistance validates a sexual identity previously considered dissident, marginalized, and sworn to secrecy. In the case of the United States— Weeks reminds us—San Francisco as a geographical location helps to organize and validate the sexual identity of a group of men and women by providing them with a place where their sexuality is validated. On a much smaller scale, gay bars, theaters, and cinemas in other cities create temporal spaces of belonging and acceptance.

Having said this, we now need to establish the way in which gays figure into the revolutionary ideology. It would be impossible to treat this question lightly. Historically in Cuba, as typically in the rest of Latin America, direct repression of gays has been openly practiced; after all, from the declaration of independence to the end of the last century, the Island was subjected to th castrating yoke of successive dictatorial regimes in which the most "macho" forcefully seized the power to govern.[9] As an inevitable consequence, from the time of its inception the Cuban revolutionary ideology has categorically rejected any dissident expression that does not adhere to its precepts, and thus, Cuban gays find themselves in the epicenter of a iron-handed official persecution, repression, and ridicule that has lasted more than two decades. In effect, in an escapist game with the intent to avoid the deliberate homophobia characteristic of the Revolution, Fidel Castro himself attributed antigay sentiment expressed by his government to traditional Latin American *machismo* during a personal interview:

> El machismo es una tradición histórica y cultural, que data quién sabe desde cuándo [. . .]. Debo decirle con toda honestidad, que nunca he compartido esos sentimientos [. . .] a pesar de haber crecido en la misma sociedad machista. Pienso que pudo haber habido un época en la que el machismo fue muy poderoso, pero no fue un producto de la revolución, sino del medio social en que vivíamos. No podemos hablar de un tiempo como el que usted describe en su pregunta, porque en realidad nunca ha habido aquí una persecución de homosexuales. (Bardach 50)[10]

However, in another interview conducted by Lee Lockwood in 1966 and cited by Ann Louise Bardach, Castro stated explicitly that homosexuality is "una desviación de la naturaleza [. . .]. Nunca pudimos llegar a creer que un homosexual pudiera encarnar las condiciones y los requerimientos de conducta que nos permitieran considerarlo un verdadero revolucionario" (50).[11] These words, articulated by Castro in the middle of the repressive process of the camps of the Unidades Militares de Ayuda a la Producción [Military Entities for the Aid of Production] (UMAP, which operated between 1965 and 1969), denote the tone of the politics taken against the sexual dissident during the 1960s, and that endure even through this decade when the "homosexual condition" is still considered an impediment for the revolutionary citizen. This is exemplified by the fact that membership in the exclusive Cuban Communist Party, sole guide for the political direction of the country, is explicitly prohibited for homosexuals.

    However, we must clarify that in continuing with the *machista*-patriarchal Latin American tradition, in Cuba a man is not categorized as homosexual for maintaining sexual relations with another man: "to have sex with another man is not what identifies one as a homosexual. For many Cubans, a man is homosexual only if he takes the passive receiving role. . . . A man is suspected of being a homosexual only if his behavior is not macho" (Leinier 22). Similarly, to cite another example of this erroneous conceptualization of gay identity, in a conversation that took place in Havana during the summer of 1994, Juan Nicolás Padrón, then editor in chief of the publishing house Letras Cubanas, discussed the topic when asked about the discrimination that Reinaldo Arenas suffered during his pilgrimage through Cuba:

> Mira, Reinaldo Arenas era un individuo que caía mal allá y aquí por una cosa muy sencilla, porque en medio de una sociedad machista como la nuestra, como lo son todas las sociedades latinoamericanas, un individuo que se ponía un pantalón de flores, unas sandalias y pregonaba su homosexualismo era un individuo chocante. Aquí, en el Vaticano, en Estados Unidos, entonces justamente si aparte de tú ser un homosexual declarado, tú también eres un hombre que pregonas tu desafecto total, figúrate tú ya te buscas un problema. (Alvarez 140)[12]

From the start, then, with its patriarchal inheritance the Revolution assumes compulsory heterosexual practices. David William Foster explains that from its inception, the Cuban Marxist-Leninist dogmatism rejecting gay culture was:

> [no] other than one of bourgeois capitalism's many diseased faces, and its failure to distinguish between homosexuality (particularly as it was viewed and consumed by the foreign tourist in Havana) as part of the corrupt market system and gay identity as a dimension of personal liberation, provided a potent substratum for homophobia of the Castro Revolution. . . . (*Sexual Textualities* 88)

We share Foster's assertion and concur that gay identity is a dimension of personal freedom, and therefore, there is no doubt that this concept is diametrically opposed to the absolute uniformity and conformity that the Revolution has always demanded of all of its citizens. In other words, here we are referring to the imposition of a so-called revolutionary identity a priori that is necessarily prejudiced and exclusive. If we want to bring our discussion from the particular case which concerns us to a more general level, we can make use of Diana Fuss's conceptualization of "political identity": "identity is always purchased at the price of the exclusion of the Other, the repression or repudiation of nonidentity" (103).

Also, we must not forget that in its most general sense, the persecution of homosexuals coincides with the persecution of the dissident: a homosexual is a dissident of the bourgeois norm of conjugal life. When the roles "revolutionary Woman-Man" which have been autocratically designated are transgressed, the power that the heterosexual hegemony attributes to itself is violated; a violation that evokes a counterattack by hegemonic reactionary forces which, besides being repressive and controlling, violently lash out upon perceiving that the sexual order is being challenged. In the Cuban case in particular—whose socialist society has perpetuated bourgeois relations among heterosexual partners—the official responses were multiple, but at the start of the 1960s for the most part they took the form of indiscriminate arrests and subsequent transfers of citizens (all men suspected of being homosexual) to the UMAP camps.[13] Lamentably, many Cuban intellectuals suffered imprisonment in these work camps. Among the most renowned were the writer Reinaldo Arenas[14] (1943-90), the poet and director of the publishing house El Puente, an independent organ of literary dissemination from 1961-1964—José Mario, the poet Jorge Ronet and the actor Rafael Polet.[15] In 1971 the First National Congress of Education and Culture took place, the repression persisted even though the UMAP camps had disappeared years before. Among the Congress's resolutions, of particular importance for our study are the ones which refer to homosexuality, since, for the first time, an official document did not allude to homosexuality in criminal terms, but rather in medical and psychological ones. The resolutions continued to be drastic for gays in that they called for their prohibition from educational forums, which deepened intellectual and political discrimination. Extracts from the multiple resolutions were printed in diverse mass media publications such as *Casa de las Américas*, *Granma*, and *Unión*. In the following excerpt we cite some of the passages that repudiate gay participation in cultural and educational revolutionary life:[16]

> The resolution was reached that flamboyant homosexuals must not be permitted to exert influence over our youth using the justification of "artistic merit."/Therefore, we call for a decision regarding how to confront the homosexual presence in the diverse institutions of our cultural sector./ Cultural forums cannot serve as a frame for the proliferation of false intellectuals that seek to convert [. . .]

homosexuality and other social aberrations, into expressions of revolutionary art, alienated from the masses and from the spirit of our Revolution. ("Declarations" 5)

Nonetheless, although in the 1970s Cuba perpetuated the hegemony of a patriarchal and compulsory heterosexual society— evident, for example, in the demography of the Politburó in the last thirty-four years,[17]—the leaders officially tried to promote certain changes. In 1974, the Family Code which "eliminates" the double work day for women, obliging men to share the housework, was approved. Likewise, in 1977 the National Cuban Group for Sex Education was created and directed by the Cuban medical doctor Celestino Lajonchere in collaboration with the German sexologist Monika Krause. This group, in conjunction with other entities for health education, is dedicated to the study and promotion of information relevant to sexuality, thus promoting a certain degree of instruction previously nonexistent for the masses. However, the Penal Code, which was established in 1978—that is, at the end of what later became known as the Decenio Negro (Black Decade) in Cuban culture. Although it provides a certain degree of flexibility in differentiating between homosexual expression in the public and private space, it puts severe restrictions on the cultural production of gay themes and content (Citron 39). For instance, a documentary about the painter René Portocarrero, filmed under the auspices of the ICAIC, omits the fact that the famous artist is gay, and one of the few able to maintain an openly gay lifestyle in Cuba due to his internationally renowned cultural work and contribution.

In *The Cultural Revolution in Cuba* (1991), Roger Reed adds that, along general lines, Castro's government accosted the gay citizenry of Cuba because "Homosexuals are rebels; they dissent from conventional morality. Therefore, they pose a challenge to any system in which all modes of behavior are supposed to be controlled by the authorities" (80). That is to say, gays do not conform to moralizing rules and laws; to put it in the vocabulary used in this study, gays articulate one of the most irreverent forms of contestatory expression. Therefore, reinforcing Foster's assertion regarding the tendency to view gay culture as the remains of bourgeois capitalism, in the initial years of the Revolution in Cuba, a hyper-masculinization of a society established on the basis of an evolving nationalist socialism was carried out. The most obvious modification could be observed in the physical appearance of the revolutionaries: the long locks sported by the Sierra rebels were replaced with Prussian haircuts that the recruits of the subsequent Fuerzas Armadas Revolucionarias (FAR, Revolutionary Armed Forces) began to wear. In turn, women now dressed in the "masculine" olive green uniforms of the campaigns began to make the rows of female militant revolutionaries. All of this was one more element that applied to the goal of putting into practice the conceptualization of the "New Man" who according to Che Guevara, should rise up from the revolutionary process.[18]

For all intents and purposes then, the only option for (intellectual) gays striving to survive in their country was self-censorship, that is, to forcibly silence their identities upon realizing that the hegemonic powers were too mighty to defeat or even to persuade. Lourdes Arguelles and Ruby Rich accurately assert that Cuban intellectual gays of the 1960s and 1970s did not organize any type of unified internal resistance that would permit them to counter the governmental assault. The aforementioned authors attribute the lack of opposition to three fundamental factors: (1) at the beginning of the 1960s, Cuba lacked a discursive feminist tradition, impeding the establishment of a base from which to discuss sexual hierarchy or gender politics; (2) the contemporary mind set concerning homosexuality did not allow for a vision much beyond the notion that homosexuality was practiced in sinister places with limited or no sexual implication; (3) many intellectuals feared the loss of privileges—the most valued being trips abroad that permitted them the freedom to explore their sexual orientation—if they vocalized their opinions against the official position regarding homosexuality (691).

We have already mentioned various young intellectuals who suffered internment in the UMAP camps after having been arbitrarily identified as "homosexuals." However, there are others who due to their intellectual maturity and international fame, could not be openly oppressed as their novice counterparts were. One case in particular involves the narrator and playwright Virgilio Piñera (1912-1979), who by the time of the triumph of the Revolution was already a recognized figure in literary circles for having published the novel *La carne de René* (René's Flesh, 1952), the short stories collection *Cuentos fríos* (Cold Tales, 1956), and dramatic works such as *Electra Garrigó, Jesús*, and *Aire frío* (Cold Breeze, 1959).[19] Like many other intellectuals, in 1959, Piñera jumped on the revolutionary bandwagon and contributed to the pages of the magazine *Revolución* and the literary supplement

Lunes, but his decadence began at the moment he was arrested and imprisoned in el Morro[20] in October 1961. From this point on, Virgilio Piñera would suffer from an internal exile that would last until his death. The only alternative left to him was to exercise a silence that would permit his survival. In the intriguing essay, "Fleshing Out Virgilio Piñera from the Cuban Closet" (1995), José Quiroga comments on the possible reasons for Piñera's silence: "depending on your political point of view, this was the silence of fear, of repression, of inner exile, the silence of the literary closet and of the refusal to come out of that closet or perhaps this was the silence of the heroic" (170). It is true that Piñera was able to publish three works at the end of the 1960s: the novel *Presiones y diamantes* (Pressures and Diamonds, 1967), the play *Dos viejos pánicos* (Two Old Panicked Men, 1968), and a collection of poems entitled *La vida entera* (The Entire Life, 1969); but after this last date of publication, on the eve of the Stalinist Quinquineo Gris [Five Gray Years], Piñera lived submerged in a forced literary silence until his death. Knowing the irreverent character of Virgilio Piñera (gay, anti-Communist, anti-Catholic), we must agree with Quiroga's final estimation of this author as heroically silent, and we add that silence is one of the few expressions of resistance that could be practiced in Cuba in the 1970s. However, Reinaldo Arenas reminds us in his autobiography, *Antes que anochezca* (Before Night Falls, 1992), that Piñera, from the closet, directly influenced subsequent generations by serving as their mentor:

> Yo visitaba a Virgilio Piñera en su casa a las siete de la mañana [. . .] sentado frente a mí, leía una copia de la novela [*El mundo alucinante*] y donde consideraba que debía añadir una coma o cambiar una palabra por otra así me lo decía [. . .]. Fue mi profesor universitario además de mi amigo. (105)[21]

We cannot conclude this section without first mentioning that the homophobic posture and the repressive measures that the Revolution assumed went beyond its own citizens. For example, let us remember that the North American poet Allen Ginsberg was thrown out of Cuba in 1965, after having been invited to participate as a judge of the Casa de las Américas poetry prize that same year, for protesting against gay persecution. Upon his return to the United States, Ginsberg admitted that the worst thing he said in Cuba was that Raúl Castro was gay[22] and that Che Guevara was very beautiful (quoted in Reed 82); that is, he struck at the heterosexual *machista* heart of the Revolution.

THREE GENERATIONS OF HOMOEROTIC WRITING IN CUBA

Homoerotic writing is not a foreign genre to Cuban literature. In 1928 the novel *Angel de Sodoma* (Angel of Sodom) was published in Madrid by the Cuban Alfonso Hernández Catá, a text that portrays the protagonist, José María, first born of the Vélez Gomara family, as a confused individual who finds himself forced into fighting against his distinct homoerotic inclinations. These "tendencias" [tendencies] are justified by the narrator, following the Spanish tradition of the era as in the case of Gregorio Marañón, by presenting them as accidents of nature: "¡Qué culpa tengo yo! [. . .] Si la naturaleza, o Dios, o Satán iban a hacerme mujer y, cuando ya estaban puestos los cimientos de mi ser, se arrepintieron y echaron de mala gana arcilla de hombre, ¿qué he de hacer yo?" (84).[23]

José María's dilemma is a vivid historical representation of the gay individual's entrapment in the codes of a patriarchal society. Throughout his life, he is forced to assume a social identity that goes against not only his sexual desire, but also against the person that he is, that obliges him to identify with those masculine values and repress his "lado femenino" (feminine side) in order to "absorber" (absorb) the masculinity of his father (85). Likewise, he submits himself to changing his physical appearance into a "masculine" one, despite the fact that this tramples his personal integrity. These practices range from a "violenta" (violent) exercise regime that he completes daily (98) to hardening his soft skin by exposing it to an abusive sun "que le abrasaba la piel, le producía tremendas cefalalgias y dejaba dentro de sus ojos un chisporroteo de estrellitas cáusticas, terribles" (98-99).[24] The protagonist convinces himself of the possibility of "regenerarse" (redemption) in the public space by means of marriage and fatherhood, confirmed by what he reads in "a science book" that he had consulted "una vez, con rubores y terrores, [en] la Biblioteca Municipal" (137)[25]: "¡En esa está la última salvación para siempre!" (136).[26] "¡Un hijo que él no dejaría criar en las faldas de su madre, como lo criaron a él; un hijo que en vez de jugar a las muñecas y andar con niñas, estaría de continuo al sol, entre pilluelos, aun cuando regresase con chichones y escalabraduras!" (137).[27]

In the pages of *Angel de Sodoma* the reader cannot ignore the reality that discourages the protagonist throughout his life. Parisian exile and the subsequent suicide that ends José María's life are the only options open to him, a gay man who after innumerable pondering cannot deny his gay identity, and even less, maintain a farce in order to placate the demands of society. It is important to note that the end of this novel satisfies the patriarchal perspective, since it climbs another rung on the ladder of homosexual extermination, the explicit goal of compulsory heterosexuality. Some ten years after the publication of Hernández Catá's novel, the narrator and journalist Carlos Montenegro wrote the novel *Hombres sin mujer* (Men without Women; 1937) in Cuba, a work which presents the theme of homosexuality closely linked to violence: the discrimination and exercise of power over the weak, the daily routine among common prisoners in Cuban jails during that era.[28] Unlike the previously discussed novel, *Hombres sin mujer* is a cruel and disturbing autobiography, full of sex from start to finish, in which *bugarronería* (anal penetration of one man by another, the latter performing the "feminine" role of receiver) is the law of prison life.[29] However, like *Angel de Sodoma*, the tragic canonized ending that characterizes Western writing cannot be escaped in this work either. In the prologue to the novel that Montenegro himself writes, he informs the reader that his work is highly testimonial, and he makes clear that his purpose is the "denuncia del sistema carcelario a que [se vio] sometido durante doce años"[30]; at the same time, he does not make any sort of apology to those who might consider the content immoral since "todo lo que dicen [las páginas] corresponde a un mal existente" (7).[31] In this case, this evil does not refer to the same-sex relations themselves that take place in the jails, but rather the violence which one is capable of perpetrating against another human being in order to derive erotic pleasure.

The novel is told in the third person by an ubiquitous narrator who frequently appears in the text itself. The physical space of the narration is the closed space of the prison, yet the characters appear in different situations in distinct spaces: the bathroom, the galley, the infirmary, their respective cells, the patio, and the workroom. Although time in the novel is linear, the narrator interrupts the chronology with flashbacks that inform the reader of previous occurrences, and the narration seems to be circular as well, since at the end of the text crazy Valentín yells out the same words that he says at the beginning of the novel, "¡Yo quiero comer gallina blanca!" (11, 216).[32]

The protagonist of *Hombres sin mujer* is Pascasio Speek, a black
Cuban who has served eight years of a prison term for having stabbed a
man who attempted to rape him. The text is very explicit in presenting
the psychological changes which haunt the protagonist, whose greatest
worry is to maintain an impeccable record of conduct in order to get out
of jail as soon as possible. Initially he cannot understand why one man
would carry on sexual relations with another, and therefore he rejects
the possibility of entering into any such situation, forcing him to satisfy
his sexual urges through masturbation:

> ¿Cómo es posible que un hombre se pusiera a enamorar a otro?. . .
> Había acabado por reirse a carcajadas . . . ¡Vamos! El también tenía
> con qué. . . Y sangre. . . Y potencia. . . Y. . . ¡rayos!. . . Mas, cuando
> estaba muy desesperado, soñaba con Encarnación, con Tomasa, con
> un palo de escoba que fuera, pero con sayas, y, listo, ¡para la
> próxima! (15)[33]

During the eight years he spends in prison, Pascasio does not merely
reject such homoerotic practices on an abstract level, but rather when
La Morita tries to force him, Pascasio gives him a ferocious beating:
"Pascasio Speek le había dado con el puño en medio de la cara y como
todavía, al sujetarlo los demás [La Morita], quedaba al alcance de su
brazo, volvió a pegarle con furia hasta que rodó por el suelo con el
rostro lleno de sangre" (42).[34] However, as the narration progresses, the
reader comes to realize that Speek's explicit homophobia stems from
his fear of his attraction to the same sex and that this is a desire that
goes beyond a simple sexual need. At the same time, from the
beginning and as the novel advances, the narration overturns that initial
conception that sex between men is "anormal" (abnormal) (16) or
perverse: "—¿Sabes lo que nos pasa a todos?—Le pregunta Matienzo
al recién ingresado Andrés—¡Que somos hombres sin mujer!. . . Aquí
no hay degenerados; solamente hombres sin mujer. . . Eso es todo"
(56),[33] and it reinforces the concept that homoeroticism does not take
the manliness out of a man:

> —Estás loco, pero. . .
> [Andrés] no pudo terminar la frase; el brazo de Pascasio lo había
> envuelto y atraído hacia sí, confundiendo las dos bocas. Andrés no
> opuso resistencia alguna; cerró los ojos abandonándose, hasta que

Pascasio asombrado de lo que hacía lo soltó. Entonces el muchacho repitió lo que había comenzado a decirle:
—Estás loco, pero eres un hombre. . . (152)[36]

The erotic-love relationship that Pascasio and Andrés establish in the course of the novel reproduces those of heterosexual relations. In particular there is the question of jealousy, which is what leads to Andrés's murder and Pascasio's suicide after having found his lover in the workshop in Manuel Chiquito's company:

Andrés, con la guerrera desabotonada, corrió hacia Pascasio y fue a decirle algo, pero no tuvo tiempo: quedó detenido de súbito, con la palabra rota en la garganta y los ojos humedecidos mirando hacia Pascasio, que con toda la fuerza de su brazo y de su salvajismo le había hundido en el cráneo el extremo cortante de la llave. (214)[37]

Cuban narrative will have to wait until after the triumph of the Revolution in 1959 for the thematic of homosexuality to present itself in another novel, in this case *Paradiso* (1966), considered to be the masterpiece of poet, narrator and essayist José Lezama Lima (1910-76). It is well known that the historical context in which this novel is published was precisely one of relentless discrimination against homosexuals. This is the apex of the UMAP camps years(1965-69) to which it is estimated that thousands of gays—and those arbitrarily designated as such for having long hair or walking a particular way; that is, for whims of the homophobic military and police—were sent.[38] Also, it is during these years that the government dismantles the independent editorial group El Puente, and its director, José Mario, along with other members, was sent to the UMAP camps. During the First Congress of Education and Culture in 1971 the Cuban government adopted the official stance of open rejection of gays; in cultural and educational spheres they were altogether excluded.

Within this historical Cuban context, *Paradiso* appeared seven years after Batista's fall, that is during the years when the aureola of initial enthusiasm was being put to the test by the protests in Escambray, general disenchantment, the exile or death of some of the pioneers of the Revolution who fought alongside Fidel in the Sierra, and internal opposition, including the exile of well-known intellectuals who had at first collaborated on the reforms. In terms of literature in particular, the year that this work appeared is of specific importance in demarcating the beginning of what will later come to be known as "el Quinquenio de Oro" of the Cuban short story, inaugurated by Jesús Díaz's prize-winning collection of stories *Los años duros* (The Harsh Years, 1966). It is important to note that until this time almost all of the works published in Cuba, including the films produced, exalted the Revolution one way or another. It is in the atmosphere of tension between the historical moment and the literary production that had been published up until this moment that *Paradiso* appeared, a work of profound universal content that did not pay any attention whatsoever to the historical events that had transpired in Cuba during the five years previous to its publication. In other words, with *Paradiso*, Lezama Lima, instead of reflecting on the history that circumscribed his era, mentioning names, events, or nationalist/pseudopatriotic examples, drew references from the Bible, Asia, the Romans, the Egyptians, and from Greek mythology. Socratian thought, which sees the world as something larger than a simple and tangible reality, consistently runs through the works of I *e*zama Lima:

> According to Lezama, it is a matter of looking for the absolute and the comprehension of the world beyond appearances. Such thinking reveals that the writer is confident in the existence of a reality hidden behind the appearances of the physical world. Consequently, a constant feature in his essays is the search for concealed connections and unexpected linkings that move away from the linearity of rationalistic thought. (Altamiranda 203)

In addition to the hermetism and the apparent verbal obscurity with which Lezama Lima writes (circumlocution, periphrase, prosopopoeia, all elements that form part of the narrative technique of baroque writing), it is also important to note his great literary license which does not fix itself to set structures, and juxtaposes narratives that have no outward relation, giving the readers the impression that at times they face a block of pages lacking a common thread. As the Argentine writer Julio Cortázar—one of the first to write about *Paradiso* in the same year as its publication[39]—says, the novel works on different levels, from familiar narrations to which we easily relate, to erotic and imaginary ones that border on magical/fantastic literature. In reference to the characters of *Paradiso*, Cortázar comments that we have to take into account that all of them are viewed in "esencia" (essence) rather than "presencia" (presence); they are archetypes, not types. We have to accept that these characters present themselves and speak from the "imagen" (image) cloistered in the Lezamian poetic system. The characters themselves are not important for Lezama, rather what is crucial is the complete mystery that encloses human experience (137-44).

The novel is divided into three parts, connected by the events in the life of the protagonist, José Cemí, and more specifically, his awakening to his sexual identification. In the first section (chapters one to six), the narrator focuses on providing the ancestral history of the Cemí family. In the next section (chapters eight to eleven), the narrator presents the protagonist's adolescent years in high school and college. In these candid passages, Cemí's philosophical and sexual initiation in the company of his classmates Fronesis and Foción is portrayed. In the rest of the novel, the text first presents four dreams that the protagonist experiences (chapter twelve) and to conclude the work, he develops the character Oppiano Licario (13-14), who becomes Cemí's "lazarillo" (person who guides the blind) during the last years of his philosophical formation, and who provides the title for Lezama's last work, which he never finishes due to his death.

On a level of cultural politicking that starts to become institutionalized in the mid-1960s in Cuba, when no one cared to make the distinction between politics and aesthetics, one of the errors[40] that Lezama Lima made with his publication of *Paradiso* was to neglect any credit or reference to the revolutionary process.[41] Furthermore, and in direct relation to this study, the Cuban writer did not only allude to and present homoerotic space (along with heterosexual, incestuous, voyeuristic, adulterous, exhibitionist, and sadomasochistic spaces), but rather more importantly, in my opinion, he did so on the same level as heterosexual eroticism, thus validating that which the Revolution—and the patriarchal hegemony itself—attempted to punish. This is to say that, as we will see in our analysis of chapter 8, the narration does not concern itself with making gender distinctions between the two bodies that make love. However, in terms of the entirety of the novel, we agree with the Cuban-American critic Gustavo Pérez Firmat who proposes that the main protagonist's "attainment of Paradise entails a concomitant affirmation of his homosexuality" (247).[42]

The chapter in question could very well orient itself under the title, "Sex: presence and reality in human beings." This estimation diametrically opposes the commentary that José Prats Sariol makes in the critical edition to *Paradiso* edited by Cintio Vitier, and the one to which we make reference in this work, when he writes in relation to chapter eight: "Si leemos con cuidado las respectivas descripciones, podemos observar cómo un signo de bestialidad envuelve las relaciones homosexuales, mientras un signo festivo, casi humorístico, cubre las heterosexuales" (662).[43] A detailed comparison reveals that in this chapter, for example, the narrator presents us with a total of five erotic episodes which include sexual intercourse: three are heterosexual and two homosexual encounters. These latter are preceded and comple- mented by a passage in which the narrator describes an occasion where one of the students, Leregas, brags publicly in geography class about his "potencia fálica [que] reinaba como la vara de Aarón,"[44] which brings the narrator to affirm that: "Su gladio demostrativo era la clase de geografía" (200).[45] During the (doubly) pedagogic session and under the attentive eyes of fifty or sixty classmates, the narrator tells us: "Leregas extraía su falo y sus testículos, adquiriendo como un remolino que se trueca en columna, de un solo ímpetu el reto de un tamaño excepcional" (201).[46] In the page that precedes this description, the narrator explains: "Leregas extraía su verga—con la misma indiferencia majestuosa del cuadro velazqueño donde se entrega la llave sobre un cojín—, breve como un dedal al principio, pero después impulsada como un viento titánico, cobraba la longura de un antebrazo de trabajador manual" (200).[47] We repeat that in the images represented by the narrative text there does not exist any indication that might suggest some type of jest or degradation. On the contrary, the group of spectators that "contemplaba[n]—el desafío de Leregas con—aquel tenaz cirio dispuesto a romper su valano envolvente, con un casquete sanguíneo extremadamente pulimentado—con el cual—imantó con más decisión la ceñida curiosidad de aquellos peregrinos inmóviles [..] pero sin ninguna socarronería ni podrida sonrisilla" (201)[48] is formed by young people that, like José Cemí, are in a process of sexual self- discovery, of self-definition where sexual curiosity is not biased by any homophobic expression characteristic of patriarchal society. Indeed it can be said to be a utopic Lezamian configuration that refutes the analysis of Prats Sariol.

We have mentioned that in this chapter five distinct episodes of sexual intercourse take place in a period of three consecutive Sundays, with Farraluque—the other character possessing sexual prowess—the main protagonist. Farraluque's erotic encounters, treated all on the same semantic level, sustain our previous statement. Supporting Pérez Firmat's previously cited stance, the Argentine critic Daniel Altamiranda affirms that in those prolongedly descriptive sequences, "the narrator establishes a principle of social behavior that seems omnipresent in Lezama Lima's universe: sexual indefinition as a distinctive factor in adolescence" (207). The first two erotic encounters that Farraluque has are heterosexual, with the director's cook and the maid on the first Sunday. We are told that his youth permitted him "que una vez terminada la conjugación normal [con la cocinera], pudiera comenzar otra *per angostam viam*" (204).[49] The next Sunday Farraluque has his first homoerotic encounter after having gone to bed with "la señora de la casa de enfrente,"[50] an episode that is distinct from "sus dos anteriores encuentros [que] habían sido bastos y naturalizados, [porque] ahora entraba en el reino de la sutileza y de la diabólica especialización" (207).[51] Afterwards, he has a sexual experience with Adolfito (el miquito [the little monkey]), the cook's brother, and it is this character with whom Farraluque begins what we could call an erotic game of intense seduction between two bodies; here we enter into what the narrator designates "the kingdom of subtlety." The Farraluque-Adolfito encounter is one of extreme refinement; the archaic schema "passive-active," or the possession of one (female-weak) by another (male-strong), has no resonance whatsoever in this description. The mutual pleasure between two bodies that is portrayed is an exemplary image of what Foster calls "dos cuerpos que se quieren,"[52] and, as Altamiranda articulates in the aforementioned quote, the universe of lezamian sexual indefinition, concomitant with the utter lack of homophobic prejudice, permit the narrator to express sexual curiosity and to enjoy both bodies in the same way that he had during the descriptions of heterosexual coitus: "cuando Farraluque buscaba apuntalarlo, hurtaba la ruta de la serpiente, y cuando con su aguijón se empeñaba en sacar el del otro [el pene] de su escondite, rotaba de nuevo, prometiéndole más remansada bahía a su espolón" (207).[53] As we note, Farraluque is interested in establishing something that goes far beyond a mere sexual satisfaction on his part, a sexual schema much more common in Latin American literature—such as in Montenegro's novel, for example. The previous passage presents us with a scene of mutual eroticism and pleasure, in which Farraluque wants to share the erect penis of the opposite body, while the latter eroticizes the experience more by rotating his body and concealing his penis.

Paradiso is one of the first works (and one of the few in reality) of Latin American literature in which a preconception of what it is like, or what it should be like to be gay does not exist; that is, it does not contain a biased perspective in regard to homoeroticism. In his novel, Lezama Lima leads us through a oscillation of episodes, some humorous, others dramatic, in which he portrays the crises which affect a human being, any human, in the search for a personal sexual identity. Such an interwoven baroque work ends with the hopeful words, "podemos empezar" (we can begin); José Cemí's life, for all of its sexual dichotomies, has yet to begin.

The official attitude that created an ambience of extreme oppression towards any dissidence persisted and intensified throughout the 1970s (el Decenio Negro [the Black Decade], as the critic Ambrosio Fornet will christen it), which were crucial years in the intellectual formation of writers born between 1950 and 1958, such as Francisco López Sacha, Leonardo Padura Fuentes, and Senel Paz, and those of the Novísima generation, born between 1959 and 1972.

As we write these lines, we find ourselves in the middle of an *ajiaco* of contradictions as Gustavo Pérez Firmat would say. Initial readings of short stories written and published in Cuba during the last seven years, which at first glance can make one think were texts that transgressed the habitual politico-ideological parameters inscribed within the historico-social dialect of the Cuban Revolution, proved themselves to the contrary upon a second reading. Among other elements we find the strong homophobic sentiment that has flourished in our countries, and overall in the first three decades of the Cuban revolutionary process. I am referring specifically to the stories "El cazador" (The Hunter; 1991) from the fiction writer-journalist Leonardo Padura Fuentes, and to the already very famous novella by Senel Paz, *El lobo, el bosque y el hombre nuevo* (The Wolf, the Forest and the New Man; 1990), the latter serving as a base for the script of the film, *Fresa y chocolate* (Strawberry and Chocolate; 1993). It is important to note that both works were winners of literary prizes in México and the film was nominated for Hollywood's Oscar for best foreign film of 1995. Also, the first story won honorary mention in *Plural* magazine's literary contest in 1990, and the second received the prestigious Juan Rulfo award in the same year. However, if we submit these narrations to a second, more mature reading, we conclude that our first estimation had been hasty. In retrospect, our error can be attributed to, among other factors, the incorporation into the plot of the character of the "other," which leads the studious reader of Cuban literary production towards the discovery of a theme not previously explored. That is to say, the subject who in Senel Paz's short story declares himself homosexual and Catholic, but also a revolutionary with conviction, who jumped on the progressive revolutionary train by participating in the Literacy Campaigns of the 1960s, captures the imagination of the reader by presenting a perspective, to a certain extent, critical of the Revolution. Therefore, it is easy to conclude that the aforementioned text portrays a social judgment previously ambiguous or nonexistent, and is thus a progressive text in the politico-ideological field. However, once the story is deconstructed, the reader realizes something very evident: what strives to be a vanguard text in reality is a textually homophobic representation within the very same character who openly declares himself homosexual, which, of course, authorizes the rhetoric. Furthermore, I suggest that this novella, and later the script for the film as well, once again reproduces the cultural proposals of the heterosexual bourgeois society mimesis of Castro's Cuba where expressions distinct from those practiced by the hegemonic culture have always been marginalized or punished.

My second readings have followed Gloria Anzaldúa's arguments suggested in her article, "To(o) Queer the Writer: loca, escritora y chicana" (1991). Anzaldúa suggests that the reader should read with what she calls *facultad* (257); that is to say, "to 'see into' and 'see through' unconscious falsifying disguises by penetrating the surface and reading underneath the words and between the lines" (238). In other words, my work has taken the form of a contestatory reader who, according to what Alberto Julián Pérez writes in "Tipología histórica de la lectura: lectores europeos y lectores latinoamericanos" (Historical Typology of Reading: European and Latin American Readers; 1991), "critica la autoridad del modelo hegemónico que se le quiere inculcar y la vision del mundo que éste transmite y pretende legitimar" (287).[54]

Our purpose in this segment is twofold: first, as we have previously mentioned, we have attempted to present a reading that goes beyond a primary or superficial analysis motivated by pseudointellectual sentiment; secondly, and perhaps most crucially, we wish to highlight the literary criticism interested in the specific component of queer themes in recent Cuban narrative, which is difficult to locate in libraries, as this body of criticism has been only fragmentarily published in Cuba and/or abroad. We do this in hopes of promoting a genuine dialogue that will enrich our perspectives.

After the debut of *Paradiso*, it is not until the publication of the short story "¿Por qué llora Leslie Caron?" (Why Does Leslie Caron Cry; 1988) by Roberto Urías that a text appears in Cuba whose central theme is the dilemma of a gay character. In 1986 Urias's story wins a national prize for literature, and it is published for the first time in the journal *Letras cubanas* in 1988, twenty-two years after the publication of Lezama Lima's novel.[55] Even though it is the first short story that revisits the theme of the homosexual in the Revolution, a motif begun by Lezama Lima, Virgilio Piñera, and Reinaldo Arenas (his fiction with the exception of *Celestino antes del alba* (*Singing from the Well*; 1967) is published in its entirety abroad and therefore we do not address it here), among others, Urias's story is the most human of its contemporaries in that it presents a nonhomophobic vision, one that is not biased against the gay individual within the post-revolutionary Cuban society. The protagonist, Francisco, defines his own identity by telling us that he prefers the name Leslie Caron, since "mis compinches admiten que entre ella, la actriz, y yo existe un gran parecido, la misma gracia y la misma condición etérea" (236).[56] Through the voice of this gay character, the author both deconstructs the hegemonic heterosexual parameters of bourgeois society that have been reproduced in Castroist Cuba, and satirizes the trite and tired Marxist-Leninist rhetoric. At the start of the story the protagonist admits to having a "sacred" family: "una madre, un padre, adorable hermanita, un perro y muchas plantas [. . .] el clásico nidito decorado y decoroso" (236).[57] That , he refers to the scenario of the supposedly perfect heterosexual bourgeois existence. Nevertheless, what is presented initially as the ideal in reality is a satire of a deplorable situation: a father who keeps mistresses and never remembers his children's birthdays, a mother who leaves the house to put an end to her sorrows, and a sister who "se casa con un tipo sólo porque tiene una casa en Miramar y un carro y una videocasetera" (238).[58] In this short story, unlike others that treat gay themes (such as the one by Senel Paz), the protagonist has his own legitimate voice and in no way needs to perform self-criticism nor apologizes for his gay identity. Rather, from his position outside the heterosexist hegemony, the protagonist is better able to critique those he observes: "la mayor parte de las gentes me inspira lástima; son vacías, tan falsos; que se mueven a través de los estrechos márgenes de los esquemas que les imponen" (238),[59] that is, the heterosexual world that surrounds him.

     If it is true that *El lobo, el bosque y el hombre nuevo* (1990) and *Fresa y chocolate* (1993) are texts which advocate tolerance towards the Other in an oppressive and intransigent society, as both the film's director Tomás Gutiérrez Alea and author/screenwriter Senel Paz have contended, I have to ask myself: in the process of arguing for this much needed tolerance in Cuba, why is it that the gay character is mocked, stereotyped, and ultimately sacrificed? As much in the story as in the film, the gay character is the one who seems preoccupied with sex, and therefore, the eroticism between two bodies portrayed in *Paradiso* is noticeably absent: "si te vas conmigo a la casa y me dejas abrirte la portañuela botón por botón, te la presto [la novela de Vargas Llosa]" (14),[60] Diego says to David in the Coppelia ice cream parlor when they meet for the first time. On another occasion, Diego's discourse in the film projects a self-deprecating message: "Sé que la bondad de los maricones es de doble filo."[61]

At the start of this essay, the official Cuban mind-set of the 1960s is evidenced and documented as one that conveys the incompatibility of homosexuality and the Revolution. In these two texts that we are analyzing, this ideology is reinforced by the portrayal of homosexuals whose conduct is improper according to revolutionary doctrine: Diego, the gay protagonist gets hold of censored books, he does business in the black market with dollars, he has meetings with foreign diplomats, he is an unfaithful friend. Germán, a gay sculptor, is silenced by the regime, and he sells himself in exchange for a trip off the Island. All of the previous characteristics catalogued under the revolutionary conscience as highly counterrevolutionary are part of the image of the gay that exudes from Gutiérrez Alea's film and Paz's short story, both from the early 1990s. On another level, and following the tradition of compulsory heterosexual narrative of the Western world, in these texts the gay characters are those who perform the duties of the *celestina* to resolve the erotic "problems" of the heterosexual characters. Despite the evident attraction and erotic-love desire that Diego has for David, the discourse of the former constantly represses that desire, a sacrifice that is complemented by Diego who asks his friend Nancy to sleep with David in order to initiate him into heterosexual sexuality—"como debe ser" (as it should be). In a failed attempt to lessen the gap between these two erotic worlds, at the conclusion of the film, moments before Diego's departure, David, by Diego's request, hugs his gay friend after recounting the details of his first sexual encounter with Nancy. It is this minimal expression of affection that the gay character must conform to. Diego's exile, represented similarly in *Fresa y chocolate* and in *El lobo, el bosque y el hombre nuevo*, as well as in Hernández Catá's 1928 novel mentioned earlier, fulfills the desire of heterosexual society in the sense that gays disappear leaving ample room for the propagation of heterosexuality.

Writing on homosexual themes in Cuba during the last ten years, of course, is not limited to short story and cinema. Without entering into a discussion of great detail, we could mention the poetry and drama of Abilio Estévez: *Manual de tentaciones* (Manual of Temptations; 1989), *La verdadera culpa de Juan Clemente Zenea* (The True Guilt of Juan Clemente Zenea; 1986) and *Juego con Gloria* (I Play with Gloria; 1986). This young writer presents the first case of openly homosexual poetry that has been published in Cuban journals.[62] Unlike Senel's short story, Estévez's poems contain verses in which the poet clearly acknowledges his homosexuality; that is, he expresses with a gender marker his attraction for a person of the same sex without having to make apologies.

In the field of music, it is important to note the song written and performed in concerts by singer-songwriter Pedro Luis Ferrer, "Amor de hombres," which serves as a precursor to the defense of gays who have been accused of being false revolutionaries and persecuted because of their sexual orientation: "Lo discriminan por ser así/siempre al acecho de un similar/que culpa tiene si en su sentir/pusieron el peso de otra moral [. . .] tan evidente en sus emociones"[63] when in reality it is the opposite since "el muchacho resulta al fin/un excelente trabajador [. . .] y no se fijan en los demás/como lo llaman para el fusil/trabajo extra y hora puntual."[64] Ferrer takes another step on the contestatory ladder when he criticizes Cuban patriarchal heterosexuality that perseveres through the Revolution by denouncing the "machitos que suelen tratar a sus mujeres como esclavistas"[65] and the official cupola of "los poderosos que escandalizan al vecindario/dándole a sus hijos autos lujosos."[66] This song by Ferrer encourages a reconceptualization of the revolutionary individual that from the outset excluded homosexuals. In 1994, the famous troubadour Pablo Milanés, who incidentally was one of the many young artists forced into the work camps of the UMAP in the 1970s, composed a song entitled "El pecado original" (Original Sin) in which he presents "Dos almas, dos cuerpos,/dos hombres que se aman"[67] who "van a ser expulsados/del paraíso que les tocó vivir"[68] and consequently he asks the audience to consider that "No somos Dios/no nos equivoquemos otra vez."[69]

The long process of the evolution of homoerotic texts in Cuba is finally reclaiming its legitimate space within Cuban literature with the publication of works that will continue to be a source of inquiry and dialogue, and is not simply a "temporary fad" in the contemporary culture of the Island, as some have argued (see my interview with

Salvador Redonet, "Ruptura"). So the many years of official repression that negated, penalized, and ridiculed any cultural artistic expression that manifests a vision different from that of the institution have not been able to annihilate the human emotion for the civil right to be different.

NOTES

1. Power always seeks an antagonism with some stratum of society. The homosexual is a persone who questions the context in which he lives.

2. Apparently, a good Marxist, besides knowing *Das Kapital*, must demonstrate an impeccable endocrine system. The Party owns his body and soul. The body also includes his genitals and his excretory orifice.

3. the construction of what does not exist, or that still does not predominantly exist in civil society.

4. How can historical reality so radically change by force?, how can one go to bed convinced of the fact that s/he has defended a democratic revolution to wake up the next day having defended a communist one that s/he is not even familiar with?

5. The Cuban leaders subscribe to the precepts established by Carl Marx and Vladimir Lenin. The former believed that a transformation of the economic system would produce cultural change. Lenin, however, argued that cultural change was only possible if intellectuals and leaders of the party molded the conscience of the masses (Gurley 72-74).

6. According to Julie Marie Bunck, "The government established the Committees for the Defense of the Revolution [CDR] as a system to mobilize and reeducate citizens, to publicize official goals and to promote and organize cooperatives, civil defense, and first-aid projects" (9).

7. The *actos de repudio* (acts of repudiation) were meetings presided over by Communist party leaders that were officially enacted in work and study centers with the express objective of renouncing the conduct of a colleague.

8. Throughout this study we use the term "gay" as a theoretico-cultural concept instead of the official term "homosexual," in an attempt to avoid any possible stereotype that is associated with the latter's medico-juridical classification. Furthermore, we do not refer to the parallel lesbian terms, since within the Cuban patriarchy such relations are not rejected; they are not deemed as a threat to the Cuban patriarchy, and thus do not form part of the revolutionary ethic/code of conduct.

9. Cuban homophobia transcends temporal (pre/post Castro) and spatial (Havana/Miami) frontiers. The homosexual in Miami suffers the same affronts

as those on the Island. This similarity has inspired a popular saying that the only thing Havana and Miami have in common is the explicit hatred and persecution that gays suffer in both places.

10. *Machismo* is an historical and cultural tradition, that dates back to who knows when . . . I must tell you in all honesty that I have never shared those sentiments . . . in spite of having grown up in this same machista society. I believe that there could have been an era in which machismo was very powerful, but it was not a product of the Revolution, but rather of the social environment in which we live. We cannot speak of a time like the one you describe in your question, because in reality there never has been a persecution of homosexuals here.

11. a deviation of nature. . . . We could never come to believe that a homosexual would embody the conditions and conduct requirements that could permit us to consider him a true revolutionary.

12. Look, Reinaldo Arenas was an individual who no one liked because of one simple reason, because in the middle of a *machista* society like ours, like all of the rest of Latin American society, a person who wore flowered pants, sandals and who proclaimed his homosexuality was a shocking individual. Here, in the Vatican, in the United States, if apart from the fact that you are a declared homosexual, you also are a man who publicly announces your total disaffection, then it shouldn't surprise you that you're already looking for trouble.

13. It is estimated that before the dismantling of UMAP camps in December of 1969, more than 35,000 homosexuals, religious followers (primarily Jehovah's witnesses), and counterrevolutionaries suffered mandatory sentences there.

14. In his novel *Arturo la estrella más brillante* (Arthur, the Brightest Star; 1984), Arenas fictionalizes much of his experiences in the UMAP camps.

15. See the film *Conducta impropia* (Improper Conduct; 1984).

16. These quotes were taken from *Granma Weekly Review*, the English edition of the official newspaper of the Cuban Communist Party, from the ninth of May, 1971.

17. In 1975, Carlos Montaner points out that in that era, of the one hundred members comprising the Politburo, the Secretariat and the Central Committee of the Communist Party, only five were women.

18. Montaner states with justifiable conviction: "Guevara fue el primer, el último y único 'hombre nuevo' que dio el proceso revolucionario. Ese cubano del futuro, desinteresado, laborioso, honesto, crítico, era él mismo" (Guevara was the first, the last, and the only New Man that the revolutionary process

created. The disinterested, hard-working, honest, critical, future Cuban was [Che] himself; 70).

19. Piñera also formed part of the exclusive group of contributors to the journal *Orígenes*. Immediately after its disappearance, he founded the journal *Ciclón* with José Rodríguez Feo. According to Reinaldo Arenas, the latter was "otra revista mucho más irreverente, prácticamente homosexual, dentro de una dictadura como la de Batista, reaccionaria y burguesa. Lo primero que hizo Virgilio [...] fue publicar *Las ciento veinte jornadas de Sodoma y Gomorra* del Marqués de Sade" (another journal much more irreverent than the first, practically a homosexual one, and all under Batista's reactionary bourgeois dictatorship. The first thing Virgilio did [...] was publish the Marquis de Sade's *The One Hundred and Twenty Days of Sodom and Gomorra* 106).

20. This is the same prison that would incarcerate his disciple, Reinaldo Arenas, for eighteen months after being sentenced in 1974.

21. I used to visit Virgilio Piñera at home at seven in the morning . . . sitting in front of me, he read a copy of the novel [*El mundo alucinante*] and where he thought that I should add a comma or change one word for another, he told me so. . . . He was my university professor as well as my friend.

22. Ginsberg makes reference to a rumor circulating for many years. It was not uncommon to hear that the second in command of the Revolution was seen frequenting gay hangouts such as El Floridita and Las Casa de las Infusiones [The House of Infusions].

23. What fault is it of mine? . . . If Nature, or God, or Satan were going to make me a woman and, when the seeds of my being were already planted, they changed their minds and in bad faith they threw in clay belonging to men, what am I to do?

24. that burned his hide, produced tremendous blisters and left a sparking of caustic, terrible little stars in his eyes.

25. one time, with shame and terror, [in] the Municipal Library

26. That's where the ultimate salvation forever is.

27. A son that he would not raise in the folds of his mother's skirts, like he was raised; a son who instead of playing with dolls and hanging around with girls, would be continually in the sun, among mischievous boys, even when he would return with bumps and blisters!

28. In the entry that Alfredo Villanueva writes about Carlos Montenegro in *Latin American Writers on Gay and Lesbian Themes: A Bio-Critical Source Book*, he accurately point out that *Hombres sin mujer* (Men without Women) resembles Adolfo Caminha's novel *Bom-Crioulo* (*The Cabin Boy*; 1895) in that it presents a homoerotic relationship between a black man (strong and older) and a white boy (weak and young) which terminates in the death of both

protagonists because of jealousy towards a third party. The critic argues that *Othello* is the model for this type of writing which treats interracial relations between protagonists and ends in tragedy: "Thus one may venture the hypothesis that in relationships between whites and members of any other racial group, the expected outcome is rupture, separation and personal tragedy for both partners, or at least the nonwhite partner [...], irrespective of the gender of the individuals concerned" (250).

29. This work by Montenegro anticipates the theme of the prison in connection with homosexuality that will later be addressed by the narrations of other authors: José María Arguedas, *El sexto* (The Sixth One; 1961); Manuel Puig, *El beso de la mujer araña* (*Kiss of the Spider Woman*; 1976. In 1966, the Chilean writer José Donoso publishes his novel *El lugar sin límites* (*The Place without Limits*; 1965) in which he elaborates the story of La Manuela, the transvestite protagonist. But unlike the novels already mentioned, he does so in an open space.

30. denouncing of a prison system to which he found himself subjected for twelve years.

31. everything the [pages] say correspond to an existing evil

32. I want to eat white chicken!

33. How is it possible that one man can propose to make another fall in love with him?...He had ended up laughing himself to hysterics. . . . Come on! He also possessed the means. . . . And blood. . . . And power. . . . And . . . lightning! . . . But, when he was really desperate, he dreamed of Encarnación, of Tomasa, with whatever broomstick was around, but with skirts, and ready, on to the next one!

34. Pascasio Speek gave him a punch right in the face, and as he was still close enough since the others were holding [La Morita] up, he hit him again with fury until [La Morita] was rolling around on the floor with his face full of blood.

35. "Do you know what the deal is with all of us?" Matienzo asks the recently jailed Andrés. "It's that we are men without women! There are no perverts here; only men without women. . . . That's all."

36. "You're crazy, but. . . ." [Andrés] couldn't finish his sentence; Pascasio's arm had encircled him and brought him closer to himself, confusing their two mouths. Andrés did not put up any sort of a fight; he closed his eyes, abandoning himself, until Pascasio, astounded by what he himself was doing, let [Andrés] go. Then the boy repeated what he had begun to say to him: "You're crazy, but you're a man. . . .

37. Andrés, with his pants unzipped, ran towards Pascasio and was about to tell him something, but he didn't have time: he stopped all of a sudden, with

broken words in his throat and eyes wet with tears looking at Pascasio, who had dug the cutting edge of a key into [Andrés'] cranium with all the might of his arm and of his savagery.

38. See the documentary *Conducta impropia*, in which various individuals interviewed elaborate in detail the selective proceedings used by state security agencies to arrest young people who would later be sent to the UMAP camps.

39. The essay cited here originally appeared in the journal *Unión* 4 (1966): 36-60.

40. Due to Lezama Lima's universal status, the Stalinist-Cuban censorship could not penalize him to the same degree as it would later do so with Reinaldo Arenas and Heberto Padilla. However, his literary audacity would cost him the strictest limit on the copies of his novel (only 4,000 printings were allowed) and the repeated rejection of his applications to leave the country, despite frequent international invitations.

41. Lezama Lima never took a directly antagonistic stance against the Revolution. In fact, he was one of the intellectuals who initially supported the cultural direction of the Revolution: in January of 1959 he signed, along with other intellectuals, a public document supporting the Revolution; in 1960 he is named Director of Literature and Publications of the Dirección Nacional de Cultural [National Agency for Culture]; and in 1961 he was elected as one of six vice-presidents of the Cuban Writers and Artists Union, under the leadership of the poet Nicolás Guillén. Recently, *La gaceta de Cuba* published a letter written by Lezama to Fidel Castro on 1 February 1959 in which this great master of letters expressed gratitude towards the revolutionaries for their efforts: "Ud. con sus heroicos 'barbudos,' ha sembrado con raíz, *directa*, bien potente, el árbol de la Libertad, en el fértil terreno de la conciencia pública" [You, sir, have sown the tree of Liberty with roots *firmly* and powerfully planted in the fertile terrain public conscience] (Bianchi 18).

42. Pérez Firmat argues that José Cemí's sexual position is, up to the end of the novel, quite undecided, almost androgenous. If it is true that his homosexuality is ambiguous, it is also true that he does not establish any heterosexual relations, even though he does have visions and erotic dreams about his mother, dolphins, etc. Pérez Firmat contends that with Cemí's descent into "las profundidades" (the depths), the last scene of the novel fixes his acceptance of his homosexual desire.

43. If we read carefully the respective descriptions, we can note that a sense of bestiality envelops homosexual sex acts, whereas a festive, almost comical, sense surrounds the heterosexual ones.

44. phallic potency which reigns like Aaron's rod

45. His demonstrative gladiolus was the geography class.

46. Leregas revealed his penis and testicles, acquiring with only one single impetus the transformation of his genitals into a column and the achievement of exceptional size.

47. Leregas exposed his penis, with the same majestic indifference contained in the Velázquez painting in which the key is given over and placed on the pillow, at first, as small as a thimble, but afterwards impelled like a titanical wind, it achieved the length of a manual laborer's forearm.

48. contemplated—Leregas's defiance with—that tenacious cereus ready to break its wrapping at any moment, with an extremely polished blood-red helmet—with which—magnetized with even more force the attentive curiosity of those frozen pilgrims [...] but without any sarcasm nor mocking little grins

49. once he was finished with the normal intercourse [with the cook], he could then begin another *per angostam viam*

50. the woman who lived across the street

51. his two previous encounters which had been rough and clumsy, because now he was entering into the kingdom of subtlety and of diabolical specialization

52. two bodies that love each other

53. when Farraluque tried to take aim, he twisted away from the serpent's path, and when with his stinger he was determined to tease the other's penis from its hiding place, the latter would roll over again, with the promise of a calmer harbor for his prow.

54. criticizes the authority of the hegemonic model that seeks to inculcate itself and its vision of the world which this model transmits and strives to legitimate.

55. According to a comment made by Francisco López Sacha published in *La Gaceta de Cuba* (marzo-abril 1993): 43, in 1984, the Novísimo writer Miguel Mejides published a lesbian short story entitled "Mi prima Amanda" (My cousin Amanda) in the journal *Bohemia*. We have not, unfortunately, been able to locate this text, in part due to the lack of an index for this journal.

56. my pals admit that she, the actress, and I have a lot in common, we have the same grace and the same ethereal air

57. a mother, a father, an adorable little sister, a dog and lots of plants . . . the classic decorous and decorated nest.

58. is marrying some guy just because he has a house in Miramar and a car and a VCR.

59. the majority of people are pitiful; they are empty, and so false; they move only within the narrow limits of the paradigms imposed upon them.

60. If you come home with me and you let me open your fly button by button, I'll lend [Vargas Llosa's novel] to you.

61. I know that the goodness of fags is a double-edged sword.

62. In a prose poem entitled "Mis tentaciones" (My Temptations), Estévez writes "Yo quisiera decir, nombrar todas mis tentaciones, mis pasiones tan simples. Que no hay mayor dicha que tenderse y ver cómo crece la mata de limón, y desear la lluvia, una lluvia sin violencia, cayendo sobre un cuerpo hermoso que baila para mí, y una música suave—Vivaldi, Marcello, Frescobaldi—y una voz de contralto" (I would like to tell, to name all of my temptations, my very simple passions. There is no greater happiness than to lie oneself down to watch the lemon shrub grow, and to wish for the rain, a rain without violence, falling over the beautiful body that dances for me, and a soft music—Vivaldi, Marcello, Frescobaldi—and a contralto voice, 63).

63. they discriminate against him because he is that way/always waiting for someone similar/what fault is it of his if in his feelings/they put the weight of other morals [...] so evident in his emotions.

64. the kid turns out to be/an excellent worker . . . and they don't rely on the others/when they call him to the guns/extra work and on time.

65. the little macho men who are used to treating their wives like slavedrivers.

66. the powerful ones that scandalize the neighborhood/by giving their children luxury cars.

67. Two souls, two bodies,/two men who love each other.

68. are going to be expelled/from the paradise in which they were made to live.

69. We are not God/let's not make another mistake.

Ana María Fagundo's
Poetry Revisited
Language and the Body
Carmen de Urioste

Ana María Fagundo was born in Santa Cruz de Tenerife, Spain, in 1938. She studied business in Spain, but at the age of twenty she moved to the United States with an Anne Simpson scholarship to study English and Spanish Literature at the University of Redlands. She received a doctorate in Comparative Literature from the University of Washington (Seattle) with a thesis on the life and works of Emily Dickinson. Since 1967, Fagundo has been teaching twentieth-century Spanish Literature at the University of California at Riverside. Fagundo's writing covers poetry, short stories, essay, and criticism. She has published nine poetry books: *Brotes* (Sprouts; 1965), *Isla adentro* (Inland in the Island; 1969), *Diario de una muerte* (Diary of a Death; 1970), *Configurado tiempo* (Configuration of Time; 1974), *Invención de la luz* (Invention of Light; 1978), with which she won the Carabela de Oro Prize in Spain in 1977, *Desde Chanatel, el canto* (From Chanatel, the Chant; 1981), *Como quien no dice voz alguna al viento* (As One Who Doesn't Say Anything to the Wind; 1984), *Retornos sobre la siempre ausencia* (Return over the Forever Absence; 1989), and *El sol, la sombra, en el instante* (The Sun, the Shadow, in the Moment; 1994). Her poems can also be found in three anthologies: *Obra poética: 1965-1990* (Poetic Work: 1965-1990; 1990), with an introduction by Candelas Newton, *Isla en sí: 1965-1989* (Island itself; 1992), and *Antología (1965-1989)* (Anthology [1965-1989]), edited by Antonio Martínez Herrarte in 1994. She is the founder of the literary journal *Alaluz*.

When analyzing Ana María Fagundo's poetry, some of the aspects more widely studied by the critics are the relationship between the poetic voice and the act of creation, the foundation of a feminine world through the body, and her unique "poetic cartography," which manifests itself in the use of elements such as "island" and "sea." For example, Candelas Newton claims that "la triada poesía-fisiología-geografía, y sus derivados poema-cuerpo-isla, constituyen los polos en torno a los cuales gira y se sustenta la reflexión poética de Fagundo" (22). At the same time, this triad also represents the axis around which the patriarchal ideology rotates as it enforces its power and control over the individuals: the fixation of the language (e.g., the resolution of all possible ambiguities that could challenge the dominant view; the unity and purity of the language, which standardizes the individuals so that the exercise of power becomes more effective); the restrictions imposed on the use of the body at different levels of representation: political, ideological, and sexual; and the demarcation of the territory in order to establish an in and an out and control the margins (cartographic borders) where transgressions normally take place. In a conventional analysis of Fagundo's poetry, her poems would fall within the context of a patriarchal framework of conduct and her poetic creation would be reduced to an ontological search based on the word as the principle for experimentation. The use of a masculine language to express a feminine conception of the world reveals the appropriation of the language by men and the corresponding subordination of women. To verbalize their being, their feelings, or their world conception, women employ a feminine dialect (consciously or unconsciously), which contains strategies to subvert and evade the patriarchal world organization. As Lucía Guerra Cunningham points out:

> [E]n el texto producido por la mujer se observa una diglosia fundamental en la cual la escritura adopta y se asimila a un espacio intertextual de carácter masculino y dominante estratégicamente ubicando elementos de una visión del mundo subordinada a través de márgenes, vacíos, silencios, inversiones y mímicas con un valor subversivo.[1] (25)

For this reason, in the light of queer criticism, it is possible to analyze Fagundo's poetry not as the perpetuation of patriarchy, but as the representation of a social and sexual identity search, considering identity as a matter of desire. Here I understand queer not only as an openness to sexual alternatives, but also to the construction of a new Subject—not opposed to the Other—liberated from the patriarchal rules of behavior. This new Subject will avoid being constrained within rigid social definitions which would make it appear as a finished product instead of something in progress. From this perspective, the poem and the very act of creation wouldn't be considered as a "finished product," but as "something in the making," always in progress, always changing and mutating its significance. This alternative reading gives us a better understanding of the metaphor used by Fagundo to denote the relationship between the poet and the poem. For example the final stanza in "Poeta"—"Ilusa espera del que sabe/que no se apresa la brisa/en cordones de palabras,/¡que no hay poema!/que la lucha es simple y vieja/eterno diálogo del poeta con el Poeta"[2] (*Brotes* 11)— indicates the progress of the creation, the impossible identification of the poet with the Ideal, and, therefore, the endless construction of the poetic voice. Similarly, this alternative view provides a better understanding of the use of phallic symbols in her metaphors—"De espada en despunte/de torre truncada, de canto./De todo/extendida hasta lo sumo/me crezco, me elevo por lo filo/de lo básico[3] (*Brotes* 29)— which show not the masculine impersonation of the poetic voice, exclusive space to speak about desire (this would be a traditional reading), but the desire of the poetic voice itself. The recurrent utilization of the neuter—"¡A puñados de lo pétalo quiero serte!"[4] (*Brotes* 28)—can also be viewed from a queer perspective as a way to express the no-sex and, consequently, all the sexes, in an attempt to subvert the rigid cultural categorization of the two sexual constructs and indicate the possible openness to alternative sexualities. In the present article, I will study some of the options employed by Fagundo to break the rules and find fissures and displacement in the patriarchal value system and how the poetic voice conceptualizes the poem/the poetry as a body of desire, since, according to Fagundo, the poet's trade consists in "[c]ercar, acariciar, penetrar el cuerpo cambiante y sugerente del idioma a sabiendas de que nunca se podrá poseerlo en su totalidad porque ese cuerpo familiar y amante es, a la vez, extraño, mágico y lejano"[5] ("Lo mío" 16).

Fagundo's poetry could be located, provisionally, within the platonic school of thought where language is attached to desire and where it is precisely the desire which obscures the language: because normal language is inadequate to utter desire, the language has recourse to symbols and allegories. From this point of view, desire as well as language is contemplated as a deficiency, as an open space that cannot be satisfied or can only be ephemerally filled. This conception of desire gives rise to the binary theory of language as well as of desire: masculine/feminine, active/passive, presence/absence, subject/object, full/empty. As Hélène Cixous claimed in *La Jeune née* (*The Newly Born Woman*; 1975), in the formulation of binarism lies the foundation of the concept of power, since one of the opposition terms becomes the archetype and the other represents the absence or lack thereof. Thus, this other term is forced to believe that the path to perfection consists in acquiring the properties of the first. As Zelda I. Brooks affirms in *Struggle for Being: An Interpretation of the Poetry of Ana María Fagundo* (1994) "the poem itself, as an act of creation, lives and brings an intense feeling and desire for a search beyond the ordinary boundaries and methods for knowledge" (23) and this quest will be similar to the journey of the mystic writers in search of God. Fagundo's strategy to break away from the confinement imposed by the patriarchal binary conception of language and desire is the continuous displacement of significations. This displacement is a direct challenge to the patriarchal authority, which attempts to determine the language. I will focus my analysis, primarily, on Fagundo's first book—*Brotes*, which appears divided into four parts: Búsqueda (Search), Caos (Chaos), Remanso (Heaven), and Camino abierto (Open Way)—but I will make references to other texts whenever necessary. In *Brotes*, the poetic voice is captured in its search for identity as it goes through the four stages highlighted in the book in an attempt to apprehend the quintessence of poetry. The recurrence of this idea in the poem titles makes evident an obsession: "Mi poesía," "Poeta," "La página en blanco," "Parto o poema," "Mansedumbre," and "La noche" (My Poetry, Poet, The Blank Page, Labor or Poem, Meekness, and The Night). The first four poems can be read as a traditional journey of the poet trying to give expression to the poetry. One finds echoes of the poetic conception of Juan Ramón Jiménez and his comparison of the poem with the perfection of a rose: "Es como si la rosa/pétalo a pétalo/fuera desnudando su fragante ternura/y se quedara limpia/e infinita en la soledad" (10).[6] But Fagundo, leaving behind this natural conception of poetry, equates the creation of a poem with the experience of childbearing labor, since the relationship between woman and language is based on "a systematic experimentation with the bodily functions" (Cixous 78): "El lento parirse inacabado/de todo lo que se siente rebullendo,/que se palpa en carne viva, que nos sangra" (13).

With "Mansedumbre" (Meekness) the poetic voice forsakes the feminine sphere of pregnancy, childbearing, and suckling as it shifts to a defiance against the rules by abandoning even the conventionalism of being a woman, with an eagerness to find the poetic body outside all binary formulations of masculine/ feminine:

> Saber que la pauta
> la vamos deshenebrando a cada instante
> y que no cabe volver
> sobre lo destrenzado
> que nuestro paso es un rasgar
> de tinieblas,
>   un descubrir a tirones
> nuestro cuerpo y un quehacer desnudo
> ante la soledad desnuda.
> Saber que nuestro grito
> es algodón tierno
>   y que nuestra voz más íntima
> es un caracol muerto.
> ¡Que toda nuestra angustia
> se limita a un diálogo con el silencio!
> Saber lo irremediable del vivir,
> y aplacar el aullido
> y seguir viviendo. [7](77)

The title, "Mansedumbre," seems to indicate submission and moderation, but on the contrary, the texts show rebelliousness against the establishment. The poem addresses the preoccupation with identity and advocates a personal liberation from sociosexual guidelines ("descubrir a tirones nuestro cuerpo") even as it acknowledges that this is a no-return trip. In "Meekness," the poetic voice doesn't identify its product (the poem) with the result of an "uterine social organization" (Spivak 103) such as the childbearing labor, but takes a stand against patriarchal rules ("la pauta"). The search for poetry becomes a search for one's own body and one's own sexuality. In this journey, the poetic voice is not alone: it utilizes the first person plural to represent an entire dissident group with a common antagonism against the binary representation. Two feminine keywords: "trenzar" (to plait/to braid) and "enhebrar" (to thread) represent conformity with a rational behavior. The struggle against this conformity is expressed with the prefix "des-"

(un- in English) in both words—"destrenzar" and "deshenebrar"—expressing the disintegration of the feminine sphere and the adoption of a model of conduct that involves "un rasgar de tinieblas,"[8] "un descubrir a tirones nuestro cuerpo,"[9] and "un quehacer desnudo."[10] Still lacking its own language to be able to express these dissident bodies, the poetic voice uses the masculine one, since the quest entails the admission into a masculine world expressed in the metaphor "deflowering the nighttime." But in the end, the poetic voice feels the anguish of living, of living without hope, because of the impossible dialogue between the dissident bodies with the silence of society. Still—*Brotes* was written in 1965—the fate of these dissenting bodies is the end of a dead snail, that is, nothingness.

The displacement from a patriarchal organization to an open dissidence seems evident in the poem entitled "Transición" (Transition) in "Remanso," the third part of *Brotes*. After the chaos of the second part, the poetic voice announces in the poem "Retorno" (Return): "Ya me vuelvo a lo mi yo,"[11] but with the use of the Spanish neuter "lo," the verse acquires the sense of vacuum or absence of all meanings. At the same time—and most importantly—"lo" is the no-sex, the displacement of the binary conception of masculine/feminine. The use of the neuter indicates Fagundo's desire to escape the sex-gender system as a "sociocultural construct and a semiotic apparatus, a system of representation which assigns meaning [. . .] to individuals within the society" (De Lauretis, *Technologies of Gender* 5). In "Transición," the reader finds the characteristics of this return. The poetic voice has suffered a transformation and now it explains the reasons: The first stanza represents the poetic voice's desire for an existence without regulations: "Entonces todo lo imaginaba suave,/limpio, ceñido de no sé qué,"[12] but in the second and third stanza, the poetic voice feels the overwhelming weight of social demands and chooses to follow the rules: "Entonces me crecieron raíces/y me afinqué a lo cuadrado y exacto."[13] But one day the transmutation occurs and the poetic voice again leaves behind the feminine sphere and unbraids its roots, opening them to the breeze and to the wind (both in neuter, expressing again the no-sex):

> Pero un día no sé cómo
> destrencé mi raíz, mis raíces
> y quedé para siempre
> entraña abierta a lo briso y a lo viento.[14] (34)

Fagundo performs another displacement of meanings in the poem entitled "Conjunción" (Synthesis): here the poetic voice states the relation between poet and poetry, between poem and poetry, between the I and the Other not as an end, but as a uninterrupted displacement:

> Tú la voz
> yo el silencio a grupas de tu voz,
> el jinete ensimismado
> con todo el potro de la palabra
> entre mis muslos de sombras.
> Los dos conjuntados eternamente,
> separados.
> Tú: el poema.
> Yo: la poesía. (53)[15]

In a traditional reading, the binary concept of the language can be seen in the pairs: "yo/tú" (I/you), "voz/silencio" (voice/silence), "jinete/potro" (rider/colt), "conjuntados/separados" (joined/separated). However, when we look at the disposition of genders to describe the elements of the synthesis, we find a gender displacement in which the poem (masculine) is compared to voice (feminine), and poetry (feminine) to silence (masculine), whereas the fusion of the two has the metaphorical representation of a masculine rider riding a colt (masculine). The colt and the rider's thighs—both masculine—are determined by two feminine nouns working as adjectives—"palabra" (word) and "sombra" (darkness) respectively—suggesting the fusion of the two genders into one, neither masculine nor feminine. Therefore, the lack of gender of I/you becomes all the genders or the alternative of genders, that is, their indeterminacy:

Tú (no genre) <->voz (feminine) <->p otro (masculine) <->poema (masculine)
Yo (no genre) <>silencio (masculine) <>jinete (masculine) <->poesía (feminine)

Moreover, this nonassociative identification of genders—for I and you—is not identical in all of Fagundo's books. In "Proximidad de la poesía" (Proximity of the Poetry), from *Invención de la luz*, poetry appears not as a masculine rider, but first as a girl and then as a "mujer cabal" (upright women), that is, the feminine subject or poetry gives herself up to the poetic voice who enjoys the defloration of the first night:

Tenerte así tan cerca, tan vibrante, tan mía
poder convocarte a mi concierto de luces
y sentir tu turgente cuerpo de palabras,
tu voz más íntima restallando sobre la página
. . . .
y haber estrenado tu primer pudor de adolescente,
haberte sentido niña enarbolada
y luego mujer cabal en la alegría y el dolor,
haber probado tu primer amor,
haberte herido con el primer desconcierto. (17)[16]

This poem serves as a bridge to a second topic worthy of analysis
in Fagundo's poetic thinking: the meaning of the body in her poetry.
The body appears in Fagundo's poems as an obsession, and many critics
have studied the body's textuality in her poetry. For example, in "La
textualización del cuerpo femenino en la poesía de Ana María
Fagundo," Antonio Martínez claims that Fagundo:

> no cuestiona el pasado erótico-discursivo del lenguaje. Lo asimila en
> sus entrañas por el simple hecho de asumir las diferencias en sí
> misma: 'Eres mi amada,/mi amante,/mujer mía,/hombre mío,/isla
> mía, acantilado mío,/voz de mi voz,/palabra mía de siglos:/poema,
> caricia, poesía.' ("A la poesía") Proclamando a la mujer y a la poeta
> como fuente de vida, sin pretenderlo, destruye esas estructuras
> binarias machistas de paradigma activo/pasivo, logos/pathos,
> positivo/negativo, que siempre terminan abocando a la pareja
> fundamental masculino/femenino [. . .] (331)[17]

I believe that Fagundo's goal is more radical than claimed by
Martínez. She consciously seeks to challenge the erotic discursivity of
the language and to eliminate not only its inherent masculinism, but
also its patriarchal binarism. In the poem quoted by Martínez and in
other poems that I will analyze later, the poetic voice and its partner
have no predetermined body, but rather an evasive and changeable one.
In order to transgress the patriarchal dualism of the language, it is
essential not only to bring down the binary system of thoughts, but also
to create a new notion of body. For Deleuze and Guattari this new
body's conception is attached to "a discontinuous, nontotalizable series
of processes, organs, flows, energies, corporeal substances and
incorporeal events, speeds and durations" (Grosz 164). According to

them, it becomes necessary to abandon a series of dualistic concepts such as mind/body, spirit/body, soul/body, spirituality/biology, in favor of a view of the body as a space for transformations, for performances, for endless interrelations. In regards to this concept of body, desire is now seen from a entirely different perspective "as what produces, what connects, what makes mechanic alliances" (Grosz 165). Therefore, desire will not be perceived as a lack of the Ideal, but as a concept that makes, that functions, that creates. At the same time, the woman's body will not be framed as a privation of the man's attributes. With this new conceptualization of body and desire, the notion of sexuality also changes. Sexuality is not attached exclusively to sex, biology, and genetics, but it is open to all bodily manifestations, either cultural, social, political, or biological. The bodies must be refigured and specially those bodies which are in the margins—either sexual, political, economical, racial, social, religious, or cultural—must look for diverse dimensions of retheorization. One of the dimensions to consider is the space in which the body develops itself: the body does not exist in vacuum, but it settles in a space which it is necessary to reconsider as a part of the body, since "we do not grasp space directly or through our senses but through our bodily situation" (Grosz 90). It becomes necessary to respect the body-space symbiosis, since intrusion in this space will be equal to an act of taking possession of the body. The objects incorporated to the body are in close connection with the space where the body moves. These objects change from being accessories to being part of the body-image, its representation, its volume, its value, its function, its use, among others. The patriarchal dualism of subject/object is eliminated: the new subject incorporates the objects, which shape the body as much as any body part. The objects mark the body's presence, even when the body can be absent.

The body-space continuity is reflected in Fagundo's poetry book *Isla adentro* as a complete identification of body with an island, the island of Tenerife in Spain. The book, divided into four parts—Isla-poesía, Isla-hombre, Isla-amor, and Isla-muerte (Island-poetry, Island-man, Island-love, and Island-death)—has been extensively studied by critics and, for this reason, I will center my analysis on the above-mentioned *Invención de la luz*. In several poems of this book, Fagundo elaborates on her conception of the body. For example, in "A modo de explicación" (By Way of Explanation) the poem, envisioned as an object, creates a space for the development of the body. However, borders between body, space, and poem don't exist, they are conceived as a continuum. The poetic voice proclaims that the poem is "inside but under the blood" ("dentro pero por debajo de la sangre"), but the same poem creates time and space for the body and for the body senses: the touch ("el tacto") and the taste (represented by the lip, "labio"). In spite of the continuous poem-body space, the poem is not capable of explaining the being-body continuum, symbolized by the objects that, normally, come with the body: name, clothes, shoes sizes, purse, passport, job, and date ("nombre," "ropas," "número de zapatos," "bolso," "pasaporte," "profesión," and "fecha"):

> Llevarte dentro pero por debajo de la sangre
> . . . .
> Habitar así el tiempo no habitable
> y crear espacios concretos donde el cuerpo
> pueda decir que existe
> porque el labio palpa la brisa de la piel
> . . . .
> y no saber decir el por qué del ser
> que lleva mi nombre, que viste mi ropa,
> que calza mi número de zapato,
> que en el bolso guarda un pasaporte para llegar a cualquier tierra;
> y que tiene un nombre, una profesión,
> y una fecha de comienzo;
> . . . . (35-36)[18]

The poetic voice uses the senses of touch and taste to affirm the existence of the body-space: "Pueda decir que existe/porque el labio palpa la brisa de la piel."[19] The binary opposition senses/knowledge has also been erased in the poem, since the poetic voice can arrive at the knowledge of the space through the experience accumulated by the senses. In Fagundo's poetry, touch is the privileged sense: "Inventamos el tacto vibrante de los cuerpos"[20] ("Soledad de los cuerpos"/Bodies in Solitude, *Invención* 20); "Yo toco aquí" ("Pálpito"/Feeling, *Invención* 33); "Dije «tacto», «abril»/dije «las manos»/[. . .] Dije «toda la piel», toda la orgía de la mirada"[21] ("Visitación"/Visitation, *Invención* 31). The way the sense of touch gathers information is extremely complex, since it puts surfaces in contact while providing diachronic notions of form, temperature, and texture (Grosz 98). But in order to obtain a more extensive knowledge, the body-space-poem continuum utilizes a combination of the senses, as in "Nombres" (Names):

Estoy nombrándome un universo de tactos,
ojos, piel, labios,
pasos que comparten otros pasos,
mi cuerpo despertando otro cuerpo,
mi voz en otra voz nombrando
. . . .(81)[22]

Here, the body awakens another body inside a universe of senses in
contact: "tactos" (touchings; touch), "ojos" (eyes; sight), "piel" (skin;
touch), "labios" (lips; taste), "pasos" (steps; hearing), and "voz" (voice;
hearing). With the ability of the intertwining senses to create
knowledge, the supremacy of language disappears and the communication between bodies acquires a dimension beyond the world of
words. At the same time, this independence of knowledge from the
sphere of language implies the autonomy of pleasure, which can be
attached to multiple dimensions of exchange, for example, pain.
Culturally, pain has been seen as a negative concept, although typically
acceptable in the religious sphere as a means to arrive to superior levels
of spirituality: the bodily pain was merely observed as adequate when
addressed to God. From the perspective of Catholic discourse, it is
reasonable to represent the saints in pain, as suffering bodies waiting
for the divine recompense in form either of love or the pleasure of
heaven. Beyond the mystic world organization and before the cultural
limitation of the body concept, the body was a tabula rasa opened to the
senses' experimentation. Thus, pain was observed as a currency
(Deleuze, cited by Grosz 132) and appropriated by the justice inside a
principle of socioeconomic contract. The reintegration of pain to the
sphere of bodily pleasures has been observed by Fagundo in her poem
"Amando" (Loving):

Erguirse enhiesto.
Clavar el dardo de la fé.
Herirse.
Sentir el bisturí del tiempo abrir surcos profundos,
el tajo del cuchillo hendirse en el beso
y abrir el cuerpo entregándose.
Estar dispuesto a la ternura,
                    al dolor,
al puñal que clava su luz en nuestro centro
. . . .(87-88)[23]

Here pain—produced by an erect member/"enhiesto," by the faith dart/ "dardo de la fé" [sic], by a scalpel/"bisturí," and by a dagger/"puñal"— has the same value as tenderness. Understanding *puñal* as a symbolization of justice, pain will have the meaning of tenderness within the human, mystic, medical, and justice discourses.

As a conclusion of this rereading of Ana María Fagundo's poetry, where we have seen that language renounces the binary system limitation, liberating notions such as desire, body, body-image, objects, senses, pain, from the patriarchal conceptualization of the world, the poem "La canción del estreno"/The Song of Inaguration from *Invención de la luz* serves as a exemplary recapitulation:

> Ya vuelvo a estrenar los labios,
> la redondez de los hombros,
> los senos, las manos,
> las manos para darle forma a otro cuerpo,
> los labios para que moldeen mis labios.
> Y todo único, nuevo, infinito:
> el vientre estrenando el temblor;
> los muslos al son de un nuevo canto.
> Estoy estrenando el tacto de la piel,
> el de los ojos, el del paso,
> el de mi huella y mi sombra,
> el de mi sangre alborotada en otra sangre.
> . . . .(25)[24]

The body of the poetic voice is not terminated with the first sexual performance, but from its fragmentation into lips ("labios"), shoulders ("hombros"), breasts ("senos"), and hands ("manos"), it still can orient itself toward other bodies through the senses of touch ("manos") and taste ("labios"). The broken body and its parts are articulated again from the stomach ("el vientre") and the thighs ("los muslos") for a new and eternal song. The reconfigured body—the skin ("la piel"), the eyes ("los ojos"), the step ("el paso"), the footprint ("la huella"), the shadow ("la sombra")—dialogues with the other body through the fluids—the blood ("la sangre")—which mark both bodies as women's bodies. Inside the practice of a dissident sexuality—structured alongside to the heterosexual male concept of desire—women can redefine the zones of their bodies that produce pleasure. In addition , it is possible to emanci- pate woman's body from patriarchal beliefs—such as virginity, deflowering, marriage, illness, honor, pregnancy, among others—which served, for centuries, to center the feminine sexuality, while reinforcing women's oppression by tying them to bodily functions.

NOTES

1. In texts written by women, one observes a fundamental diglossia in which the writing adopts and assimilates itself to an intertextual space of masculine and dominant character, but strategically scattering elements of a subordinate vision of the world through margins, gaps, silences, inversions, and mimes with subversive value.

2. Deluded wait of he who knows/that the breeze cannot be seized/in ropes of words,/that there is no poem!/that the struggle is simple and ancient;/ eternal dialogue of the poet with the Poet. Translated into English by Zelda I. Brooks in her book *Struggle for Being* (24).

3. Of sword sprouting/of truncated tower,/of chant./Of everything/spread until the summit/I grow myself, I raise myself by the edge/of the basic.

4. By the handful of the petal I want to be yourself!

5. [t]o enclose, to caress, to penetrate the moody and suggestive body of the language knowingly that never one can possess it totally because that familiar and loving body is, at the same time, odd, magic, and distant.

6. It is as if the rose/petal by petal/were revealing its fragrant smoothness/ and was left cleansed/and infinite in its loneliness. Translated into English by Z. Brooks in her book *Struggle for Being* (22).

7. To know that we unthread the the guideline/at every moment/and that it is not possible to return/to the unbraided/that every step is a tearing/of the darkness/a discovery of our bodies in one go/and a naked chore/ facing the naked loneliness./To know that our cry/is tender cotton/and that our most private voice/is a death snail./To know that all our entire anguish/is limited to a dialogue with silence!/To know how irremediable is living/and to soothe the howl/ and to go on with living.

8. tearing of the darkness.

9. discovering our bodies in one go.

10. a naked work.

11. Now I return to my I.

12. Then I imagined everything soft,/clean, tight by I don't know what.

13. Then roots grew on me/and I settled to the square and exact.

14. But one day I don't know how/I unthreaded my root, my roots/and I stayed forever/with entrails open to breeze and to wind.

15. You the voice/me the silence riding your voice,/the rider deep in thought/with all the colt of the word/between my thighs of shadows./Both eternally joined,/separated./You: The poem./Me: The poetry.

16. To have you so close, so vibrant, so mine/to be able to call you to my lights concert/and to feel your turgid body of words/your more private voice glittering over the page/[. . .]/and to have been the first to test your adolescent modesty/to have felt you as a raised girl/and then as an upright woman in joy and in pain,/to have tasted your first love,/to have wounded you with the first confusion.

17. [Fagundo] doesn't question the erotic-discursive past of the language. She makes it part of her flesh by accepting the differences within herself: "You are my love,/my lover,/my woman,/my man,/my island,/my cliff,/voice of my voice,/my word of centuries:/poem, caress, poetry." ("To Poetry") Proclaiming woman and poetry as springs of life, without actually intending it, she destroys those binary sexist structures of active/pasive, logos/pathos, positive/negative paradigm which always lead toward the basic masculine/feminine pair [. . .]

18. To carry you inside but under the blood/[. . .]/and in this way to reside in the unlivable time/and create concrete spaces where the body/can say that it exists/ because the lip senses the skin breeze/[. . .]/and not to know how to express the purpose of the human being/who wears my name, who wears my clothes,/who takes my shoe size,/who keeps a passport in the purse to arrive to any land;/and who has a name, a profession,/and a beginning date;/[. . .]

19. One can say that it exists/because the lip touches the skin breeze.

20. We invent the vibrant touch of the bodies.

21. I touch here.

22. I said "touch," "April"/I said "the hands"/[. . .] I said "all the skin," all the look orgy.

23. I am naming myself a universe of touches,/eyes, skin, lips,/steps which share other steps,/my boy awakening another body,/my voice in other voice naming/[. . .]

24. To stand erect./To thrust in the dart of faith./To wound oneself./To feel the sharp blade of time opening deep furrows,/the cut of a knife cleaving its way in a kiss/and to open our body surrendering,/to be ready for terderness,/for pain,/for the dagger which stabs its light in our core/[. . .]

25. I am now returning to wear my lips for the first time,/the shoulders´ roundness,/the breasts, the hands,/the hands, so that they form another body,/the lips, so that they shape my lips./And everything unique, new, countless:/the stomach shaking for the first time;/the thighs dancing to the sound of a new song./I am using the skin touch for the first time,/that of the eyes, that of the step,/that of my footprint and my shadow,/that of my blood excited by some other blood/[. . .]

Building a Research Agenda on U. S. Latino Lesbigay Literature and Cultural Production

Texts, Writers, Performance Artists, and Critics

Manuel de Jesús Hernández-G.

*In twenty years, we will have degree-granting programs
in lesbian and gay studies, but there are no guarantees
that they will be headed by people whose work
incorporates an awareness of race. Lesbians and
gays of color and their allies need constant vigilance,
networking, and organizing to ensure that lesbian and
gay studies will be a site for what it purports to do: study
lesbians and gays (not just white, middle-class lesbians
and gays).*
—Yvonne Yarbro-Bejarano, "Expanding the Categories" 126

A growing bibliography materially marks the maturing of homoerotic cultural production among U. S. Latinas/os at both the creative and critical level. In creative writing, a number of leading lesbigay voices have surfaced in three of the major U.S. Latino ethnic groups: Chicanas/os, AmeRícans,[1] and Cuban-Americans. Among Chicanas/os, we have John Rechy (b. 1934), Gloria Anzaldúa (b. 1942), Cherríe Moraga (b. 1952), Richard Rodriguez[2] (b. 1944), Michael Nava (b. 1954), and Francisco X. Alarcón (b. 1956).[3] Among AmeRícans, there are Luz María Umpierre-Herrera (b. 1947) and Carlos A. Rodríguez-Matos (b. 1949). As for Cuban Americans, Elías Miguel Muñoz (b. 1954) and Mireya Robles (b. 1934) are the leading figures. Luis Alfaro

(b. 1964) is the leading lesbigay performance artist. Along with these leading writers and performance artists, there are several important critics (to be later identified within this essay). In the near future, publication of one theoretical book on U.S. Chicano/Latino gay writing and one on U.S. Chicana/Latina lesbian letters will contain these critical voices, currently noticed for their silence in over sixty-five critical books published in the last twenty-three years on Chicano/U.S. Latino criticism.[4]

LEADING CHICANA/O LESBIGAY WRITERS

Fortunate to sign a contract in 1959 with Grove Press,[5] a then unknown but today a mainstream publisher, John Rechy began his publishing career in 1963—two years before the beginning of contemporary Chicano literature in 1965.[6] By acquiring such a contract, he achieved—a first—something unrepeated by other Mexican American writers until the 1990s: publishing in a mainstream Anglo-American press.[7] In fact, Grove Press printed Rechy's first five novels and a documentary: *City of Night* (1963), *Numbers* (1967), *This Day's Death* (1969), *Vampires* (1971), *Rushes* (1979), and *The Sexual Outlaw: A Documentary* (1977). Moreover, Rechy represents another first among Chicano/U.S. Latino writers: having a best seller across America (Castillo 118).[8] With Grove Press's decline as a major publisher, due in part to expensive court battles incurred from fighting censorship, Rechy continued publishing his novels with other Anglo presses in New York and Los Angeles: *Bodies and Souls* (1983), *Marilyn's Daughter* (1988), *The Miraculous Day of Amalia Gómez* (1991), and *Our Lady of Babylon* (1996) (see bibliographic appendeix, below).[9] *The Miraculous Day of Amalia Gómez* links directly to contemporary Chicana/o literature.

In Chicano gay writing, only Michael Nava (b. 1954), a new and younger writer, has matched Rechy's accomplishment of publishing with Anglo-American presses and becoming a prolific writer. In a brief, ten-year period, 1986 to 1996, Nava published five detective novels— *The Little Death* (1986), *Goldenboy* (1988), *How Town* (1990), *The Hidden Law* (1992), and *The Death of Friends* (1996)—whose protagonist is gay, one collection of suspense short stories entitled *Finale: Short Stories of Mystery and Suspense* (1989), and one gay-rights book, *Created Equal: Why Gay Rights Matter to America* (1994). Comparable to Rechy's success, three of these novels went into a second or third printing: *The Little Death, Goldenboy*, and *How Town*. Nava's latest novel is *The Burning Plain* (1997).

1981: THE YEAR OF THE CHICANA/O LESBIGAY VOICE

With their own prize-winning and commercially successful works, Cherríe Moraga, Gloria Anzaldúa, and Richard Rodriguez attained leading roles in contemporary Chicana/o literature. Concomitantly, they have influenced mainstream Anglo writing, Anglo feminist and lesbian letters, and literature by other writers of color. Historically, all three began publishing U.S. Latino literature in the same year, 1981, with the following works: *This Bridge Called My Back: Radical Writings by Women of Color* edited by Moraga and Anzaldúa,[10] and *Hunger of Memory: The Education of Richard Rodriguez* (1981) by Rodriguez.[11] *Hunger of Memory* had the most immediate impact on Chicanos and the general U.S. society. Rodriguez's autobiography was central both as a leading genre and as a critical discourse in Chicano literature;[12] moreover, with the essay "Late Victorians: San Francisco, AIDS, and the Homosexual Stereotype" (1990), published originally in *Harper's Magazine* and then included in the essay collection *Days of Obligation: An Argument with My Mexican Father* (1992), Rodriguez drew attention to the impact of AIDS on gays.[13]

Co-editors of *This Bridge Called My Back: Radical Writings by Women of Color*, Moraga and Anzaldúa represent Chicana/o literature concerning the issues of feminism, sexuality, and gender. They enabled Chicanas to take the lead in mainstreaming Chicana/o writing.[14] Six years later, Anzaldúa published her own original work, *Borderlands/La Frontera: The New Mestiza*, which soon became the central text in borderlands writing and critical discourse.[15] In 1990, she edited the collection *Making Face, Making Soul/Haciendo Caras: Creative and Critical Perspectives by Women of Color.*[16] Since co-editing *This Bridge Called My Back*, Moraga remains at the center of Chicana/o literature with her books *Loving in the War Years: lo que nunca pasó por sus labios* (1983) and *The Last Generation* (1992), that contain three essays now considered canonical in Chicana/o literature: respectively, "A Long Line of Vendidas" (1983), "Art in América con Acento" (1992), and "Queer Aztlán: the Reformation of Chicano Tribe" (1992).

Finally, Francisco Alarcón, a poet, barrio activist, teacher, and gay advocate, has become, in less than ten years, the leading Chicano poet of homoerotic verse and social commitment (Hernández-Gutiérrez 7-8). His human and artistic image of the Chicano/U.S. Latino homosexual appears in two of his most important poetry collections: *Body in Flames/Cuerpo en llamas* (1990) and *Snake Poems* (1992). From 1980 to the early 1990s, Alarcón's socially organic verse helped fill the vacuum left by *engagé* poets of the 1960s and 1970s. With *Snake Poems*, he also surpasses the indigenist voice found in early barrio poetry. Moreover, with the publication of *De amor oscuro/Of Dark Love* (1991) Alarcón gained the recognition of Chicano critical acclaim for writing the best love poetry book, if not in the history of Mexican American literature since 1848, in all contemporary Chicano Chicana/o literature. Many Chicana/o heterosexual poets write poetry questioning traditional sex roles; thus, they seem to overlook producing quality love poetry.

LEADING AMERÍCAN AND CUBAN AMERICAN LESBIGAY WRITERS

Among leading AmeRícan lesbigay writers, the poet, Luz María Umpierre-Herrera, represents the lesbian voice and the poet, Carlos A. Rodríguez-Matos, the gay male voice. Like in the case of Chicana lesbian writers, Third Woman Press makes available works by Umpierre-Herrera. In the 1980s this press published three of her works: *En el país de las maravillas* (1982), *. . .Y otras desgracias/And Other Misfortunes* (1985), and *The Margarita Poems* (1987). According to George Klawitter, this last collection contains Umpierre-Herrera's fully defined lesbian voice with the poem "Immanence" as the most representative (435). On the other hand, her three volumes of poetry feature a certain reserve in using the lesbian voice.[17] With two poetry books written in Spanish, *Matacán* (1982) and *Llama de amor vivita: jarchas* (1988), Rodríguez-Mato's production is limited. However, in sharp contrast to Umpierre-Herrera, the gay male voice seems to exude expressiveness. Ana Sierra claims that Rodríguez-Matos openly writes, without sacrificing his sense of humor, on "the impact of societal repression on homosexuals" (375). In writing uninhibited gay male poetry, he confesses experiencing "the feeling of stirring up mischief" (quoted in Sierra 375).

Within Cuban-American lesbigay writing, Elías Miguel Muñoz represents the most outspoken voice and Mireya Robles Cuban-American lesbians. To date, Muñoz has published three novels and two poetry collections, and Mireya Robles represents Cuban-American lesbians. The leading Cuban-American press, Editorial Universal, published in Spanish Muñoz's first novel *Los viajes de Orlando Cachumbambe* (1984). However, Arte Público Press published English versions of his next two works, which develop a gay male voice: *Crazy Love* (1989) and *The Greatest Performance* (1991). According to John C. Miller, Muñoz's three novels "move from assured heterosexuality to bisexuality to homosexuality, as they go from Spanish to English" (276), exploring not only gay male identity but also lesbian, heterosexual, and bisexual. As a group, Muñoz's three novels display an evolution of sexuality. In addition to examining the following issues, lesbian and gay life, Chicano power, political exile, and Hispanic acculturation into U.S. society, *The Greatest Performance* covers in detail the impact of AIDS on the U.S. Latino society. Written exclusively in Spanish, Muñoz's poetry collections also expose multiple facets of gay life. In contrast with Muñoz's substantial production, Mireya Robles has published only two significant homoerotic works (both in Spanish): a poetry collection entitled *En esta aurora* (1978) whose protagonist's love desire is an absent lesbian lover, and the novel *Hagiografía de Narcisa la bella* (1985) whose protagonist, according to Karen S. Christian, develops her lesbian identity "more through her fantasies than through actual homoerotic encounters" (368). The lesbian Cuban-American voice has a minimal representation in U.S. Latino literature, a view reinforced by the Cuban-American lesbian critic, Lourdes Argüelles.

ALFARO: LEADING LESBIGAY PERFORMANCE WRITE

Regarding cultural production, the best known gay contribution comes from performance art. A recipient of the MacArthur Award, Luis Alfaro is the leading figure in this field. Born and raised in East Los Angeles, he has been a performance artist since the 1980s. To date, he has one outstanding CD, *down town* (1994), which dramatizes his barrio childhood, his coming out and life as a gay man, his fear of AIDS, and his participation in cultural and social struggles. Alfaro's notable contribution both in art and social activism was recognized in the recently released critical article "Teatro Viva! Latino Performance and the Politics of AIDS in Los Angeles" (1995) by David Román. Alfaro is expected to produce greater work, especially since the MacArthur Award guarantees economic independence for five years.

THIRD WOMAN PRESS: THE LEADING PRESS
FOR U.S. LATINO LESBIGAY WRITING

Although small presses founded contemporary Chicana/o literature
with an ethnic social base as a world literary discourse in the 1960s and
1970s, they also made an effort, though minor in quantitative terms, to
extend a space for lesbian and gay writers.[18] The new, small presses
that today maintain U.S. Latino literature as a viable and living
discourse also continue to publish lesbigay writing.[19] From its founding
in 1981, Third Woman Press led in publishing U.S. Latino gay and
lesbian writing, particularly Latina lesbian letters. This press remains at
the forefront with the publication of such titles as: *En el país de las
maravillas* (1982), . . . *Y otras desgracias/And Other Misfortunes*
(1985), and *The Margarita Poems* (1987) by Luz María Umpierre-
Herrera; *The Sexuality of Latinas* (1993) edited by Norma Alarcón, et
al.; *Chicana Critical Issues* (1993) edited by Norma Alarcón, et al.;
Chicana Lesbians: The Girls Our Mothers Warned Us About (1991)
edited by Carla Trujillo; and *Living Chicana Theory* (1998) edited by
Carla Trujillo.[20] Notwithstanding, other presses contribute historically
to publishing U.S. Latino lesbigay writing. Headed by two leading
Chicano critics, Nicolás Kanellos and Gary Keller, Arte Público Press
and Bilingual Press continue to make a contribution to U.S. Latino
lesbigay writing. Bilingual Press has published: *The Mixquihuala
Letters* (1986) by Ana Castillo; *Beggar on the Córdoba Bridge/Three
Times a Woman: Chicana Poetry* (1989) by Alicia Gaspar de Alba; *En
estas Tierras/In This Land* (1989) by Elías Miguel Muñoz; and *The
Mystery of Survival and Other Stories* (1993) by Alicia Gaspar de Alba.
Arte Público Press has published: *Crazy Love* (1989) and *The Greatest
Performance* (1991) by Elías Miguel Muñoz, and *Tommy Stands Alone*
(1995) by Gloria Velásquez. Apparently a small feminist press, West
End Press, has published *Giving Up the Ghost: Teatro in Two Acts*
(1986) and *Heroes and Saints and Other Plays* (1994) by Cherríe
Moraga. In Watertown, Massachusetts, Persephone Press published the
first edition of *This Bridge Called My Back*, whose subsequent editions
were produced by Kitchen Table Press.[21] Along with U.S. Latino and
small Anglo feminist presses, journals have dedicated special issues to
Latino lesbigay writing: in 1979 *Minority Voices* featured a special
section on John Rechy; in 1995 *Diacritics* also featured three articles
about him;[22] and in 1993 *Signs* published a special number entitled
"Theorizing Lesbian Experience."[23]

In reviewing the publishing of lesbigay writing by U.S. Latino presses, it is apparent that Chicana/Latina lesbian writers, in comparison to gay Chicano/Latino male gays, have met with greater success in publishing their work, because of Third Woman Press, who from its modest beginnings in 1981 has committed space for U.S. Latina lesbians. Although individuals may be featured as contributing writers or guest editors in mainstream Anglo feminist journals and books, U.S. Latina lesbians guarantee the survival of their literary expression through their own presses and journals. On the other hand, U.S. Latino gays have relied on short-lived presses, on small Chicano/Latino presses, publication abroad, or acceptance of a space within small Anglo presses. Along with two other Chicano gay poets, Francisco X. Alarcón helped found the press, Humanizarte, which published the first openly gay poetry collection *Ya vas, carnal* (1985) in contemporary Chicano literature, edited by Rodrigo Reyes, Alarcón and Juan Pablo Gutiérrez. Carlos A. Rodríguez-Matos and Elías Miguel Muñoz each published a poetry book in Madrid, Spain; respectively, *Matacán* (1982) and *No fue posible el sol* (The Sun Was Not Possible, 1989). Arturo Islas published the first edition of *The Rain God: A Desert Tale* (1984), with Alexandrian Press—a small Anglo press. In 1990 Francisco Alarcón published *Body in Flames/Cuerpo en llamas* through Chronicle Books, a San Francisco press. Within the publication world of U.S. Latino lesbigay writing, John Rechy and Michael Nava are exceptions: they have succeeded in publishing with mainstream Anglo presses, especially Rechy, who had three openly gay novels as bestsellers across the United States. On the other hand, due in part to publishing in Anglo presses and his reluctance to interact with the writers of contemporary Chicano and U.S. Latino literature, Rechy's work took fifteen years to earn a place in contemporary Chicano literature. Michael Nava has not been recognized as part of Chicano literature.[24]

THE RISE AND CONTRIBUTION
OF U.S. LATINO LESBIGAY CRITICISM

Critical analysis of U.S. Latino/Hispanic homoerotic literature includes four significant theoretical articles, several leading critics, two noteworthy responses from leading Anglo-lesbian critics, and one theoretical challenge from a renowned Latin American critic.

An original proponent of internal-colony theory in Chicana/o Studies, Tomás Almaguer (b. 1948) is author of the leading theory on Chicano gay sexuality, "Chicano Men: A Cartography of Homosexual Identity and Behavior" (1991), that originally appeared in the journal *différences: A Journal of Feminist Cultural Studies* and has been reprinted in the leading anthology *The Lesbian and Gay Studies Reader* (1993) edited by Henry Abelove, et al. and in *Social Perspectives in Lesbian and Gay Studies: A Reader* (1998) edited by Peter M. Nardi and Beth E. Scheneider.[25] A marked achievement, Almaguer mainstreamed Chicano gay theory.[26] Notwithstanding, the article "Chicano Men: A Cartography of Homosexual Identity and Behavior" has been criticized by, among others, David William Foster and the gay Chicano poet Francisco Alarcón, who criticize the article's use of binary thinking. Nontheless, Almaguer's essay has not been challenged by another Chicano gay writer, displacing Almaguer's theoretical article as the leading one.[27] A possible exception would be Michael Nava's book *Created Equal: Why Gay Rights Matter to America* (1994).

In the field of Chicana/U.S. Latina lesbian theory, Gloria Anzaldúa, Cherríe Moraga, Emma Pérez, and Lourdes Argüelles remain leading figures. The first three have produced the respective texts: "La conciencia de la mestiza: Towards A New Consciousness" (1987), "Queer Aztlán: The Re-formation of Chicano Tribe" (1993), and "Irigaray's Female Symbolic in the Making of Chicana Lesbian *Sitios* y *Lenguas* (Sites and Discourses)" (1998). Argüelles is co-author with B. Ruby Rich of the two-part article entitled "Homosexuality, Homophobia, and Revolution: Notes toward an Understanding of the Cuban Lesbian and Gay Male Experience," published respectively in *Signs* 9.4 (Summer 1984) and *Signs* 11 (1985).[28] She was also co-guest editor for *Signs*'s special issue entitled "Theorizing Lesbian Experience" (18.4, Summer 1993). Anzaldúa produced the leading article in Chicana lesbian theory, making a global impact among both feminist Anglo and minority lesbians, and abroad in Mexico and Europe. Specifically, "La conciencia de la mestiza: Towards A New Consciousness," a chapter of *Borderlands/La Frontera*, has influenced two leading white lesbian critics: Annamarie Jagose and Shane Phelan. They each wrote a chapter in a recent critical book: "Slash and Suture: The Border's Figuration of Colonialism, Homophobia, and Phallo-centricism in *Borderlands/La Frontera: The New Mestiza*" (1994) and "Lesbians and Mestizas: Appropriation and Equivalence" (1994). Although claiming not to find the touted transcendency in Anzaldúa's borderlands theory, Phelan does value, in contrast to Jagose, its transgression regarding race (Phelan 74) and considers it highly instrumental in building "coalitional identity politics" (Phelan 58). Since the mid-1980s, Chicana and other U.S. Latina lesbians have maintained a dialogue with Anglo-American feminists and lesbians through journals such as *Signs*,[29] anthologies such as *The Lesbian and Gay Studies Reader*, and organizations such as the National Women's Studies Association. In 1988 the latter's annual conference featured Anzaldúa as a plenary speaker (Phelan 68). Contributing to Chicano lesbigay writing, the essay "Queer Aztlán: The Re-formation of Chicano Tribe" by Moraga represents an invitation for Chicano readers to recognize gays and lesbians as part of the community and, as such, is an attempt to dialogue with mainstream Chicano thought. Finally, in the essay "Irigaray's Female Symbolic in the Making of Chicana Lesbian *Sitios y Lenguas* (Sites and Discourses)," Emma Pérez blends feminist symbolic criticism and historical materialism in order to fashion a new, alternative Chicana lesbian theory alongside Anzaldúa's derridean one.

LEADING U.S. LATINO HOMOEROTIC CRITICS

A review of Chicano/U.S. Latino homoerotic criticism reveals as leading voices the following critics: Juan Bruce-Novoa, Yvonne Yarbro Bejarano, David William Foster, Arnaldo Cruz Malavé, and John C. Miller. With the article "Homosexuality and the Chicano Novel," first published in 1986 in the journal entitled *Confluencia: revista hispánica de cultura y literatura* (Confluence: Hispanic Journal of Culture and Literature) and then reprinted in both *European Perspectives on Hispanic Literature in the United States* (1988) edited by Genvieve Fabre and *Homosexual Themes in Literary Studies* (1992) edited by Stephen Donaldson, Bruce-Novoa represent the most successful Chicano critic who, aided by Charles Tatum and Carlos Zamora, expanded the Chicana/o literary canon to include both gay and lesbian writers.[30] In this now canonical article, Bruce-Novoa openly criticizes homophobia among Mexican American critics and convincingly argues for including John Rechy, Sheila Ortiz Taylor, and Arturo Islas in Chicana/o literature. Few can deny that since the publication of "Homosexuality and the Chicano Novel," Chicano gay and lesbian writers have been an integral part of the Chicano literary canon.[31]

Critic Yarbro-Bejarano has written nine articles on Chicana lesbian writing with five dedicated to work by Cherríe Moraga (see bibliography in this volume). A significant achievement, Yarbro-Bejarano contributed the article entitled "Expanding the Categories of Race and Sexuality in Lesbian and Gay Studies" to the noteworthy anthology *Professions of Desire: Lesbian and Gay Studies in Literature* (1995) edited by George E. Haggerty and Bonnie Zimmerman and published by the Modern Language Association. Yarbro-Bejarano has contributed, like Anzaldúa and Moraga in the creative field, to the inclusion of Chicano/U.S. Latino literature into mainstream homoerotic writing and criticism. Moreover, Yarbro-Bejarano's nine articles could be published as a critical book on Chicana lesbian writing.

David William Foster is the undisputed leader regarding encyclopedia work on Chicana(o)/U.S. Latina(o) writers. His bio-critical sourcebook entitled *Latin American Writers on Gay and Lesbian Themes* (1994) includes twenty-one U.S. Latino writers, among them: Francisco Alarcón, Gloria Anzaldúa, Cherríe Moraga, Elías Miguel Muñoz, Michael Nava, Achy Obejas, Sheila Ortiz Taylor, Terri de la Peña, John Rechy, Mireya Robles, Carlos A. Rodríguez-Matos, and Luz María Umpierre-Herrera. Unlike the literary biography written on some of the same Chicano authors in the two volumes entitled *Chicano Writers: First Series* (1989) and *Chicano Writers: Second Series* (1992), edited by Francisco Lomelí and Carl R. Shirley, which emphasize the ethnic dimension, Foster includes biographies which directly and uninhibitedly discuss lesbian and gay issues, works, and themes. In fact, some of the entries examine homophobia in such heterosexual writers as Oscar Zeta Acosta, Estela Portillo Trambley, and Piri Thomas. With three entries, John C. Miller represents the largest contribution to Foster's *Latin American Writers on Gay and Lesbian Themes.*

AmeRícan lesbigay critical writing is done by Arnoldo Cruz-Malavé, and Cuban-American by Lourdes Argüelles. Cruz-Malavé's 1995 article "Towards an Art of Transvestism: Colonialism and Homosexuality in Puerto Rican Literature" considers Neo-Rican gay and lesbian literature as an extension of writing in the island and thereby ideologically anticolonialist.[32] Cuban-American writers, as well as other U.S. Latino writers, recognize Lourdes Argüelles as an ally of lesbian critical discourse. She has made two significant contributions: 1) her two-part essay entitled "Homosexuality, Homophobia, and Revolution: Notes toward an Understanding of the Cuban Lesbian and Gay male Experience" (1984 and 1985) and 2) her co-editing in 1993 of the special *Signs* number, "Theorizing Lesbian Experience."

CONCLUSION

Without a doubt, U.S. Latina/o lesbigay cultural production has earned a place locally, nationally, and internationally in creative and critical discourse. However, it took over twenty-four years of conscious efforts—from *City of Night* by John Rechy in 1963 to *Borderlands/La Frontera* by Gloria Anzaldúa in 1987—to establish such a voice among U.S. Latinos, mainstream Americans in general, and academia. Those years are marked by a marginal existence for the work by U.S. Latino lesbigay writers. The consequences of this situation continues to linger, for these works are found primarily in gay and lesbian studies, some sectors in Chicano/U. S. Latino studies, women studies, and poststructuralist critics in literary and cultural studies. That is, U.S. Latina/o lesbigay cultural production is not fully mainstreamed.

The initial literary and commercial success of U.S. Latino lesbigay discourse, *City of Night*, opened in blockbuster fashion. By 1965, Rechy's first novel had been translated into Brazilian and German, in addition to remaining seven weeks as a best-seller across America. The inclusion of the 1964 essay "Rechy and Gover" by Terry Southern in the critical collection *Contemporary American Novelists*, edited by Harry T. Moore, promises a place in the canon for Rechy alongside Walt Whitman, Thomas Clayton Wolfe, and Carl Sandburg. Southern praises Rechy for earning a place in "the self-revelatory school of Romantic Agony" (222) in American letters. It is a thesis implied once again in the 1990 article "Dionysus in Publishing: Barney Rosset, Grove Press, and the Making of a Countercanon" by S. E. Gontarski. Unfortunately, existing bibliography on U.S. Latino lesbigay creative writing reveals that no other critic of American literature took Southern's and Moore's early enthusiasm and inclusion of Rechy seriously.[33] In retrospect, a leading critic of the Chicana/o literary project (Hernández-Gutiérrez 51-53), Juan Bruce Novoa, rescued Rechy's work for Chicana/o literature, U.S. Latino literature, and American literature in general. Rechy's novels now form part of literature classes in Chicana/o studies programs across the country. Rechy himself can be found in books of literary biography like *Chicano Writers: Second Series* and has been the object of major discussion in conferences on Chicano literature like "New Perspectives on Chicano/a Cultures: An Interdisciplinary Conference," held at the University of California in Los Angeles on May 15, 1997.

Ironically, inconsistency marks Rechy's inclusion. In spite of publishing nine novels and one documentary, with three of these texts earning best-seller status, Rechy's creative work, as well as the respective critical work, have been excluded from the groundbreaking 1993 anthology *The Lesbian and Gay Studies Reader* edited by Henry Abelove, et al.. Mainstream critics also seem reluctant to include new and younger Chicano gay writers like Michael Nava. The silencing and/or glossing of the U.S. Latino lesbigay voice in over sixty-five critical works on Chicano/U.S. Latino literature needs to be addressed. This critical task will shed greater understanding on the contributions by AmeRícans, Cuban-Americans, and other U.S. Latino gay writers.

U.S. Latina lesbian literature and criticism appears to have the widest acceptance among mainstream Americans in general, particularly by Chicanas/os and U.S. Latinas/os, Anglo feminists and lesbians, and women of color. Both Third Woman Press and the journal *Signs* have played a significant role. Among countless works, the now classic essay collection *Borderlands/La Frontera* by Gloria Anzaldúa is considered the textual link. Cherríe Moraga's work also appears to have been accepted. Moreover, Cuban-American Lourdes Argüelles has played an important role in achieving such acceptance.

Concerning critical discourse, the bibliography expands daily. The short encyclopedia, *Latin American Writers on Gay and Lesbian Themes: A Bio-Critical Sourcebook*, edited in 1994 by David William Foster, represents the leading critical text. However, its collection of critical biographies does not fulfill the need for theoretical or critical work focused primarily on U.S. Latino gay and lesbian discourse. At this point in time, the 1991 essay "Chicano Men: A Cartography of Homosexual Identity and Behavior" by Tomás Almaguer appears to be the leading theoretical article on gay Chicano writers and all gay male Latino artists. Because of her nine essays on U.S. Latina lesbians, Yvonne Yarbro-Bejarano could publish the pioneering critical text on Chicana lesbian writing, an understanding that would influence additional critical work on U.S. Latina lesbians. Only time will tell what contribution will come from other prominent Chicanas in lesbian theory, such as Chela Sandoval and Carla Trujillo. David William Foster's forthcoming work on gay Chicano writers may begin a series of critical books on such writing.

While scrutinizing past and current critical work, the future requires a more concerted and focused scholarship to document and critically interpret U.S. Latino lesbigay cultural production. It is an unprecedented opportunity for scholars. There is a need to increase the number of studies on U.S. Latino lesbigay cultural production and critical work by AmeRícans, Cuban Americans, and other U.S. Hispanic groups—including lesbigay performance artists like Luis Alfaro—to study its literary/cultural impact and its relation to mainstream, and Afro-American, gay and lesbian literary production. In the area of cultural production, researchers and critics need to identify and document other expressions such as film, painting, sculpture, photography, comic books, crafts, and so forth. Finally, the large and significant account of Chicano lesbigay writing cannot encompass an understanding of all U.S. Latino homoerotic cultural production.

NOTES

1. An identity term developed by the New York poet Tato Laviera, *AmeRícan* refers to Puerto Ricans raised or born on the mainland. See Tato Laviera, *AmeRícan* (Houston: Arte Público P, 1985).

2. Richard Rodriguez insists in writing his last name without the written accent required in the Spanish language.

3. The homoerotic voice in Chicana/o literature is one of the many voices that emerged or realigned themselves with Southwest Mexican letters: identity, feminism, conservatism, revisionism, internationalism. Most critics agree that contemporary Chicana/o literature began in 1965.

4. Some of the leading critical books are: Francisco Jiménez, ed., *The Identification and Analysis of Chicano Literature* (New York: Bilingual P/Editorial Bilingüe, 1979); Juan Bruce-Novoa, *Chicano Authors: Inquiry by Interview* (Austin: U of Texas P, 1980); Juan Bruce-Novoa, *Chicano Poetry: A Response to Chaos* (Austin: U of Texas P, 1982); Vernon E. Lattin, ed., *Contemporary Chicano Fiction: A Critical Survey* (Binghamton: Bilingual P/Editorial Bilingüe, 1986); Ramón Saldívar, *Chicano Narrative: The Dialectics of Difference* (Madison: U of Wisconsin P, 1990); Héctor Calderón, and José David Saldívar, eds., *Criticism in the Borderlands: Studies in Chicano Literature, Culture and Ideology* (Durham: Duke UP, 1991); Alfred Arteaga, ed., *An Other Tongue: Nation and Ethnicity in the Linguistic Borderlands* (Durham: Duke UP, 1991); Juan Flores, *Divided Borders: Essays on Puerto Rican Identity* (Houston: Arte Público P, 1993); Manuel de Jesús Hernández-Gutiérrez, *El colonialismo interno en la narrativa chicana: el barrio, el anti-barrio y el exterior* (Tempe: Bilingual P/Editorial Bilingüe, 1994); Carl Gutiérrez-Jones, *Rethinking the Borderlands: Between Chicano Cultural and Legal Discourse* (Berkeley: U of California P, 1995); Rafael Pérez-Torres,

Movements in Chicano Poetry: Against Myths, Against Margins (Cambridge: U of Cambridge P, 1995); Tey Diana Rebolledo, *Women Singing in the Snow: A Cultural Analysis of Chicana Literature* (Tucson: U of Arizona P, 1995); Alvina E. Quintana, *Home Girls: Chicana Literary Voices* (Philadelphia: Temple UP, 1996); and Teresa McKenna, *Migrant Song: Politics and Process in Contemporary Chicano Literature* (Austin: U of Texas P, 1997). All these critical books bypass or merely gloss the presence of lesbigay writers in U.S. Latino literature and culture. For a specific lesbian critique of such silencing, see Deena J. González, "Masquerades: Viewing the New Chicana Lesbian Anthologies." *Out/Look* 15 (1991): 80-83.

5. For a detailed history of John Rechy with Grove Press, see John Rechy, "On Being a 'Grove Press Author.'" A history of the press itself will also help understand Rechy's writing career; see S. E. Gontarski, "Dionysus in Publishing: Barney Rosset, Grove Press, and the Making of a Countercanon." *The Review of Contemporary Fiction* 10.3 (Fall 1990): 7-19.

6. In Chicano literary criticism, most critics agree that 1965 is the birth of contemporary Chicana/o writing. See Francisco Lomelí, "An Overview of Chicano Letters: From Origins to Resurgence."

7. Beginning in 1991 with the reprinting of Sandra Cisneros's *The House on Mango Street* (1985) by Vintage Books, a division of Random House, reputable or mainstream Anglo presses have consciously marketed—in reprint or original work—three Chicana writers among both Chicana/o and general American readers. The writers, works, and presses are: *The House on Mango Street* and *Woman Hollering Creek and Other Stories* (1991) by Sandra Cisneros, Random House; *The Mixquihuala Letters* (1986; 1992) by Ana Castillo, Anchor Books, and *So Far From God* (1993) by Ana Castillo, W. W. Morton; and *Face of An Angel* (1994) by Denise Chávez, Farrar, Straus and Giroux. A central and major Chicano writer who began his career in the 1970s, Rudolfo Anaya has also benefited from mainstream Anglo presses that are marketing Mexican American writers: in 1994 Warner Books reprinted in both hard and soft cover *Bless Me, Última*, originally published by Quinto Sol Publications in 1972. Integral to the same marketing are: (1) Puerto Rican Esmeralda Santiago, who in 1994 reprinted *When I Was a Puerto Rican* (1993) with Vintage Books (Random House) and published the original *America's Dream* (1996) with HarperCollins Publishers, and (2) the Dominican American Julia Alvarez who in 1992 reprinted *How the Garcia Girls Lost Their Accent* (1991) with Plume and in 1995 reprinted with the same press *In the Time of the Butterflies* (1994).

8. With each one having a Mexican American protagonist, *City of Night* was a top national best-seller for seven months and *Numbers* and *The Sexual*

Outlaw made the national best-sellers. For more information, see Debra Castillo: "Interview: John Rechy."

9. Reflecting a corpus of thirty-five years of writing, John Rechy remains one of the most prolific Chicano writers: nine novels and one documentary on the sexual underground (see bibliography in this volume).

10. In co-editing in 1981 *This Bridge Called My Back: Radical Writings by Women of Colors*, Anzaldúa and Moraga brought to the center in Chicana/o letters feminism, solidarity between U.S. minority women of color, sexuality, gender issues, and lesbianism. The essay collection *Borderlands/La Frontera: The New Mestiza* (1987) by Gloria Anzaldúa instituted borderlands writing in Chicana/o literature. It also became the central text in borderlands critical discourse. In this critical strain, *Borderlands/La Frontera* occupies a similar role to *I Am Joaquín* (1967) by Rodolfo "Corky" Gonzales in Chicano criticism of the 1960s and 1970s.

11. On Rodriguez's impact on Chicano/U.S. Latino criticism, see Ramón Saldívar, "Ideologies of the Self: Chicano Autobiography." Although aligned with the conservative right at the time of promoting *Hunger of Memory*, Rodriguez is today a self-declared left-of-center writer and an advocate of gay rights.

12. On the controversial side, Rodriguez also sharpened the debate on bilingual education, affirmative action, and ethnic studies. In this debate, Anglo conservatives helped him through access to journals and speaker honorariums. Today his position on all three issues continues to have repercussions within the greater educational issue of access for young U.S. Latinas/os.

13. Over the years, Rodriguez has earned the right to speak for gays. Since publishing *Days of Obligation* and earning an essayist position in *The Lehrer News Hour*, shown on PBS, he apparently has ceased to be a protegé of the conservative right and identifies politically as center-left. During the Los Angeles rebellion triggered by the beating received by Rodney King, Rodriguez corrected an interpretation of the rioting as simply a black/white issue, pointing out that the majority of the rioters arrested were U.S. Latinos. On the occasion of the Pope's recent visit to America, he appeared as a consultant and criticized the Catholic Church's antigay policies. He has also presented several television essays on the AIDS crisis and gay men.

14. As mentioned in footnote eight, reputable or mainstream Anglo-American presses, such as Random House, Anchor Books, and Farrar, Straus and Giroux, began consciously in 1991 to market reprinted or original works by Sandra Cisneros, Ana Castillo, and Denise Chávez.

15. In 1987, the same year in which Anzaldúa published *Borderlands/La Frontera* Héctor Calderón and José Saldívar, respectively a Ford Fellow at the

Stanford Humanities Center and a National Research Council Fellow at the Stanford Center for Chicano Research, organized the conference entitled "Chicano Literary Criticism in a Social Context," whose selected proceedings led to the critical anthology entitled *Criticism in the Borderdlands: Studies in Chicano Literature, Culture, and Ideology* (1991), edited by both organizers. In the same year, E. Emily Hicks published *Border Writing: The Multidimensional Text* (1991)—another key text in borderlands critical discourse. To date, borderlands writing and critical discourse remains at the center of the critical work *Rethinking the Borderlands: Between Chicano Culture and Legal Discourse* (1995) by Carl Gutiérrez-Jones, joined by a special issue entitled "Remapping the Border Subject" from the journal *Discourse*. See *Discourse* 18.1-2 (Fall-Winter 1995-96). An interview with Gloria Anzaldúa is the first entry. See Ellie Hernández, "Re-Thinking Margins and Borders: An Interview."

    16. This book appears to be a sequel to *This Bridge Called My Back*.

    17. Such reserve stands in sharp contrast with its expressiveness in the recent video *Brincando el Charco: Portrait of a Puerto Rican* (1994) by Frances Negrón-Muntaner (b. 1966), a younger and new leading voice in AmeRícan lesbian cultural production.

    18. Quinto Sol Publications published in 1972 the play entitled *The Day of the Swallows* by Estela Portillo, which features a tragic lesbian protagonist named Josefa. See Estela Portillo, "The Day of the Swallows," *El espejo/The Mirror: Selected Chicano Literature*, 5th ed., Ed. by Octavio Ignacio Romano-V. and Herminio Ríos-C. (Berkeley: Quinto Sol, 1972): 147-93. Prior to going out of business, Editorial Justa Publications published a gay theater collection entitled *The False Advent of Mary's Child and Other Plays* (1979) by Alfonso C. Hernández.

    19. The leading presses are Bilingual Press and Arte Público Press. The latter has published: *Crazy Love* (1989) and *The Greatest Performance* (1991) by Elías Miguel Muñoz, and *Tommy Stands Alone* (1995) by Gloria Velásquez. Bilingual Press has printed: *The Mixquihuala Letters* (1986) by Ana Castillo, *Beggar on the Córdoba Bridge/Three Times a Woman: Chicana Poetry* (1989) by Alicia Gaspar de Alba, *En estas tierras/In This Land* (1989) by Elías Miguel Muñoz, and *The Mystery of Survival and Other Stories* (1993) by Alicia Gaspar de Alba.

    20. These titles feature either a subdued or an open lesbian literary expression.

    21. A small press named Ism Press/Editorial "Ismo" published a translation of *This Bridge Called My Back*. See Cherríe Moraga and Ana Castillo, eds., *Esta puente mi espalda: voces de mujeres tercermundistas en los*

Estados Unidos. Trads. Ana Castillo y Norma Alarcón (San Francisco: Ism Press/Editorial "Ismo," 1988).

22. In May 1997, a special section was dedicated to John Rechy in the scholarly event, New Perspectives on Chicano/a Cultures: An Interdisciplinary Conference, held at the University of California in Los Angeles.

23. Respectively, see *Minority Voices* 3.1 (Fall 1979): 37-45; *Diacritics* 25.1 (Spring 1995): 99-130; and *Signs* 18.4 (Summer 1993). In this last special number, Gloria Anzaldúa and Lourdes Argüelles served as two of the four invited guest editors. See *Signs* 18.4 (Summer 1993).

24. In spite of his prolific production, Michael Nava is not included in the two standard dictionaries of literary biography dedicated to Chicana/o writers. See Francisco Lomelí and Carl R. Shirley. *Chicano Writers: First Series.* Dictionary of Literary Biography, vol. 82 (Detroit: Gale Research, 1989); and Francisco Lomelí and Carl R. Shirley, *Chicano Writers: Second Series.* Dictionary of Literary Biography, vol. 122 (Detroit: Gale Research, 1992).

25. Ironically, *The Lesbian and Gay Studies Reader* ignores John Rechy's work and the articles by Juan Bruce-Novoa. In a token gesture, Bruce-Novoa's essay, "Homosexuality and the Chicano Novel," is listed in a reference bibliography given in the back pages.

26. Ironically, Almaguer appears not to be aware of the substantial bibliography in Chicano/U.S. Latino lesbigay writing, cultural production, and criticism.

27. For the moment David William Foster, offers the best challenge. See "Homoerotic Writing and Chicano Authors."

28. See Lourdes Argüelles, and B. Ruby Rich. "Homosexuality, Homophobia, and Revolution: Notes Toward an Understanding of the Cuban Lesbian and Gay Male Experience, Part I" and "Homosexuality, Homophobia, and Revolution: Notes toward an Understanding of the Cuban Lesbian and Gay Male Experience, Part II."

29. In 1984, Chicana Chela Sandoval wrote to *Signs* and criticized the article "Lesbian Identity and Community: Recent Social Science Literature" by Susan Krieger (1982). See Chela Sandoval. "Comments on Krieger's 'Lesbian Identity and Community: Recent Social Science Literature.'" *Signs: Journal of Women in Culture and Society* 9.4 (Summer 1984): 725-29. In the same issue of *Signs* 9.4 (Summer 1984), Lourdes Argüelles and B. Ruby Rich published the article entitled "Homosexuality, Homophobia, and Revolution: Notes Toward an Understanding of the Cuban Lesbian and Gay Male Experience, Part I." In 1993, Gloria Anzaldúa and Lourdes Argüelles were two of four guest editors who edited a special *Signs* issue entitled "Theorizing Lesbian Experience." See *Signs* 18.4 (Summer 1993). In this same special issue, Alicia

Gaspar de Alba contributed the noteworthy article, "Tortillerismo: Work by Chicana Lesbians," 956-63.

30. See special section on John Rechy in *Minority Voices* 3.1 (Fall 1979). The three articles which make up the special section—"In Search of the Honest Outlaw: John Rechy" by Juan Bruce-Novoa, 37-45, "The Sexual Underworld of John Rechy" by Charles Tatum, 47-52, and "Odysseus in John Rechy's *City of Night*: The Epistemological Journey" by Carlos Zamora, 53-62—represent the first critical effort to include John Rechy as part of the canon in Chicana/o literature.

31. Soon after 1986, a Lesbian Caucus and a Joto Caucus emerged and eventually established themselves inside the National Association for Chicano Studies (NACS)—now known as the National Association for Chicana and Chicano Studies (NACCS) in order to code the participation of women scholars. Held in Spokane, Washington in 1995, the twenty-second national annual conference featured the theme "Expanding Raza World View: Sexuality and Regionalism" and saw a strong participation on the part of Chicano gays and Chicana lesbians in panels and workshops. The forthcoming volume of selected proceedings will reflect their contribution.

32. Apparently in agreement with Juan Flores, Cruz-Malavé believes that Puerto Rican literature from the island and the mainland make up one continuous body of work. See Juan Flores, *Divided Borders: Essays on Puerto Rican Identity* (Houston: Arte Público Press, 1993).

33. A critic of Anglo-American lesbigay writing, James Levin made an effort in 1983 to include John Rechy as a mainstream gay novelist. See Levin, James, *The Gay Novel: The Male Homosexual Image in America* (New York: Irvington, 1983); particularly several pages in chapter five, "The Sixties: Time of Transition," 215-79, and chapter 7, "Gay Man as Everyman: Into the Eighties," 281-367.

Appendix
U. S. Latina/o Lesbigay Research Bibliography: Literature, Culture, and Criticism

Dedicated primarily to U.S. Latino homoerotic writing and cultural production, this bibliography also includes some creative and critical work by Latin Americans and Spaniards since there is a marked cultural link as identified and claimed by both artists and critics, such as Cherríe Moraga, Tomás Almaguer, Carlos A. Rodríguez-Matos, Lourdes Argüelles, and others.

LITERATURE AND CULTURE
(in chronological order and alphabetically by year)

Rechy, John. *City of Night*. New York: Grove P, 1963. Rpt. with trans. *As cidades da noite*. by Fernando Teles de Castero. Rio de Janeiro: Editora Civilização Brasileira, 1964. Rpt. with trans. *Nacht in der Stadt: Roman*. Munchen: Droemer Knaur, 1965. Rpt. with trans. *La ciudad de la noche*. México: Edivisión, 1987.

———. *Numbers*. New York: Grove P, 1967. Rpt. with trans. *Nummern*. Darmstadt: Melzer, 1968. Rpt. with intro. by John Rechy New York: Grove P, 1984.

———. *This Day's Death: A Novel*. New York: Grove P, 1969. Rpt. London: MacGibbon & Kee, 1970.

———. *The Vampires*. New York: Grove P, 1971.

Portillo, Estela. *The Day of the Swallows. El espejo/The Mirror: Selected Chicano Literature*. Ed. Octavio Ignacio Romano-V. and Herminio Ríos. Berkeley: Quinto Sol Publications, 1972. 150-93.

Rechy, John. *The Fourth Angel*. New York: Viking P, 1972.

Mohr, Nicholasa. "Herman and Alice." *El Bronx Remembered: A Novella and Stories*. New York: Harper & Row, 1975. Rpt. Houston: Arte Público P, 1986.

Mohr, Nicholasa. "The Perfect Little Flower Girl." *In Nueva York*. New York: Dial P, 1977. Rpt. Houston: Arte Público P, 1988. 73-99.

Rechy, John. *The Sexual Outlaw: A Documentary; A Non-Fiction Account, with Commentaries, of Three Days and Nights in the Sexual Underground*. New York: Grove P, 1977. Rpt. and enlarged New York: Grove P, 1984.

Robles, Mireya. *En esta aurora*. San Antonio: M & A Editions, 1978.

Hernández, Alfonso. *The False Advent of Mary's Child and Other Plays*. Berkeley: Editorial Justa Publications, 1979.

McCaskell, Tim. "We Will Conquer a Space Filled With Light." *The New Gay Liberation Book: Writings and Photographs about Gay (Men's) Liberation*. Ed. Len Richmond, with Gary Noguera. Foreword by Bruce Voeller. Palo Alto: Ramparts P, 1979. 111-20.

Rechy, John. *Rushes: A Novel*. New York: Grove P, 1979. Distributed by Random House.

———. "An Open Letter to Anita Bryant." *The New Gay Liberation Book: Writings and Photographs about Gay (Men's) Liberation*. Ed. Len Richmond, with Gary Noguera. Foreword by Bruce Voeller. Palo Alto: Ramparts P, 1979. 213-19.

Moraga, Cherríe and Gloria Anzaldúa, eds. *This Bridge Called My Back*. Watertown, MA: Persephone P, 1981. Rpt. Kitchen Table/ Women of Color P, 1983. Rpt. *Esta puente, mi espalda: voces de mujeres tercermundistas en los Estados Unidos*. Ed. Cherríe Moraga y Ana Castillo. Trans. Ana Castillo y Norma Alarcón. San Francisco: ISM P/Editorial "Ismo," 1988.

Rodriguez, Richard. *Hunger of Memory: The Education of Richard Rodriguez*. Boston: D.R. Godine, 1981. Rpt. New York: Bantam Books, 1983.

Ortiz Taylor, Sheila. *Faultline: A Novel*. Tallahassee: Naiad P, 1982.

Rodríguez-Matos, Carlos A. *Matacán*. Madrid: Playor, 1982.

Umpierre-Herrera, Luz María. *En el país de las maravillas*. Bloomington: Third Woman P, 1982.

Anzaldúa, Gloria. "El Paisano Is a Bird of Good Omen." *Cuentos: Stories by Latinas*. Ed. Alma Gómez, Cherríe Moraga, and Mariana Romo-Carmona. New York: Kitchen Table/Women of Color P, 1983. 153-75.

Moraga, Cherríe. *Loving in the War Years: lo que nunca pasó por sus labios*. Boston: South End P, 1983.

———. "Sin luz." *Cuentos: Stories by Latinas*. Ed. Alma Gómez, Cherríe Moraga, and Mariana Romo-Carmona. New York: Kitchen Table/Women of Color P, 1983. 136-37.

Rechy, John. *Bodies and Souls: A Novel*. New York: Carroll & Graf; Distributed by Publishers Group West, 1983.

Islas, Arturo. *The Rain God: A Desert Tale*. Palo Alto: Alexandrian P, 1984. Rpt. New York: Avon Books, 1991.

Reyes, Ricardo, Francisco X. Alarcón and Juan Pablo Gutiérrez. *Ya vas, carnal*. San Francisco: Humanizarte Publications, 1985.

Mohr, Nicholasa. "Brief Miracle." *Rituals of Survival: A Woman's Portfolio*. Houston: Arte Público P, 1985. 75-73.

Ortiz Taylor, Sheila. *Spring Forward/Fall Back*. Tallahassee: Naiad P, 1985.

Robles, Mireya. *Hagiografía de Narcisa la bella*. Hanover, NH: Ediciones del Norte, 1985.

Castillo, Ana. *The Mixquihuala Letters*. Tempe: Bilingual P/Editorial Bilingüe, 1986. Rpt. New York: Anchor Books, 1992. Rpt. with trans. *Las cartas de Mixquiahuala*. México, DF: Consejo Nacional para la Cultura y las Artes/Grijalbo, 1994.

García Ramis, Magali. *Felices días, Tío Sergio*. Río Piedras: Editorial Antillana, 1986. 1992. Reimpr. 5a ed. 1992.

Moraga, Cherríe. *Giving Up the Ghost: Teatro in Two Acts*. Los Angeles: West End P, 1986. Rpt. in *Heroes and Saints & Other Plays*. Albuquerque: West End P, 1994. Rpt. in *The Actor's Book of Gay and Lesbian Plays*. Ed. Eric Lane and Nina Shengold. New York: Penguin Books, 1995. 380-416. Rev. and rpt. in *Literatura chicana, 1965-1995: An Anthology in Spanish, English, and Caló*. Ed. Manuel de Jesús Hernández-Gutiérrez and David William Foster. New York: Garland, 1997. 301-30.

Nava, Michael. *The Little Death*. Boston: Alyson Publications, 1986. Rpt. Boston: Alyson Publications, 1996. Rpt. Los Angeles: Alyson Publications, 1997.

Anzaldúa, Gloria. *Borderlands/La Frontera: The New Mestiza*. San Francisco: Spinsters/Aunt Lute, 1987.

Ramos, Juanita, ed. *Compañeras: Latina Lesbians: An Anthology*. New York: Latina Lesbian Project (LLHJP), 1987. For copies, write: LLHP, c/o Latina Women's Educational Resources, P.O. Box 627, Peter Stuyvesant Station, NY, NY 10009.

Umpierre-Herrera, Luz María. *The Margarita Poems*. Bloomington: Third Woman P, 1987.

Velásquez, Gloria. "Fugitive." *Cuentos chicanos II*. El Paso: Dos Pasos Editores, 1987. 119-24. Rpt. in *Literatura chicana, 1965-1995: An Anthology in Spanish, English, and Caló*. Ed. Manuel de Jesús Hernández-Gutiérrez and David William Foster. New York: Garland Publishing, 1997. 163-67.

AIDS in the Barrio: eso no me pasa a mí. Prod. by Alba Martínez and Frances Negrón-Muntaner. Dir. by Peter Biella and Frances Negrón-Muntaner. Cinema Guild, 1988.

Nava, Michael. *Goldenboy*. Boston: Alyson, 1988. Rpt. 1991. Los Angeles: Alyson Publishers, 1996.

Rechy, John. *Marilyn's Daughter: A Novel*. New York: Carroll & Graf Publishers, 1988.

Rodríguez-Matos, Carlos A. *Llama de amor vivita. Jarchas*. South Orange, NJ: Ediciones Ichali, 1988.

Anzaldúa, Gloria E. "Life Line." *Lesbian Love Stories*. Ed. Irene Zahara. Freedom, CA: The Crossing P, 1989. 1-3.

Gaspar de Alba, Alicia. "Beggar on the Córdoba Bridge." *Three Times A Woman: Chicana Poetry*. Tempe: Bilingual P, 1989. 1-50.

Muñoz, Elias Miguel. *Crazy Love*. Houston: Arte Público P, 1989.

———. *En estas tierras/In This Land*. Tempe: Bilingual P/Editorial Bilingüe, 1989.

———. *No fue posible el sol*. Madrid: Editorial Betanía, 1989.

Nava, Michael, ed. *Finale: Short Stories of Mystery and Suspense*. Boston: Alyson, 1989. Rpt. Los Angeles: Alyson, 1989.

Ortiz Taylor, Sheila. *Slow Dancing at Miss Polly's*. Tallahassee: Naiad P, 1989.

Alarcón, Francisco. *Body in Flames/Cuerpo en llamas*. San Francisco: Chronicle Books, 1990. Trans. *Kropp I Lägor* by Ulla Nätterqvist-Sawa. Drottninggatan: Fabians Förlag, 1991. Trans. *Colainn ar Bharr Lasrach* by Gabriel Rosenstock. Indreabhán, Conamara, Ireland: Cló Iar-Chonnachta, 1992.

Alfaro, Luis. *Downtown*. Performed at Highway Performance Space in Santa Monica, CA. 30 November, 1-2, 7-9 December 1990.

Anzaldúa, Gloria (ed.). *Making Face, Making Soul/Haciendo caras: Creative and Critical Perspectives by Women of Color*. San Francisco: Aunt Lute Foundation Books, 1990.

———. "She Ate Horses." *Lesbian Philosophies and Cultures*. Ed. Jeffner Allen. New York: State U of New York P, 1990. 371-88.

Lugones, María. "Playfulness, 'World'—Travelling, and Loving Perception." *Lesbian Philosophies and Cultures.* Ed. Jeffner Allen. New York: State U of New York P, 1990. 159-80.

Ortiz Taylor, Sheila. *Southbound.* Tallahassee: Naiad P, 1990.

Castillo, Ana. "La Macha: Toward a Beautiful Whole Self." *Chicana Lesbians: The Girls Our Mothers Warned Us About.* E. Carla Trujillo. Berkeley: Third Woman P, 1991. 24-48. Rpt. *Massacre of the Dreamers: Essays on Xicanisma.* Albuquerque: U of New Mexico P, 1994. 121-43.

Nava, Michael. *How Town.* New York: Harper & Row, 1990. Rpt. New York: Ballantine Books, 1991.

Navarro, Martha. "Interview with Ana Castillo." *Chicana Lesbians: The Girls Our Mothers Warned Us About.* E. Carla Trujillo. Berkeley: Third Woman P, 1991. 113-32.

Ortiz Taylor, Sheila. *Southbound.* Tallahassee: Naiad P, 1990.

Rodriguez, Richard. "Late Victorians: San Francisco, AIDS, and the Homosexual Stereotype." *Harper's Magazine* (Oct. 1990): 57-66. Rpt. as "Late Victorians." *Days of Obligation: An Argument with my Mexican Father.* New York: Viking, 1992. 26-47.

———. "Masculinity, Femininity, and Homosexuality: On the Anthropological Interpretation of Sexual Meanings in Brazil." *Blackwood* (1991?): 155-64.

Alarcón, Francisco. *De amor oscuro/Of Dark Love.* Santa Cruz: Moving Parts P, 1991. Trans. *Um An Ngrá Dorcha* by Gabriel Rosenstock. Indreabhán, Conamara, Ireland: Cló Iar-Chonnachta, 1992.

Anzaldúa, Gloria. "To(o) Queer the Writer—Loca, escritora, chicana." *Inversions: Writing by Dykes, Queers, and Lesbians.* Ed. Betsy Warland. Vancouver: Press Gang, 1991. Rpt. in *Living Chicana Theory.* Ed. Carla Trujillo. Berkeley: Third Woman P, 1998. 263-76.

Berubé, Allan and Jeffrey Escoffier. "Queer/Nation." *Out/Look* 11 (1991): 14-16.

Fernández, Charles. "Undocumented Aliens in the Queer Nation." *Out/Look* 12 (1991): 20-23.

Gordon, Linda. "On Difference." *Genders* 10 (1991): 91-111.

Hernández, E. D. "Discussion, Discourse and Direction: The Dilemmas of a Chicana Lesbian." *Chicana Lesbians: The Girls Our Mothers Warned Us About.* Ed. Carla Trujillo. Berkeley: Third Woman P, 1991. 138-40.

Islas, Arturo. *Migrant Souls: A Novel.* New York: Morrow, 1990. Rpt. New York: Avon Books, 1991.

Muñoz, Elías Miguel. *The Greatest Performance.* Houston: Arte Público P, 1991.

Saalfield, Catherine and Ray Navarro. "Shocking Pink Praxis: Race and Gender on the ACT UP Frontlines." *Inside/Out: Lesbian Theories, Gay Theories.* Ed. Diana Fuss. New York: Routledge, 1991. 341-69.

Trujillo, Carla. "Chicana Lesbians: Fear and Loathing in the Chicano Community." *Chicana Lesbians: The Girls Our Mothers Warned Us About.* Ed. Carla Trujillo. Berkeley: Third Woman P, 1991. 186-94. Rpt. in *Chicana Critical Issues.* Ed. Norma Alarcón et al. Berkeley: Third Woman, 1993. 117-25.

———, ed. *Chicana Lesbians: The Girls Our Mothers Warned Us About.* Berkeley: Third Woman P, 1991.

Rechy, John. *The Miraculous Day of Amalia Gómez.* New York: Arcade, 1991.

Alarcón, Francisco. *Poemas zurdos.* México, DF: Editorial Factor, 1992.

Alfaro, Luis; Alberto Araiza, and Monica Palacios. *Deep in the Crotch of My Latino Psyche.* Performed at Highways Performance Space, 9-11 and 14-16 July 1992.

Alfaro Luis. "Pico Union." *Men on Men 4: Best New Gay Fiction.* Ed. George Stambolian. Intro. by Felice Picano. Afterword by Andrew Holleran. New York: Plume, 1992. 268-83.

Moraga, Cherríe. "Arte in América con Acento." *Frontiers: A Journal of Women Studies* 12.3 (1992). Rpt. in *Other Words: Literature by Latinas of the United States.* Ed. Roberta Fernández. Houston: Arte Público P, 1994. 300-306. Rpt. in *Latina: Women's Voices from the Borderlands.* Ed. Lillian Castillo-Speed. New York: Touchstone, 1995. 211-20.

Nava, Michael. *The Hidden Law.* New York: HarperCollins, 1992.

Peña, Terri de la. *Margins.* Seattle: Seal P, 1992.

Rechy, John. "Love in the Backrooms." *Men on Men 4: Best New Gay Fiction.* Ed. George Stambolian. Intro. by Felice Picano. Afterword by Andrew Holleran. New York: Plume, 1992. 10-18.

Rodriguez, Richard. *Days of Obligation: An Argument with my Mexican Father.* New York: Viking, 1992.

Anzaldúa, Gloria. *Friends from the Other Side/Amigos del otro lado.* Pictures by Consuelo Méndez. San Francisco: Children's Book P, 1993.

Argüelles, Lourdes. "Crazy Wisdom: Memories of a Cuban Queer." *Sisters, Sexperts, Queers: Beyond the Lesbian Nation.* Ed. Arlene Stein. New York: Plume, 1993. 196-204. Rpt. in *The Latino Studies Reader: Culture, Economy and Society.* Ed. Antonia Darder and Rodolfo D. Torres. Malden, Mass.: Blackwell, 1998. 206-10.

Gaspar de Alba, Alicia. *The Mystery of Survival and Other Stories.* Tempe: Bilingual P, 1993.

González Paz, Juana María. "Where Do Dreams Go When They Die?" *Lesbian Culture: An Anthology: The Lives, Work, Ideas, Art and Visions of Lesbians Past and Present.* Ed. Julia Penelope and Susan Wolfe. Freedom, CA: Crossing P, 1993. 420-23.

Moraga, Cherríe. *The Last Generation: Poems and Essays.* Boston: South End P, 1993.

———. "Queer Aztlán: the Reformation of the Chicano Tribe." *The Last Generation: Poems and Essays.* Boston: South End P, 1993. 145-74. Rpt. in *The Material Queer: A LesBiGay Cultural Studies Reader.* Ed. Donald Morton. Boulder: Westview P, 1996. 297-304.

Román, David. "*Fierce Love* and Fierce Response: Intervening in the Cultural Politics of Race, Sexuality, and AIDS." *Critical Essays: Gay and Lesbian Writers of Color.* Ed. Emmanuel S. Nelson. New York: Haworth P, 1993.

Alfaro, Luis. *CD: down town.* New Alliance/SST Records, 1994.

———. "Cuerpo Politizado." Uncontrollable Bodies: Testimonies of Identity and Culture. Ed. Rodney Sappington and Tyles Stallings. Seattle: Bay P, 1994. 217-41. "Cuerpo Politizado" is a section that includes the following poems, "Vistiendo en Drag," "Abuelita," and "Orphan of Aztlán." It also contains one short biographical narrative, "Deseo Es Memoria."

Brincando el Charco: Portrait of a Puerto Rican. Produced, written, and directed by Frances Negrón-Muntaner. Women Make Movies, 1994.

Carmelita Tropicana: Your Kunst Is Your Waffen. Screenplay by Carmelita Tropicana and Ela Troyano. Dir. Ela Troyano. Perf. Carmelita Tropicana. First Run/ICARUS Films, 1994.

Graziano C., Rodolfo. *Amos de la noche: conversaciones con homosexuales, tramposos, prostitutas, ladrones, lesbianas.* Caracas, Venezuela: Editorial Planeta Venezolana, 1994.

Molina, María Luisa. "Papusa." "Fragmentation: Meditations on Separatism." *Signs* 19.2 (Winter 1994): 449-57.

Moraga, Cherríe. *Heroes and Saints & Other Plays.* Albuquerque: West End P, 1994. Anthology features the plays: *Giving Up the Ghost, Shadow of a Man,* and *Heroes and Saints.*

Nava, Michael and Robert Dawidoff. *Created Equal: Why Gay Rights Matter to America.* New York: St. Martin's P, 1994

Negrón-Muntaner, Frances. *Los límites del silencio/Shouting in a Whisper (Latino Poets in Philadelphia).* Santiago, Chile: Cuarto Proprio, 1994.

Peña, Terri de la. *Latin Satins: A Novel.* Seattle: Seal P, 1994.

Peña, Terri de la. *Life: A Celebration of the Lesbian Experience.* Ed. Karla Jay. New York: Basic Books, 1995. 27-32.

Pérez, Laura M. "Go Ahead: Make My Movement." *Bisexul Politics: Theories, Queries, and Visions.* Ed. Naomi Tucker. New York: The Haworth P, 1995. 109-14.

Rechy, John. "From *Autobiography: A Novel.*" *Diacritics* 25.1 (Spring 1995): 126-30.

Reyes, Guillermo. "Allende by Pinochet" (1995). Unpublished manuscript.

———. "The Seductions of Johnny Diego" (1995). Unpublished manuscript.

Sánchez, Edwin. *Trafficking in Broken Hearts.* In *The Actor's Book of Gay and Lesbian Plays.* Ed. Eric Lane and Nina Shengold. New York: Penguin Books, 1995. 431-81.

Velásquez, Gloria. *Tommy Stands Alone.* Houston: Piñata Books, 1995.

Alfaro, Luis. "Orphan of Aztlán." *The United States of Poetry.* Eds. Joshua Blum, Bob Homan, and Mark Pellington. New York: Harry N. Abrams, 1996. 88-89.

Islas, Arturo. *La Mollie and the King of Tears.* Edited with afterward by Paul Skenazy. Albuquerque: U of New Mexico P, 1996.

Nava, Michael. *The Death of Friends.* New York: G.P. Putnam's, 1996.

Pérez, Emma. *Gulf Dreams.* Berkeley: Third Woman P, 1996.

Rechy, John. *Our Lady of Babylon: A Novel.* New York: Arcade, 1996.

Reyes, Guillermo. *Men on the Verge of a His-Panic Breakdown.* In *Staging Gay Lives: An Anthology of Contemporary Gay Theater.* Boulder: Westview P, 1996. 401-24. Westview is a division of HarperCollins Publishers. *Men on the Verge of a His-Panic Breakdown* premiered 6 June 1994 at the Celebration Theater in Los Angeles.

———. "Miss Consuelo" (1996). Unpublished manuscript.

———. "The Deporting of the Divas" (1996). Unpublished manuscript.

Alarcón, Francisco. *Laughing Tomatoes and Other Spring Poems/ Jitomjates risueños y otros poemas de primavera.* Illustrations by Maya Christina González. San Francisco: Children's Book P/Libros Primarios, 1997.

Giard, Robert. *Particular Voices: Portraits of Gay and Lesbian Writers.* Cambridge: MIT P, 1997. Contains brief, self-portraits of several writers taken from author's own writing, such as, Francisco X. Alarcón, Luis Alfaro, Gloria Anzaldúa, Rafael Campo, María Irene Fornes, Michael Nava, Achy Obejas, Terri de la Peña, Juanita (Díaz) Ramos, and Mariana Romo-Carmona.

Nacho. "Personal Vocies: Nacho." *Invented Identities? Lesbians and Gays Talk about Migration.* Ed. Bob Cant. London: Cassel, 1997. 57-66.

Nava, Michael. *The Burning Plain.* New York: G. P. Putnam's, 1997.

Reyes, Guillermo. "A Southern Christmas" (1997). Unpublished manuscript.

———. "The Hispanick Zone" (1997). Unpublished manuscript.

———. "The Latin American Writer: Writing in English." *Latin American Theatre Review* 31.1 (1997): 113-15.

Chávez Leyva, Yolanda. "Listening to the Silences in Latina/Chicana Lesbian History." *Living Chicana Theory.* Ed. Carla Trujillo. Berkeley: Third Woman P, 1998. 429-34.

Gaspar de Alba, Alicia. "The Politics of Location of the Tenth Muse of America: An Interview with Sor Juana Inés de la Cruz." *Living Chicana Theory.* Ed. Carla Trujillo. Berkeley: Third Woman P, 1998. 136-65.

Moraga, Cherríe. "Free at Last." *Living Chicana Theory.* Ed. Carla Trujillo. Berkeley: Third Woman P, 1998. 166-88.

Palacios, Mónica. "Tomboy." *Living Chicana Theory.* Ed. Carla Trujillo. Berkeley: Third Woman P, 1998. 306-309.

Trujillo, Carla, ed. *Living Chicana Theory.* Berkeley: Third Woman P, 1998.

CRITICISM
(in chronological order and alphabetically by year)

Southern, Terry. "Rechy and Gover." *Contemporary American Novelists.* Ed. Harry T. Moore. Cardbondale & Edwardsville: Southern Illinois UP, 1964. 222-27.

Lemon, Lee T. "You May Have Missed These." *Prairie Schooner* 45 (Fall 1971): 270-72.

Giles, James R., and Wanda Giles. "An Interview with John Rechy." *Chicago Review* 25 (Summer 1973): 19-31.

Leyland, Winston, ed. "John Rechy." *Gay Sunshine Interviews*, vol. 2. San Francisco: Gay Sunshine, 1978. 251-68.

Bruce-Novoa, Juan. "In Search of the Honest Outlaw: John Rechy." *Minority Voices* 3.1 (Fall 1979): 37-45. Special Section: Focus on John Rechy.

Tatum, Charles M. "The Sexual Underground of John Rechy." *Minority Voices* 3.1 (Fall 1979): 47-52. Special Section: Focus on John Rechy.

Zamora, Carlos. "Odysseus in John Rechy's *City of Night*: The Epistemological Journey." *Minority Voices* 3.1 (Fall 1979): 53-62. Special Section: Focus on John Rechy.

Reinhardt, Karl J. "The Image of Gays in Chicano Prose Fiction." *Explorations in Ethnic Studies* 4.2 (1981): 41-55.

Kriegar, Susan. "Lesbian Identity and Community: Recent Social Science Literature." *Signs: Journal of Women in Culture and Society* 8.1 (Autumn 1982): 91-108. Rpt. in *The Lesbian Issue: Essays from Signs*. Ed. Estelle B. Freedman et al. Chicago: U of Chicago P, 1985. 223-40.

Satterfield, B. "John Rechy's Tormented World." *Southwest Review* 67 (Winter 1982): 78-85.

Fone, Byrne R. S. "This Other Eden: Arcadia and the Homosexual Imagination." *Essays on Gay Literature*. Ed. Stuart Kellog. New York: Harrington Park P, 1983. 13-34.

Levin, James. *The Gay Novel: The Male Homosexual Image in America*. New York: Irvington Publishers, 1983. Levin dedicates several pages to Rechy's early work, particularly in chapter five, "The Sixties: Time of Transition," 215-79, and chapter seven, "Gay Man as Everyman: Into the Eighties," 281-367.

Nelson, E. S. "John Rechy, James Baldwin and the American Double Minority Literature." *Journal of American Culture* 6 (Summer 1983): 70-74.

Argüelles, Lourdes and B. Ruby Rich. "Homosexuality, Homophobia, and Revolution: Notes toward an Understanding of the Cuban Lesbian and Gay Male Experience, Part I." *Signs: Journal of Women in Culture and Society* 9.4 (Summer 1984): 683-99. Rpt. in

The Lesbian Issue: Essays from **Signs**. Ed. Estelle B. Freedman et al. Chicago: U of Chicago P, 1985. 169-85.

Kriegar, Susan. "Reply to Sandoval and Bristow and Pearn." *Signs: Journal of Women in Culture and Society* 9.4 (Summer 1984): 732-33. Rpt. in *The Lesbian Issue: Essays from* **Signs**. Ed. Estelle B. Freedman et al. Chicago: U of Chicago P, 1985. 248-49.

Sandoval, Chela. "Comment on Krieger's 'Lesbian Identity and Community: Recent Social Science Literature.'" *Signs: Journal of Women in Culture and Society* 9.4 (Summer 1984): 725-29. Rpt. in *The Lesbian Issue: Essays from* **Signs**. Ed. Estelle B. Freedman et al. Chicago: U of Chicago P, 1985. 241-45.

Argüelles, Lourdes and B. Ruby Rich. "Homosexuality, Homophobia, and Revolution: Notes toward an Understanding of the Cuban Lesbian and Gay Male Experience, Part II." *Signs: Journal of Women in Culture and Society* 11 (1985): 120-36.

Carrasco, Rafael. *Inquisición y represión sexual en Valencia: Historia de los sodomitas (1565-1785)*. Barcelona: Laertes S. A. de Ediciones, 1985.

Bruce-Novoa, Juan. "Homosexuality and the Chicano Novel." *Confluencia: revista hispánica de cultura y literatura* 2.1 (1986): 69-77. Rpt. in *European Perspectives on Hispanic Literature of the United States*. Ed. Genvieve Fabre. Houston: Arte Público P, 1988. 98-106. Rpt. in *Homosexual Themes in Literary Studies*. Ed. Stephen Donaldson. New York: Garland P, 1992.

Steuervogel, T. "Contemporary Homosexual Fiction and the Gay Rights Movement." *Journal of Popular Culture* 20 (Winter 1986): 125-34.

Yarbro-Bejarano, Yvonne. "Cherríe Moraga's *Giving Up the Ghost*: The Representation of Female Desire." *Third Woman* 3.1-2 (1986): 113-20.

Anzaldúa, Gloria E. "Bridge, Drawbridge, Sandbar or Island: Lesbians-of-Color *Hacienda Aliance*." *Social Perspectives in Lesbian and Gay Studies: A Reader*. Ed. Peter M. Nardi and Beth E. Schneider. New York: Routledge, 1988. 527-36.

Kanellos, Nicolás. *Biographical Dictionary of Hispanic Literature in the United States: The Literature of Puerto Ricans, Cuban Americans and other Hispanic Writers*. New York: Greenwood, 1988.

Martínez, Maza, Otoniel, Diana M. Shin, and Helen F. Banks *Latinos and AIDS: A National Strategy Symposium*. Los Angeles: Center for Interdisciplinary Research in Immunology and Disease (CIRID), 1989.

Wescott, Gloria. ["Interview: Francisco X. Alarcón."] *Tiempo Latino* (5 July 1989).

Woods, Richard D. "Richard Rodriguez (31 July 1944 -)." *Chicano Writers: First Series*. Dictionary of Literary Biography, vol. 80. Eds. Francisco Lomelí and Carl R. Shirley. Detroit: Gale Research, 1989. 214-16.

Yarbro-Bejarano, Yvonne. "Cherríe Moraga (25 September 1952 -)." *Chicano Writers: First Series*. Dictionary of Literary Biography, vol. 80. Eds. Francisco Lomelí and Carl R. Shirley. Detroit: Gale Research, 1989. 165-77.

Martínez, Julio A., ed. *Dictionary of Twentieth-Century Cuban Literature*. New York: Greenwood P, 1990.

Rechy, John. "On Being a 'Grove Press Author.'" *The Review of Contemporary Fiction* 10.3 (Fall 1990): 137-42.

Almaguer, Tomás. "Chicano Men: A Cartography of Homosexual Identity and Behavior." *différances* 3.2 (1991): 75-100. Rpt. in *The Lesbian and Gay Studies Reader*. Ed. Henry Abelove, Michele Aina Barale, and David M. Halperin. New York: Routledge, 1993. 255-73. Rpt. in and with trans. "Hombres chicanos: una cartografía de la identidad y del comportamiento homosexual." *Debate feminista* 6.11 (1995): 46-77. Rpt. in *Social Perspectives in Lesbian and Gay Studies: A Reader*. Ed. Peter M. Nardi and Beth E. Schneider. New York: Routledge, 1998. 537-52.

Bruce-Novoa, Juan. "Sheila Ortiz Taylor's *Faultline*: A Third-Woman Utopia." *Confluencia* 6.2 (Spring 1991): 75-87.

Gontarski, S. E. "Dionysus in Publishing: Barney Rosset, Grove P, and the Making of a Countercanon." *The Review of Contemporary Fiction* 10.3 (Fall 1990): 7-19.

González, Deena J. "Masquerades: Viewing the New Chicana Lesbian Anthologies." *Out/Look* 15 (1991): 80-83.

Pérez, Emma. "Sexuality and Discourse: Notes from a Chicana Survivor." *Chicana Lesbians: The Girls Our Mothers Warned Us About*. E. Carla Trujillo. Berkeley: Third Woman P, 1991. 159-84.

Piedra, José. "Literary Whiteness and the Afro-Hispanic Difference." *The Bounds of Race: Perspectives on Hegemony and Resistance*. Ed. Dominick La Capra. Ithaca: Cornell UP, 1991. 278-310.

Sandoval, Chela. "U.S. Third World Feminism: The Theory and Method of Oppositional Consciousness in the Postmodern World." *Genders* 10 (1991): 1-24.

Yarbro-Bejarano, Yvonne. "De-constructing the Lesbian Body: Cherríe Moraga's *Loving in the War Years.*" *Chicana Lesbians: The Girls Our Mothers Warned Us About*. Ed. Carla Trujillo. Berkeley: Third Woman P, 1991. 143-55. Rpt. in *The Lesbian and Gay Studies Reader*. Ed. Henry Abelove, Michele Aina Barale, and David M. Halperin. New York: Routledge, 1993. 595-603.

———. "Reclaiming the Lesbian Body: Cherríe Moraga's *Loving in the War Years.*" *Out/Look* 12 (1991): 74-79.

Negrón-Muntaner, Frances. "Echoing Stonewall and Other Dilemmas: The Organizational Beginnings of a Gay and Lesbian Agenda in Puerto Rico, 1972-1977." *Centro* 4.1 (Winter 1991-92): 76-95; and 4.2 (Spring 1992): 98-115.

Bustamante, Nuria. "Alfonso C. Hernández (18 September 1938 -)." *Chicano Writers: Second Series*. Dictionary of Literary Biography, vol. 122. Ed. Francisco Lomelí and Carl R. Shirley. Detroit: Gale Research, 1992. 127-31.

Cantú, Roberto. "Arturo Islas (24 May 1938 - 15 February 1991)." *Chicano Writers: Second Series*. Dictionary of Literary Biography, vol. 122. Ed. Francisco Lomelí and Carl R. Shirley. Detroit: Gale Research, 1992. 146-54.

Christian, Karen. "Will the 'Real Chicano' Please Stand Up? The Challenge of John Rechy and Sheila Ortiz Taylor to Chicano Essentialism." *Americas Review* 20.2 (Summer 1992): 89-104.

Jaén, Didier. "John Rechy (10 March 1934 -)." *Chicano Writers: Second Series*. Dictionary of Literary Biography, vol. 122. Ed. Francisco Lomelí and Carl R. Shirley. Detroit: Gale Research, 1992. 212-19.

Maldonado, Miguelina. "On the Out Side: Latinos and Clinical Trials." *SIDAhora* 11 (1992): 13.

Rodríguez del Pino, Salvador. "Francisco X. Alarcón (21 February 1954 -)." *Chicano Writers: Second Series*. Dictionary of Literary Biography, vol. 122. Eds. Francisco Lomelí and Carl R. Shirley. Detroit: Gale Research, 1992. 3-7.

Román, David. "Performing All Our Lives: AIDS, Performance, Community." *Critical Theory and Performance*. Ed. Janelle Reinelt and Joseph Roach. Ann Arbor: U of Michigan P, 1992.

————. "Performing All Our Lives: AIDS, Performance, Community." *Critical Theory and Performce*. Ed. Janelle Reinelt and Joseph Roach. Ann Arbor: U of Michigan P, 1992.

Torres, Héctor A. "Experience, Writing, Theory: The Dialects of Mestizaje in Gloria Anzaldúa's *Boderlands/La Frontera: The New Mestiza*." *Understanding Others: Cultural and Cross-Cultural Studies and the Teaching of Literature*. Ed. Joseph Trimmer and Tilly Warnock. Urbana: National Council of Teachers of English, 1992.

Torres, Héctor A. "Gloria Anzaldúa (26 September 1942 -)." *Chicano Writers: Second Series*. Dictionary of Literary Biography, vol. 122. Ed. Francisco Lomelí and Carl R. Shirley. Detroit: Gale Research, 1992. 8-17.

Abelove, Henry; Michele Aina Barale, David M. Halperin, eds. *The Lesbian and Gay Studies Reader*. New York: Routledge, 1993.

Anzaldúa, Gloria; Lourdes Argüelles et al. "Editorial." *Signs* 18.4 (Summer 1993): 757-64.

Alonso, Ana María and María Teresa Koreck. "Silences: 'Hispanics,' AIDS, and Sexual Practices." *The Lesbian and Gay Studies Reader*. Ed. Henry Abelove, Michele Aina Barale, and David M. Halperin. New York: Routledge, 1993. 110-26.

Argüelles, Lourdes. "Crazy Wisdom: Memories of a Cuban Queer." *Sisters, Sexperts, and Queers*. Ed. Arlene Stein. New York: Dutton, 1993.

Gaspar de Alba, Alicia. "*Tortillerismo*: Work by Chicana Lesbians." *Signs* 18.4 (Summer 1993): 956-63.

Moraga, Cherríe. "Queer Aztlán: the Reformation of the Chicano Tribe." *The Last Generation: Poems and Essays*. Boston: South End P, 1993. 145-74.

Negrón-Mutaner, Frances. "Interview: Magali García Ramis." *Hispanoamérica* 22.64-65 (1993): 89-104.

Peña, Terri de la. "Tortilleras." *Lesbian Culture: An Anthology: The Lives, Work, Ideas, Art and Visions of Lesbians Past and Present*. Ed. Julia Penelope and Susan Wolfe. Freedom, CA: Crossing P, 1993. 304-308.

Román, David. "*Fierce Love* and Fierce Response: Intervening in the Cultural Politics of Race, Sexuality, and AIDS." *Critical Essays: Gay and Lesbian Writers of Color*. Ed. Emmanuel S. Nelson. New York: Haworth P, 1993.

Ríos Avila, Rubén (interview). "El Show de Cristina." *Piso 13* (Edición Gay) 2.3 (September-December 1993): 6.

Yarbro-Bejarano, Yvonne. "Cherríe Moraga's *Shadow of a Man*: Touching the Wound in Order to Heal." *Acting Out: Feminist Performances*. Ed. Lynda Hart and Peggy Phelan. Ann Arbor: U of Michigan P, 1993.

Borim, Jr., Dário. "Thomas, Piri (pseud. of John Peter Thomas; United States; 1928)." *Latin American Writers on Gay and Lesbian Themes: A Bio-Critical Sourcebook*. Ed. David William Foster. Westport, CT: Greenwood P, 1994. 427-31.

Castillo, Ana. "La Macha: Toward an Erotic Whole Self." *Massacre of the Dreamers: Essays on Xicanisma*. Albuquerque: U of New Mexico P, 1994. 121-43.

Christian, Karen S. "Ortiz Taylor, Sheila (United States; 1939)." *Latin American Writers on Gay and Lesbian Themes: A Bio-Critical Sourcebook*. Ed. David William Foster. Westport, CT: Greenwood P, 1994. 300-304.

———. "Robles, Mireya (Cuba; 1934)." *Latin American Writers on Gay and Lesbian Themes: A Bio-Critical Sourcebook*. Ed. David William Foster. Westport, CT: Greenwood P, 1994. 366-70.

Díaz, Luis Felipe. "Ideología y sexualidad en *Felices días, Tío Sergio* de Magali García Ramis." *Revista de Estudios Hispánicos* 21 (1994): 325-41.

Foster, David William. *Latin American Writers on Gay and Lesbian Themes: A Bio-Critical Sourcebook*. Westport, CT: Greenwood P, 1994.

Hernández, Linda. "Obejas, Archy [sic] (Cuba; ca. 1950)." *Latin American Writers on Gay and Lesbian Themes: A Bio-Critical Sourcebook*. Ed. David William Foster. Westport, CT: Greenwood P, 1994. 294-97.

Hernández-Gutiérrez, Manuel de Jesús. "Alarcón, Francisco X. (United States; 1954)." *Latin American Writers on Gay and Lesbian Themes: A Bio-Critical Sourcebook*. Ed. David William Foster. Westport, CT: Greenwood P, 1994. 7-13.

Jaén, Didier T. "Rechy, John (United States; 1934)." *Latin American Writers on Gay and Lesbian Themes: A Bio-Critical Sourcebook*. Ed. David William Foster. Westport, CT: Greenwood P, 1994. 349-56.

Jagose, Annamarie. "Slash and Suture: The Border's Figuration of Colonialism, Homophobia, and Phallocentrism in *Borderlands/La*

Frontera: The New Mestiza." Lesbian Utopics. New York: Routledge, 1994. 137-57.

Keating, AnnLouise. "Anzaldúa, Gloria E. (United States; 1942)." *Latin American Writers on Gay and Lesbian Themes: A Bio-Critical Sourcebook.* Ed. David William Foster. Westport, CT: Greenwood P, 1994. 15-22.

——. "Chávez, Denise (United States; 1948)." *Latin American Writers on Gay and Lesbian Themes: A Bio-Critical Sourcebook.* Ed. David William Foster. Westport, CT: Greenwood P, 1994. 108-10.

——. "Peña, Terri de la (United States; 1947)." *Latin American Writers on Gay and Lesbian Themes: A Bio-Critical Sourcebook.* Ed. David William Foster. Westport, CT: Greenwood P, 1994. 311-13.

Klawitter, George. "Nava, Michael (United States; 1954)." *Latin American Writers on Gay and Lesbian Themes: A Bio-Critical Sourcebook.* Ed. David William Foster. Westport, CT: Greenwood P, 1994. 286-88.

——. "Umpierre-Herrera, Luz María (Puerto Rico; 1947)." *Latin American Writers on Gay and Lesbian Themes: A Bio-Critical Sourcebook.* Ed. David William Foster. Westport, CT: Greenwood P, 1994. 434-36.

Miller, John C. "Acosta, Oscar Zeta (United States; 1935-1974?)." *Latin American Writers on Gay and Lesbian Themes: A Bio-Critical Sourcebook.* Ed. David William Foster. Westport, CT: Greenwood P, 1994. 1-3.

——. "Mohr, Nicholasa (United States; 1938)." *Latin American Writers on Gay and Lesbian Themes: A Bio-Critical Sourcebook.* Ed. David William Foster. Westport, CT: Greenwood P, 1994. 236-39.

——. "Muñoz, Miguel Elías [*sic*] (Cuba; 1954)." *Latin American Writers on Gay and Lesbian Themes: A Bio-Critical Sourcebook.* Ed. David William Foster. Westport, CT: Greenwood P, 1994. 274-77

Negrón-Muntaner, Franes. "Moraga, Cherríe (United States)." *Latin American Writers on Gay and Lesbian Themes: A Bio-Critical Sourcebook.* Ed. David William Foster. Westport, CT: Greenwood P, 1994. 254-62.

Núñez Noriega, Guillermo. *Sexo entre varones: poder y resistencia en el campo sexual.* Hermosillo, Sonora, México: El Colegio de Sonora, 1994.

Ocasio, Rafael. "Portillo Trambley, Estela (United States; 1936)." *Latin American Writers on Gay and Lesbian Themes: A Bio-Critical Sourcebook.* Ed. David William Foster. Westport, CT: Greenwood P, 1994. 336-39.

———. "Salas, Floyd (United States; 1931)." *Latin American Writers on Gay and Lesbian Themes: A Bio-Critical Sourcebook.* Ed. David William Foster. Westport, CT: Greenwood P, 1994. 394-96.

Phelan, Shane. "Lesbians and Mestizas: Appropriation and Equivalence." *Getting Specific: Postmodern Lesbian Politics.* Minneapolis: U of Minnesota P, 1994. 57-75.

Rechy, John. *Bodies and Souls: A Novel.* New York: Carroll & Graf, 1983.

———. *City of Night.* New York: Grove P, 1963.

———. *Marilyn's Daughter: A Novel.* New York: Carroll & Graf, 1988.

———. *The Miraculous Day of Amalia Gómez.* New York: Arcade, 1991.

———. *Numbers.* New York: Grove P, 1967.

———. *Our Lady of Babylon: A Novel.* New York: Arcade, 1996.

———. *Rushes: A Novel.* New York: Grove P, 1979.

———. *The Sexual Outlaw: A Documentary; A Non-Fiction Account, with Commentaries, of Three Days and Nights in the Sexual Underground.* New York: Grove P, 1977. Rpt. and enlarged New York: Grover P, 1984.

———. *This Day's Death: A Novel.* New York, Grove P, 1969.

———. *The Vampires.* New York, Grove P, 1971.

Rodríguez-Matos, Carlos A. "Negrón-Muntaner, Frances (Puerto Rico; 1966)." *Latin American Writers on Gay and Lesbian Themes: A Bio-Critical Sourcebook.* Ed. David William Foster. Westport, CT: Greenwood P, 1994. 288-90.

———. "Sandoval-Sánchez, Alberto (Puerto Rico; 1954)." *Latin American Writers on Gay and Lesbian Themes: A Bio-Critical Sourcebook.* Ed. David William Foster. Westport, CT: Greenwood P, 1994. 405-406.

Sierra, Ana. "Rodríguez-Matos, Carlos A. (Puerto Rico; 1948)." *Latin American Writers on Gay and Lesbian Themes: A Bio-Critical*

Sourcebook. Ed. David William Foster. Westport, CT: Greenwood P, 1994. 374-77.

Soto, Francisco. "Arenas, Reinaldo (Cuba; 1943-1990)." *Latin American Writers on Gay and Lesbian Themes: A Bio-Critical Sourcebook.* Ed. David William Foster. Westport, CT: Greenwood P, 1994. 24-36.

Torres, Daniel. "An AIDS Narrative." *Centro Bulletin* 6.1-2 (1994): 179.

Yarbro-Bejarano, Yvonne. "Gloria Anzaldúa's *Borderlands/La frontera:* Cultural Studies, 'Difference,' and the Non Unitary Subject." *Cultural Critique* (Fall 1994): 5-28.

Almaguer, Tomás. "Hombres chicanos: una cartografía de la identidad y del comportamiento homosexual." *Debate feminista* 6.11 (1995): 46-77.

Bergmann, Emilie L. and Paul Julian Smith, eds. *¿Entiendes?: Queer Readings, Hispanic Writings.* Durham: Duke UP, 1995.

Castillo, Debra. "Interview: John Rechy." *Diacritics 25.1* (Spring 1995): 113-25.

Cruz-Malavé, Arnoldo. "Toward an Art of Transvestism: Colonialism and Homosexuality in Puerto Rican Literature." *¿Entiendes?: Queer Readings, Hispanic Writings.* Durham: Duke UP, 1995. 137-67. Rpt. in *Queer Representations: Reading Lives, Reading Cultures.* Ed. Martin Duberman. New York: New York UP, 1997. 226-44.

Gutiérrez-Jones, Carl. "Desiring B/orders." *Diacritics 25.1* (Spring 1995): 99-112.

Lugo-Ortiz, Angnes. "Community at Its Limits: Orality, Law, Silence, and the Homosexual Body in Luis Rafael Sánchez's '¡Jum!'" *¿Entiendes?: Queer Readings, Hispanic Writiings.* Durham: Duke UP, 1995. 115-36.

Piedra, José. "Nationalizing Sissies." *¿Entiendes? Queer Readings, Hispanic Writings.* Ed. Emile L. Bergmann and Paul Smith. Durham: Duke UP, 1995. 370-409.

Román, David. "Teaching Differences: Theory and Practice in a Lesbian and Gay Studies Seminar." *Professions of Desire: Lesbian and Gay Studies in Literature.* Ed. George E. Haggerty and Bonnie Zimmerman. New York: Modern Language Association of America, 1995. 113-23.

―――. "Teatro Viva!: Latino Performance and the Politics of AIDS in Los Angeles." *¿Entiendes? Queer Readings, Hispanic Writings.*

Ed. Emile L. Bergmann and Paul Smith. Durham: Duke UP, 1995. 346-69. Rpt. in *The Latino Studies Reader: Culture, Economy and Society*. Ed. Antonia Darder and Rodolfo D. Torres. Malden, MA: Blackwell Publishers, 1998. 211-27.

Tabuenca Córdoba, María Socorro. "Teoría y creación en la prosa de Gloria Anzaldúa." *Las formas de nuestras voces: Chicana and Mexicana Writers in Mexico*. Ed. Claire Joysmith. México: Universidad Nacional Autónoma de México, 1995. 153-65.

Umpierre, Luz María. "Lesbian Tantalizing in Carmen Lugo Filippi's "Milagros, Calle Mercurio." *¿Entiendes? Queer Readings, Hispanic Writings*. Ed. Emilie L. Bergmann and Paul Julian Smith. Durham: Duke UP, 1995. 306-14.

Yarbro-Bejarano, Yvonne. "Expanding the Categories of Race and Sexuality in Lesbian and Gay Studies." *Professions of Desire: Lesbian and Gay Studies in Literature*. Ed. George E. Haggerty and Bonnie Zimmerman. New York: Modern Language Association of America, 1995. 124-35.

———. "The Lesbian Body in Latina Cultural Production." *¿Entiendes? Queer Readings, Hispanic Writings*. Ed. Emilie L. Bergmann and Paul Julian Smith. Durham: Duke UP, 1995. 181-97.

Bleys, Rudi C. *The Geography of Perversion: Male-to-Male Sexual Behaviour Outside the West and the Ethnographic Imagination, 1750-1918*. London: Cassell, 1996. Specifically, see the section entitled "Constructing the New World's Sexuality," 22-36.

Foster, David William. "Homoerotic Writing and Chicano Authors." *The Bilingual Review/La Revista Bilingüe* 21.1 (January-April 1996): 42-51. Special Focus: Papers from the Aquí/A Key Conference, edited by Manuel de Jesús Hernández-G.

Madden Arias, Rose Mary. "Outraging Public Morality: The Experience of a Lesbian Feminist Group in Costa Rica." *Amazon to Zami: Towards a Global Lesbian Feminism*. Ed. Monika Reifelder. New York: Cassell, 1996. 130-37.

Csömyei, Claudia and Silvia Palumbo. "Las lunas y las otras." Trans. Vivien Hughes. *Amazon to Zami: Towards a Global Lesbian Feminism*. Ed. Monika Reifelder. New York: Cassell, 1996. 152-60.

García, J. Neil C. *Philippine Gay Culture: The Last Thirty Years*. Diliman, Quezon City: U of the Philippines P, 1996.

Rivera Fuentes, Consuelo. "'Todas locas, todas vivas, todas libres': Chilean Lesbians 1980-95." *Amazon to Zami: Towards a Global Lesbian Feminism.* Ed. Monika Reifelder. New York: Cassell, 1996. 138-51.

Schaefer, Claudia. *Danger Zones: Homosexuality, National Idenity, and Mexican Culture.* Tucson: U of Arizona P, 1996.

Skenazy, Paul. "Afterword: The Long Walk Home." *La Mollie and the King of Tears.* Arturo Islas. Albuquerque: U of New Mexico P, 1996. 167-98.

Conner, Randy P., David Hatfield Sparks, and Mariya Sparks, eds. *Cassell's Encyclopedia of Queer Myth, Symbol, and Spirit: Gay, Lesbian, Bisexual, and Transgender Lore.* Foreword by Gloria E. Anzaldúa. London: Cassell, 1997.

Montero, Oscar. "Notes for a Queer Reading of Latin American Literature." *Queer Representations: Reading Lives, Reading Cultures.* Ed. Martin Duberman. New York: New York UP, 1997. 216-25.

Romo-Carmona, Mariana. "Latina Lesbians." *A Queer World.* Ed. Martin Duberman. New York: New York UP, 1997. 35-38.

Sifuentes Jáuregui, B. "National Fantasies: Peeking into a Latin American Closet." *Queer Representations: Reading Lives, Reading Cultures.* Ed. Martin Duberman. New York: New York UP, 1997. 290-301.

Szymczak, Jerome. "Cherríe Moraga." *Outstanding Lives: Profiles of Lesbian and Gay Men.* Ed. Michale Bronski. Detroit: Visible Ink P, 1997. 270-73.

Trujillo, Carla M. "Sexual Identity and the Discontents of Difference." *Ethnic and Cultural Diversity among Lesbians and Gay Men.* Thousand Oaks: Sage, 1997. 266-78.

Esquivel, Catrióna Rueda. "Memories of Girlhood: Chicana Lesbian Fictions." *Signs: Journal of Women in Culture and Society* 23.3 (1998): 645-82.

Baulio, Mildred. "Challenging the Sodomy Law in Puerto Rico." *NACLA Report on the Americas* 31.4 (Jan/Feb 1998): 33.

Pérez, Emma. "Irigaray's Female Symbolic in the Making of Chicana Lesbian *Sitios* y *Lenguas* (Sites and Discourses)." *Living Chicana Theory.* Ed. Carla Trujillo. Berkeley: Third Woman P, 1998. 87-101.

Román, David. *Acts of Intervention: Performance, Gay Culture, and AIDS.* Bloomington: Indiana UP, 1998.

Sánchez, Margarita. "Racismo y sexismo en Puerto Rico." *Claridad* (San Juan, Puerto Rico, Feb. 6-12, 1998): 32.

Trujillo, Carla. "La Virgen de Guadalupe and Her Reconstruction in Chicana Lesbian Desire." *Living Chicana Theory*. Ed. Carla Trujillo. Berkeley: Third Woman P, 1998. 214-31.

Yarbro-Bejarano, Yvonne. "Laying It Bare: The Queer/Colored Body in Photography by Laura Aguilar." *Living Chicana Theory*. Ed. Carla Trujillo. Berkeley: Third Woman P, 1998. 277-305.

Works Cited

Abbe, Elfrieda. "Creating Images Where There Were None." *Angles* (January 1997): 8-12.

Abelove, Henry, Michele Aina Barale, and David M. Halperin. *The Lesbian and Gay Studies Reader.* New York: Routledge, 1993.

Alarcón, Francisco X. *Canto hondo/Deep Song.* unpublished manuscript.

———. *De amor oscuro. Of Dark Love.* Santa Cruz: Moving Parts P, 1991, 1992.

———. *Body in Flames. Cuerpo en llamas.* Trans. by Francisco Aragón. San Francisco: Chronicle Books, 1990.

———. *No Golden Gate for Us; Poems by Francisco X. Alarcón.* With an introduction by Juan Felipe Herrera. Tesuque, NM: A Pennywhistle Chapbook, 1993.

———. *Poemas zurdos.* Naucalpan de Juárez, México: Editorial Factor, 1992.

———. *Snake Poems; An Aztec Invocation.* San Francisco: Chronicle Books, 1992.

Alarcón, Norma, Ana Castillo, and Cherríe Moraga, eds. "Introduction." *The Sexuality of Latinas.* Berkeley: Third Woman P, 1993. 8-10. Orig. special issue, *Third Woman* 4 (1989).

———, et al. *Chicana Critical Issues.* Berkeley: Third Woman P, 1993.

Alegre Barrios, Mario. "Credos en conflicto." *El nuevo día* [San Juan, PR] (5 oct. 1997): 7.

———. "Llegó la hora de la solidaridad." *El nuevo día* [San Juan, PR] (5 oct. 1997): 6.

———. "Tras la verdad de su cuerpo." *El nuevo día* [San Juan, PR] (6 oct. 1997): 18.

Allen, Mike. "A Heated Hearing on Partner Rights." *New York Times* (3 June 1998): B5.

Almaguer, Tomás. "Chicano Men: A Cartography of Homosexual Identity and Behavior." *différences* 3.2 (1991): 75-100. Rpt. in *The Lesbian and Gay Studies Reader*. Ed. Henry Abelove, Michele Aina Barale, and David M. Halperin. New York: Routledge, 1993. 255-73. Rpt. in *Social Perspectives in Lesbian and Gay Studies: A Reader*. Ed. Peter M. Nardi and Beth E. Schneider. New York: Routledge, 1998. 537-52. In Spanish as "Hombres chicanos: una cartografía de la identidad y del comportamiento homosexual." *Debate feminista* 11 (abril 1995): 46-77.

Altamiranda, Daniel. "Lezama Lima, José." *Latin American Writers on Gay and Lesbian Themes: A Bio-Critical Sourcebook*. Ed. David William Foster. Westport, CT: Greenwood P, 1994. 202-11.

Alvarez IV, José B. "Desarrollo de la narrativa cubana de las últimas décadas: el Quinquenio Gris y sus consecuencias." *Mester* 23.2 (1994): 129-56.

———. "Ruptura en la narrativa social cubana: novísimos y novísimas." *Torre de papel* 4.4 (1995): 61-75.

Alvarez, Julia. *How the García Girls Lost Their Accent*. Chapel Hill: Algonquin Books of Chapel Hill, 1991.

Anaya, Rudolfo. *Bless Me, Ultima*. Berkeley: Quinto Sol, 1972.

Anzaldúa, Gloria. *Borderlands/La Frontera*. San Francisco: Spinsters/Aunt Lute, 1987.

Anzaldúa, Gloria. "La conciencia de la mestiza: Towards a New Consciousness." *Borderlands/La Frontera: The New Mestiza*. San Francisco: Spinsters/Aunt Lute, 1987. 77-98.

———. "To(o) Queer the Writer: Loca, escritora y chicana." *InVersions: Writings by Dykes, Queers and Lesbians*. Ed. Betsy Warland. Vancouver: Press Gang, 1991. 249-63.

———, ed. *Making Face, Making Soul. Haciendo caras. Creative and Critical Perspectives by Feminists of Color*. San Francisco: Aunt Luke Books, 1990.

Aponte-Parés, Luis. "Organizing Against All Odds: Latino Gay Organizations and Community Identity Building in New York City, 1987-1995." LASA International Conference. Guadalajara, Mexico, 17-19 Apr. 1997.

——— and Jorge B. Merced. "Páginas Omitidas. Building Puerto Rican Gay Organizations in New York City: Boricua Gay and Lesbian Forum." Unpublished essay.

Arenas, Reinaldo. *Antes que anochezca*. Barcelona: Tusquets Editores, 1992.

——. *Arturo la estrella más brillante*. Barcelona: Montesinos, 1984.

——. *Celestino antes del alba*. La Habana: UNEAC, 1967.

——. *Singing from the Well*. Trans. Andrew Hurley, New York: Viking, 1987.

Arguedas, José María. *El sexto*. Lima: Librería Editorial Juan Mejía Baca, 1961.

Arguelles, Lourdes, and B. Ruby Rich. "Homosexuality, Homophobia, and Revolution: Notes Toward an Understanding of the Cuban Lesbian and Gay Male Experience, Part I." *Signs* 9.4 (1984): 683-99. Rpt. in *The Lesbian Issue: Essays from Signs*. Ed. Estelle B. Freedman et al. Chicago: U of Chicago P, 1985. 169-85.

——. "Homosexuality, Homophobia, and Revolution: Notes toward an Understanding of the Cuban Lesbian and Gay Male Experience, Part II." *Signs: Journal of Women in Culture and Society* (1985): 120-36.

Arteaga, Alfred. *Chicano Poetics; Heterotexts and Hybridities*. Cambridge: Cambridge UP, 1997.

——, ed. *An Other Tongue: Nation and Ethnicity in the Linguistic Borderlands*. Durham: Duke UP, 1991.

Astor del Valle, Janis. *Fuschia*. Peformance, Nuyorican Poets Cafe, New York City, April 1996. In *Intimate Acts: Eight Contemporary Lesbian Plays*. Nancy Dean and M.G. Soares. Eds. New York: Brito; Atlanta: Lair, 1997. 85-110.

——. *I'll Be Home para la Navidad. Torch to the Heart: Anthology of Lesbian Art and Drama*. Ed. Sue McConnell-Celi. Red Bank, N.J.: Lavender Crystal, 1994. 97-113.

——. *Where The Señoritas Are. Torch to the Heart: Anthology of Lesbian Art and Drama*. Ed. Sue McConnell-Celi, Red Bank, N.J.: Lavender Crystal, 1994. 82-96.

Avilés, Arthur. *Arturella*. Dance/Theater Performance. Repertory Theater, Hostos Community College, The Bronx, New York. 1-2 Nov. 1996.

Bakhtin, Mijail. *La cultura popular en la Edad Media y en el Renacimiento. El contexto de François Rabelais*. México, DF: Alianza Universidad, 1990.

Bardach, Ann Louise. "Fidel Castro, a los 67 años: 'debemos preocuparnos más por el destino de las ideas que por el destino de los hombres.'" *Proceso internacional* 919 (1994): 50-51.

Barnet, Miguel *Canción de Rachel*. México: Alfaguara, 1996.

Barry, Kathleen, Charlotte Bunch, and Shirley Castley, eds. *International Feminism: Networking against Female Sexual Slavery*. New York: International Women's Tribune Center, 1984.

La bella del Alhambra. Dir. Enrique Pineda Barnet. Perf. Cecilia Valdés, César Evora. Instituto de Cinematografía Cubana. 1995.

Belsey, Catherine. *Desire: Love Stories in Western Culture*. Oxford: Blackwell, 1994.

————. "Postmodern Love: Questioning the Metaphysics of Desire." *New Literary History* 25.3 (Summer 1994): 683-705.

Bhabha, Homi K. *The Location of Culture*. London: Routledge, 1994.

Bianchi Ross, Ciro. "Como las cartas no llegan: correspondencia trunca, olvidada o perdida que descubre preocupaciones, odios y amores del autor de *Paradiso*." *La gaceta de Cuba* 3 (1994): 15-20.

Binding, Paul. *García Lorca o la imaginación gay*. Barcelona: Laertes, 1985? Orig. *Lorca: The Gay Imagination*. London: GMP, 1985.

Birtha, Becky. "Johnnieruth." 1981. *Breaking Ice: An Anthology of Contemporary African American Fiction*. Ed. Terry McMillan. New York: Penguin, 1990. 71–76.

Blasor, Lorraine. "Rejection of Gay Cops in P.R. May Spark a Tourist Boycott." *San Juan Star* (13 Feb. 1995): 2.

Bliss, Peggy Ann. "A Cloud Over the Gayest Little Island." *San Juan Star* (20 Feb. 1995): 22.

Braulio, Mildred. "Challenging the Sodomy Law in Puerto Rico." *NACLA Report on the Americas* 31.4 (Jan.-Feb. 1998): 33.

Brooks, Zelda I. *Struggle for Being: An Interpretation of the Poetry of Ana María Facundo*. Miami: Universal, 1994.

Bruce-Novoa, Juan. *Chicano Authors: Inquiry by Interview*. Austin: U of Texas P, 1980.

————. *Chicano Poetry: A Response to Chaos*. Austin: U of Texas P, 1982.

————. "In Search of the Honest Outlaw: John Rechy." *Minority Voices* 3.1 (Fall 1979): 37-45. Special Section: Focus on John Rechy.

————. "Homosexuality and the Chicano Novel." *Confluencia: revista hispánica de cultura y literatura* 2.1 (1986): 69-77. Rpt. in *European Perspectives on Hispanic Literature of the United States*. Ed. Genvieve Fabre. Houston: Arte Público P, 1988. 98-106. Rpt.

in *Homosexual Themes in Literary Studies*. Ed. Stephen Donaldson. New York: Garland, 1992. 33-41.

—. *Retrospace: Collected Essays on Chicano Literature*. Houston: Arte Público P, 1990.

Bunck, Julie Marie. *Fidel Castro and the Quest for a Revolutionary Culture in Cuba*. University Park: Pennsylvania State UP, 1994.

Butler, Judith. *Bodies That Matter: On the Discursive Limits of "Sex."* New York: Routledge, 1993.

—. *Gender Trobule, Feminism and the Subversion of Identity*. New York: Routledge, 1990.

—."Imitation and Gender Insubordination." *The Material Queer: A LesBiGay Cultural Reader*. Ed. Donald Morton. Boulder: Westview P, 1996. 180-92. Also *Inside/Out: Lesbian Theories, Gay Theories*. Ed. Diana Fuss. New York and London: Routledge, 1991. 13–31.

Cabrera, Jorge Mario. "En el labertino de la universalidad: una charla con Francisco X. Alarcón." *De ambiente; la revista bisexual, lésbica, y gay latina de Los Angeles* 5 (1994): 24-25, 41-42.

Cabrera Infante, Guillermo. Interview in *Conducta impropia*. Dirs. Néstor Almendros y Orlando Jiménez Leal. 1984.

Calderón, Héctor, and José David Saldívar, eds. *Criticism in the Borderlands: Studies in Chicano Literature, Culture and Ideology*. Durham: Duke UP, 1991.

Castillo, Ana. *Massacre of the Dreamers. Essays on Xicanisma*. Albuquerque: U of New Mexico P, 1994.

—. *The Mixquiahuala Letters*. 1986. New York: Anchor Books, 1992.

—. *So Far From God*. New York: Anchor Books, 1993.

Castillo, Debra. "Interview: John Rechy." *Diacrtics* 25.1 (Spring 1995): 113-25.

Castillo-Speed, Lillian, ed. *Latinas: Women's Voices from the Borderlands*. New York: Touchstone, 1995.

Chávez, Denise. *The Face of an Angel*. New York: Warner Books, 1995.

Chávez, Denise. *The Last of the Menu Girls*. Houston: Arte Público, 1987.

Chávez-Silverman, Susana. "Tropicolada: Inside the U.S. Latino Gender B(l)ender." *Tropilcalizations: Transcultural Representations of Latinidad*. Ed. Frances R. Aparicio and Susana Chávez-

Silverman. Dartmouth: Darmouth College/UP of New England, 1997. 101-18.

Christian, Karen S. "Robles, Mireya (Cuba; 1934)." *Latin American Writers on Gay and Lesbian Themes: A Bio-Critical Sourcebook.* Ed. David William Foster. Wesport, CT: Greenwood P, 1994. 366-70.

Cisneros, Sandra. *The House on Mango Street.* 1984. New York: Vintage, 1991.

———. *Loose Woman.* New York: Knopf, 1994.

———. *My Wicked, Wicked Ways.* Bloomington: Third Woman P, 1987.

Cisneros, Sandra. *Woman Hollering Creek and Other Stories.* New York: Random House, 1991.

Citron, Michael et al. "Homosexuality in Cuba." *Jump Cut* 19 (1978): 38-39.

Cixous, Hélène. "The Laugh of the Medusa." *The Women and Language Debate. A Sourcebook.* Eds. Camille Roman, Suzanne Juhasz and Cristanne Miller. New Brunswick: Rutgers UP, 1994. 78-93.

——— and Catherine Clément. *La Jeune née.* 1975. *The Newly Born Woman.* Trans. Betsy Wing. Minneapolis: U Minnesota P, 1986.

Clarke, Cheryl. "Lesbianismo: un actos de resistencia." *Esta puente mi espalda.* Eds. Cherríe Moraga and Gloria Anzaldúa. San Francisco: Ism P, 1998. 99-107.

Compañeras: Latina Lesbians. Ed. Juanita Ramos. New York: Routledge, 1994.

Conducta impropia. Almendros, Néstor y Orlando Jiménez Leal, dirs. 1984.

Córdova, Jeanne. *Kicking the Habit.* Los Angeles: Multiple Dimensions, 1990.

Cortázar, Julio. *Vuelta al día en ochenta mundos.* México, DF: Siglo Veintiuno Editores, 1969.

Craddock, Catherine and Claudia Meléndez. "The Right to a Life of Letters: A Few Words with Sandra Cisneros." *El Andar* (March 1995): 12-19.

Cruz-Malavé, Arnoldo. "Toward an Art of Transvestism: Colonialism and Homosexuality in Puerto Rican Literature." *¿Entiendes?: Queer Readings, Hispanic Writiings.* Durham: Duke UP, 1995. 137-67. Rpt. in *Queer Representations: Reading Lives, Reading*

Cultures. Ed. Martin Duberman. New York: New York UP, 1997. 226-44.

———. "'*What a Tangled Web!*': masculinidad, abyección y la fundación de la literatura puertorriqueña en los Estados Unidos." *Revista de critica literaria latinoamericana* 45 (1997) 327-40.

Daly, Mary Ann. Rev. of *Margins*, by Terri de la Peña. *Lambda Book Report* 3.5 (1992): 15.

Daniel, Yvonne. *Rumba: Dance and Social Change in Contemporary Cuba.* Bloomington: Indiana UP, 1995.

Danzón. Dir. María Novaro. Perf. María Rojo, Tito Vasconcelos. Instituto Mexicano de Cinematografía, 1991.

Dauster, Frank. *Xavier Villaurrutia.* New York: Twayne, 1971.

Dávila, Jesús. "Proponen legalizar la 'convivencia.'" *El vocero de Puerto Rico* (11 oct. 1997): 19.

De Jongh, Nicholas. *Not in Front of the Audience.* London: Routledge, 1992.

De Lauretis, Teresa. *The Practice of Love: Lesbian Sexuality and Perverse Desire.* Bloomington: Indiana UP, 1994.

———. "Queer Theory: Lesbian and Gay Sexualities." *différences* 5.2 (1991): i-xviii.

———. Rev. of *Gulf Dreams* by Emma Pérez. *Lesbian Review of Books* 2.4 (1996): 4.

———. *Technologies of Gender. Essays on Theory, Film, and Fiction.* Bloomington: Indiana UP, 1987.

"Declarations of the First National Congress of Education and Culture." *Granma Weekly Review* (9 de mayo de 1971): 5.

Del Toro and Santana, Attorneys and Counselors at Law. Documents regarding Dr. Rosalina Ramos Padró et al. v. Commonwealth of Puerto Rico et al., Civil No. 95-1770 (HL). 21 Feb. 1996.

Delaup, Rick. Unpublished interview with John Waters, June 1997.

Diacritics 25.1 (Spring 1995): 99-130. Special section on John Rechy.

Díaz, Jesús. *Los años duros.* La Habana: Casa de las Américas, 1966.

Díaz, Luis Felipe. "Ideología y sexualidad en *Felices días, tío Sergio* de Magali García Ramis." *Revista de estudios hispánicos* 21 (1994) 325-41.

Díaz Varcárcel, Emilio. *Harlem todos los días.* Río Piedras: Huracán, 1978.

Donoso, José. *El lugar sin límites.* Barcelona: Bruguera, 1965.

Doty, Alexander. *Making Things Perfectly Queer: Interpreting Mass Culture.* Minneapolis: U of Minnesota P, 1993.

Duberman, Martin. *Stonewall*. New York: Plume, 1994.

Duning, Jennifer. "Role in *Rent* as Path to Self-Acceptance." *New York Times* (1 Jan. 1998: E3). Online. Nexis. 4 June 1998.

Dyer, Richard. "Believing in Fairies: The Author and the Homosexual." *Inside/Out: Lesbian Theories/Gay Theories*. Ed. Diana Fuss. New York: Routledge, 1991. 185-201.

———. *Only Entertainment*. London: Routledge, 1992.

———. "The Role of Stereotypes." *The Matter of Images*. London: Routledge, 1993. 11-18.

Eisenberg, Daniel. "Federico García Lorca." *Spanish Writers on Gay and Lesbian Themes; A Bio-Critical Sourcebook*. Ed. David William Foster. Westport, CT: Greenwood P, forthcoming.

Engelbrecht, P. J. "López Becomes 1st Openly Lesbian Latina Elected to Office in U.S." *En la vida* [Chicago] (Dec. 1997): 6.

¿Entiendes? Queer Readings, Hispanic Writings. Eds. Emilie Bergmann and Paul Julian Smith. Durham: Duke UP, 1995.

Epstein, Steven. "Gay Politics, Ethnic Identity: The Limits of Social Constructionism." *Socialist Review* 17.3-4 (1987): 9-54.

Estévez, Abilio. *Juego con Gloria*. La Habana: Editorial Letras Cubanas, 1987.

———. *Manual de las tentaciones*. La Habana: Editorial Letras Cubanas, 1989.

———. *La verdadera culpa de Juan Clemente Zenea*. La Habana: UNEAC, 1987.

Fagundo, Ana María. *Antología (1965-1989)*. Ed. Antonio Martínez Herrarte. Islas Canarias: Viceconsejería de Cultura y Deportes, 1994.

———. *Brotes*. La Laguna: Litografía Maype, 1965.

———. *Como quien no dice voz alguna al viento*. Santa Cruz de Tenerife: Junta de Publicaciones de la Caja de Ahorros, 1984.

———. *Configurado tiempo*. Madrid: Oriens, 1974.

———. *Desde Chanatel, el canto*. Sevilla: Ángaro, 1981.

———. *Diario de una muerte*. Madrid: Agora, 1970

———. *Invención de la luz*. Barcelona: Vosgos, 1978.

———. *Isla adentro*. Santa Cruz de Tenerife: Gaceta semanal de las Artes, 1969.

———. *Isla en sí: 1965-1989*. Madrid: Rialp, 1992.

———. "Lo mío es el poema." *Ana María Fagundo: texto y contexto de su poesía*. Ed. Antonio Martínez Herrarte. Madrid: Verbum, 1993. 15-17.

————. *Obra poética: 1965-1990*. Madrid: Endimyon, 1990.

————. *Retornos sobre la siempre ausencia*. Riverside, CA: Alaluz, 1989.

————. *El sol, la sombra, en el instante*. Madrid: Verbum, 1994.

Faludi, Susan. "The Money Shot." *The New Yorker* 71.34 (October 30, 1995): 64-87.

Farwell, Marilyn R. "Toward a Definition of the Lesbian Literary Imagination." 1988. *Sexual Practice, Textual Theory: Lesbian Cultural Criticism*. Ed. Susan J. Wolfe and Penelope Stanley. Cambridge, MA: Blackwell, 1993. 66–84.

Farr, Jory. "Through It All, His Life's On A Role [Theater: *Rent*]." *Press-Enterprise* [Riverside, Calif.] (28 Sept. 1997): E1. Online. Nexis. 4 June 1998.

Farwell, Marilyn R. "Toward a Definition of the Lesbian Literary Imagination." *Sexual Practice, Textual Theory: Lesbian Cultural Criticism*. Ed. Susan J. Wolfe and Julia Penelope. Oxford: Blackwell, 1993. 66-84.

Fernández Retamar, Roberto. *Calibán y otros ensayos*. La Habana, Editorial Arte y Literatura, 1979.

Fleites-Lear, Marisela y Enrique Patterson. "Teoría y praxis de la revolución cubana: apuntes críticos." *Nueva sociedad* 123 (1993): 50-64.

Flores, Juan. *Divided Borders: Essays on Puerto Rican Identity*. Houston: Arte Público P, 1993.

Foster, David William. "Erótica lesbiana: unos ejemplos de la poesía de latinas." *Culturadoor* 3.31 (enero/febrero1997): 1, 13.

————. *Gay and Lesbian Themes in Latin American Writing*. Austin: U of Texas P, 1991.

————. "Homoerotic Writing and Chicano Authors." *The Bilingual Review/La Revista Bilingüe* 21.1 (January-April 1996): 42-51. Special Focus: Papers from the Aquí/A Key Conference, edited by Manuel de Jesús Hernández-G.

————. "El homoerotismo y la lucha por el espacio en Buenos Aires: dos muestras cinematográficas." *Tramas* 6 (1997): 13-42.

————. "El lesbianismo multidimensional: conflicto lingüístico, conflicto cultural y conflicto sexual en *Giving up the Ghost; teatro in two acts* de Cherríe Moraga." *XVIII Simposio de Historia y Antropología de Sonora*. Hermosillo, Sonora: Instituto de Investigaciones Históricas de la Universidad de Sonora, 1994. 2.331-40.

——. *Producción cultural e identidades homoeróticas: teoría y aplicaciones*. San José: Editorial Universitaria de Costa Rica, 1998 (in press).

——. *Sexual Textualities; Essays in Queer/ing Latin American Writing*. Austin: U of Texas P, 1997.

Foucault, Michel. *The History of Sexuality: An Introduction*. Vol. 1. New York: Random House, 1978.

Fresa y chocolate. Dir. Tomás Gutiérrez Alea. Perf. Jorge Perrugoria, Vladimir Cruz, Mirtha Ibarra. ICAIC Instituto Cubano de las Artes y la Industria Fílmica. 1993.

Freud, Sigmund. "Three Essays on the Theory of Sexuality." *The Standard Edition of the Complete Psychological Works of Sigmund Freud*. Trans. and ed. James Strachey. London: Hogarth, 1953. 123-243.

Fry, Joan. "An Interview with John Rechy." *Poets & Writers Magazine* 20/3 (May/June 1992): 25-37.

Fuego, Laura de. *Maravilla*. Encino, CA: Floricanto P, 1989.

Fuss, Diana. *Essentially Speaking: Feminism, Nature and Difference*. New York: Routledge, 1989.

Garber, Marjorie. *Vested Interests: Cross-Dressing & Cultural Anxiety*. New York: Routledge, 1992.

García Lorca, Federico. *Poema del cante jondo/Poem of Deep Song*. San Francisco: Citylights, 1990.

——. *Sonetos del amor oscuro*. Buenos Aires: Instituto de Estudios de Literatura Latinoamericana, 1984?

García Ramis, Magali. *Felices días, Tío Sergio*. 5a ed. Río Piedras: Editorial Antillana, 1992.

——. *Happy Days, Uncle Sergio*. Trans. Carmen C. Esteves. Fredonia, NY: White Pine, 1995.

——. "Magali García Ramis." Interview by Frances Negrón-Muntaner. *Hispamérica* 22.64-65 (1993) 89-104.

Gaspar de Alba, Alicia. *Beggar on the Córdoba Bridge. Three Times a Woman*. With María Herrera-Sobek and Demetria Martínez. Tempe: Bilingual P, 1989.

——. *The Mystery of Survival and Other Stories*. Tempe: Bilingual P, 1993.

——. "Tortillerismo: Work by Chicana Lesbians." *Signs*. 18.41 (1993): 956-68.

Gay Cuba. Prod. Sonja de Vries. New York: Center for Cuban Studies, 1995.

Gibson, Ian. *Granada en 1936 y el asesinato de Federico García Lorca.* Barcelona: Crítica, 1979.

Gil, Carlos. *El orden del tiempo: Ensayos sobre el robo del presente en la utopía puertorriqueña.* San Juan: Postdata, 1994.

Goffman, Erving. *Stigma: Notes on the Management of Spoiled Identity.* Englewood Cliffs, NJ: A Spectrum Book, 1963.

Goldberg, Jonathan. *Sodometries: Renaissance Texts, Modern Sexualities.* Stanford: Stanford UP, 1992.

Goldstein, Richard. "Crossover Dreams: Two Gay Candidates Win Where They Weren't Supposed To—In the Barrios." *Village Voice* (23 Sept. 1997): 44-45.

Gontarski, S. E. "Dionysus in Publishing: Barney Rosset, Grove Press, and the Making of a Countercanon." *The Review of Contemporary Fiction* 10.3 (Fall 1990): 7-19.

Gonzales, Rodolfo "Corky." *Yo soy Joaquín/I Am Joquín.* Denver, 1967.

González, Deena J. "Masquerades: Viewing the New Chicana Lesbian Anthologies." *Out/Look* 15 (1991): 80-83.

González, María C. *Contemporary Mexican-American Women Novelists: Towards a Feminist Identity.* New York: Peter Lang, 1996.

Graham, Jefferson. "*So-Called Life* Mirrors Cruz's Own." *USA Today* (22 Dec. 1994): D3. Online. Nexis. 4 June 1998.

Griggers, Cathy. "Lesbian Bodies in an Age of (Post) Mechanical Reproduction." *The Lesbian Postmodern.* Ed. Laura Doan. New York: Columbia UP, 1994. 118-33.

Grosfoguel, Ramón. "The Divorce of Nationalist Discourses from the Puerto Rican People: A Sociohistorical Perspective." In Negrón-Muntaner and Grosfoguel, 57-76.

Grosz, Elizabeth. *Volatile Bodies. Toward a Corporeal Feminism.* Bloomington: Indiana UP, 1994.

Guerra Cunningham, Lucía. "Silencios, disidencias y claudicaciones: los problemas teóricos de la nueva crítica feminista." *Discurso femenino actual.* Ed. Adelaida López de Martínez. San Juan, PR: Editorial de la Universidad de Puerto Rico, 1995. 21-32.

Gurley, John G. *Challengers to Capitalism: Marx, Stalin, Lenin, and Mao.* New York: Norton, 1979.

Gutiérrez-Jones, Jones. *Rethinking the Borderlands: Between Chicano Cultural and Legal Discourse.* Berkeley: U of California P, 1995.

Guzmán, Manuel. "'Pa La Escuelita Con Mucho Cuida'o y por la Orillita': A Journey through the Constested Terrains of the Nation and Sexual Orientation." In Negrón-Muntaner and Grosfoguel, 209-28.

Hammonds, Evelynn. "Black (W)holes and the Geometry of Black Female Sexuality." *différences* 6:2-3 (1994): 126-45.

Handbook of Hispanic Cultures in the United States: Literature and Art. Ed. Francisco Lomelí. Houston: Arte Público P, 1993.

Hennessy, Rosemary. "Queer Theory: A Review of the *differences* Special Issue and Wittig's *The Straight Mind.*" *Signs* (Summer 1993): 964-73.

Hernández, Alfonso. *The False Advent of Mary's Child and Other Plays.* Berkeley: Editorial Justa Publications, 1979.

Hernández, Ellie. "Re-Thinking Margins and Borders: An Interview." *Discourse* 18.1-2 (Fall-Winter 1995-96): 7-15.

Hernández Catá, Alfonso. *El ángel de Sodoma.* Madrid: Editorial Mundo Latino, 1928.

Hernández-Gutiérrez, Manuel de Jesús. "Alarcón, Francisco X. (United States; 1954)." *Latin American Writers on Gay and Lesbian Themes: A Bio-Critical Sourcebook.* Ed. David William Foster. Westport, CT: Greenwood P, 1994. 7-13.

———. *El colonialismo interno en la narrativa chicana: el barrio, el anti-barrio y el exterior.* Tempe: Bilingual P/Editorial Bilingüe, 1994.

———. "El proyecto ideológico: la autorrepresentación chicana en la narrativa." *El colonialismo interno en la narrativa chicana: el barrio, el anti-barrio y el exterior.* Tempe: Bilingual P/Editorial Bilingüe, 1994. 28-56.

Herrera-Sobek, María. "The Politics of Rape: Sexual Transgression in Chicana Fiction." *Americas Review* 15.3-4 (1987): 171–88.

Hicks, Emily. *Border Writing: The Multidimensinal Text.* Minneapolis: U of Minnesota P, 1991.

Huisman, Mark J. "Coloring Blind." *Village Voice* (26 May 1998): 136f.

Jacobs, Andrew. "Loved and Hated, He Wants To Be Borough President." *New York Times* (17 Nov. 1996): sec. 13, 8.

———. "Natural Allies? Guess Again." *New York Times* (11 May 1997), sec. 13:3.

Jagose, Annamarie. *Queer Theory.* Washington Square: New York UP, 1996.

―――. *Lesbian Utopics.* New York: Routledge, 1994.

―――. "Slash and Suture: The Border's Figuration of Colonialism, Homophobia, and Phallocentrism in *Borderlands/La Frontera: The New Mestiza.*" *Lesbian Utopics.* New York: Routledge, 1994. 137-57.

Jameson, Fredric. *Signatures of the Visible.* New York: Routledge, 1990.

Jay, Karla and Joanne Glasgow. *Lesbian Texts and Contexts: Radical Revisions.* New York: New York UP, 1990.

Jiménez, Francisco, ed. *The Identification and Analysis of Chicano Literature.* New York: Bilingual P/Editorial Bilingüe, 1979.

Johnson, Allan. "A 'So-Called Break': Actor's Not Ready To Call It Quits With Special Role." *Chicago Tribune* (24 Jan. 1995): C7. Online. Nexis. 4 June 1998.

Johnson, Marsha. Interview. "Rapping with a Street Transvestite Revolutionary." Karla Jay and Allen Young, eds. *Out of the Closets: Voices of Gay Liberation.* New York: New York UP, 1992.

Jones, Andrea. "As Last Show Airs, Gay Teens Discover Themselves On *My So-Called Life.*" *Pacific News Service* (16 Jan. 1995). Online. Nexis. 4 June 1998.

Jones, Ann Rosalind. "Writing the Body: Toward an Understanding of l'Ecriture féminine." *The New Feminist Criticism: Essays on Women, Literature, & Theory.* Ed. Elaine Showalter. New York: Pantheon, 1985, 361-77.

Kiss of the Spider Woman. Dir. Héctor Babenco. Perf. Sonia Braga, Raúl Juliá, William Hurt. Island Alive and Film Dallas Investment, 1985.

Klawitter, George. "Umpierre-Herrera, Luz María (Puerto Rico; 1947)." *Latin American Writers on Gay and Lesbian Themes: A Bio-Critical Sourcebook.* Ed. David William Foster. Westport, CT: Greenwood P, 1994. 434-36.

Kriegar, Susan. "Lesbian Identity and Community: Recent Social Science Literature." *Signs: Journal of Women in Culture and Society* 8.1 (Autumn 1982): 91-108.

―――. "Reply to Sandoval and Bristow and Pearn." *Signs: Journal of Women in Culture and Society* 9.4 (Summer 1984): 732-33.

The Last of the Boricuas. Lamonte, dir. New York: The Latin Connection, 1994.

Latex. Michael Nunn, dir. Los Angeles: Excalibur Films, 1995.

Latin American Writers on Gay and Lesbian Themes. Ed. David William Foster. Westport, CT: Greenwood, 1995.

Lattin, Vernon E., ed. *Contemporary Chicano Fiction: A Critical Survey.* Binghamton, NY: Bilingual P/Editorial Bilingüe, 1986.

Laviera, Tato. *AmeRícan.* Houston: Arte Público Press, 1985.

Lehman, Peter. "Revelations about Pornography." *Film Criticism* 20.1-2 (Fall 1995): 3-16.

Leinier, Marvin. *Sexual Politics in Cuba: Machismo, Homosexualty and AIDS.* Boulder: Westview P, 1994.

Levin, James. "Gay Man as Everyman: Into the Eighties." *The Gay Novel: The Male Homosexual Image in America.* New York: Irvington, 1983. 281-367.

———. "The Sixties: Time of Transition." *The Gay Novel: The Male Homosexual Image in America.* New York: Irvington, 1983. 215-79.

Lezama Lima, José. *Paradiso.* Ed. Cintio Vitier. Nanterre, Francia: Université Paris X, Centre de Recherches Latino-Américaines, 1988.

Liskow, Samantha. "His So-Called Lifestyle: Actor Wilson Cruz Tells Students What It's Like To Grow Up Gay." *Kansas City Star* (11 Feb. 1997): 1. Online. Nexis. 4 June 1998.

Littlefield, Kinney. "Episode About Gay Teen May Be Last For *Life*." *Orange County Register* (22 Dec. 1994): F3. Online. Nexis. 4 June 1998.

Lombardi, Frank. "Recount Hands López Win." *Daily News* [New York] (18 Sept. 1997): 2.

Lomelí, Francisco. "An Overview of Chicano Letters: From Origins to Resurgence." *Chicano Studies: A Multidisciplinary Approach.* Ed. Eugene E. García, Francisco Lomelí and Isidro D. Ortiz. New York: Teachers College P, 1984. 103-19.

——— and Carl R. Shirley. "Alma Luz Villanueva." *Chicano Writers: Second Series.* Detroit: Gale Research, 1992. 313-17.

———. *Chicano Writers: First Series.* Detroit: Gale Research, 1989.

———. *Chicano Writers: Second Series.* Detroit: Gale Research, 1992.

López, Margarita. Candidate Statement. In New York City Campaign Finance Board. *1997 Primary Voter Guide.* 48.

López Sacha, Francisco. "Mi prima Amanda." *La gaceta de Cuba* (marzo-abril 1993): 43-45.

Lord, M.G. "Pornutopia: How Feminist Scholars Learned to Love Dirty Pictures." *Linguafranca* 7.4 (April/May 1997): 40-48.

Lugo Bertrán, Dorian. "*Brincando el charco*: primer largometraje de Frances Negrón Muntaner." *Nómada* [San Juan, PR] 3 (June 1997): 137-40.

Lugo-Ortiz, Agnes I. "Community at Its Limits: Orality, Law, Silence, and the Homosexual Body in Luis Rafael Sánchez's '¡Jum!.'" *¿Entiendes? Queer Readings, Hispanic Writings*. Eds. Emilie L. Bergman and Paul Julian Smith. Durham: Duke UP, 1995. 115-36.

——. "Sobre el tráfico simbólico de mujeres: Homosocialidad, identidad nacional y modernidad literaria en Puerto Rico (apuntes para una relectura de *El puertorriqueño dócil* de René Marqués)." *Revista de crítica literaria latinoamericana* 23.45 (1997): 261-78.

Mariposa en el andamio. n.p. n.d.

Marrero, María Teresa. "Chicano Self-representation in Theater and Performance Art." *Gestos: teoría y práctica del teatro hispánico* 11 (abril 1991): 147-62.

Martin, Biddy. "Lesbian Identity and Autobiographical Difference[s]." *The Lesbian and Gay Studies Reader*. Ed. Henry Abelove, Michele Aina Barale, and David M. Halperin. New York: Routledge, 1993. 274-93.

Martínez, Antonio. "La textualización del cuerpo femenino en la poesía de Ana María Fagundo." *Inti* 40-41 (Fall 1994-Spring 1995): 327-31.

McKenna,Teresa. *Migrant Song: Politics and Process in Contemporary Chicano Literature*. Austin: U of Texas P, 1997.

McNair, Brian. *Mediated Sex: Pornography and Postmodern Culture*. London: Arnold, 1996.

Medin, Tzvi. *Cuba: the Shaping of the Revolutionary Consciousness*. Trans. Martha Grenzback. Boulder: Lynne Rienner, 1990.

Meese, Elizabeth A. *(Sem)erotics. Theorizing Lesbian: Writing*. New York: New York UP, 1992.

Mendoza, Manuel. "Young Actor Finds *Life* Imitates Life." *Dallas Morning News* (22 Dec. 1994): C1. Online. Nexis. 4 June 1998.

Miller, John C. "Muñoz, Elías Miguel (Cuba; 1954)." *Latin American Writers on Gay and Lesbian Themes: A Bio-Critical Sourcebook*. Ed. David William Foster. Westport, CT: Greenwood P, 1994. 274-77.

Mintority Voices 3.1 (Fall 1979): 37-45. Special section on John Rechy.

Monclova, Héctor Iván. "Entrevista. Frances Negrón: la realizadora y las muchas voces." *Diálogos* (Río Piedras, PR) (January 1996): 32.

Montaner, Carlos Alberto. *Informe secreto sobre la revolución cubana*. Madrid: Ediciones Sedmay, 1976.

Montenegro, Carlos. *Hombres sin mujer*. México: Editorial Oasis, 1981.

Montero, Oscar. *Erotismo y representación en Julián del Casal*. Amsterdam: Rodopi, 1993.

Moraga, Cherríe. *Giving Up the Ghost: Teatro in Two Acts*. Los Angeles: West End, 1986.

———. *Heroes and Saints & Other Plays*. Albuquerque: West End P, 1994.

———. *Loving in the War Years; lo que nunca pasó por sus labios*. Boston: South End P, 1983.

———. "Queer Aztlán: the Re-formation of Chicano Tribe." *The Last Generation*. Boston: South End P, 1993. 145-74. Rpt. *The Material Queer: A LesBiGay Cultural Studies Reader*. Ed. Donald Morton. Boulder: Westview P, 1996. 297-304.

——— and Gloria Anzaldúa, eds. *This Bridge Called My Back: Writings by Radical Women of Color*. New York: Kitchen Table Women of Color P, 1981.

——— and Ana Castillo. *Esta puente, mi espalda*. San Francisco: Ism P/Editorial "Ismo," 1988. Spanish translation, with revisions, of previous entry.

Mott, Luiz. *Escravidão, homossexualidade e demonologia*. São Paulo: Icone Editora, 1988.

———. *O sexo proibido: virgens, gays e escravos nas garras da Inquisição*. Campinas: Papirus Editora, 1988.

Muñoz, Elías Miguel. *Crazy Love*. Houston: Arte Público P, 1989.

———. *En estas tierras/In This Land*. Tempe, AZ: Bilingual P/Editorial Bilingüe, 1989.

———. *The Greatest Performance*. Houston: Arte Público P, 1991.

———. *No fue posible el sol*. Madrid: Editorial Betanía, 1989.

———. *Los viajes de Orlando Cachumbambe*. Miami: Editorial Universal, 1984.

Murray, Stephen O. and Manuel Arboleda G. "Stigma Transformation and Relexification: *Gay* in Latin America." *Latin American Male Homosexualities*. Ed. Stephen O. Murray. Albuquerque: U of New Mexico P, 1995. 138-44.

Musto, Michael. "Lost in Yonkers. Sylvia Rivera May Be the Rosa Parks of Gay Rights, But on the Streets, She's Just Another Homeless Queen." *Village Voice* (30 May 1995): 25.

My Deep Dark Pain Is Love; A Collection of Latin American Gay Fiction. Ed. Winston Leyland. San Francisco: Gay Sunshine P, 1983.

Nandino, Elías. *Erotismo al rojo vivo.* México, DF: Editorial Katún, 1983.

———. *The Burning Plain.* New York: G. P. Putnam's, 1997.

———. *The Death of Friends.* New York: G.P. Putnam's, 1996.

———, ed. *Finale: Short Stories of Mystery and Suspense.* Boston: Alyson, 1989.

———. *Goldenboy.* Boston: Alyson, 1988.

———. *The Hidden Law.* New York: HarperCollins, 1992.

———. *How Town.* New York: Harper & Row, 1990.

———. *The Little Death.* Boston: Alyson, 1986.

——— and Robert Dawidoff. *Created Equal: Why Gay Rights Matter to America.* New York: St. Martin's P, 1994.

Nardi, Peter M., and Beth E. Schneider. *Social Perspectives in Lesbian and Gay Studies: A Reader.* New York: Routledge, 1998. 537-52.

Negrón de Montilla, Aida. *Americanization in Puerto Rico and the Public School System 1900-1930.* Río Piedras: U of Puerto Rico, 1971.

Negrón-Muntaner, Frances, dir. *Brincando el charco: Portrait of a Puerto Rican.* 1994.

———. "Echoing Stonewall and Other Dilemmas: The Organizational Beginnings of a Gay and Lesbian Agenda in Puerto Rico, 1972-1977." *Centro* 4.1 (1992): 77-95; 4.2 (1992): 98-115.

———. "Twenty Years of Puerto Rican Activism: An Interview with Luis 'Popo' Santiago." *Radical America* 25.1 (Jan.-Mar. 1991 [Sept. 1993]): 39-51.

Newton, Candelas. Introducción. "La poesía de Ana María Fagundo; poniéndole hechura al ser por la palabara." Ana María Fagundo, *Obra poética: 1965-1990.* Madrid: Endymion, 1990. 21-65.

Olivares, Julián, ed. *The Americas Review* 16.3-4 (Fall-Winter 1988). Special issue entitled "U.S. Hispanic Autobiography."

———. "Sandra Cisneros' *The House on Mango Street,* and the Poetics of Space." *Americas Review* 15.3-4 (1987): 160–70.

Ordónez, Elizabeth J. "Narrative Texts By Ethnic Women: Rereading The Past, Reshaping the Future." *Melus: The Journal of the Society for the Study of the Multi-Ethnic Literature of the United States* 9.3 (Summer 1982): 19-27.

Ortiz, Mimi. "Esclavos de su corazón." *El nuevo día* [San Juan, PR] (5 oct. 1997): 5.

———. "Trastocadas las fotos en el álbum familiar." *El nuevo día* [San Juan, PR] (6 oct. 1997): 16-17.

———. "Una unión más allá del clóset. . ." *El nuevo día* [San Juan, PR] (5 Oct. 1997): 4.

Ortiz Taylor, Sheila. *Faultline*. Tallahassee, FL: The Naiad P, 1982.

Owens, Craig. *Beyond Recognition: Representation, Power, and Culture*. Berkeley: U of California P, 1992.

Padura Fuentes, Leonardo. "El cazador." *La Puerta de Alcalá y otras cacerías*. Madrid: Ediciones Olalla, 1998. 187-201.

Pagán, Antonio. Candidate Statement. In New York City Campaign Finance Board. *1997 Primary Voter Guide*. 37.

Paris is Burning. Dir. Jenny Livingston. 1990.

Paz, Octavio. *El laberinto de la soledad*. México: Fondo de Cultura Económica, 1959.

Paz, Senel. "El lobo, el bosque y el hombre nuevo." *Antología de cuento*. Concurso Internacional Juan Rulfo. Premios 1984-1992. México, D.F.: Editorial Diana, 1993. 154-75. Also as *El lobo, el bosque y el hombre nuevo*. Mexico: Ediciones Era, 1991.

Pedreira, Antonio S. *Insularismo*. Río Piedras: Edil, 1969.

Peña, Terri de la. "Beyond El Camino Real." *Chicana Lesbians*. Ed. Carla Trujillo. Berkeley: Third Woman P, 1991. 85–94.

———. "Blue." *Riding Desire*. Ed. Tee Corinne. Austin: Banned Books, 1990. 149–53.

———. "Desert Quartet." *Lesbian Love Stories, Volume 2*. Ed. Irene Zahava. Freedom, CA: The Crossing P, 1991. 154–61.

———. "La Maya." *Intricate Passions*. Ed. Tee Corinne. Austin: Banned Books, 1989. 1–10.

———. "Labrys." *Word of Mouth*. Ed. Irene Zahava. Freedom, CA: The Crossing P, 1990. 31.

———. *Latin Satins*. Seattle: The Seal P, 1994.

———. *Margins*. Seattle: Seal P, 1992.

———. "Mariposa." *Lesbian Bedtime Stories 2*. Ed. Terry Woodrow. Willits, CA: Tough Dove Books, 1990. 7–19.

———. "Mujeres Morenas." *Lesbian Love Stories, Volume 2*. Ed. Irene Zahava. Freedom, CA: The Crossing P, 1991. 85–93.

———. "Once a Friend." *The One You Call Sister*. Ed. Paula Martinac. San Francisco: Cleis P, 1989. 49–62.

———. "A Saturday in August." *Finding Courage.* Ed. Irene Zahava. Freedom, CA: The Crossing P, 1989. 141–50.

———. "Tortilleras." *Lesbian Bedtime Stories.* Ed. Terry Woodrow. Willits, CA: Tough Dove Books, 1989. 83–92.

Pérez, Alberto Julián. "Tipología histórica de la lectura: lectores europeos y lectores latinoamericanos." *Revista de crítica literaria latinoamericana* 15.33 (1991): 281-90.

Pérez, Emma. *Gulf Dreams.* Berkeley: Third Woman P, 1996.

———. "Irigaray's Female Symbolic in the Making of Chicana Lesbian *Sitios* y *Lenguas* (Sites and Discourses)." *Living Chicana Theory.* Ed. Carla Trujillo. Berkeley: Third Woman P, 1998. 87-101.

Pérez Firmat, Gustavo. "Descent Into *Paradiso*: A Study of Heaven and Homosexuality." *Hispania* 59 (1976): 247-57.

Pérez-Torres, Rafael. *Movements in Chicano Poetry: Against Myths, Against Margins.* Cambridge: U of Cambridge P, 1995.

Phelan, Shane. "Lesbians and Mestizas: Appropriation and Equivalence." *Getting Specific: Postmodern Lesbian Politics.* Minneapolis: U of Minnesota P, 1994. 57-75.

Piñera, Virgilio. *La carne de René.* Buenos Aires: Ediciones Siglo Veinte, 1952.

———. *Cold Tales.* Trans. Mark Schafer. Hygiene, Colorado; New York: Eridanos P, 1988.

———. *Cuentos fríos.* Buenos Aires: Editorial Losada, 1956.

———. *Dos viejos pánicos.* Buenos Aires: Centro Editor de América Latina, 1968.

———. *Presiones y diamantes.* La Habana: UNEAC, 1967.

———. *Rene's Flesh.* Trans. Mark Schafer. Boston: Eridanos P, 1989.

———. *Teatro completo.* La Habana: Ediciones R, 1960.

———. *La vida entera.* La Habana: UNEAC, 1969.

Portillo, Estela. "The Day of the Swallows." *El espejo/The Mirror: Selected Chicano Literature.* 5th ed. Ed. by Octavio Ignacio Romano-V. and Herminio Ríos-C. Berkeley: Quinto Sol, 1972. 147-93. Also *Contemporary Chicano Theater.* Ed. Roberto J. Garza. Notre Dame: U of Notre Dame P, 1976. 206–45.

Praschak, Andrew. "P.R. Candidates in N.Y. Vie to End Stereotypes." *San Juan Star* (18 Apr. 1997): 68.

Prats Sariol, José. Cap VIII de los "Resúmenes críticos de los capítulos Erotismos." *Paradiso.* José Lezama Lima. Ed. Cintio Vitier. Nanterre, Francia: Université Paris X, Centre de Recherches Latino-Américaines, 1988. 661-62.

Puerto Rican Jam: Essays on Culture and Politics. Eds. Negrón-Muntaner, Frances and Ramón Grosfoguel. Minneapolis: U of Minnesota P, 1997.

"Puerto Rico Police Accused of Harassing a Gay Group." *New York Times* (14 Feb. 1995): A14.

Puig, Manuel. *El beso de la mujer araña.* Barcelona: Seix Barral, 1976.

———. *Kiss of the Spider Woman.* Trans. Thomas Colchie. New York: Knopf, 1979.

Pujals, Enrique J. *La obra narrativa de Carlos Montenegro.* Miami: Ediciones Universal, 1981.

Quintana, Alvina. *Home Girls: Chicana Literary Voices.* Philadelphia: Temple UP, 1996.

Quiroga, José. "Fleshing Out Virgilio Piñera from the Cuban Closet." *¿Entiendes? Queer Readings, Hispanic Writings.* Eds. Emilie L. Bergman and Paul Julian Smith. Durham: Duke UP, 1995. 168-80.

"Race for City Hall: The Council. Error May Change Result." *New York Times* (11 Sept. 1997): B4.

"Race for City Hall: Vote Correction Reverses Election Result." *New York Times* (17 Sept. 1997): B2.

Ramos, Juanita. *Compañeras: Latina Lesbians.* New York: Latina Lesbian History Project, 1987.

Ramos Otero, Manuel. *Cuentos de buena tinta.* San Juan: Instituto de Cultura Puertorriqueña, 1992.

———. *Invitación al polvo.* Madrid: Plaza Mayor, 1991.

———. *El libro de la muerte.* Río Piedras: Cultural; Maplewood, NJ: Waterfront, 1985.

———. *La novelabingo.* New York: Editorial El Libro Viaje, 1976.

———. *Página en blanco y staccato.* 2a ed. Madrid: Playor, 1988.

Raymond, Janice. "The Politics of Transgenderism." *Blending Genders: Social Aspects of Cross-Dressing and Sex-Changing.* Ed. Richard Ekins and Dave King. London: Routledge, 1996. 217-23.

Rebolledo, Tey Diana. *Women Singing in the Snow: A Cultural Analysis of Chicana Literature.* Tucson: U of Arizona P, 1995.

Rechy, John. *City of Night.* New York: Grove P, 1963,

———. "On Being a 'Grove Press Author.'" *The Review of Contemporary Fiction* 10.3 (Fall 1990): 75-87.

Reed, Roger. *The Cultural Revolution in Cuba.* Geneva: Latin American Round Table, 1991.

"Remapping the Border Subject." *Discourse* 18.1-2 (Fall-Winter 1995-96). Special issue.

Rev. of *Margins*, by Terri de la Peña. *Publishers Weekly* 239.15 (1992): 66.

Reyes, Guillermo. *Deporting the Divas.* Manuscript.

———. "The Latin American Writer: Writing in English." *Latin American Theatre Review* 31.1 (Fall 1997): 113-15.

Reyes, Rodrigo, Francisco Alarcón and Juan Pablo Gutiérrez. *Ya vas, carnal.* San Francisco: Humanizarte, 1985.

Rich, Adrienne. "Compulsory Heterosexuality and Lesbian Existence." *Powers of Desire: The Politics of Sexuality.* Ed. Ann Sitnow, Christine Stansell, and Sharon Thompson. New York: Monthly Review P, 1983.

Ríos Avila, Rubén (interview). "El Show de Cristina." *Piso 13* (Edición Gay) 2.3 (September-December 1993): 6.

Rivas, Lillian. "A ponerle candado a la ley de los hombres." *El nuevo día* [San Juan, PR] (6 oct. 1997): 2.

———. "Un amor que no conoce de sexos." *El nuevo día* [San Juan, PR] (5 oct. 1997): 8.

———. "Intocable el derecho a escoger." *El nuevo día* [San Juan, PR] (6 oct. 1997): 4.

Rivera, Sylvia. "The Drag Queen: Rey 'Sylvia Lee' Rivera." Interview by Eric Marcus. *Making History: The Struggle for Gay and Lesbian Equal Rights, 1945-1990 (An Oral History).* New York: Harper Perennial, 1993. 187-96.

Robinson, Regan. Rev. of *Margins*, by Terri de la Peña. *Library Journal* 117.5 (1992): 124.

Robles, Mireya. *En esta aurora.* San Antonio: M & A Editions, 1978.

———. *Hagiografía de Narcisa la bella.* Hanover, NH: Ediciones del Norte, 1985.

Rodríguez, Dinah E. "Un cine sospechoso: conversando con Frances Negrón-Muntaner." *Revista de crítica literaria latinoamericana* 45 (1997): 411-20.

Rodriguez, Richard. *Days of Obligation: An Argument with my Mexican Father.* New York: Viking, 1992.

———. *Hunger of Memory: The Education of Richard Rodriguez.* Boston: D.R. Godine, 1981.

———. "Late Victorians: San Francisco, AIDS, and the Homosexual Stereotype." *Harper's Magazine* (Oct. 1990): 57-66. Rpt. as "Late Victorians." *Days of Obligation: An Argument with my Mexican Father.* New York: Viking, 1992. 26-47.

Rodríguez-Matos, Carlos A. *Llama de amor vivita. Jarchas.* South Orange, N.J.: Ediciones Ichali, 1988.

———. *Matacán.* Madrid: Playor, 1982.

Román, David. "Teatro Viva!: Latino Performance and the Politics of AIDS in Los Angeles." *¿Entiendes? Queer Readings, Hispanic Writings.* Ed. Emile L. Bergmann and Paul Smith. Durham, NC: Duke UP, 1995. 346-69. Rpt. *The Latino Studies Reader: Culture, Economy and Society.* Ed. Antonia Darder and Rodolfo D. Torres. Malden, MA: Blackwell, 1998. 211-27.

Rosaldo, Renato. "Fables of the Fallen Guy." *Criticism in the Borderlands.* Ed. Héctor Calderón and José David Saldívar. Durham, NC: Duke UP, 1991. 84–93.

Ross, Karl. "Gay Cops Get Cold Shoulder From P.R. Police Officers." *San Juan Star* (10 Feb. 1995): 2f.

Saldívar, Ramón. *Chicano Narrative: The Dialectics of Difference.* Madison: U of Wisconsin P, 1990.

Saldívar, Ramón. "Ideologies of the Self: Chicano Autobiography." *Diacritics* 15.3 (1985): 25-34.

———. "Narrative, Ideology and the Reconstruction of American Literary History." *Criticism in the Borderlands: Studies in Chicano Literature, Culture and Ideology.* Ed. Héctor Calderón and José David Saldívar. Durham: Duke UP, 1991. 11-20.

Salessi, Jorge. *Médicos maleantes y maricas: higiene, criminología y homosexualidad en la construcción de la nación argentina (Buenos Aires: 1871-1914).* Rosario: Beatriz Viterbo, 1995.

Sánchez de León, Margarita. "Racismo y sexismo en Puerto Rico." *Claridad* [San Juan, PR] (6-12 feb. 1998): 32.

Sandoval, Chela. "Comment on Krieger's 'Lesbian Identity and Community: Recent Social Science Literature.'" *Signs: Journal of Women in Culture and Society* 9.4 (Summer 1984): 725-29.

Sandoval Sánchez, Alberto. "Puerto Rican Identity Up in the Air: Air Migration, Its Cultural Representations, and Me 'Cruzando el Charco." In Negrón-Muntaner and Grosfoguel, 189-208.

Santiago, Esmeralda. *When I Was a Puerto Rican.* Reading, MA: Addison-Wesley, 1993.

Satterfield, B. "John Rechy's Tormented World." *Southwest Review* 67 (Winter 1982): 78-85.

Schaefer, Claudia. *Danger Zones: Homosexuality, National Identity, and Mexican Culture.* Tucson: U of Arizona P, 1996.

Seda, Marisol. "Choque verbal 'gays' y religiosos." *El vocero de Puerto Rico* [San Juan, PR] (11 oct. 1997): 7.

———. "Proyecto matrimonios 'gays': baja la temperatura del debate." *El vocero de Puerto Rico* [San Juan, PR (11 oct. 1997: 15.

Sedgwick, Eve Kosofsky. *Epistemology of the Closet.* Berkeley: U of California P, 1990.

Shanahan, Ed. "Give'em Hell, López." *Village Voice* (23 Sept. 1997): 22.

———. "Machine vs. Reformer." *Village Voice* (9 Sept. 1997): 27.

Shister, Gail. "*My So-Called Life* Imitates His Own Life For Wilson Cruz." *Orlando Sentinel* (30 Nov. 1994): A2. Online. Nexis. 4 June 1998.

———. "*Rent* Standout Is On Cruz Control." *Arizona Republic* (22 Feb. 1998): 18. Online. Nexis. 4 June 1998.

Sierra, Ana. "Rodríguez-Matos, Carlos A. (Puerto Rico; 1948)." *Latin American Writers on Gay and Lesbian Themes: A Bio-Critical Sourcebook.* Ed. David William Foster. Westport, CT: Greenwood P, 1994. 374-77.

Signs 18.4 (Summer 1993). Special issue on "Theorizing Lesbian Experience."

Silverman, Kaja. *The Threshold of the Visible World.* New York: Routledge, 1996.

Smith, Barbara. "Toward a Black Feminist Criticism." *All the Women Are White, All the Blacks Are Men, But Some of Us Are Brave: Black Women's Studies.* Ed. Gloria T. Hull, Patricia Bell Scott and Barbara Smith. New York: Feminist P, 1982. 157–175.

Smith, Paul Julian. "Néstor Almendros/Reinaldo Arenas: Documentary, Autobiography and Cinematography." *Vision Machines: Cinema, Literature and Sexuality in Spain and Cuba, 1983-93.* London: Verso, 1996. 59-80.

Sobchack, Thomas. "Genre Film: A Classical Experience." *Film Genre Reader II.* Austin: U Texas P, 1995. 102-13.

Somerville, Siobhan. "Scientific Racism and the Invention of the Homosexual Body." *Queer Studies: A Lesbian, Gay, Bisexual, and Transgender Anthology.* Ed. Brett Beemyn and Michey Eliason. New York: New York UP, 1996. 241-61.

Soto, Pedro Juan. *En busca de J.I. de Diego Padró.* Río Piedras: Universidad de Puerto Rico, 1990.

———. *Spiks.* 7a ed. Río Piedras: Cultural, 1985.

Southern, Terry. "Rechy and Gover." *Contemporary American Novelists.* Ed. Harry T. Moore. Cardbondale: Southern Illinois UP, 1964. 222-27.

Spivak, Gayatri Chakravorti. "Can the Subaltern Speak?" *Marxism and the Interpretation of Culture.* Eds. Cary Nelson and Lawrence Grossberg. Urbana: U of Illinois P, 1988. 271-313.

———. "French Feminism in an International Frame." *The Women and Language Debate. A Sourcebook.* Eds. Camille Roman, Suzanne Juhasz, and Cristanne Miller. New Brunswick: Rutgers UP, 1994. 101-04.

Tatum, Charles. "The Sexual Underworld of John Rechy." *Minority Voices* 3.1 (Fall 1979): 47-52.

Taylor, Diana. "Opening Remarks." *Negotiating Performance: Gender, Sexuality, and Theatricality in Latino/o America.* Ed. Diana Taylor and Juan Villegas. Durham: Duke UP, 1994. 1-16.

Tisdale, Sallie. *Talk Dirty to Me.* New York: Doubleday, 1994.

"Toledo Orders Investigation of Raid at Santurce Gay Bar." *San Juan Star* (18 Feb. 1995): 4+.

Torres, Daniel. "An AIDS Narrative." *Centro Bulletin* 6.1-2 (1994): 179.

Trevisan, João Silvério. *Devassos no paraíso: a homossexualidade no Brasil, da colônia à atualidade.* São Paulo: Max Limonad, 1986.

Trinh, T. Min-ha. "The Language of Nativism." *American Feminist Thought a Century's End: A Reader.* Ed. Linda S. Kauffman. Massachusetts, 1993. 107-39.

Trujillo, Carla, ed., *Chicana Lesbians: The Girls Our Mothers Warned Us About.* Berkeley: Third Woman P, 1991.

———, ed. *Living Chicana Theory.* Berkeley: Third Woman P, 1998.

Udis-Kessler, Amanda. "Present Tense: Biphobia as a Crisis of Meaning." *The Material Queer: A LesBiGay Cultural Studies Reader.* Ed. Donald Morton. Boulder: Westview P, 1996. 297-304.

Umpierre-Herrera, Luz María. *En el país de las maravillas.* Bloomington: Third Woman P, 1982.

———. *The Margarita Poems.* Bloomington: Third Woman P, 1987.

———. *. . . Y otras desgracias/And Other Misfortunes.* Bloomington: Third Woman P, 1985.

Urías, Roberto. "¿Por qué llora Leslie Caron?" *Letras cubanas* 9 (1988): 236-39.

Velásquez, Gloria. *Tommy Stands Alone.* Houston: Piñata Books, 1995.

Villanueva, Alfredo. "Carlos Montenegro." *Latin American Writers on Gay and Lesbian Themes: A Bio-Critical Sourcebook.* Ed. David William Foster. Westport, CT: Greenwood P, 1994. 250-51.

Villanueva, Alma Luz. *Naked Ladies.* Tempe: Bilingual P/Editorial Bilingüe, 1994.

———. Villanueva, Alma Luz. *Weeping Woman: La Llorona and Other Stories.* Tempe, AZ: Bilingual P/Editorial Bilingüe, 1994.

Villaurrutia, Xavier. *Obras.* México, DF: Letras Mexicanas, 1996.

Vivas Maldonado, J. L. *A vellón las esperanzas o Melania (Cuentos de un puertorriqueño en Nueva York).* Long Island City: Las Americas, 1971.

Warner, Michael. "Introduction." *Fear of a Queer Planet: Queer Politics and Social Theory.* Ed. Michael Warner. Social Text Collective, Cultural Politics Series. Minneapolis: U of Minnesota P, 1993. vii-xxxi.

Waugh, Thomas. "The Third Body." *Queer Looks: Perspectives on Lesbian and Gay Film Video.* Ed. Martha Gever, John Greyson and Pratibha Parmar. New York: Routledge, 1993. 141-61.

Weeks, Jeffrey. *Against Nature.* London: Rivers Oram P, 1991.

"We'll Always Wonder. . ." *St. Louis Post-Dispatch* (29 June 1995): 45. Online. Nexis. 4 June 1998.

West, Cornel. "The new Cultural Politics of Difference." *Out There: Marginalization and Contemporary Cultures.* Ed. Russell Ferguson, Martha Gever, Trinh T. Minh-ha, and Cornel West. Cambridge: MIT P, 1990. 19-36.

Williams, Linda. *Hard Core: Power, Pleasure, and the Frenzy of the Visible.* Berkeley: U of California P, 1989.

Williams, Patricia J. "On Being the Object of Property." *Writing on the Body.* Ed. Katie Conboy, Nadia Medina, and Sarah Stanbury. New York: Columbia UP, 1997. 155-75.

Wolf, Mary Ellen. "Out of Frame: Border(line) Images." *Critical Inquiry* 23 (1997): 494-508.

Wolff, Janet. *Feminine Sentences: Essays on Women and Culture.* Berkeley: U of California P, 1990.

Wolverton, Terry. Rev. of *Margins*, by Terri de la Peña. *Advocate* 604 (1992): 40.

Woo, Merle. "Letter to Ma." *This Bridge Called My Back: Writings by Radical Women of Color.* Ed. Cherríe Moraga and Gloria Anzaldúa. New York, Kitchen Table Women of Color P, 1981. 140-47.

Woodlawn, Holly and Jeff Copeland. *A Low Life in High Heels: The Holly Woodlawn Story.* New York: Harper Perennial, 1991.

Xavier, Emanuel. "Motherfuckers." *Best Gay Erotica 1997.* Ed. Richard Labonté. Pittsburg: Cleis, 1997. 112-116.

———. *Pier Queen.* New York: Pier Queen Productions, 1997.

Yakowar, Maurice. *The Films of Paul Morrissey.* Cambridge: Cambridge UP, 1993.

Yarbro-Bejarano, Yvonne. "Chicana Literature From a Chicana Feminist Perspective." *Review* 15.3–4 (1987): 139–45. Also *Chicana Creativity and Criticism: Charting New Frontiers in American Literature.* Ed. María Herrera Sobek. Houston: Arte Público P, 1988. 139-45.

———. "Expanding the Categories of Race and Sexuality in Lesbian and Gay Studies." *Professions of Desire: Lesbian and Gay Studies in Literature.* Ed. George E. Haggerty and Bonnie Zimmerman. New York: Modern Language Association of America, 1995. 124-35.

———. "The Lesbian Body in Latina Cultural Production." *¿Entiendes? Queer Readings, Hispanic Writings.* Ed. Emilie L. Bergmann and Paul Julian Smith. Durham: Duke UP, 1995. 181-97.

Zamora, Carlos. "Odysseus in John Rechy's *City of Night*: The Epistemological Journey." *Minority Voices* 3.1 (Fall 1979): 53-62.

Zavarzadeh, Mas'ud. *Seeing Films Politically.* New York: State U of New York P, 1995.

Zimmerman, Bonnie. "Exiting from Patriarchy: The Lesbian Novel of Development." *The Voyage In: Fictions of Female Development.* Ed. Elizabeth Abel, Marianne Hirsch, and Elizabeth Langland. Hanover, NH: UP of New England, 1983. 244-57.

———. "Perverse Reading: The Lesbian Appropriation of Literature." 1991. *Sexual Practice, Textual Theory: Lesbian Cultural Criticism.* Ed. Susan J. Wolfe and Penelope Stanley. Cambridge, MA: Blackwell, 1993. 135–49.

———. "What Has Never Been: An Overview of Lesbian Feminist Criticism." 1981. *Sexual Practice, Textual Theory: Lesbian Cultural Criticism.* Ed. Susan J. Wolfe and Penelope Stanley. Cambridge, MA/Oxford: Blackwell, 1993. 33-54.

Contributors

Francisco X. Alarcón, Chicano poet and educator, was born in Wilmington, California in 1954. Together with poets Rodigo Reyes and Juan Pablo Gutiérrez, he published *Ya vas, carnal* (1985), one of the first collections of homoerotic poetry by Chicanos. He is also the author of ten volumes of poetry, including *Body in Flames/Cuerpo en llamas* (1990), *De amor oscuro/Of Dark Love* (1991). *Snake Poems: An Aztec Invocation* (1992), and *No Golden Gate for Us* (1993). Alarcón has been a recipient of the Danforth and Fulbright fellowships and has been awarded several literary prizes, including the 1993 American Book Award, the 1993 Pen Oakland Josephine Miles Awad, and the 1984 Chicao Liteary Prize. Alarcón did his undergraduate studies at California State University, Long Beach, and his graduate studies at Stanford University. He currently teaches at the University of California, Davis, where he directs the Spanish for Native Speakers Program.

José B. Alvarez IV is an Assistant Professor of Spanish at the University of Georgia, where he teaches courses in Latin American literature and film. He is also founding director of Grupo Teatro TUNANTA, a theater group dedicated to the performance of Latin American and Spanish plays that present marginal themes.

Cristina Buckley received her Ph.D. in August 1998 from Tulane University, and she is currently an Assistant Professor at Furman University. Her dissertation was "Seen and Heard: Silence and Speech in Spanish Women's Postwar Short Stories and Film," and her main areas of interest are nineteenth- and twentieth-century Spanish Peninsular literature and contemporary Spanish and Latin American film and popular culture.

Susana Chávez-Silverman is Associate Professor of Spanish and Chair of the Latin American Studies Program at Pomona College. She is the editor, with Frances Aparicio, of *Troplicalizations: Transcultural Representations of Latinidad* (Dartmouth C/U P of New England) and editor, with Librada Hernández, of *En el ambiente: Queer Sexualities in Latino, Latin American and Spanish Writing & Culture* (U Wisconsin P). She has published essays on gender, sexuality, and queer theory on Latin American and U.S. Latino literary and cultural texts. Her current project is a book, *Desire In/Verse: Readings in Argentine Women's Poetry from Pizarnik to the Millennium.*

Beatriz Cortez is a doctoral student in Spanish at Arizona State University. She is currently completing her dissertation on testimonial and postrevolutionary narrative in Central America.

David William Foster is Chair of the Department of Languages and Literatures and Regents' Professor of Spanish, Humanities, and Women's Studies at Arizona State University. His research interests focus on urban culture in Latin America, with emphasis on issues of gender construction and sexual identity, as well as Jewish culture. His most recent publications include *Violence in Argentine Literature; Cultural Responses to Tyranny* (University of Missouri Press, 1995); *Cultural Diversity in Latin American Literature* (University of New Mexico Press, 1994); *Contemporary Argentine Cinema* (University of Missouri Press, 1992); and *Gay and Lesbian Themes in Latin American Writing*. Austin: University of Texas Press, 1991). He is also the editor of *Latin American Writers on Gay and Lesbian Themes; A Bio-Critical Sourcebook* (Greenwood Press, 1994). *Sexual Textualities: Essays on Queer/ing Latin American Writing* was published in Fall 1997 by the University of Texas Press. *Buenos Aires: Perspectives on the City and Cultural Production* was published in Fall 1998 by the University of Florida Press.

Manuel de Jesús Hernández-Gutiérrez is an Associate Professor of U.S. Latino/a Literature and a Research Faculty member of the Hispanic Research Center at Arizona State University. He has contributed article to various journals and books, including *The Bilingual Review, Culturas hispanas de los Estados Unidos* (1990), *Chicano Discourse* (1992), *Mexican Literature: A History* (1994), *Latin American Writers on Gay and Lesbian Themes: A Bio-Critical Sourcebook* (1994), and *Humanism and the Good Life* (1998). In 1994 he published the postcolonial study *El colonialismo interno en la narrativa chicana* and in 1997 he co-edited the historic collection *Literatura chicana, 1965-1995: An Anthology in Spanish, English, and Caló*. He is presently writing a postcolonial and postmodernist theory of U.S. Latina/o literature.

Lawrence M. La Fountain-Stokes was born in Puerto Rico in 1968 and received his Ph.D. from Columbia University in 1998 with a dissertation on "Culture, Representation, and the Puerto Rican Queer Diaspora." He is currently a professor of Latino/a Studies in the Department of Spanish and Portuguese at Ohio State University.

Daniel Enrique Pérez is a graduate student in the Department of Languages and Literatures at Arizona State University, where he is working in comparative literature with an emphasis on a Chicano literature. He has published in *The Americas Review* and *Escritura*.

Antonio Prieto holds a Ph.D. in Latin American Studies from the National Autonomous University of Mexico and a Master's in Performance Studies from New York University. He is the author of *El teatro como vehículo de comunicación* (Editorial Trillas, 1992). He is the author of several essays on border-crossing performance art and gay Chicano performance. Prieto is currently project director for Data-Center's Information Services Latin America (ISLA).

Sandra Quinn is from White Bread, America. She went to art school in Chicago, worked as an exhibit designer, a filmmaker, a courtroom artist, and in her present incarnation is working on a Ph.D. in Justice Studies at Arizona State University. Her research considers how queer theory, race theory, and theories of masculinity might converge to inflect subtle readings of popular images of masculinity.

Guillermo Reyes is a Chilean-born U.S. playwright whose works include the off-Broadway hit *Men on the Verge of a His-panic Breakdown* and *Deporting the Divas, A Southern Christmas, Chilean Holiday*, among others. His plays have been seen across the country. The full text is available in the theater journal *Gestos*, published by the Department of Spanish and Portuguese at the University of California-Irvine. Reyes is an Assistant Professor of Theatre at Arizona State University.

Cecilia Rosales is completing her doctorate in Spanish at Arizona State University.

Catrióna Rueda Esquibel is a Ph.D. candidate in the History of Consciousness Program at the University of California, Santa Cruz, where she is completing her dissertation on Chicana Lesbian fictions. She is a Chicana of Mexican and Nuevomejicana ancestry and is active in the Research Cluster for the Study of Women of Color. She has published poetry in *Frontiers: A Journal of Women Studies* and critical writing in *SIGNS* and *New Perspectives on Women and Comedy*. Her monologue "La Karla" was performed by El Centro Su Teatro in Denver as part of the series of one-acts on Latinas and love: *Amor Picante Pero Sabroso* (1991). Her play *Familia Is a Story We Make Up* was awarded second prize in the Chicano/Latino Literary Contest in 1998. She makes her home and her life with Luz Calvo in Watsonville, CA.

Trino Sandoval is a Professor of Spanish at Phoenix College.

Kanishka Sen is completing his doctorate in Spanish at Arizona State University.

Juana Suárez is a doctoral candidate at Arizona State University, where she is specializing in Latin American literature and film.

Carmen de Urioste is Assistant Professor of Spanish at Arizona State University. Her main interest is contemporary Peninsular literature, cultural studies, and women's cultural productions. She is the author of *Literatura andaluza (1900-1936). Erotismo, feminismo y regionalismo* (1997) and the co-editor of *Literatura española: una antología* (1995). Her articles have been published, among other journals, in *Confluencia, Letras Peninsulares, Revista hispánica moderna,* and *Hispanic Journal.*

Index

For Product Safety Concerns and Information please contact our EU
representative GPSR@taylorandfrancis.com
Taylor & Francis Verlag GmbH, Kaufingerstraße 24, 80331 München, Germany